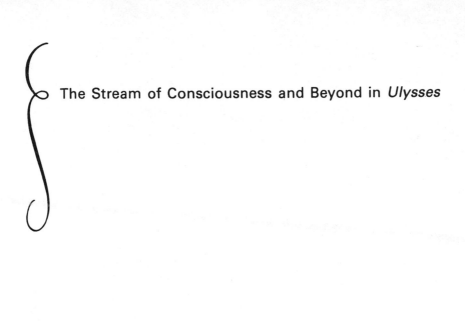 The Stream of Consciousness and Beyond in *Ulysses*

ERWIN R. STEINBERG

The Stream of Consciousness and Beyond in *Ulysses*

UNIVERSITY OF PITTSBURGH PRESS

Library of Congress Catalog Card Number 72-78932
ISBN 0-8229-3245-8
Copyright © 1958, 1973, Erwin R. Steinberg
All rights reserved
Media Directions Inc., London
Manufactured in the United States of America

Grateful acknowledgment is made to Random House, Inc., and The Bodley Head for permission to quote material from *Ulysses* by James Joyce. Copyright 1914, 1918 by Margaret Caroline Anderson and renewed 1942, 1946 by Nora Joseph Joyce. Reprinted by permission of Random House, Inc., and The Bodley Head.

Grateful acknowledgment is made to the following for permission to quote material that appears in this book:

American Psychological Association for excerpts from J. P. Guilford, "Three Faces of Intellect," *American Psychologist* 14 (1959).

Chatto and Windus Ltd., London, and Barnes and Noble Books, New York, for excerpts adapted from *The Classical Temper* by S. L. Goldberg, 1961.

E. P. Dutton & Co., Inc., and William Heinemann Ltd., for excerpts from the book *The Symbolist Movement in Literature* by Arthur Symons, rev. ed. copyright 1919 by E. P. Dutton & Co., Inc., renewal, 1946, by Nona Hill. Used by permission of the publisher.

Harcourt Brace Jovanovich, Inc., and The Hogarth Press, Ltd., for excerpts from *The Common Reader* by Virginia Woolf, published 1925 by Harcourt Brace.

Jonathan Cape Ltd., Viking Press, Inc., The Society of Authors as the literary representative of the Estate of James Joyce, and the Poetry Collection of the Lockwood Memorial Library, State University of New York at Buffalo, for excerpts from *Exiles* by James Joyce, edited by Padraic Colum, copyright 1951 by The Viking Press, Inc.

Kraus Reprint Company and Marie Jolas for permission to reprint in full "Proclamation," *transition*, nos. 16-17, June 1929.

McGraw-Hill Book Company for excerpts from *The Psychology of Thinking* by W. Edgar Vinacke, 1952. Used by permission of McGraw-Hill Book Company.

MIT Press for excerpts from Benjamin Lee Whorf, *Language, Thought, and Reality*, ed. John B. Carroll, 1956.

Murnat Publications, and Abelard-Schuman Ltd., for excerpts from *Claybook for James Joyce* by Louis Gillet, published by Abelard-Schuman Ltd., copyright 1958.

Oxford University Press for excerpts from *The Art of James Joyce* by A. Walton Litz, published 1964 by Oxford University Press.

Psychiatry and the William Alanson White Psychiatric Foundation for excerpts from Marie Lorenz, "Expressive Behavior and Language Patterns," *Psychiatry* 18 (1955).

Psychological Reports for excerpts from H. Aronson and W. Weintraub, "Sex Differences in Verbal Behavior Related to Adjustive Mechanisms," *Psychological Reports*, 1967, 21, 965-971.

The Trustees of the Philip H. & A. S. W. Rosenbach Foundation, Philadelphia, for excerpts from the manuscript "Ulysses."

The Viking Press, Inc., and Jonathan Cape Ltd., for excerpts from *Exiles* by James Joyce, edited by Padraic Colum. Copyright 1951 by The Viking Press, Inc. Reprinted by permission of The Viking Press, Inc. and Jonathan Cape Ltd.

W. W. Norton & Company for excerpts from *Conceptions of Modern Psychiatry* by Harry Stack Sullivan, M.D., with the permission of the publisher, W. W. Norton & Company, Inc. Copyright 1940, 1945, 1947, and 1953 by the William Alanson White Psychiatric Foundation.

For all the Steinbergs

Contents

Figures

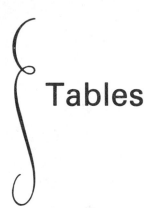

Tables

Acknowledgments

I was fortunate in having begun my study of James Joyce in the company of several colleagues at what was then Carnegie Institute of Technology. One was John A. Hart, still a friend and colleague at Carnegie-Mellon University, whose wit and wisdom helped make the initial reading of *Ulysses* a most pleasant and profitable undertaking and from whom I continue to learn. Another was William M. Schutte, no longer a colleague, but still a friend and frequent collaborator, with whom for many years I have happily shared experiences and projects in a wide variety of fields. His understanding of Joyce and his judgment and comments on the first version of this manuscript contributed in important ways to whatever value this book may have.

In its initial version this study was presented as a dissertation at New York University. To Louise M. Rosenblatt, who supervised the dissertation, I am very grateful. I learned much from her sympathetic yet rigorous approach to literature, and I am indebted to her for the way in which she helped and encouraged me, by challenging questions and comments, to chart my course and to carry out what I had planned. During that period the encouragement and support of Austin Wright, Elliott Dunlap Smith, and Glen U. Cleeton of Carnegie Institute of Technology were important. I am also grateful for the later encouragement and support of Edward R. Schatz. At critical times research and leave funds available at Carnegie Institute of Technology (subsequently Carnegie-Mellon University) proved most helpful.

As I prepared for the expansion and revision of my original manuscript, I benefitted greatly from the detailed comments and encouragement of Thomas F. Staley. I was fortunate, too, to be appointed a visiting scholar at the Center for Advanced Study in the Behavioral Sciences for the academic year 1970-71. The

warm and helpful staff at the Center, the interested and
friendly colleagues there, and the pleasant surroundings all
combined to provide ideal conditions for completing this book.

I am, of course, indebted to many librarians and other
benefactors for their help in the use of Joyce materials: to
Charles D. Abbott and the staff of the Lockwood Memorial
Library at the State University of New York at Buffalo, to the
staff of the Houghton Library at Harvard University, and to
Herbert Cahoon at The New York Public Library. Lessing J.
Rosenwald very kindly arranged for me to use the *Ulysses*
manuscripts which belong to the Philip and A. S. W. Rosenbach
Foundation of Philadelphia. Mary Scarlott and other members
of the staff of the Hunt Library at Carnegie-Mellon University
have given me invaluable support over the years, and Betty
Calloway and Betsy Hastorf helped in many ways to make my
year at the Center for Advanced Study a productive one. I am
also indebted to Random House and The Bodley Head for the
many quotations from *Ulysses*.

Statistical advice and assistance from David B. Peizer at the
Center and statistical assistance from Ann L. Rice were very
helpful, as was clerical assistance from two students, Carol
Kruger of Carnegie-Mellon University and Cora Presley of
Stanford University.

Many editors have been helpful. Over the years portions of
this study have appeared in the Carnegie Series in English,
*ETC; A Review of General Semantics; James Joyce Quarterly;
The James Joyce Review; Modern Fiction Studies; Style;* Thomas
F. Staley and Bernard Benstock, eds., *Approaches to "Ulysses":
Ten Essays* (Pittsburgh: University of Pittsburgh Press, 1970);
and Fritz Senn, ed., *Spotlight on Joyce: The Dublin Symposium*
(Bloomington: University of Indiana Press, 1972). I am also
indebted to Eleanor M. Walker and M. Louise Craft for their care
in editing my manuscript.

I must also record my gratitude to Lea N. Steinberg, who
several times attended meetings of the James Joyce Society at
the Gotham Book Mart in New York City and sent me detailed
notes of the proceedings and who has helped in other ways;
Virginia Y. Schenck and Anne Ramey of Carnegie-Mellon
University, who have helped—and continue to help—much
beyond the call of duty; and Estella M. Krebs, who typed this
manuscript.

To my wife and sons, for whom this study must have been an endless undertaking and who not only tolerated but forgave the absences (and absentmindedness) it caused, I can only record my very humble thanks and ask continued forgiveness for future ventures. They have shown a warm forbearance and understanding.

Technical Note

Since this study was begun before the appearance of the 1961 revision of the Random House (Modern Library) *Ulysses*, many of the analyses were based on the 1934 Random House (Modern Library) text. When the 1961 edition appeared, it would have been simple enough to change page references to refer to that edition, but two considerations militated for an alternate solution. First, many of the analyses made were based on eighteen half-page sample passages (six each for Proteus, Lestrygonians, and Penelope—chapters three, eight, and eighteen of *Ulysses*; see the appendix for a description of these samples). It was simplest to report the samples that way. A second point is probably more important. Many people are still using the 1934 edition. Quotations from *Ulysses* are therefore from the 1934 edition, but page and line references are given to *both* editions. Thus the figures in the reference " 'no pun intended' (649:7/665:4)" mean that the phrase "no pun intended" appears on the seventh line of page 649 in the 1934 edition and in the fourth line of page 665 in the 1961 edition.

References are also made throughout this book to the manuscript version of *Ulysses* in the Lockwood Memorial Library at the State University of New York at Buffalo, to the Rosenbach manuscript version of *Ulysses* at Philadelphia, and to the page proofs of *Ulysses* in the Houghton Library at Harvard University. The Buffalo collection is described by John J. Slocum and Herbert Cahoon in their *Bibliography of James Joyce, 1882-1941* (New Haven: Yale University Press, 1953), pp. 140-41. (See also Peter Spielberg, ed., *James Joyce's Manuscripts and Letters at the University of Buffalo* (Albany: State University of New York Press, 1962). The most useful manuscript in that collection for this study was an early version of Proteus. The Rosenbach manuscript (described by Slocum and

Cahoon on pp. 138-40) is now the property of the Philip and
A. S. W. Rosenbach Foundation of Philadelphia. It contains,
among other documents, full versions of Proteus and
Lestrygonians and a version of Penelope through "O but then
what am I going to do about him though" (761:22/776:19)—
roughly 85 percent of that chapter. The page proofs at the
Houghton Library (described by Slocum and Cahoon on pp.
141-42), on which Joyce made many additions, include at least
two successive proofs for most of the book and as many as six
proofs for some sections of it. There were no gaps for the
Proteus, Lestrygonians, or Penelope chapters.

Throughout I have employed the commonly accepted custom
of referring to the chapters of *Ulysses* by the Homeric titles
which Joyce gave them:

1. Telemachus
2. Nestor
3. Proteus
4. Calypso
5. Lotus-Eaters
6. Hades
7. Aeolus
8. Lestrygonians
9. Scylla and Charybdis
10. The Wandering Rocks
11. The Sirens
12. Cyclops
13. Nausicaa
14. Oxen of the Sun
15. Circe
16. Eumaeus
17. Ithaca
18. Penelope

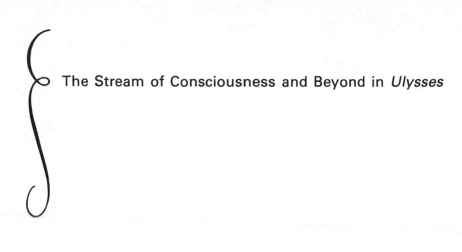 The Stream of Consciousness and Beyond in *Ulysses*

1
Introduction

When one reads what Joyce, his friends, and the critics said and wrote about *Ulysses* while it was appearing in serial form in the *Little Review* and after it was published in 1922, it is clear that they thought that Joyce had developed a technique for presenting to the reader exactly what happens inside a person's mind. Not a simulation, but a presentation.

For example, Joyce told Djuna Barnes, "In *Ulysses* I have recorded, simultaneously, what a man says, sees, thinks, and what such seeing, thinking, saying does, to what you Freudians call the subconscious."[1] And to Frank Budgen he said, "I try to give the unspoken, unacted thoughts of people in the way they occur."[2] In an early review of *Ulysses* which, according to Mary Colum, pleased Joyce very much, Edmund Wilson wrote, "It is, in short, perhaps the most faithful X-ray ever taken of the ordinary human consciousness."[3]

Statements prepared under Joyce's tutelage repeated the claim. In a lecture (prepared with Joyce's help) delivered just before *Ulysses* appeared, Valery Larbaud said of it: "For us the readers, Bloom and Stephen are, so to speak, the vehicles in which we pass across the book. Stationed in the intimacy of their minds, and sometimes in the minds of other characters, we see through their eyes and hear through their ears what happens and what is said about them."[4] Stuart Gilbert, a friend of Joyce and an early commentator on his writings, called the "monologue intérieur" in *Ulysses* "une reproduction exacte et quasi-photographique des pensées, telle qu'elle prennent forme dans le conscience du penseur"—an exact and quasi-photographic reproduction of thoughts of the kind which take form in the consciousness of the thinker.[5] And Frank Budgen, a close friend to whom Joyce talked and wrote at considerable length about *Ulysses*, said: "There is nothing from beginning to end of *Proteus*

3

that is not thought or sensation. Other characters who come into the picture do so only as part of the contents of Stephen's mind. Through his senses the seashore comes to life."[6]

Even those who were critical of *Ulysses* when it appeared tended to agree. Arnold Bennett, for example, wrote:

> Of course the author is trying to reproduce the thoughts of the personage [Bloom in Lestrygonians], and his verbal method can be justified—does indeed richly justify itself here and there in the story. But upon the whole, though the reproduction is successful, the things reproduced appear too often to be trivial and perfectly futile in the narrative.[7]

And Louis Gillet wrote:

> I do not believe a writer has ever clung more closely to the desire fearlessly to portray a man, his body and soul, guts and bowels, to turn him inside-out, to represent with more details and less reticence all the interior movement, the physical and moral substance, the depth of feelings and images, of appetites and tendencies, of impurities, desires, obsessions, manias and needs, of stray impulses and thoughts, which all constitute the living texture, physiology and psychology of a single individual. . . . Imagine the cover lifted from a man's brain, so that you could watch the brain, its entrails functioning and steaming and you will then have an idea of this portrait of Mr. Bloom.[8]

Some years later, after he had spent many hours talking with Joyce about his writing and had become a Joyce enthusiast, the same critic wrote: "This technique was new, free from all the chains of logic and even from the rules of syntax. It represented thought grasped in its nascent, elementary state and close to pure sensation, before it was clarified and solidified by the thinking mind."[9]

The fullest early analysis of the need for and function of what soon came to be called the stream-of-consciousness technique—and in many ways still the best—was written by Virginia Woolf, herself a practitioner of that technique. By March 1919 there had appeared in the *Little Review* the first eight chapters of *Ulysses*: Telemachus, Nestor, Proteus, Calypso, Lotus-Eaters, Hades, Aeolus, and Lestrygonians.[10] In April Mrs. Woolf wrote:

> Examine for a moment an ordinary mind on an ordinary day. The mind receives a myriad impressions—trivial, fantastic,

evanescent, or engraved with the sharpness of steel. From all sides they come, an incessant shower of innumerable atoms; and as they fall, as they shape themselves into the life of Monday or Tuesday, the accent falls differently from of old. . . . Life is not a series of gig lamps symmetrically arranged; but a luminous halo, a semi-transparent envelope surrounding us from the beginning of consciousness to the end. Is it not the task of the novelist to convey this varying, this unknown and uncircumscribed spirit, whatever aberration or complexity it may display, with as little mixture of the alien and external as possible? We are not pleading merely for courage and sincerity; we are suggesting that the proper stuff of fiction is a little other than custom would have us believe it.[11]

The concluding sentence makes the claim of at least a new beginning, if not a new method of writing.

Of the work "of several young writers, among whom Mr. James Joyce is most notable," she found:

They attempt to come closer to life [than their predecessors], and to preserve more sincerely and exactly what interests and moves them, even if to do so they must discard most of the conventions which are commonly observed by the novelists. Let us record the atoms as they fall upon the mind in the order in which they fall, let us trace the pattern, however disconnected and incoherent in appearance, which each sight or incident scores upon the consciousness.

She found that Joyce in particular

is concerned at all costs to reveal the flickerings of that innermost flame which flashes its messages through the brain, and in order to preserve it he disregards with complete courage whatever seems to him adventitious, whether it be probability, or coherence or any other of these signposts which for generations have served to support the imagination of a reader when called upon to imagine what he can neither touch nor see.

Finally,

for the moderns . . . the point of interest . . . lies very likely in the dark places of psychology. At once, therefore, the accent falls a little differently; the emphasis is upon something hitherto ignored; at once a different outline of form becomes necessary, difficult for us to grasp, incomprehensible to our predecessors.[12]

The statement that the new approach is "incomprehensible to our predecessors" clearly overshadows the more ladylike demurrers that the new "stuff of fiction" is only "a little other than custom would have us believe" and that the new accent falls only "a little differently." The modern writer, and particularly Joyce, was concerned with the "myriad impressions [the mind receives]—trivial, fantastic, evanescent, or engraved with the sharpness of steel"; with "the atoms as they fall upon the mind"; with "the flickerings of that innermost flame which flashes its messages through the brain"; with "the dark places of psychology." There has been no better operational definition of the stream-of-consciousness technique.

There was at least one early dissenter to the validity of the stream-of-consciousness technique. Four years after the publication of *Ulysses*, Wyndham Lewis wrote:

> [Joyce] had to pretend that we were really surprising the private thought of a real and average human creature, Mr. Bloom. But the fact is that Mr. Bloom was abnormally *wordy*. He *thought in words*, not images, for our benefit, in a fashion as unreal, from the point of view of the strictest naturalist dogma, as a Hamlet soliloquy.[13]

Lewis was arguing that thought is more than just words, that it includes images. But no one seems to have paid much attention to the point.

In *James Joyce's "Ulysses,"* which he indicated he wrote under Joyce's supervision, Gilbert simply dismissed the argument:

> Mr. Wyndham Lewis suggested . . . that, as thoughts are not always verbal and we can think without words, the technique of the silent monologue is misleading. Against this, however, there is the equally tenable hypothesis that 'without language there can be no thought', and the ineluctable fact, that even if we do not *think*, we certainly must *write* in words.[14]

He did not indicate how his defense invalidates Lewis's criticism. Joyce, too, seems to have brushed the ciriticism aside without answering it. According to Gilbert he said, "From my point of view, it hardly matters whether the technique is 'veracious' or not; it has served me as a bridge over which to march my eighteen episodes."[15]

Some time later William York Tindall renewed the discussion:

> No longer looking through [the author's] eyes into the observer's
> mind, we occupy that mind. Its total contents of thought,
> sensation, and memory pass through us. Thought is by image as
> well as word, and the tone of experience is neither verbal nor
> imagistic. The author must not only record his observer's
> verbalized thought but, since books consist of words, must
> verbalize what his observer feels.[16]

Here the problem is made explicit, but just how Joyce was able
to accomplish the transmutation from image to word is not
discussed.

At about the same time, René Wellek and Austin Warren
offered still another description of the stream-of-consciousness
technique:

> If one examines "stream of consciousness" novels, one soon
> discovers that there is no "real" reproduction of the actual mental
> processes of the subject, that the stream of consciousness is rather
> a device of dramatizing the mind, of making us aware completely
> . . . of what Mrs. Bloom is like. But there is little that seems
> scientific or even "realistic" about the device.[17]

A little earlier, however, C. S. Lewis had gone even further,
claiming that verbalizing the true stream of consciousness
does, in fact, distort it: "The moment you put it into words you
falsify it."[18]

In a reissue of *James Joyce's "Ulysses,"* published after the
Tindall and Lewis statements and advertised as a "complete
revision, rewritten, and reset," Gilbert made no attempt to meet
these objections, repeating with but a single change his earlier
statement about Wyndham Lewis's criticism: "the ineluctable
fact" became "the obvious fact."[19]

Thus where Joyce, his friends, and most of the early critics
felt that Joyce's stream-of-consciousness technique *reproduces*
the psychological stream of consciousness, Tindall said that it
verbalizes it. Wellek and Warren felt that it did not reproduce
the psychological stream of consciousness, that it is not even
"realistic," but that it *dramatizes* the mind. And C. S. Lewis
insisted that it seriously distorts and misrepresents the
psychological stream of consciousness. Today, almost fifty years
after the publication of *Ulysses,* there is still no agreement
about Joyce's use of the stream-of-consciousness technique and
its relation to the psychological stream of consciousness. Nor

is there any sustained analysis of many of the statements made about it.

A slightly different problem presents itself with the early critical acclaim that Joyce found "the unique vocabulary and rhythm which will represent the thoughts of each [character]." When *Ulysses* was published, for example, Mary Colum wrote:

> James Joyce gives us the characters of Stephen and Bloom as they appear externally and in their own subconsciousness. One of the remarkable feats of the book is the manner in which the separate subconsciousnesses of Stephen and Bloom are revealed, with every aimless thought, every half-formed idea and every unformed phrase indicative of their separate character and personality, and of the influences that have gone into their making. This is most marked when they think of the same things.[20]

And Gilbert Seldes declared, "There is no mistaking the meditations of Stephen for those of Bloom, those of either for the dark flood of Marion's consciousness."[21] Contemporary critics do not disagree; but they simply assert the fact. They do not demonstrate that it is true.

Still another problem is the wide variety of terms that critics use interchangeably for what they take to be the same stylistic technique: stream of consciousness, stream of thought, *monologue intérieur*, interior monologue, silent monologue, soliloquy, silent soliloquy. It would be helpful to discriminate among them—to distinguish shades of meaning, if there are any; and to determine which are most apt, most usefully descriptive.

A pair of related problems is what led Joyce to develop the stream-of-consciousness technique so fully and why, having done so, he dropped it in the middle of *Ulysses* and moved on to other techniques. What were the forces in his own aesthetic, in his personality, and in his times that made him adopt a little-noticed technique and lavish on it the full powers of his creativity? And having perfected that technique, having developed a unique method for portraying character, why did he reject it in favor of the other techniques he used in the second half of *Ulysses* and, ultimately, the technique he used in *Finnegans Wake?*

There have been three books devoted to the stream-of-consciousness technique which have dealt with some of these matters: *Stream of Consciousness in the Modern Novel,* by Robert Humphrey (1954);[22] *Stream of Consciousness: A Study in Literary Method,* by Melvin Friedman (1955);[23] and *Bergson and the Stream of Consciousness Novel,* by Shiv K. Kumar (1962).[24] Joyce is only one of their concerns, however; the first two are over fifteen years old; and the third, a decade old, looks at the stream-of-consciousness technique from a very special point of view. It is time not only for another look, but for a closer look at Joyce's use of the stream-of-consciousness technique.

I shall attempt to answer the questions I have raised in the order in which I have raised them. In Part One, I shall consider the psychological stream of consciousness, the nature of language, and the interrelationship of the two. I shall then examine Joyce's use of the stream-of-consciousness technique, the extent to which it reproduces the psychological stream of consciousness, and how Joyce introduces the reader to it in the opening sections of *Ulysses.*

In Part Two, I shall compare the streams of consciousness of Stephen, Bloom, and Molly as Joyce presents them in three chapters of *Ulysses:* Proteus, Lestrygonians, and Penelope. By analyzing such things as content, sentence structure, vocabulary, images, and associations, I shall attempt to determine the degree to which Joyce used the stream-of-consciousness technique to project three distinctly different personalities. Novelists generally give us the shapes and idiosyncracies of the characters in their novels by what they have the characters say to one another or about one another, by what the characters do, or by omniscient author's sentences, which simply tell the reader what the novelist wants them to know. Comparing the three streams of consciousness will allow us to see whether Joyce developed the stream-of-consciousness technique as a new tool for the novelist or whether he employed standard novelistic techniques and simply used the stream-of-consciousness technique as a tour de force or for superficial surface texture. The methodology and analyses employed in this comparison should be of interest not only to students of Joyce, but to students of stylistics as well.

This close examination of the text will also help us to consider some of the disagreements among the critics about the meaning of *Ulysses* and the relationships existing among its three main characters. If we are to restore "the living balance, the poise between vital uncertainties and unanswered questions which constitute, for a classical temper, the authentic mystery of life" and which for Thomas Merton were "the very essence of the comic art" and thus of *Ulysses*, we must examine carefully what Joyce wrote. What Joyce and his friends said may be of interest along the way, but as readers and critics we must look finally to the text. Merton has charged that workers "in the Joyce industry" (as he termed it) "can get away with anything."[25] Perhaps not.

Finally, in Part Three, I shall first attempt to define the stream-of-consciousness technique and the other labels that are associated with it, distinguish among them, and make some recommendations for their use. Then I shall examine Joyce's aesthetic, the development of his prose style, and the aesthetic and intellectual movements of his time to see if I can account for his interest in and development of the stream-of-consciousness technique and for his moving beyond it to the polyphonic technique of *Finnegans Wake*.

PART I
The Stream of Consciousness and the Stream-of-Consciousness Technique

2
The Psychological Stream of Consciousness

Confronted with a stream-of-consciousness passage in a novel, many readers think that the author has presented them with an actual stream of consciousness, the flow of thought and awareness as it occurs from moment to moment in the mind. An examination of what we know about consciousness, thinking, and language, however, indicates that a stream-of-consciousness novelist can at best *simulate* the psychological stream of consciousness. Such an examination also indicates some of the problems facing him when he attempts that simulation.

Unfortunately there is no single source in which to find a summary of what the psychologists know about the stream of consciousness. One must construct an understanding of it from diverse—and often divergent—sources. I shall undertake such a construction in this chapter, perhaps in more detail than some readers may wish. Such detail is necessary, however, if we are to understand what happens in the mind, how we perceive the world, and what we read on the printed page—particularly, of course, what we read in a stream-of-consciousness novel, but also in other forms of literature; for all literature seeks to present a view of the world, widely or narrowly perceived.

Critics and plain readers tend to psychologize too glibly (and superficially) about perception, thought, and the mind, and how these all relate to the world outside. The jargon and statistics of the social scientists may make reading psychology difficult, sometimes as difficult as reading literary criticism; but just as the student of psychology has much to learn from literature about the patterns of mind and behavior he seeks to understand, so the student of literature has much to learn from psychology about the patterns of mind and behavior a writer seeks to portray.

13

An example of how far back careful attempts to describe thinking go can be found in what is perhaps the oldest of the theories about the nature of thought, association:

> Generally speaking, associationism is a mechanistic doctrine, conceiving of mental processes as the more or less automatic elaboration—combination and recombination—of materials derived from the sense organs. The development of the theory centers around the attempt to reduce the mechanism to its simplest, most concrete terms and to discover the "laws" according to which it works.[1]

We can trace the beginnings of this theory to the Greeks. Socrates says in *Phaedo*: "So much is clear—that when we perceive something, either by the help of sight, or hearing, or some other sense, from that perception we are able to obtain a notion of some other thing like or unlike, which is associated with it but has been forgotten."[2] And, too, in his *De Memoria*, Aristotle says:

> Acts of recollection, as they occur in experience, are due to the fact that one movement has by nature another that succeeds it in regular order.
> If this order be necessary, whenever a subject experiences the former of the two movements thus connected, it will invariably experience the latter; if, however, the order be not necessary, but customary, only in the majority of cases will the subject experience the latter of the two movements.[3]

The British associationists are largely responsible for developing the concept into a school of psychology. Thomas Hobbes, John Locke, David Hume, David Hartley, Thomas Brown, James Mill, and Alexander Bain, to name just the important ones, added considerably to the body of writing discussing the theory. "Since Bain's time, associationism has persisted in one form or another, but as an aspect of behavior rather than as its sum and substance."[4]

Contemporary psychology also owes much of its interest in the nature of thought and its understanding of it to William James. James begins with a very elementary statement: "*The first fact for us . . . is that thinking of some sort goes on.*" By "thinking" James means "every form of consciousness indiscriminantly." "Continuous thought" James characterizes as "the stream of thought" or "the stream of consciousness,"[5] defined as

the conscious experience of an individual, likened to a stream
in order to emphasize its continuity, in opposition to the
conception of it as a series of discrete states [a term introduced
by James].[6]

[It contains] sensations of our bodies and of the objects around
us, memories of past experiences and thoughts of distant things,
feelings of satisfaction and dissatisfaction, desires and aversions,
and other emotional conditions, together with determinations of
the will, in every variety of permutation and combination.[7]

According to James, thought has five characteristics:

1) Every thought tends to be part of a personal consciousness.
2) Within each personal consciousness thought is always
changing.
3) Within each personal consciousness thought is sensibly
continuous.
4) It always appears to deal with objects independent of itself.
5) It is interested in some parts of these objects to the exclusion
of others, and welcomes or rejects—*chooses* from among them, in
a word—all the while.[8]

Little of this material is now controversial. James argues that
every person's world is split into the "me" and the "not-me,"
and thought is an irrevocable part of the "me." Thought,
therefore, is personal. And it is never the same. Inasmuch as
it is directly connected with our sensations and feelings, which
are always undergoing change, and since it is the function of
a brain content which is ever being modified, which is never
the same, which can never return to a previous state, thought
must always change, not only from year to year, but from hour
to hour. That thought is continuous to James means the following
two things:

1. That even where there is a time-gap the consciousness after
it feels as if it belonged together with the consciousness before
it, as another part of the same self;
2. That the changes from one moment to another in the quality
of the consciousness are never absolutely abrupt.[9]

Thus thoughts color one another. We do not think thought a,
then thought b, and then thought c; but rather thought $(x)a(b)$,
then thought $(a)b(c)$, and then thought $(b)c(d)$. Even after
sleep we "mentally . . . [reach] back and . . . [make]
connection with . . . the . . . [stream] of thought which . . .

[was] broken by the sleeping hours."[10] Point four needs little expansion; in these days of the semanticist's insistence on the separation of the symbol from the object, there should be little disagreement, philosophical or psychological, about the distinction of the thought from the object. And point five has to do with the individual differences of perception and abstraction that have been dwelt on at great length by the psychologists who followed James.

That "consciousness, from our natal day, is of a teeming multiplicity of objects and relations"[11] is borne out by a contemporary psychiatrist, the late Harry Stack Sullivan, in his discussion during a lecture of a single moment of consciousness:

> I shall remember this moment as it exists, with all its implications past, present, and future—most of these implications having been present as tensional elements, and not as formulated statements. Let me illustrate: there is the spatial orientation—this beautiful and acoustically excellent auditorium; the rostrum, the microphone and its related system which tonight seems to be unmonitored, the audience as a certain amazingly large number of people, a friend who is deaf in the ear nearest me, the stenotype reporter, and many and many another detail of the geometric and local geographic situation—coupled with the *most significant* first experience of the related spatial orientation at the start of the first lecture in this series. There is the temporal orientation along several significant lines; the night after our unusually timed Thanksgiving, the "place" of the moment in the exposition that I had planned for this lecture; the "place" of the moment in a prehended durability of the lumped attention of the audience and their tolerance for my presentation; the "place" in the attention-tolerance of certain more personally significant members of the audience; and various other details. There is the orientation in terms of my personal career-line; the lucidity of my formulation, the adequacy of its verbal expression—or rather, verbal indication, for one has no time to be exact and precise, if one is to cover these topics without exhausting the auditors—the effect on this moment of gaps in the earlier presentations, the "coming" ideas that should grow out of this, its relation to the hoped-for success of the whole as an organization of all these statements and indications in terms of changes in the general audience, and new insights in the more personally significant auditors—including, very significantly, myself. I have mentioned these orientations without reference to the zones of interaction that are involved. I have omitted reference to the patterns of kinesthetic and related data that exist in me, in connection with them. I can but invite your attention

to the complex pattern of vocal—sound productive and sound receptive—past and future verbal and other voice-communicative processes concerned, and the effective or partially ineffectual and unfortunate function of these patterns in terms of what makes up this moment in each of you. I will only mention as yet other coordinates of the present moment, states of my visceral and skeletal musculature as terms in relative satisfaction or dissatisfaction with the momentary situation and with the accomplished and the potential performances of the whole lecture, the series of lectures, and with events before and to follow on the lecture. These are some of the items that may be abstracted from the momentary state of the organism—of a vast series of which one's memory is composed.[12]

If an instant of consciousness is so complex, how much more so, then, is the stream of consciousness from which such an instant has been arbitrarily torn in order to hold it up, threads trailing, for examination?

According to Sullivan, consciousness, and therefore the stream of consciousness, contains: language; spatial, temporal, and purposive orientation; kinesthetic elements and related data; vocal patterns; states of visceral and skeletal musculature; and many other items. Further, all of these items are interacting, so that even in such a suspended moment of consciousness as that described by Sullivan, to list them separately is to distort the picture.[13]

This emphasis on "the teeming multiplicity of objects and relations" in the stream of consciousness raises many problems. For example, if all these elements appear in the consciousness, how do they appear, how are they embodied; or, to put it another way, in what guise do they appear, how are they presented? At the risk of distorting, we must organize these components somehow in order to talk about them. The method involving the least risk would seem to be to describe them just as various schools of psychology claim to have found them.

The structuralists, led by Wundt and Titchener, attempted to determine the elements of consciousness by introspection:

Analysis of mental contents by this method seemed to reveal that all mental processes are composed of simple, irreducible elements, namely, sensations, affections, and images, each with characteristic dimensions, or "attributes." Sensations, the basic data arriving in the sense organs, and classified accordingly, are marked by specifiable quality, *e.g.,* cold, blue, salt, by intensity of a given amount, by variations in clearness and by a given duration. They are compounded into perceptions, following the laws of such a mixture. Similarly, affections, with their describable attributes, lacking the dimension of clearness, are compounded into feelings, or simple emotions. Images . . . are derived from sensations. They constitute the elements of which ideas are composed and thus form the basic content of thought. The differences between sensations and images grow out of their relationship, for an image has less distinctive quality, less intensity, and shorter duration than the corresponding sensation.

The structuralists explained all thinking as the occurrence of images, combining and recombining, according to requirements.[14]

Since we shall be concerned with some of these elements later, they warrant a more careful definition here:

sensation
1. (*psychol.*) an experience aroused from outside the nervous system, which is not further analyzable by introspection; i.e., an element of consciousness; 2. (*physiol.*) an afferent neural process which commences in a receptor and extends to the cerebrum.

perception
1. the awareness of external objects, qualities or relations, which ensues directly upon sensory processes, as distg. fr. memory or other central processes; 2. a mental complex or integration which has sensory experience as its core; 3. awareness of present data, whether external or intraorganic.

image
1. an element of experience which is centrally aroused and which possesses all the attributes of sensation; 2. an experience which reproduces or copies in part and with some degree of sensory realism a previous perceptual experience in the absence of the original sensory stimulation.[15]

The so-called Würzburg school, insisting that there could be imageless thought, approached the problem in a somewhat different way:

They contributed the concepts of task, set, and determining tendency. According to the usual formulation, the *task* gives the subject a particular *set*, and this set influences his associative sequence by means of unconscious *determining tendencies* that guide the process to its proper completion. . . . These concepts bear a very close resemblance to what we have called, in preceding chapters, contextual constraints or associative connections. Determining tendencies must operate in the extemporaneous patching together of words in ordinary speech.[16]

The early years of the twentieth century saw two new schools of psychology: in the United States, behaviorism; in Germany, Gestalt psychology.

The two movements were contemporaneous and each protested against the same orthodoxy. . . . Orthodox psychology in 1910 was (i) experimental, (ii) introspective, (iii) elementalistic and (iv) associationistic. Behaviorism and Gestalt psychology were agreed only on the first: both schools thought psychology should and could be experimental.[17]

The behaviorists claimed that thinking is the action of language mechanisms. J. B. Watson put it very concisely: "Thinking is then largely a verbal process; occasionally expressive movements substitutable for word movements (gestures, attitudes, etc.) enter in as part of the general stream of implicit activity."[18] The Gestaltists, in their rejection of "elementalistic psychology," announced the principle of isomorphism, "the essence of [which] is that phenomenologically ascertained forms actually correspond to psychophysical forms. Psychophysical forms in the brain are viewed as not essentially different from the physical forms of inorganic nature."[19] Perceptions and thoughts, then, may not be embodied in or composed of anything, but may simply be neural excitations or chemical changes; perhaps "the forms of experience correspond to recognizable physical forms in the nervous system."[20]

Neither school had much use for images. In the United States particularly, under the influence of behaviorism, "imagery, attention, states of consciousness, and other such central concepts of the old era were anathematized as 'mentalistic' and cast into outer darkness."[21]

It took almost fifty years to recall the image from outer darkness and reinstall it as an appropriate—and for some a significant—concern for psychology. In 1962 Robert R. Holt gave as his presidential address to Division Twelve of the American Psychological Association a paper entitled "Imagery: the Return of the Ostracized."[22] Published studies by Jerome L. Singer indicated that, for some people, at least, visual imagery is "the most pervasive underlying feature of the ongoing thought stream" and "the predominant modality for fantasy."[23] And in 1969 Alan Richardson published a book entitled *Mental Imagery*, the purpose of which was "to bring together in one place a representative sample of facts and hypotheses concerning the phenomena of mental imagery."[24]

The studies reported by Richardson show that people differ in their use of imagination imagery. Some people are primarily visualizers, and others primarily verbalizers; and still others use a mixture of both. A study of tonal memory shows that some people have more dominant auditory imagery than others.[25] Still other studies report kinesthetic images, tactile (including thermal) images, and olfactory images.[26] There is also the suggestion that image dominance may be related to personality type: visualizers tending to be active, independent, and hypersensitive; verbalizers—passive, dependent, submissive, slow, calm, and even-tempered; and those who are both—impatient, aggressive, and intolerant.[27]

I have offered this brief history to demonstrate that the psychological stream of consciousness is not merely a string of words and that therefore what the stream-of-consciousness writer writes is not a presentation but can at best be only a simulation of what occurs in the mind. The discussion serves at the same time to point out what it is that the stream-of-consciousness writer must simulate if he is to be convincing.

We must now look at the problem of simulating the "teeming multiplicity of objects and relations" in the stream of consciousness by means of only one of the components of that stream—language. Semanticists have been insisting for some time now that there is a fundamental difference between the world we live in and the language we use to describe it. For example, Alfred Korzybski makes the statement that "the common A[ristotelian]-system and language which we have inherited from our primitive ancestors *differ entirely in structure* from the well-known and established 1933 structure of the world, ourselves and our nervous systems included." The world, our perception of it, and often our thinking about it are "structural," "multi-dimensional," whereas language is linear and additive.[28] Perhaps an example will make the point more clearly. We are always highly amused at the episode in *Alice in Wonderland* in which Alice, talking to the grinning Cheshire cat, sees the

cat slowly disappear while the grin remains. How could the grin
be separated from the cat? That would be preposterous. And
yet that is exactly what our language does. In the sentence "The
cat grins," we have done precisely the same thing—separated
the cat from the grin. We were forced to do so because of the
subject-predicate pattern of our language. As Lessing puts it,
"The coexistence of the body comes into collision with the
consecutiveness of language."[29]

Benjamin Lee Whorf wrote in great detail about this problem:

> Segmentation of nature is an aspect of grammar—one as yet little
> studied by grammarians. We cut up largely because, through our
> mother tongue, we are parties to an agreement to do so, not
> because nature itself is segmented in exactly that way for all
> to see. . . . Thus English and similar tongues lead us to think
> of the universe as a collection of rather distinct objects and events
> corresponding to words. Indeed this is the implicit picture of
> classical physics and astronomy—that the universe is essentially
> a collection of detached objects of different sizes.

This is a problem that arises particularly with the
Indo-European languages:

> Some languages have means of expression—chemical combination,
> as I called it—in which the separate terms are not as separate
> as in English but flow together into plastic synthetic creations.
> Hence such languages, which do not paint the separate-object
> picture of the universe to the same degree as do English and
> its sister tongues, point toward possible new types of logic and
> possible new cosmical pictures.
>
> Our Indian languages show that with a suitable grammar we may
> have intelligent sentences that cannot be broken up into subjects
> and predicates. Any attempted breakup is a breakup of some
> English translation or paraphrase of the sentence, not of the
> Indian sentence itself.[30]

Perhaps some of the languages of the American Indians that
Whorf writes about would be better adapted than are the
Indo-European languages to the work of the physicist—and to
the problems of the stream-of-consciousness novelist! At any
rate, Whorf's analyses underline further the fact that reproducing
reality in an Indo-European language is beset with difficulties.

Actually, what is being propounded here is in one way quite

similar to Lessing's argument in *Laokoon* about the proper
subjects for painting and poetry:

> I reason thus: if it is true that painting and poetry in their
> imitations make use of entirely different means or symbols—the
> first, namely, of form and colour in space, the second of
> articulated sounds in time—if these symbols indisputably require
> a suitable relation to the thing symbolized, then it is clear that
> symbols arranged in juxtaposition can only express subjects of
> which the wholes or parts exist in juxtaposition; while consecutive
> symbols can only express subjects of which the wholes or parts
> are themselves consecutive.
>
> Subjects whose wholes or parts exist in juxtaposition are called
> bodies. Consequently, bodies with their visible properties are the
> peculiar subjects of painting.
>
> Subjects whose wholes or parts are consecutive are called
> actions. Consequently, actions are the peculiar subject of poetry.[31]

Lessing is saying here what the semanticists say in a more
technical way—that visual perception or imagining is structural,
relational, multidimensional. The stream-of-consciousness writer
must deal with this multidimensionality, however, because
unlike Lessing's poet he is not merely concerned with action
but also with *people and things in action*. Thus a stream-of-
consciousness novelist tries to depict a multidimensional
consciousness in the process of flow.

It could be argued here that all novelists have always
attempted to depict reality. But the problem is peculiarly acute
for the stream-of-consciousness writer, for he is trying to
simulate the effect of reality impinging upon the consciousness.
We have heard Virginia Woolf, herself a stream-of-consciousness
novelist, speaking of Joyce: "Let us record the atoms as they
fall upon the mind in the order in which they fall, let us trace
the pattern, however disconnected and incoherent in appearance,
which each sight or incident scores upon the consciousness."[32]
Thus, as A. A. Mendilow says, the stream-of-consciousness
novelist tries to "plumb the deeper levels of human nature, the
foreconscious, the subconscious, the depths where experience and
awareness proceed not entirely or even mainly in a verbal
medium, but are tactile and motile and visual and aural too."[33]
Other novelists attempt rather to summarize the flow of
consciousness than to simulate it and thus operate on a much
higher level of abstraction.

In order to *reproduce* reality, an author would have to have at his command a medium like the "feelies" in *Brave New World*, in which the audience sees, hears, smells, and feels what the characters in the story experience. When the lovers on the screen kiss, the audience feel the sensation on their lips; and when "a little love [is] made" on a bearskin, the audience feel "every hair . . . separately and distinctly."[34] But since the novelist has only language at his command, he cannot reproduce reality. The stream-of-consciousness writer, however, tries to simulate reality, to give the impression to the reader that he is receiving the raw data of consciousness as they arrive in the mind of the character.

The problem of the stream-of-consciousness novelist thus begins to take shape: how can he simulate multidimensional reality in a linear, additive medium? A few examples of how the nature of language similarly complicates undertakings in other fields may help to underline the problem. As Herbert J. Muller puts it, the physicist runs into this difficulty: "Another way of describing the revolution in physics is to say that key nouns have changed into verbs—to move, to act, to happen. *What* moves and acts, physicists do not care; 'matter' to them means 'to matter,' to make a difference. But our language is still geared to express 'states of being' rather than processes."[35] James encounters a similar difficulty at the beginning of his chapter on the stream of thought: "If we could say in English 'it thinks,' as we say 'it rains' or 'it blows,' we should be stating the fact most simply and with the minimum of assumption. As we cannot, we must simply say that *thought goes on*."[36] James Livingston Lowes recognizes that difficulty several times in *The Road to Xanadu*. At the beginning of the book, as he prepares to plumb the "deep well" of Coleridge's imagination, he warns: "Above all . . . , it may not be forgotten that we are disengaging the strands of an extremely complex web. . . . It is not a gratuitous precaution, therefore, to repeat that in the paragraphs which follow the whole story is not being told at once." When he examines the components of the dream that led to "Kubla Khan," he says: "That Coleridge was conscious of constituent elements in the entrancing spectacle that rose before him . . . I do not for a moment believe. . . . The cluster of images so caught together had coalesced like light, and neither the links which we have been at such pains to discover

nor the several images which we have sedulously disengaged
were present as such (we may be sure) to consciousness at all."
And, analyzing one of his own associations, he discusses
separately its several strands, but then adds in parentheses:
"although in reality the strands of recollections were
simultaneously interweaving like a nest of startled snakes."[37]
Physicists, psychologists, literary critics—their difficulties with
language because of its very nature help us to understand the
almost insurmountable problem facing the novelist who tries to
simulate the stream of consciousness.

While we are discussing the nature of language, we should
take notice of one more point made by Korzybski. He outlines
the levels of abstraction leading to speech as follows: "(1) the
event, or scientific object, or the submicroscopic physico-chemical
processes, (2) the ordinary object manufactured from the event
by our lower nervous centres, (3) the psychological centres, and
(4) the verbal definition of the term."[38] If this is the process
by which atoms of experience, falling upon the mind, come
finally to find expression in words, it is actually impossible to
"record the atoms as they fall" or to "trace the pattern," since
language is the fourth step in a process the first three steps
of which are preverbal.

A. A. Mendilow summarizes all these problems very neatly:
"Language cannot convey non-verbal experience; being successive
and linear, it cannot express simultaneous experiences; being
composed of separate and divisible units, whether of words or
groups of words, it cannot reveal the unbroken flow of the
process of living. Reality cannot be expressed or conveyed—only
the illusion of it."[39]

To return to consciousness, its focus and the direction of its
flow are a function of a bipolar regulatory system: on the one
hand is the environment with all its demands; on the other,
individual needs. Gardner Murphy's discussion of perception in
bipolar terms is applicable to all of consciousness: "an organized
process which is both outer and inner, which is organized in
terms of saliences both of the world without and of the world
within. Organization is not molded exclusively by the need
pattern or by the stimulus pattern."[40] Now the outer world
dominates, now the inner.

This bipolar regulating system results, as might be expected, in a consciousness which operates on a bipolar continuum: when the needs of the outer world dominate, consciousness is focused on problem solving; when inner needs dominate, consciousness yields to imagination and various forms of autistic thinking. "Creative thought . . . seems to be intermediate between problem solving and imagination, occurring in special situations involving nearly indistinguishably problem-solving behavior and imagination."[41] Very seldom, of course, is the state of consciousness a result of just one of the two sets of stimuli, external or internal. Although at various times one or the other dominates, any particular moment of consciousness is generally the result of a resolution of forces.

Since stream-of-consciousness writers concern themselves very little with problem solving and much with imagination, we shall focus on the latter.

Summarizing Vinacke's statements about the bipolarity of consciousness would seem to give the following continuum:

problem solving—creative thinking—imagination

Imagination, which aims at fulfilling "inner need-states," Vinacke breaks down into: 1. imaginative thinking, which "refers to mental processes in which the free activities of imagination are evoked primarily by external stimuli; typical situations of this kind are *play* and *projective tests*," and 2. autistic thinking, which "refers to mental processes in which the free activities of imagination are evoked or influenced primarily by internal stimuli, namely, *fantasy, dreams,* and *wishful thinking*." The term *fantasy* distinguishes "the wish-fulfilling mental activity of waking life from that which occurs during sleep, i.e., dreams." In *wishful thinking,* "the wish [that is, the need, impulse, feeling] may be unconscious and the manifest content of the response [may] disguise the latent content."[42]

Recent research reported by Singer supports this model of the "general pattern of self-awareness or introspective behavior. At one end of this dimension of inner experience one finds the person given to extremely fantastic, fanciful daydreams, while at the other end the pattern suggests a considerably controlled, orderly, and objective type of daydreaming." Singer reports further that both extremes represent responsiveness to internally produced cognitive experiences quite different from the extrovert's push for direct perceptual and physical contact with the environment. It is of particular interest that both poles of this dimension of daydreaming are also associated with a measure of curiosity differing chiefly in the relative interpersonal-impersonality of reported interests. Persons emphasizing control of their thought processes tend also to be curious about natural events or the physical world; by contrast, the more fanciful daydreamers appear more curious about people and their motives or characteristics.[43]

Psychologists also differentiate other states of consciousness or use other terms to characterize or to identify particular states of consciousness. For example, Murphy uses and defines:

1. thought—"all those processes by which the answer to a problem is found."
2. imageless thought—"the result of taking account of the nature of an object without the use of images."
3. memory—"function whereby past experience is revived or relived with a more or less definite realization that the present experience is a revival."
4. daydream—"a reverie or waking fantasy, particularly one in which the dreamer is represented as playing an enjoyable role."
5. reverie—"the result of dwelling upon a train of images without much attempt to control their direction."
6. hallucination—"extremely vivid image in any sensory field. Usually the term is used only when there is acceptance of the image, by the subject, as a present fact of the environment."[44]

The difficulty with all these terms and discussions of the states of consciousness they seek to identify is that in the first place they continue to be used differently by different psychologists and that secondly they have additional meanings for the layman, sometimes entirely different from the meanings of the psychologists. Vinacke thus avoids the use of the term *consciousness,* which we have used here frequently, because of its "numerous, ill-defined meanings" and resultant ambiguity.[45] It should be noted that we are not concerned here with defending any particular description of consciousness. We are attempting merely to establish an understanding and a vocabulary that will be useful later in examining Joyce's stream-of-consciousness writing.

We have said nothing yet of the differences of individual consciousnesses. Because of the differences of environment in which individuals find themselves and the differences in their personal needs, psychologists have long agreed that no two consciousnesses are alike. Thus, for example, individuals associate differently. Jung found in his experiments that "the associations vary, within the range of the normal, chiefly under the influence of: (1) Attention. (2) Education. (3) The individual peculiarity of the subject."[46] As we will see later, an individual's associations are organized into idiosyncratic structures or constellations which are released to consciousness by internal or external stimuli, or which are sometimes repressed if they are painful.[47] Perception, too, "usually occurs in association with congruent personality characteristics," so that environment and an individual's needs play determining roles in how and what he sees, literally and figuratively.[48] We have already noted above that some people think largely in images and others do not, a fact which has caused considerable controversy in psychological circles. And we have also noted that a person's inner needs and the accidents of the environment control the focus and flow of consciousness, a fact which again points to myriad individual differences, since the environment and personal needs exist and interact entirely differently for each individual.

The nature of the psychological stream of consciousness and the problems facing the writer who would simulate it should now be clear enough that we can examine Joyce's simulation and his introduction of the stream-of-consciousness technique into the early chapters of *Ulysses*. In Part Two from time to time we shall return briefly to a continued examination of the psychological stream of consciousness to see what the linguists, psycholinguists, and psychiatrists know about the language components of the stream and what tools of linguistic analysis they have developed to examine it and to characterize cognitive styles.

3
Introducing the Stream-of-Consciousness Technique in *Ulysses*

The novelist must build the world in which his characters will live. For the stream-of-consciousness novelist, this problem is one of unusual importance. He can, of course, plunge his reader immediately into the stream of consciousness of one of his characters. That method, however, is dangerous, largely because the reader who is unfamiliar with the technique and necessarily unaware of the meaning of many of the components in the stream may very well lose interest and put the book down. Without spatial, temporal, and geographic frames of reference and without some knowledge of the past to provide a context, the result of an attempt to simulate convincingly the psychological stream of consciousness might seem very much like a mere jumble of words.

There are, of course, other alternatives. The novelist might begin by using a modified stream-of-consciousness technique, enriching it as he goes along, until, with his world established, he could use the stream-of-consciousness technique in all its complexity. Such a method has two difficulties. First, a pale version of the stream of consciousness with all memory images and personal references strained out might seem incredibly naive. And, secondly, unless it were done very gradually, over many pages—more pages, perhaps, than the novelist could afford if he wanted his novel written largely in the same technique—the increasing enrichment and complication of the stream of consciousness might be noticeable and thus aesthetically bad. The writer would be caught with his technique showing, an indiscretion which the critics and the reader might not easily forgive.

Joyce chose still another alternative. He simply postponed the use of stream-of-consciousness passages of any length until he had carefully established the outlines of the characters, their relationships, and the world in which they live. Take, for example, the first chapter of *Ulysses*. The opening lines certainly show no indication of any attempt to simulate the flow of consciousness:

> Stately, plump Buck Mulligan came from the stairhead, bearing a bowl of lather on which a mirror and a razor lay crossed. A yellow dressinggown, ungirdled, was sustained gently behind him by the mild morning air. He held the bowl aloft and intoned:
> —*Introibo ad altare Dei.*
> Halted, he peered down the dark winding stairs and called up coarsely:
> —Come up, Kinch. Come up, you fearful jesuit.
> Solemnly he came forward and mounted the round gunrest. He faced about and blessed gravely thrice the tower, the surrounding country and the awaking mountains. Then, catching sight of Stephen Dedalus, he bent towards him and made rapid crosses in the air, gurgling in his throat and shaking his head. Stephen Dedalus, displeased and sleepy, leaned his arms on the top of the staircase and looked coldly at the shaking gurgling face that blessed him, equine in its length, and at the light untonsured hair, grained and hued like pale oak. (5:1-17/3:1-17)[1]

Indeed, except for one word, "Chrysostomos" (5:28/3:28), there is nothing on the first page of the novel that suggests anything other than the standard technique of the omniscient author. And the second and third pages of the novel (6, 7/4, 5) are completely void of any evidence of the stream-of-consciousness technique. On the fourth page (8/6), we enter Stephen's mind for the first time:

> Stephen bent forward and peered at the mirror held out to him, cleft by a crooked crack, hair on end. *As he and others see me. Who chose this face for me? This dogsbody to rid of vermin. It asks me too.* (8:21-24/6:27-30)[2]

But still there is nothing really unusual about the italicized sentences. They are simply soliloquy. Although the form is used, perhaps, more in the drama than in the novel and although soliloquy in the drama is perforce spoken whereas in this passage it is silent, it is nevertheless familiar. Stephen is talking, silently, to himself.

The next instance of Joyce's attempt to present Stephen's mind to the reader, at the bottom of that same page, is also soliloquy:

"Parried again. He fears the lancet of my art as I fear that
of his. The cold steelpen" (8:41/7:6).

Not until the fifth page of the novel does Joyce include
material that suggests an attempt to simulate the actual stream
of consciousness:

> Cranly's arm. His arm. (9:7/7:14)
>
> Young shouts of moneyed voices in Clive Kempthorpe's rooms.
> Palefaces: they hold their ribs with laughter, one clasping
> another, O, I shall expire! Break the news to her gently, Aubrey!
> I shall die! With slit ribbons of his shirt whipping the air he
> hops and hobbles round the table, with trousers down at heels,
> chased by Ades of Magdalen with the tailor's shears. A scared
> calf's face gilded with marmalade. I don't want to be debagged!
> Don't you play the giddy ox with me!
>   Shouts from the open window startling evening in the
> quadrangle. A deaf gardener, aproned, masked with Matthew
> Arnold's face, pushes his mower on the sombre lawn watching
> narrowly the dancing motes of grasshalms.
>   To ourselves . . . new paganism . . . omphalos. (9:13-25/7:21-33)

The rest of the chapter continues much in the same way. In
the twenty pages of the first chapter, 840 lines of text, there
are only about 100 lines that indicate any attempt on the part
of Joyce to place the reader in Stephen's mind; and one-third
of those are soliloquy.

The first attempt at simulated stream of consciousness, the
cryptic "Cranly's arm. His arm" (9:7/7:14) brings with it one
of the difficulties discussed above; the reader cannot understand
the line because it contains a personal reference about which
the preceding pages provide no information.[3] Immediately below
it, however, is a stream-of-consciousness passage which, after
very little puzzling, the reader can decipher as a scene from
the hazing of a university student.

Examination of the next stream-of-consciousness passage
shows how earlier preparation helps the reader take a stream-
of-consciousness passage in his stride:[4]

> Woodshadows floated silently by through the morning peace from
> the stairhead seaward where he gazed. Inshore and farther out
> the mirror of water whitened, spurned by lightshod hurrying feet.
> White breast of the dim sea. The twining stresses, two by two.
> A hand plucking the harpstrings merging their twining chords.

Wavewhite wedded words shimmering on the dim tide.

A cloud began to cover the sun slowly, shadowing the bay in deeper green. It lay behind him, a bowl of bitter waters. Fergus' song: I sang it alone in the house, holding down the long dark chords. Her door was open: she wanted to hear my music. Silent with awe and pity I went to her bedside. She was crying in her wretched bed. For those words, Stephen: love's bitter mystery.

Where now?

Her secrets; old feather fans, tasseled dancecards, powdered with musk, a gaud of amber beads in her locked drawer. A birdcage hung in the sunny window of her house when she was a girl. She heard old Royce sing in the pantomime of Turko the terrible and laughed with others when he sang:

> I am the boy
> That can enjoy
> Invisibility.

Phantasmal mirth, folded away: muskperfumed
> And no more turn aside and brood.

Folded away in the memory of nature with her toys. Memories beset his brooding brain. Her glass of water from the kitchen tap when she had approached the sacrament. A cored apple filled with brown sugar, roasting for her at the hob on a dark autumn evening. Her shapely fingernails reddened by the blood of squashed lice from the children's shirts.

In a dream, silently, she had come to him, her wasted body within its loose graveclothes giving off an odour of wax and rosewood, her breath bent over him with mute secret words, a faint odour of wetted ashes.

Her glazing eyes, staring out of death, to shake and bend my soul. On me alone. The ghostcandle to light her agony. Ghostly light on the tortured face. Her hoarse loud breath rattling in horror, while all prayed on their knees. Her eyes on me to strike me down. *Liliata rutilantium te confessorum turma circumdet: iubilantium te virginum chorus excipiat.*

Ghoul! Chewer of corpses!

No, mother. Let me be and let me live. (11:15-12:16 / 9:25-10:26)

Before we examine how Joyce prepared his reader for this early and comparatively long stream-of-consciousness passage (that is, comparatively long for the opening chapters), several points should be made. To begin with, of course, not all the sentences are meant to simulate the stream of consciousness. Some of them are soliloquy (for example, "Her door was open: she wanted to hear my music"—11:24/9:35). And others are omniscient author's sentences, sentences written in the third person and obviously direct statements by Joyce. These omniscient author's statements, however, tend to be of a particular kind. First, they are often summary, with no hint of the author's point of view (for example, "In a dream, silently, she had come to him"— 12:5-8/10:15-18). And second, they often function as stage directions, merely informing the reader of a character's action or describing the scene, again maintaining the author's objectivity (for example, "Woodshadows floated silently . . . where he gazed"—11:15/9:25). And, third, they are often written in the style of the character in whose stream of consciousness they are found (for example, the imagery of "the mirror of water"—11:17/9:27—and "spurned by lightshod hurrying feet"—11:22/9:33—are in the idiom of Stephen the would-be poet). Thus even where Joyce uses omniscient author's sentences in a stream-of-consciousness passage, they do not obtrude. All of this attempted self-effacement on the part of Joyce fits in with his dictum that "the artist, like the God of the creation, remains within or behind or beyond or above his handiwork, invisible, refined out of existence, indifferent, paring his fingernails."[5]

Now we return to the passage quoted above from *Ulysses.* The reader should experience no difficulty with it, for he has all the keys necessary to unlock its meaning. Four pages earlier, when Buck and Stephen were talking atop the tower, Buck looked out over Dublin Bay (6:41/5:3), spoke of it as "our great sweet mother" (7:5/5:8), and invited Stephen to "Come and look" (7:5/5:8). Seven lines later, Buck mentions for the first time the recent death of Stephen's mother. She appears again when the view of Dublin Bay upon which Stephen has been invited to gaze reminds him of an article beside her deathbed: "The ring of bay and skyline held a dull green mass of liquid. A bowl of white china had stood beside her deathbed holding the green sluggish bile which she had torn up from her rotting liver by fits of loud groaning vomiting" (7:33-37/5:38-41). The reader learns further that Stephen had refused his mother's dying wish that he "kneel down and pray for her" (7:31/5:22; also 10:19/8:29), that she had appeared to him in a dream, "mute" but "reproachful" (7:31/5:35; also 12:5-8/10:15-18), and that Stephen is particularly sensitive about the whole matter (9:39-10:40/8:38-9:4). Thus by the time that the reader reaches the first long stream-of-consciousness passage, the sea has already been described and discussed, the sea and Stephen's mother have already been related, and Stephen's uneasy conscience has been described. Despite the ellipsis which Joyce uses as part of the technique of simulating the stream of consciousness, therefore, with all the references available the reader can easily follow the passage, even though he may not fully comprehend everything in it.

Preparation for this particular stream-of-consciousness passage shows in brief how Joyce generally prepared his reader for the long stream-of-consciousness passages, which he withheld until later on in the novel. For the first full chapter of stream of consciousness, Proteus (38-51/37-51), the reader has had thirty-four pages of preparation. By the time he reaches Proteus, there has already been established in his mind a small world of ideas and images ready to be called forth by appropriate words or phrases, so that in a sense Joyce is able to raise in the reader's mind some of the same ideas and images that would appear in a character's mind, without having to take the time to do so in the stream-of-consciousness passage itself. They are available and ready to be called forth because they have been provided by Joyce earlier.

The later long passages of stream of consciousness are handled in much the same way. Despite the fact that Proteus' being all stream of consciousness prepares the reader for a continued use of that technique, Joyce opens the chapter following it (Calypso, 55-85/55-86) by introducing Bloom in the style of the omniscient author: "Mr Leopold Bloom ate with relish the inner organs of beasts and fowls. He liked thick giblet soup, nutty gizzards, a stuffed roast heart, liver slices fried with crustcrumbs, fried hencod's roes. Most of all he liked grilled mutton kidneys which gave to his palate a fine tang of faintly scented urine" (55:1-5; both editions). Since the reader is by now used to the stream-of-consciousness technique, however, Joyce does work short stream-of-consciousnesses passages into the text more quickly and more often in the first two of Bloom's chapters than he did in the first two of Stephen's. Still it is not until ninety-four pages after Joyce has introduced Bloom that he employs a chapter almost completely composed of Bloom's stream of consciousness.[6] Similarly, the reader has been prepared to recognize a good many of the references in Molly's monologue, beginning on page 723/738, by the thoughts and actions of Bloom and the other characters in the preceding seven hundred and more pages.

To a certain extent, then, Joyce is able to overcome the difficulty of translating the multidimensional real world into language, which is linear, by building a multidimensional world in the reader's mind before he attempts to simulate the stream of consciousness. By the time Joyce introduces the stream-of-consciousness technique, he can call forth an approximation of that multidimensional world of the stream of consciousness in the mind of the reader by using appropriate trigger mechanisms (words and phrases), just as in the earlier stream-of-consciousness passage discussed above (11:15-12:4/9:25-10:6), "a bowl of bitter waters" (11:22/9:33) and "her bedside" (11:25/9:36) bring to the reader's mind the whole crowd of images and meanings placed there earlier by Buck's conversation with Stephen.[7]

Even though Joyce did not open *Ulysses* with long stream-of-consciousness passages, preferring to prepare his reader for them first, he was probably concerned about not making the opening chapters seem too obviously written from the point of view of the omniscient author. For if such an impression were established in the reader, it would be difficult for Joyce to persuade him later to shift into Stephen's mind. Joyce met this problem by keeping the first two chapters of *Ulysses* heavily conversational. By burying a few scraps of stream of consciousness in a passage of dialogue, Joyce gives the impression of a longer passage of stream of consciousness. He thus gets a stream-of-consciousness effect without demanding too soon of the reader the understanding and familiarity with the technique necessary for handling long passages of stream of consciousness. For example, in the following sixteen lines of text, there are only two full lines of stream of consciousness (8:41-42/7:6-7, one and a half lines; 9:7/7:14, one half line), yet Joyce succeeds there in giving the reader the impression of being in Stephen's mind:

> —It's not fair to tease you like that, Kinch, is it? he said kindly.
> God knows you have more spirit than any of them.
> Parried again. He fears the lancet of my art as I fear that
> of his. The cold steelpen.
> —Cracked lookingglass of a servant. Tell that to the oxy chap
> downstairs and touch him for a guinea. He's stinking with money
> and thinks you're not a gentleman. His old fellow made his tin
> by selling jalap to Zulus or some bloody swindle or other. God,

Kinch, if you and I could only work together we might do
something for the island. Hellenise it.
   Cranly's arm. His arm.
   —And to think of your having to beg from these swine. I'm
the only one that knows what you are. Why don't you trust me
more? What have you up your nose against me? Is it Haines?
If he makes any noise here I'll bring down Seymour and we'll
give him a ragging worse than they gave Clive Kempthorpe.
(8:39–9:12/7:4–20)

The words which someone speaks to us do, of course, appear
in our stream of consciousness as words, accompanied by the
overtones of response that they awaken in us. The effect of
these overtones is obtained by Joyce with the scraps of
stream-of-consciousness technique. Later when Joyce has
accustomed the reader to the technique and has built up a
context of knowledge about Stephen and his activities on which
he can rely, he drops the crutch of dialogue and allows the
reader to slip farther into Stephen's mind, letting him see more
of what happens there and establishing a truer proportion
between inner and outer components. Since the reader is
accustomed to dialogue in novels, and since dialogue does appear
in the stream of consciousness, Joyce was able to use it to keep
the opening chapter of *Ulysses* from appearing to be written
too heavily from the point of view of the omniscient author
and to prepare the reader for the long stream-of-consciousness
passages which come later.

4
Simulating the Psychological Stream of Consciousness

A. Employing the Principle of Association

Of the various aspects and components of the stream of consciousness, association is the easiest to demonstrate. Take, for example, the following passage from Proteus:

> They came down the steps from Leahy's terrace prudently, *Frauenzimmer:* and down the shelving shore flabbily their splayed feet sinking in the silted sand. Like me, like Algy, coming down to our mighty mother. Number one swung lourdily her midwife's bag, the other's gamp poked in the beach. From the liberties, out for the day. Mrs. Florence MacCabe, relict of the late Patk MacCabe, deeply lamented, of Bride Street. One of her sisterhood lugged me squealing into life. Creation from nothing. What has she in the bag? A misbirth with a trailing navelcord, hushed in ruddy wool. The cords of all link back, strandentwining cable of all flesh. That is why mystic monks. Will you be as gods? Gaze in your omphalos. Hello. Kinch here. Put me on to Edenville. Aleph, alpha: nought, nought one.
>
> Spouse and helpmate of Adam Kadmon: Heva, naked Eve. She had no navel. Gaze. Belly without blemish, bulging big, a buckler of taut vellum, no, whiteheaped corn, orient and immortal, standing from everlasting to everlasting. Womb of sin.
> (38:33-39:9/37:34-38:9)

This train of thought is triggered by a perception: Stephen's seeing the midwives, one of whom he recognizes. The sight reminds him of the fact that a midwife assisted at his birth, and he wonders briefly at the miracle of birth, "Creation from nothing." The sight of the bag that one of the midwives is carrying gives his mind food for fantasy; and for some reason, perhaps because of a story he heard or read, the bag makes him think about a misbirth, and he pictures such a foetus, with its umbilical cord still attached. The cord then becomes just one of many cords, which, when twisted into a cable, connects each person to the source of life and to "all flesh," the sum and substance of all men, of mankind, perhaps.[1] Navel cords remind Stephen of navels and of the monks who gaze at them in their attempts to understand the mysteries of the gods. The monks' attempt to communicate with heaven by way of their navels brings to Stephen's mind the puckish thought of a heavenly telephone system (with navel cords as telephone wires), and he immediately puts in a call to Edenville AA 001. Edenville reminds Stephen of Adam and Eve, who, since they were not born but created, had no navels; and he pictures Eve's unmarred stomach, the image of which reminds him first of a hide-covered shield, possibly the "white heaped" *omphaloi* of the Achean shields, and then of a passage from Traherne's *Meditations* ("The corn was orient and immortal wheat").[2] From Eve to the concept of original sin and the mother of sinners is an easy step. From there Stephen's thoughts go to his own physical birth, to his relation with the God who willed that birth, and to Arius, one of the heresiarchs who was concerned with the problem of the *lex eterna* and consubstantiality (39:14-16/38:14-16). The feeling of the wind and the sight of the waves eventually break in and disrupt this particular flow of thought. In support of an earlier statement to the effect that even in omniscient author's statements Joyce attempts to maintain the flavor of the personality about whom he is writing at the moment, it should be noted here that the omniscient author's sentence which announces to the reader Stephen's becoming aware of the immediate environment is couched in language that Stephen himself might use: "Airs romped around him, nipping and eager airs" (39:22/38:22). The last phrase, "nipping and eager airs," is an echo of *Hamlet,* which Stephen has on his mind all day.[3]

The reader, accustomed by this time to the stream-of-consciousness technique, should have little trouble with the associations. It is true that they are quite personal in that an image of Eve would probably not remind most people of either the passage from the *Iliad* or of that from Traherne's *Meditations*. But the connections between the ideas, whether one recognizes the quotations or not, are understandable to the reader. Given Stephen's poetic nature and his bookish background, the reader quickly accepts this type of association from Stephen. Indeed, as we shall see later, the kinds of thoughts Stephen has and the way they relate to one another help to establish for the reader Stephen's identity and personality.[4]

Not all the associations, however, are as easy to follow as those in the passage discussed above. Some associations are not explained until later in the novel. For example, the reader may not know what to make of the last sentence in the following passage, which appears early in *Ulysses*: "Behold the handmaid of the moon. In sleep the wet sign calls her hour, bids her rise. Bridebed, childbed, bed of death, ghostcandled. *Omnis caro ad te veniet.* He comes, pale vampire, through storm his eyes, his bat sails bloodying the sea, mouth to her mouth's kiss" (48:32/47:39). The reference to the sea immediately above (*oinopa ponton,* associated earlier with Stephen's mother —7:1-13/5:5-17), "bed of death," and "ghostcandled" clearly establish that this is a reflection of Stephen's mother's death. At her death, then, she goes, like all flesh (*omnis caro*), to God.[5] But that does not explain the association of the phrase from the Bible with the vampire. Later in the book the careful reader may come to realize that for Stephen there is another possible god of the universe, the vampire-god of materialism. As William Schutte points out, the vampire theme develops, as it does throughout *Ulysses*, as another aspect of the wanton force of destruction loose in the world, which "Stephen personalizes as the *dio boia*, the hangman god, 'the lord of things as they are' " (210:36/213:22):[6]

> The vampire returns from time to time in *Ulysses*, always in a destructive role. In Stephen's discourse at the hospital on conception and contraception, conception by "potency of vampires mouth to mouth" is opposed to conception "by wind of seeds of brightness" (383). In "Circe" the vampire appears in Stephen's imitation of the Paris guide who offers to his clients more and more exotic sensual entertainment: "All chic womans which arrive full of modesty then disrobe and squeal loud to see vampire men debauch nun very fresh young with *dessous troublants*" (555). Lynch, on whose earthy nature Stephen comments in the *Portrait* (*P*, 240), characteristically interrupts to cry, "*Vive le vampire!*" In its last appearance, at the very end of "Circe," the vampire symbol is again associated with Stephen's mother. . . . Stephen is "out cold" in the street, guarded by the solicitous Bloom. Finally Bloom tries to rouse him. He bends close and calls his name. Stephen groans: "Who? Black panther vampire" (592). Then

he stretches and sings thickly snatches of Fergus' song, which
he had sung for his mother on her deathbed and which he always
associates with her death.[7]

Further, although there is some slight evidence of it ("My
tablets"—48:37/48:4; "he bent over far to a table of rock and
scribbled words"—49:5/48:13), the reader will probably not
realize until later, when some of these same words appear
italicized in stanza form (131:1-4/132:12-15), that Stephen
recognizes in the passage quoted above the germ of a poem,
which he starts to write and on which he continues to work
(136:33/138:16).

George Humphrey feels that associations not immediately
understandable to the reader serve an important function. "What
seems incoherent in the privacy of consciousness is actually only
egocentric. The basis for this is the private relationship of the
associations." The trick of making the reader wait for several
lines, pages, or even chapters for the key to the meaning of
an association serves much the same purpose: "This method of
suspending sense impressions and ideas in the memory for so
long that they reappear at unexpected and seemingly
unreasonable places is . . . to preserve the appearance of
privacy." And Humphrey feels that the stream-of-consciousness
novelist's throwing in of seemingly irrelevant details also serves

> to present the inherent discontinuity of psychic processes and to
> make it meaningful. We may think of it this way: As the
> associations of any particular moment of consciousness are
> incoherent out of the context of the mind, so the associations in
> the passage above [a passage quoted from Faulkner's *The Sound
> and the Fury*] are incoherent out of the context of the novel;
> but within the context of the novel, they are not only
> psychologically coherent, they are revealing . . . since Faulkner
> and Joyce and Woolf and some others do not write nonsensical
> fiction, they have carefully dropped clues to unravel the knots
> of privacy throughout their work. In short, for the responsible
> writer, the mind of the character is the mind which exists *in
> the novel.*[8]

That our associations do not always seem to fit neatly together
like Lowes's "hooked atoms"[9] we all know from experience.
Gardner Murphy says, for example, that intuition may be the
product "of an organized activity of which only a small fragment

flashes meteor-like through a corner of the conscious field."[10] We are all familiar not only with these often unheralded meteorlike flashes, but also with the irrelevant image that suddenly pops unbidden and often irreverently into an alien train of thought.

Unfortunately, however, Joyce does not always drop the necessary clues to unravel "the knots of privacy" in *Ulysses*. As we shall see later, obscure passages are sometimes the unintended result of Joyce's method of building *Ulysses* by an infinite number of additions, not only in manuscript, but also in proof.

A further complication is that Joyce liked his little joke and was perfectly capable of writing into a passage private meanings that no one save himself and one or two other people could understand. For example:

> Two of [Joyce's] remarks about Cranly are . . . incomprehensible solely in terms of *Ulysses*. "The Tinahely twelve" [183:1/185:1] and "Cranly's eleven true Wicklowmen to free their sireland" [182:41/184:41] refer to a remark Byrne [J. F. Byrne, a friend of Joyce's and the model for Cranly] had made to his friends Merriman and Clancy: they had agreed that twelve men with resolution and the courage to give their lives if necessary could save Ireland, and Byrne said that he thought he could find twelve such men in Wicklow. Joyce calls them "eleven" first because there are eleven players on a soccer team, and then refers to them as "the Tinahely twelve" because the railroad station where Byrne would leave the train on his visits to Wicklow was Tinahely.[11]

How much of what is obscure in *Ulysses* is a result of this trick of Joyce's we may never know. And even if the scholar does learn of all these private meanings from the research of his fellow scholars, the general public of novel readers will not find *Ulysses* much easier to read.

B. Simulating Various States of Mind

Passages in *Ulysses* suggest different states of mind, instances of imaginative thinking,[12] for example, and of autistic thinking.[13] An example of each can be found in the passage quoted above from Proteus (38:33/37:34). An external stimulus, the sight of the midwives, starts a flow of thought which leads

Stephen to put in an imaginary phone call to Edenville AA 001
(39:4/38:4), an instance of imaginative thinking. His own
problems, however, soon swing his stream of thought to more
personal matters, and he thinks of his own begetting and his
relationship with God: "Wombed in sin darkness I was too, made
not begotten" (39:10/38:10). Here is an example of autistic
thinking. This passage also exemplifies the bipolarity of thought,
yielding now more to inner needs, now more to external stimuli.

There are examples, too, in Ulysses, of other states of
consciousness. There is memory,[14] happy:

> Touched his sense moistened remembered. Hidden under wild
> ferns on Howth. Below us bay sleeping sky. No sound. The sky.
> The bay purple by the Lion's head. Green by Drumleck.
> Yellowgreen towards Sutton. Fields of undersea, the lines faint
> brown in grass, buried cities. Pillowed on my coat she had her
> hair, earwigs in the heather scrub my hand under her nape, you'll
> toss me all. O wonder! Coolsoft with ointments her hand touched
> me, caressed: her eyes upon me did not turn away. Ravished over
> her I lay, full lips full open, kissed her mouth. Yum. Softly she
> gave me in my mouth the seedcake warm and chewed. Mawkish
> pulp her mouth had mumbled sweet and sour with spittle. Joy:
> I ate it: joy. Young life, her lips that gave me pouting. Soft,
> warm, sticky gumjelly lips. Flowers her eyes were, take me,
> willing eyes. (173:21-34/175:42-176:14)

and unhappy:

> Wait. The full moon was the night we were Sunday fortnight
> exactly there is a new moon. Walking down by the Tolka. Not
> bad for a Fairview moon. She was humming: The young May
> moon she's beaming, love. He other side of her. Elbow, arm. He.
> Glowworm's la-amp is gleaming, love. Touch. Fingers. Asking.
> Answer. Yes.
> Stop. Stop. If it was it was. Must. (165:3-9/167:19-25)

There are also examples of reverie.[15] In one of the longest
of these passages (43:25-45:7/42:27-44:9), Stephen daydreams
about Paris, Kevin Egan, and Irish revolutionary activity. There
the first indication of a shift from simple memory is the
different treatment of dialogue. Whereas in the rest of the
chapter the lines of remembered and imagined dialogue are
clearly set off, generally as a new paragraph introduced by a
dash, in this passage, except for two lines of song, all the lines

of remembered and imagined dialogue are buried in large
paragraphs of other material.

> Noon slumbers. Kevin Egan rolls gunpowder cigarettes through
> fingers smeared with printer's ink, sipping his green fairy as
> Patrice his white. About us gobblers fork spiced beans down their
> gullets. *Un demi setier!* A jet of coffee steam from the burnished
> caldron. She serves me at his beck. *Il est irlandais. Hollandais?*
> *Non fromage. Deux irlandais, nous, Irlande, vous savez? Ah oui!*
> She thought you wanted a cheese *hollandais.* Your postprandial,
> do you know that word? Postprandial. (43:34-42/42:36-43:2)

Although this is all Stephen's memory, the scramble of the
visual aspects of that memory and the phrases of Kevin Egan's
remarks blurs the edges of the scene for the reader and gives
the impression of a daydream. The effect is noticeable when
one compares this passage with ones in which Joyce treats
dialogue in the usual way, first in a remembered scene:

> Patrice, home on furlough, lapped warm milk with me in the
> bar MacMahon. Son of the wild goose, Kevin Egan of Paris. My
> father's a bird, he lapped the sweet *lait chaud* with pink young
> tongue, plump bunny's face. Lap, *lapin.* He hopes to win in the
> *gros lots.* About the nature of women he read in Michelet. But
> he must send me *La Vie de Jesus* by M. Leo Taxil. Lent it to
> his friend.
> —*C'est tourdant, vous savez. Moi je suis socialiste. Je ne crois*
> *pas en l'existence de Dieu. Faut pas le dire à mon père.*
> —*Il croit?*
> —*Mon père, oui.*
> *Schluss.* He laps. (42:14-25/41:16-27)

and then in an imagined one:

> I pull the wheezy bell of their shuttered cottage: and wait. They
> take me for a dun, peer out from a coign of vantage.
> —It's Stephen, sir.
> —Let him in. Let Stephen in.
> A bolt drawn back and Walter welcomes me.
> —We thought you were someone else.
> In his broad bed nuncle Richie, pillowed and blanketed, extends
> over the hillock of his knees a sturdy forearm. Cleanchested. He
> has washed the upper moiety. (39:38-40:4/38:38-39:4)

In the passage of reverie discussed above, the highly compressed
tangle of the visual elements of Stephen's memory and his

memory of Egan's remarks continues for the rest of the long paragraph.

The next paragraph brings another type of compression similar in effect to that of the preceding paragraph:

> The blue fuse burns deadly between hands and burns clear. Loose tobacco shreds catch fire: a flame and acrid smoke light our corner. Raw facebones under his peep of day boy's hat. How the head centre got away, authentic version. Got up as a young bride, man, veil, orangeblossoms, drove out the road to Malahide. Did, faith. Of lost leaders, the betrayed, wild escapes. Disguises, clutched at, gone, not here. (44:20-26/43:22-28)

The first seven lines of this paragraph seem to be an abstraction of the stories that Egan told, highly elliptical, and heightened by Stephen's imagination. In the last two sentences of the paragraph, Stephen presents the *quidditas* of all such episodes. The paragraph is really a masterpiece of compression, a snapshot story with appropriate romantic overtones, and with just a touch of Stephen's ironic attitude ("How the head centre got away, authentic version"; this statement also has the flavor of the newsboy's shout). The next paragraph continues in the same vein, running together Egan's remarks ("I was a strapping young gossoon"), Stephen's summarizing of other parts of Egan's story ("he prowled with colonel Richard Burke"), and Stephen's present thoughts about Egan ("In gay Paree he hides. . . . Loveless, landless, wifeless"):

> Spurned lover. I was a strapping young gossoon at that time, I tell you, I'll show you my likeness one day. I was, faith. Lover, for her love he prowled with colonel Richard Burke, tanist of his sept, under the walls of Clerkenwell and, crouching, saw a flame of vengeance hurl them upward in the fog. Shattered glass and toppling masonry. In gay Paree he hides. Egan of Paris, unsought by any save by me. Making his day's stations, the dingy printingcase, his three taverns, the Montmartre lair he sleeps short night in, rue de la Goutte-d'Or, damascened with flyblown faces of the gone. Loveless, landless, wifeless. (44:27-36/43:29-39)

The juxtaposition of past and present, the running together of dialogue with memory images and comment, and the use of a few details to tell a highly compressed story all give the effect of a person immersed in a quickly moving stream of thought, in which ideas and images jostle each other or merge into one another as they go by to blur the edges of the scene. In short, here is a mind in reverie, oblivious of the world outside, allowing images to come and go as they will, "without much attempt to control their direction."

Ulysses, too, has its examples of hallucinations, but these are largely in Circe, not a stream-of-consciousness chapter. A stream-of-consciousness passage which approaches hallucination will be discussed later.

C. Components of the Stream

There are examples, too, of some of the components of the stream of consciousness to which Sullivan referred in his discussion of a single moment of consciousness (see chapter two).

1. Words

The most obvious of these, of course, is words. Almost any page of stream of consciousness will offer examples of words in a character's stream of consciousness, instances in which the character speaks to himself—either aloud or silently:

Stephen	Here, I am not walking out to the Kish lightship, am I? (45:11/44:13)
	That's twice I forgot to take slips from the library counter. (49:6/48:14)
Bloom	I'll take my oath that's Alf Bergan or Richie Goulding. (157:33/160:3)
	Now that I come to think of it, that ball falls at Greenwich time. (164:27/167:1)
Molly	I hope I'll never be like her. (723:13/738:14)
	I wish someone would write me a loveletter. (743:28/758:30)

People talk to themselves on occasion, and Joyce's characters are no exceptions.

2. Sensations

Other aspects of the stream of consciousness must be simulated, however, and are therefore more difficult to present. There are moments of apprehension, for example, when the components of the psychological stream of consciousness are preverbal, consisting almost entirely of visceral sensations. Joyce attempts to present such moments. Here, for example, is Bloom startled by the fear that Boylan, who will surely become Molly's lover that afternoon, might infect her:

> That quack doctor for the clap used to be stuck up in all the greenhouses. . . . Just the place too. POST NO BILLS. POST NO PILLS. Some chap with a dose burning him.
> If he. . .
> O!
> Eh?
> No . . . No.
> No, no. I don't believe it. He wouldn't surely?
> No, no.
> Mr Bloom moved forward raising his troubled eyes.
> (151:28-42/153:41-154:3)

"If he. . ." records the sudden arrival of the thought as Bloom is caught up short. "O!" and "Eh?" are the analogues of visceral sensations as his fear expresses itself preverbally.

We have here a good demonstration of the writer's difficulty in simulating the psychological stream of consciousness. Psychologists have examined with some care human response to being startled and have described the startle pattern. Carney Landis and William A. Hunt speak of it as "a general flexion response." The eyes blink, the mouth widens, and the teeth bare. Frequently, also, there is movement of shoulders, arms, elbows, hands, knees, abdomen, and trunk.[16] Donald R. Lindsley calls it "a higher order of reflex adjustment, and one we commonly accept as a form of emotional response (probably a primitive form of fear)." It "is apparently a somato-viscero-somatic response, since both visceral and somatic reactions occur. For example, a strong, unexpected auditory stimulus produces a generalized body response, predominantly of flexion. Visceral manifestations are increased blood pressure, heart rate, and galvanic skin response, to mention only a few."[17] We have all experienced the startle pattern: a lurch in the stomach, a catch somewhere in the breathing apparatus, a sudden pounding of the heart, general tension, and perhaps an awareness of warmth on the cheeks and sweaty palms.

When we compare the attempt above (151:28/153:41) by Joyce to simulate the startle pattern with one that comes later in the same chapter, we realize that the second attempt is more successful:

Mr Bloom came to Kildare street. First I must. Library.

Straw hat in sunlight. Tan shoes. Turnedup trousers. It is. It is.

His heart quopped softly. To the right. Museum. Goddesses. He swerved to the right.

Is it? Almost certain. Won't look. Wine in my face. Why did I? Too heady. Yes, it is. The walk. Not see. Not see. Get on.

Making for the museum gate with long windy strides he lifted his eyes. Handsome building. Sir Thomas Deane designed. Not following me?

Didn't see me perhaps. Light in his eyes.

The flutter of his breath came forth in short sighs. Quick. Cold statues: quiet there. Safe in a minute.

No, didn't see me. After two. Just at the gate.

My heart!

His eyes beating looked steadfastly at cream curves of stone. Sir Thomas Deane was the Greek architecture.

Look for something I.

His hasty hand went quick into a pocket, took out, read unfolded Agendath Netaim. Where did I?

Busy looking for.

He thrust back quickly Agendath.

Afternoon she said.

I am looking for that. Yes, that. Try all pockets. Handker. *Freeman*. Where did I? Ah, yes. Trousers. Purse. Potato. Where did I?

Hurry. Walk quietly. Moment more. My heart.

His hand looking for the where did I put found in his hip pocket soap lotion have to call tepid paper stuck. Ah, soap there! Yes. Gate.

Safe! (180-81/183)

Bloom is moving quickly here, of course, which partly accounts for his physical state; but Joyce is also simulating Bloom's being startled by the unexpected sight of Boylan.

There are several important differences between the two passages. In the first, Joyce relies for his simulation largely on an abortive sentence, a few simulated grunts, and a train of no's to suggest desperate rejection of the idea. In the second he uses omniscient author's sentences to report Bloom's quopping heart, the fluttering of his breath, and his awareness of a pulse in his eyes; and he records twice Bloom's awareness of the quopping with "My heart." In addition, he provides: the staccato effect of the short sentences, some of which are incomplete; the confusion of the longish sentence near the end, which seems

to be a condensation of phrases from omniscient-author and
stream-of-consciousness sentences; and the climax of the final
short phrase followed by three monosyllabic words concluding
with an exclamation mark. By the time the reader reaches the
end of the passages, he may well find himself like Bloom,
holding his breath and having to try to quiet himself down.
The second simulation of the startle pattern is very effective.

3. Images

Joyce also suggests visual memory images. When Buck leaves,
after having reminded Stephen atop the Martello tower of the
death of his mother, Stephen's thoughts of the deathbed scene
are presented first as soliloquy, in complete sentences: "Fergus'
song: I sang it alone in the house, holding down the long dark
chords. Her door was open: she wanted to hear my music. Silent
with awe and pity I went to her bedside. She was crying in
her wretched bed. For those words, Stephen: love's bitter
mystery" (11:22-26/9:33-38). The next dozen lines continue
much the same way, although they contain a few elliptical
sentences, one of which anticipates the passage we shall discuss
next ("Her secrets: old feather fans, tasseled dancecards,
powdered with musk, a gaud of amber beads in her locked
drawer"—11:28/9:40). Joyce then informs the reader that
"Memories beset his [Stephen's] brooding brain" (11:38/10:9).
And then the passage continues: "Her glass of water from the
kitchen tap when she had approached the sacrament. A cored
apple, filled with brown sugar, roasting for her at the hob on
a dark autumn evening. Her shapely fingernails reddened by
the blood of squashed lice from the children's shirts"
(11:39-12:4/10:10-14). These elliptical sentences function as
memory images, snapshot scenes of specific details that appear
in Stephen's mind to characterize for him—and for the
reader—May Dedalus. Joyce cannot present them as they appear
in the mind, for they appear as pictures. To suggest their
appearance, therefore, he presents them as a series of elliptical
sentences. The several grammatically complete sentences of
soliloquy just before this passage and the omniscient author's
sentence, again grammatically complete (and, in this instance,
long and involved), following it heighten the effect of the
ellipsis, pointing up these three sentences as something

different; obviously they are neither Stephen talking to himself, as in the sentence preceding, nor the author talking to the reader, as in the sentence following.

It may be argued that each of these elliptical sentences is too long to reproduce successfully the immediacy of a memory image. In the light of some of the later reproduction of Stephen's memory images, such criticism would seem valid: "Hunger toothache. *Encore deux minutes.* Look clock. Must get. *Fermé.* Hired dog!" (42:41/42:1), and "After he woke me up last night same dream or was it? Wait. Open hallway. Street of harlots. Remember. Haroun al Raschid. I am almosting it. That man led me, spoke. I was not afraid. The melon he had he held against my face. Smiled: creamfruit smell. That was the rule, said. In. Come. Red carpet spread. You will see who" (47:39-48:2/47:4-9). Indeed, despite the long initial sentence, the last passage quoted averages slightly under four words between periods, whereas the passage about May Dedalus averages fifteen.

It should be remembered, however, as has been pointed out above, that in the first two chapters of *Ulysses*, Joyce introduces the stream-of-consciousness technique gradually. And the passage of Stephen's memory images of his mother comes from the very first chapter of the book, from the seventh page of text, in fact. Thus they are early attempts at reproducing images, precursers of the more complete ellipsis, as evidenced by the two passages quoted above (42:41/42:1; 47:39/47:4), that Joyce employs later when he has accustomed his reader to the stream-of-consciousness technique.

The fact that this early attempt at using ellipsis to present images is associated with a series of symbols of May Dedalus' life makes it easier for the reader to accept them. He may see them merely as symbols and he may see the ellipsis as an attempt to heighten their effect, to make them stand out by stripping from them as many words as possible and yet retaining their complete description. Having accepted the use of ellipsis in the early passage about May Dedalus, however, in a connection that he can understand, the reader will be better able to accept the later and more severe ellipsis when it is used just to represent images.

Each of these three elliptical sentences about Stephen's mother is also what Joyce would call an epiphany: "a sudden spiritual manifestation, whether in the vulgarity of speech or of gesture or in a memorable phase of the mind itself."[18] These are not just random impressions from the life of May Dedalus, but rather symbols of the three most important things in her life: the glass of water for the sacrament standing for her religion; the apple on the hearth, her home; and the stained fingernails on what was once an attractive (shapely) hand, her work and sacrifice for her children. Joyce, in choosing from a host of memory images that he might have paraded through Stephen's mind, chooses three that typified Mrs. Dedalus for Stephen and for the reader and thus helped to project her personality.

In the next one-sentence paragraph (12:5-8/10:15-18), Joyce summarizes a dream that Stephen had about his mother. There is no attempt at simulating here either soliloquy or memory image, Joyce feeling perhaps that a single omniscient author's sentence could quickly and efficiently set the stage for the ensuing dramatization of Stephen's remorse of conscience without destroying the effect of privacy that was built up by the preceding stream-of-consciousness passage. The sentence, however, is strictly summary and reporting, the omniscient author even here seeking to remain as much as possible invisible.

The next paragraph returns quite appropriately to elliptical sentences. The reader will feel Stephen's remorse more acutely if he receives it as a simulation of what Stephen is experiencing personally than as a third person summary by an omniscient author:

> Her glazing eyes, staring out of death, to shake and bend my soul. On me alone. The ghostcandle to light her agony. Ghostly light on the tortured face. Her hoarse loud breath rattling in horror, while all prayed on their knees. Her eyes on me to strike me down. *Liliata rutilantium te confessorum turma circumdet: iubilantium te virginum chorus excipiat.*[19]
> Ghoul! Chewer of corpses!
> No, mother. Let me be and let me live. (12:9-16/10:19-26)

For this passage, therefore, Joyce returns to the stream-of-consciousness technique, using elliptical sentences to simulate memory images and drawing on the relatively staccato effect of these sentences (that is, relatively staccato by juxtaposition with the immediately preceding omniscient author's sentence, which runs for three and a half lines) to give the effect of the intensity of Stephen's feeling. The sonorous Latin sentence at the end of the paragraph, by comparison, also serves to increase the staccato effect of the preceding six elliptical sentences.

Stephen's reaction to the memory of his mother's ghost indicates that that memory is so real to him that it approaches hallucination: "Ghoul! Chewer of corpses!/No, mother. Let me be and let me live." At the peak of his emotion, while Stephen is "still trembling at his soul's cry" (12:19/10:29), instead of allowing the intensity of feeling to relax slowly, dissipating the emotional charge and thus destroying the effectiveness of the dramatic presentation, Joyce abruptly breaks into the scene with a shout from Mulligan: "—Kinch ahoy!" (12:17/10:27). The unexpectedness of the interruption, the abruptness of the two short words, and the exclamation point provide one further turn of the screw, heightening the intensity of an already intense scene, wrenching both Stephen and the reader away from Stephen's "agenbite of inwit"; and before either has a chance to take a breath, a new scene is under way.

While we have the analyses of several highly emotional scenes close at hand, the two startle passages for Bloom and the scene for Stephen we have just analyzed, we should note a fact that supports the psychological validity of Joyce's stream-of-consciousness passages: Joyce's characters react to the world differently, much as people actually do, showing in their streams of consciousness various proportions of such components as visceral sensation and emotion, two components which are not necessarily different or mutually exclusive but which represent two significantly different levels of abstraction. Joyce emphasizes Bloom's visceral sensations rather than what he is thinking or reacting to. For Stephen, the intellectual, however, Joyce emphasizes meaning rather than visceral sensation. Comparing the two passages reveals first that whereas Joyce takes great care in describing for the reader the dream and memory which upset Stephen, he only hints at what upsets Bloom ("Some chap with a dose burning him"; "Straw hat in sunlight"). Further, Stephen's emotional reaction follows logically for the reader from the description of the dream and the memory. Bloom's emotional reaction, however, is unexpected; the fear to which he reacts is tangential to the line of his

thought that the reader has been following and not something
which the reader would expect and for which he would thus
be prepared. And, in addition, for Bloom, Joyce uses syllables
of exclamation and one-syllable words for their exclamatory
effect ("If he . . ./O!/Eh?/No . . . No"—151:36-39/153:39-42).
But for Stephen all of the words Joyce uses carry a heavy
burden of idea (several levels of abstraction higher than Bloom's
visceral reaction) and demonstrate Stephen's horror by
explaining completely to the reader the cause and meaning of
Stephen's reaction and not just simulating the visceral
sensations themselves.

The device that Joyce uses to represent Stephen's emotional
reaction is subtler than the one he uses for the first startle
passage for Bloom and potentially more effective. In the passage
from Bloom's stream of consciousness, the reader is presented
with symbolic printed analogues for Bloom's visceral sensations
(that is, exclamations and one-syllable words). As we have seen,
the second startle passage from Bloom's stream of consciousness
is more effective than the first one; but like the first it too
emphasizes visceral sensation. In the highly emotional passage
from Stephen's stream of consciousness, however, Joyce may
achieve something different. If by the immediately preceding
stream-of-consciousness passages Joyce has lured the reader into
accepting the fiction that he is in Stephen's mind and has thus
caused the reader to identify with Stephen, Stephen's emotional
outburst will have a similar emotional effect on the reader,
causing him literally to experience Stephen's emotion, or at least
a reasonable facsimile of it. Thus where Joyce uses simulation
and omniscient author's sentences to present Bloom's visceral
sensations, for Stephen's emotions he supplies the reader with
an objective correlative.

4. Perceptions

Joyce also simulates perceptions of sight, smell, taste, touch,
and sound. Although some of the things that characters in
Ulysses see are presented to the reader as they are in most
novels by the omniscient author ("A point, live dog, grew into
sight running across the sweep of sand"—45:42/45:3), Joyce
sometimes attempts to simulate perceptions as they impinge
upon the consciousness. The device he employs is the same as
the one he uses for presenting images: phrases and elliptical

sentences. He often first sets the stage with an omniscient author's sentence, explaining where the characters are or what they are doing; and then he presents the items that they see. Sometimes he lists the items separately, perhaps seeking to give the impression of a moving gaze: "He passed, dallying, the windows of Brown Thomas, silk mercers. Cascades of ribbons. Flimsy China silks. A tilted urn poured from its mouth a flood of bloodhued poplin: lustrous blood" (165:41-166:2/168:17-20). Sometimes, however, Joyce attempts to give the effect of multidimensional reality by jamming a number of visual perceptions together: "With a keep quiet relief, his eyes took note: this is street here middle of the day Bob Doran's bottle shoulders" (165:12/167:28). He cannot, of course, present the perceptions as they actually appear in the consciousness simultaneously, because of the additive nature of language. Jamming together visual perceptions by presenting them one immediately after another with no punctuation between is as close to simultaneity as he can come. His success in simulating multidimensional reality thus depends upon his earlier success in accustoming the reader to the stream-of-consciousness technique; for the more at ease the reader is with the technique, the faster he will read, and the faster he reads, the less the components will impinge upon his mind as a series of discrete items. Something of an analogy can be drawn between the stream-of-consciousness technique and a motion picture. If a film is run very slowly, the viewer sees each individual frame as a discrete item. If the speed is increased, he begins to get the impression of movement, although he sees considerable flicker and jumpy motion. And if the film is run at the proper speed, he receives a reasonably good impression of normal movement and action. Probably, however, even the phenomenally rapid reader cannot make a stream-of-consciousness passage approach any closer to reality than the stage that would compare to the flicker stage of a film.

A further fact that helps give the scene in which Bloom sees Bob Doran's bottle shoulders a sense of multidimensional reality is that, unlike the passage about the windows of Brown Thomas, it mingles visual perceptions on various levels of abstraction. "This is street here" is almost soliloquy, and thus a high level of abstraction. The next phrase, "middle of the day," reads less like soliloquy and begins to give the impression of stream of consciousness, but even it is on a relatively high level of abstraction, since, like the previous phrase, it is a judgment based on a series of perceptions of a lesser degree of abstraction: the position of the sun overhead; the absence of shadows; the temperature. The final phrase, "Bob Doran's bottle shoulders," comes closest of the three to a simulation of a perception as it occurs in the stream of consciousness, since it is an item that Bloom sees. It is thus, according to the abstraction ladder of Korzybski that we saw earlier, preverbal. As we learned from Harry Stack Sullivan, a moment of consciousness actually does include all levels of abstraction, from sensations on up through perceptions to judgments.

Similarly, Joyce's presentation of sound is often by omniscient author's sentence: "The dog's bark ran towards him, stopped, ran back" (46:18/45:21). Often, too, sound is presented more directly as it impinges upon consciousness as a line of dialogue: "—Tatters! Out of that, you mongrel" (47:26/46:32). And to add to the impression of the reality of a line of dialogue, Joyce may write it as it sounds: "Getonouthat" (125:28/126:28): "Iiiiiichaaaaaaach!" (175:17/177:39). Sometimes he tries to reproduce a sound, as in the newspaper pressroom: "Sllt. The nethermost deck of the first machine jogged forward its flyboard with sllt the first batch of quirefolded papers" (120:19/121:22). And he will occasionally attempt to simulate a sound as a component of consciousness, using again the short phrase or elliptical sentence: "jingle of harnesses, hoofthuds lowringing" (165:35/168:11). But he does not attempt to produce a chorus of sounds the way he does a confusion of visual perceptions.

Joyce's presentation of smell follows much the same pattern. He uses summary presentation by the omniscient author: "Hot mockturtle vapour and steam of newbaked jampuffs rolypoly poured out from Harrison's. The heavy noonreek tickled the top of Mr. Bloom's gullet" (155:16/157:23). He presents smells as components in the stream of consciousness by itemizing them in a series of phrases: "Smells of men. His gorge rose. Spaton sawdust, sweetish warmish cigarette smoke, reek of plug, spilt beer, men's beery piss, the stale of ferment" (167:12/169:30). And he tries to give the impression of many smells at the same time by jamming several together without punctuation: "Pungent mockturtle oxtail mulligatawny" (156:19/158:28).

Taste gets similar treatment. Here is a sentence which

combines both the omniscient author's sentence and the use of ellipsis to simulate the perception itself: "Mr Bloom ate his strips of sandwich, fresh clean bread, with relish of disgust, pungent mustard, the feety savour of green cheese" (171:12/ 173:31).

Touch, feel, and texture are handled the same way. For these Joyce employs the omniscient author's sentence ("Airs romped around him, nipping and eager airs"—39:22/38:22) as well as attempts to present the perception more directly ("Soft, warm, sticky gumjelly lips"—173:33/176:12).

D. Approaching Multidimensional Reality

As we have seen, Joyce sometimes strings a number of memory images or perceptions of sight or smell together, sometimes without punctuation to give the effect of a multiplicity of images, sights, or smells. He also, however, juxtaposes perceptions of different senses. Here, for instance, is an example of the mixing of simulated tastes and feelings of texture: "Wine soaked and softened rolled pith of bread mustard a moment mawkish cheese" (172:6/174:25). Joyce here also adds an additional dimension by attempting to give the sentence the actual feeling of a mouthful of partially chewed sandwich. The deletion of the word *the* from between "Wine soaked and softened" and "rolled pith of bread"; the abrupt shift, without punctuation or transition, from "pith of bread" to "mustard a moment" and from "mustard a moment" to "mawkish cheese"; the repetition of the mumbling *m* sound; and, should the reader mouth the sentence, the feeling that he would get as he shifts from *m* at the very front of his mouth to a vowel sound farther back in "mustard," "moment," and "mawkish"—all of these add to the actual feeling of a mouthful of food.

Joyce also mixes simulated perceptions of sight and sound together to add to the realism of a stream-of-consciousness passage: "Grafton street gay with housed awnings lured his senses. Muslin prints silk, dames and dowagers, jingle of harnesses, hoofthuds lowringing in the baking causeway" (165:34/168:10).[20] And here is a passage mixing sight and sound, omniscient author's sentences and simulated perceptions; and as in the sentence quoted which suggests a mouthful of half-chewed sandwich, it is reinforced by onomatopoeia: "Listen: a fourworded wavespeech: seesoo, hrss, rsseeiss ooos. Vehement breath of waters amid seasnakes, rearing horses, rocks. In cups of rocks it slops: flop, slop, slap: bounded in barrels. And, spent, its speech ceases. It flows purling, widely flowing, floating foampool, flower unfurling" (50:20/49:29).

As one can see from the examples quoted above, there is no consistency to the various composites of perceptions that Joyce presents or to his use of onomatopoeia as reinforcement. Nor should there be; for psychology tells us that the complexion and constitution of the stream of consciousness is always changing and that it differs for different people. In the first half of *Ulysses*, Joyce generally manages these composites so as to give the reader a minimum awareness of the author's manipulation, except in such instances as the mouthful of sandwich, where he purposely provides an awkward mouthful of words to simulate what the character is feeling. On occasion, however, he does allow his method to become obvious, as for example, when to his statement that "Davy Byrne smiledyawnednodded" (175:16/ 177:38) he adds "all in one."

E. Additional Devices

Joyce has still other devices to help give the semblance of reality to stream-of-consciousness passages. Sometimes, for example, he will give only a portion of a sentence, just enough for the reader to be able to complete the thought by himself, in order to obtain from time to time the slightly disjointed effect of the darting of a thought: "Sheet of her music blew out of my hand against the high school railings. Lucky it didn't" (154:7/156:13), and "Keyes: two months if I get Nannetti to. That'll be two pounds ten, about two pounds eight" (177:29/ 180:12).

Joyce also tries to simulate the feeling of having a name teasingly on the tip of one's tongue but not being able quite to remember it: "What was the name of that priestylooking chap was always squinting in when he passed? Weak eyes, woman. Stopped in Citron's saint Kevin's parade. Pen something. Pendennis? My memory is getting. Pen . . . ? of course it's years ago. Noise of the trams probably" (153:37/155:42).[21] The three dots are meant to represent what James called "a gap that is intensively active . . . [with a] sort of wraith of the name . . . in it."[22]

Joyce also employs traditional literary devices. As Gilbert demonstrates with a passage from Aeolus, that chapter is "a veritable thesaurus of rhetorical devices."[23] But as Humphrey points out, the display is largely tour de force and is not really inherent in the technique of the chapter. Humphrey goes on to show, however, in his analysis of the section from Proteus quoted below, that Joyce sometimes uses rhetoric "not for its own sake, but as a device for capturing the actuality of psychic processes; . . . for producing the texture of discontinuity that is a quality of consciousness":

> Ineluctable modality of the visible [epigram]: at least that if no more, thought through my eyes [metaphor]. Signatures of all things I am here to read [hyperbaton], seaspawn and seawrack, the nearing tide, that rusty boot. Snotgreen, bluesilver, rust: coloured signs. Limits of the diaphane. But he adds: in bodies. Then he was aware of them bodies before of them coloured [anastrophe]. How? By knocking his sconce against them, sure [dialect]. Go easy. Bald he was and a millionaire, *maestro di color che sanno.* Limit of the diaphane in. Why in? Diaphane, adiaphane [euphony]. If you can put your five fingers through it, it is a gate [enthymeme], if not a door. Shut your eyes and see.
>
> Stephen closed his eyes to hear his boots [synesthesia] crush crackling wrack and shells [onomatopoeia]. You are walking through it howsomever. I am, a stride at a time. A very short space of time through very short times of space [chiasmus]. Five, six: the *nacheinander.* Exactly: and that is the ineluctable modality of the audible. Open your eyes. No. Jesus! If I fell over a cliff that beetles o'er his base, fell through the *nebeneinander* ineluctably [protasis]. I am getting on nicely in the dark. My ash sword hangs at my side. Tap with it: they do. My two feet in his boots are at the end of his legs [metonymy], *nebeneinander.* Sounds solid: made by the mallet of *Los Demiurgos.* Am I walking into eternity along Sandymount strand? Crush, crack, crik, crick [alliteration and onomatopoeia]. Wild sea money. Dominie Deasy kens [archaism] them a'.
>
> *Won't you come to Sandymount,*
> *Madeline the mare?*
>
> Rhythm begins, you see. I hear [brachylogy]. A catalectic tetrameter of iambs marching [personification]. No, agallop [archaism]: *deline the mare* [ellipsis].

> I have in this short passage indicated twenty instances of the
> use of rhetorical figures and devices. There are probably as many
> more that could be found. I suspect that Joyce seldom did so well
> in the "Aeolus" episode, which was consciously devoted to them.[24]

On occasion Joyce uses allusions that call forth in the reader's
mind certain images that are probably there as a result of our
common cultural heritage. For example, most schoolchildren at
some time or another come into contact with Coleridge's "Kubla
Khan," and people of higher education, from among whom the
readers of *Ulysses* largely come, might be expected to be familiar
with it. Joyce, giving us Bloom's stream-of-consciousness view
of himself as a traveler "Somewhere in the east," builds into
the scene echoes of the Coleridge poem that arouse images
previously established in the reader's mind by his study of
"Kubla Khan." Here is the passage from Bloom's stream of
consciousness:

> Walk along a strand, strange land, come to a city gate, sentry
> there, old ranker too, old Tweedy's big moustaches leaning on
> a long kind of a spear. Wander through awned streets. Turbaned
> faces going by. Dark caves of carpet shops, big man, Turko the
> terrible, seated crosslegged smoking a coiled pipe. Cries of sellers
> in the streets. Drink water scented with fennel, sherbet. Wander
> along all day. Might meet a robber or two. Well, meet him.
> Getting on to sundown. The shadows of the mosques along the
> pillars: priests with a scroll rolled up. A shiver of the trees,
> signal, the evening wind. I pass on. Fading gold sky. A mother
> watches from her doorway. She calls her children home in their
> dark language. High wall: beyond strings twanged. Night sky
> moon, violet, colour of Molly's new garters. Strings. Listen. A girl
> playing one of these instruments what do you call them:
> dulcimers. I pass. (57:16/57:18)

In this passage Coleridge's "caves of ice" become "Dark caves
of carpet shops." "The shadow of the dome of pleasure" is echoed
in Joyce's "shadows of the mosques"; "many an incensebearing
tree" in Joyce's reference to trees; "walls and towers" in "High
wall"; "a waning moon" in "Night sky moon, violet"; and "A
damsel with a dulcimer" in "A girl playing one of those
instruments what do you call them: dulcimers." There are, too,
some humorous transpositions. Coleridge's "Ancestral voices
prophesying war" are represented by Molly's father, Major Brian
Tweedy, propped up by a spear. Coleridge's "woman wailing for

her demon lover" appears as a mother calling her children home, and "honey-dew" and "the milk of Paradise" as "sherbet" and "water scented with fennel."

Joyce may have meant these clues to suggest to the reader that Bloom was drawing here upon his own experience with "Kubla Khan" as a "schoolpoem" in building the scene in his mind.[25] But they also serve other purposes. To the reader aware of the echoes, the irony of the comparison provides a further dimension of meaning to the passage, just as do the parallels between episodes in the *Odyssey* and episodes in Joyce's novel. Secondly, the clues evoke in the reader's mind images of the Near East planted there by Coleridge, whether the *reader* is conscious of their origin or not. These allusions are not a means of simulating the stream of consciousness, but rather control and enrich the stream of consciousness of the reader as he reads a particular passage. The appearance of a particular set of images in his mind at the same time that he is reading a passage of simulated stream of consciousness encourages imaginative activity in the reader and thus provides him with a context and a receptive attitude for the simulated images in the stream-of-consciousness passages.[26]

Joyce's recurrent themes operate in much the same way. Earlier in this chapter we saw how a discussion between Stephen and Buck Mulligan in the opening chapter of *Ulysses* prepared the reader for the description of Stephen's vision of his mother's ghost a few pages later. Because of its carefully chosen detail and its use of images, the ghost passage makes a strong impression on the mind of the reader. Humphrey says of the "image-ridden passage": "Because the particulars are psychological phenomena, these private images (combined with the intense rhetoric) come as close as imaginable to an exact rendering of the phenomena—unless it were to be in terms from the psychoanalyst's chamber." Humphrey feels that the images Joyce uses here are also calculated "to convince the reader of the privacy and the actuality of the mind being represented . . . [and] to stand for ideas peculiar to that mind."[27] The passage, therefore, not only gives the impression of privacy, but it communicates the meaning of Stephen's private image to the reader and implants it in the reader's mind, making it his own, ready to be called forth by a reference or a suggestion. As a recurring theme, the ghost of Stephen's mother continues to

appear through the novel. Directly and by suggestion she
appears in Proteus, for example: "a ghostwoman with ashes on
her breath" (39:11/38:11); "I could not save her" (46:41/46:4);
and: "Behold the handmaid of the moon. In sleep the wet sign
calls her hour, bids her rise. Bridebed, childbed, bed of death,
ghostcandled" (48:32/47:39). The last two of these allusions
Joyce enriches further by association with the mention of the
sea. The references thus evoke in the reader's mind the image
of the ghostwoman left there by Stephen's highly dramatic
recoiling from his memory of his dream (12:5-15/10:15-25); and
the last two in addition recall Stephen's introductory discussion
with Buck Mulligan. Each reference to the ghost image also
carries with it the echoes of the variations on the theme rung
by the previous allusions; so that each succeeding allusion
evokes in the reader's mind a richer and richer response. Like
the images implanted in the mind of the reader by "Kubla
Khan," these images also serve to prepare the reader to accept
Joyce's simulation of the stream-of-consciousness technique by
enriching and stimulating his imaginative activity.

The symbolism involved in the image of the ghostwoman is
an example of a further device used by Joyce. Not only does
an allusion to her stir up her image in the reader's mind, but
that image brings with it a mantle of meaning. In this instance,
as most critics point out, the image is a symbol of Stephen's
"agenbite of inwit," his remorseful conscience. Humphrey
attributes the frequent use of this symbolism by the
stream-of-consciousness novelist to "his dilemma . . . [of having]
chosen words to express . . . [the] nonverbal area of mind,"
a problem presented at some length in the preceding chapter.[28]

Finally, there are several matters that should be made explicit
here that are implicit in the discussion above of all the devices
considered. First, many passages analyzed above attest to the
bipolarity of the consciousness simulated in *Ulysses*. We have
noted, for example, how external stimuli start trains of thought
which then are guided by inner tensions and need patterns: the
sea evoking Stephen's memories of his mother; and Stephen's
glimpse of the midwives starting a train of thought that leads
through Edenville to the *lex eterna*. And we have seen moments
in which a character sunk completely in his own private
thoughts and oblivious to the world around him is jostled out
of those thoughts by an intrusion from the environment: for

example, Buck's shout of "Kinch ahoy!" after Stephen envisions his mother's deathbed scene. We have seen moments in which perceptions (outer stimuli) hold sway; and we have also seen moments in which reverie (the result of inner needs) holds sway. The second matter is that although a stream-of-consciousness passage may simulate the quite unselective meanderings of consciousness, in putting it together the author must be highly selective. He must choose from an infinite number of details carefully, must distribute his choices judiciously, and must return to them artfully. His work may give the impression of automatic writing, but it is an impression that is calculated.

The matter of individual differences, discussed briefly in connection with the comparison of the treatment of emotional reaction in passages of streams of consciousness of Bloom and Stephen, is also implicit in many of the other discussions above, and will be made explicit later. Treatment of pattern in the stream of consciousness, important in the discussion of individual differences, will thus be left until later.

F. Conclusion and Summary

Thus Joyce introduces his reader carefully to his stream-of-consciousness technique. First of all, he prepares him by supplying him with a context out of which he can draw the necessary references and understanding for the stream-of-consciousness passages to come. And second, he prepares him for the stream-of-consciousness technique by relying heavily on dialogue in the introductory chapters.

Joyce also shows his characters in various states of mind: imaginative thinking, memory, reverie, and hallucination; relative placidity and strong emotion. His stream-of-consciousness passages show the mind flowing from one state to another, inner and outer stimuli governing the various states of mind, and individual differences creating different streams of consciousness.

Like the psychological stream of consciousness, Joyce's simulated stream of consciousness is made up of a complex interrelationship of many components: words, sensations, perceptions, images. Words he need not simulate; he can present them directly. Sensations, perceptions, and images, however, he cannot present directly; they are not only nonverbal, but also generally preverbal. To present all three of these, Joyce uses the same device, a phrase or an elliptical sentence. In simulating the stream of consciousness, he runs together words and simulations of sensations, perceptions, and images of various levels of abstraction, sometimes with and sometimes without punctuation. His use of various literary devices adds to the complexity of his simulated stream of consciousness.

Another device that Joyce employs is the calling forth in the mind of the reader of a series of images in addition to the ones he suggests by ellipsis. This encouraging of the imaginative thinking of the reader should help to make him receptive to Joyce's attempted simulation of the stream of consciousness.

No one of these devices in itself is enough to simulate the psychological stream of consciousness. When they are all operating together, however, they create an impression of complexity and multidimensionality despite the linear nature of language.

PART II
The Streams of Consciousness of Stephen, Bloom, and Molly

5
The Intellectual Content of Proteus, Lestrygonians, and Penelope

In the chapters in Part Two, the streams of consciousness of Stephen, Bloom, and Molly are analyzed and compared. The results show to what extent Joyce actually used the stream-of-consciousness technique to differentiate his characters and project their personalities. They also shed light on several critical problems.

Many of the analyses are of the kind frequently made by students of literary texts: sentence length and structure; word length and derivation; poetic images and sound correspondences. Others, however, borrowed from psychology, psycholinguistics, and psychiatry, are relatively new to literary criticism and may be of interest to students of stylistics as well as to students of *Ulysses* and of the stream-of-consciousness technique: association patterning; proportion of content words to function words; type-token ratios; words and phrases which reveal personality patterns.

The analyses are based to a large extent on three chapters of *Ulysses*—Proteus (Stephen), Lestrygonians (Bloom), and Penelope (Molly). The three were designated as stream-of-consciousness chapters early in the history of Joyce criticism, and critics have continued to accept that designation. In Proteus (chapter three, 38-51/37-51), Stephen walks along Sandymount strand, looking about him and thinking. In Lestrygonians (chapter eight, 149-81/151-83), Bloom wanders through the streets of Dublin searching for a restaurant in which to eat and thinking of his problems. In Penelope (chapter eighteen, 723-68/738-83), Molly lies in bed thinking over the occurrences of the day and of her lifetime. All three chapters provide typical examples of the unfettered flow of the stream of consciousness. Each chapter is long enough to give a good picture of the character concerned, and the ideas which reoccur in each character's simulated stream of consciousness throughout the day appear and reappear in these passages just as they do elsewhere in the novel.

For some of the analyses, it was appropriate to use a sampling technique. In comparing word lengths, for example, by the employment of certain statistical procedures I could use sample passages of the three chapters. The sampling procedures are discussed in the appendix. I will note for each analysis whether it was made of the full chapter or of a sampling.

A. Stephen (in Proteus)

Gilbert says of the opening of Proteus, "Surely the 'signature' of Bishop Berkeley is on this passage."[1] But the maestro here is Aristotle rather than Berkeley, for Stephen's concern with the relationship of color, transparency, and visibility echoes closely sections of *De Anima*. Aristotle says there, for example, "Whatever is visible is colour and colour is what lies upon what is in its own nature visible."[2] Stephen may also be thinking of the *Commentary* on *De Anima* by Aquinas, which he—or rather Joyce—may well have read. Saint Thomas's comments on this same problem include statements like "The eye would never perceive size or shape if it did not perceive colour," clearly the same concept which Stephen ponders as he walks along Sandymount strand musing of color, form, and the diaphane (38:1-10/37:1-10).[3]

Even Stephen's later reference to Berkeley's philosophy ("The good bishop of Cloyne"—49:16/48:25) involves Aristotle, for just a few lines before he thinks, "Endless, would it be mine, form of my form?" (49:13/48:22), an obvious echo of Aristotle's "It follows that the soul is analogous to the hand; for as the hand is a tool of tools, so the mind is the form of forms and sense the form of sensible things."[4] In two earlier references, Stephen's thoughts run closer to the original: "The soul is in a manner all that is: the soul is the form of forms" (27:3/26:3), and "My soul walks with me, form of forms" (45:24/44:26). Ernst Cassirer writes of Aristotle's view of knowledge and life: "Sense perception, memory, experience, imagination and reason are all linked together by a common bond; they are merely different stages and different expressions of one and the same fundamental activity, which attains the highest perfection in man." True of Aristotle, this statement is also true of Stephen's

stream of consciousness in Proteus, which begins with Stephen's
musing on Aristotle's *De Anima*. Cassirer adds: "If we were to
adopt this biological view we should expect that the first stages
of human knowledge would deal exclusively with the external
world."[5] Quite appropriately, therefore, Proteus opens with
Stephen's pondering of the nature of the external world and
Aristotle's discussion of it. He even tries a little experiment,
closing his eyes and walking amid the "crush crackling wrack
and shells" to show that Aristotle could have been "aware of
them bodies before of them coloured" (38:5/37:5). And his
musings continue a while on primary matters, for opening his
eyes upon the conclusion of the experiment, Stephen sees two
midwives, who make him think of birth and creation.

From there, however, he leaps to heaven with a phone call
to Edenville AA 001 (39:4/38:4); and the pattern for Proteus
is set: Stephen's thoughts will concern themselves with
everything from the most elementary to the most abstruse, from
the most common to the most esoteric, from the most
materialistic to the most spiritual. But simple or complex, his
thoughts are always concerned with the meaning of life and
the meaning of his own life. Everything that he sees he
relates to himself, and all his thoughts, even his "medieval
abstrusiosities," are organized sooner or later about his own
insecurity.

As Tindall points out, there seems also to be a reference to
Jacob Boehme, the seventeenth-century Christian mystic, in the
opening lines of Proteus: "Signatures of all things" (38:2/37:2)
is the title of what is probably Boehme's best-known work,
Signatura Rerum.[6] Although Boehme seems not to have been
an Aristotelian, his concept of *signature* is not opposed to
Aristotle's concept of the *soul*.[7] To Aristotle, soul is form. For
Boehme, too, the outer is formed by and is a manifestation of
the inner: "The whole outward visible world with all its being
is a signature, or figure of the inward spiritual world; whatever
is internally, and however its operation is, so likewise it has
its character externally."[8]

It would be difficult to determine how much Boehme
influences Stephen's thoughts in Proteus without a careful
examination of Boehme's writings. Tindall feels that Joyce was
thoroughly versed in mysticism.[9] Certainly "Signatures of all
things I am here to read, seaspawn and seawrack, the nearing

tide, that rusty boot" (38:2/37:2) is more understandable after one has read in Boehme: "For nature has given to everything its language according to its essence and form . . . and the fiat of that essence forms the quality of the essence in the voice or virtue which it sends forth, to the animals in the sound, and to the essentials [vegetables] in smell, virtue, and form."[10] As might be expected, Stephen does not restrict himself to the exact application of Boehme's categories. While Boehme assigns voice to animals and "smell, virtue, and form" to essentials (vegetables), even Stephen's essentials have voice: "sigh of leaves and waves" (50:30/49:40).

The ideas of another Christian mystic are also interwoven into the opening passage of Proteus, although Joyce, in his endless textual revisions, obscured the reference. In the second paragraph of the chapter, Stephen, closing his eyes to "see" whether that action will cause the world to cease to exist (an old idealist controversy), thinks, "Sounds solid: made by the mallet of *Los Demiurgos*" (38:20/37:20). The reader might think the italicized words to be merely a casual reference in Spanish to those gods in Greek mythology who were supposed to have made the world. The word "mallet," however, strikes an odd note. It is appropriate enough in the sense that it is a tool used by artists and craftsmen such as sculptors and carpenters (that is, creators) and would thus fit the image of the demiurges as fashioners of the world. But that Joyce should have mentioned a particular tool at all suggests that he had something particular in mind, a picture perhaps, or an episode from Greek mythology. The puzzle disappears when one examines the Buffalo manuscript. There the line reads "Solid no doubt: made by the hammer of Los," to which has been appended with an asterisk the word "Demiurgos."[11]

The hammer of Los appears several times in Blake's prophetic books: "Los . . . built / Furnaces: he formed an Anvil, / A Hammer of adamant; then began / The binding of Urizen day and night."[12] And: "In terrors Los shrunk from his task: / His great hammer fell from his hand."[13] In "The Book of Los," Los forms "an immense Orb of fire," a "round Globe," with his hammer.[14] Inasmuch as Urizen, whom Los (Imagination) imprisons in this globe, is generally taken to represent Reason, Joyce may well have taken the globe to represent the earth.[15] Support for such a theory can be found in the last lines of the poem, which ascribe to this globe rocks and rivers, darkness and deep clouds (figurative as well as literal, perhaps?), and call the whole a "Human Illusion":

> here Urizen lay
> In fierce torments on his glowing bed,
>
> Till his Brain in a rock, & his Heart
> In a fleshy slough formed four rivers
> Obscuring the immense Orb of fire
> Flowing down into night; till a Form
> Was completed, a Human Illusion
> In darkness and deep clouds involv'd.[16]

Sometime before he wrote his final handwritten draft of the Proteus episode, Joyce changed the line to read the way it does in the published form.[17] Knowing Joyce's interest in double meanings, an interest which found full expression in *Finnegans Wake,* one can assume that he intended both meanings of the line, that the earth was made solid by the demiurges, and by the mallet of Los, the demiurge. Whether or not he realized that he was obscuring the reference to Blake, however, it would be difficult to say.

Blake's ideas are appropriate at the beginning of Proteus for two reasons. In the first place, Blake was concerned with some of the same problems of which Stephen read in Aristotle; for example, form. Max Plowman says: "Blake regards life as the descent of spirit into matter in order that spirit may achieve form. . . . He looked upon human life, not as the discontinuous appearance of phenomena, but as a particular manifestation of eternal being.[18] Secondly, we know from students of Blake and from Blake's own writings that he knew and greatly admired the works of Boehme, the seventeenth-century mystic discussed above. In "The Marriage of Heaven and Hell," we find:

> Any man of mechanical talents may, from the writings of Paracelsus or Jacob Behmen [a variation of Boehme], produce ten thousand volumes of equal value with Swedenborg's, and from those of Dante and Shakespeare an infinite number.
> But when he has done this, let him not say that he has done better than his master, for he only holds a candle in sunshine.[19]

Aristotle, then, who was the master, and the group of lesser philosophers, Berkeley, Blake, and Boehme, provide both the guideposts and the yardsticks for Stephen's inquiring and speculative mind in Proteus.

Another major motif in Proteus is change. At the beginning of his discussion of that chapter, Gilbert speaks of "a triad of directive themes that permeate its fabric": the story of Proteus (in Book IV of the *Odyssey*); metempsychosis; and philology.[20] Budgen reports that Joyce himself said about this chapter: "You catch the drift of the thing? . . . It's the struggle with Proteus. Change is the theme. Everything changes—sea, sky, man, animals. The words change, too."[21] And change does occur in many ways. The effects of the tide are noted (44:34/45:40). Stephen speaks of himself as a changeling (46:16/45:19). The dog as he frisks about the beach changes from buck to bear to wolf to calf to fox to leopard to panther (47/46). A corpse suffers a "seachange" (51:8/50:19) and becomes "saltwhite" (50:39/50:7). And "God becomes man becomes fish becomes barnacle goose becomes featherbed mountain" (51:3/50:13). Language goes through protean transformation too. "Trudges" becomes "schlepps, trains, drags, trascines" (48:29/47:36).[22] Words give way to elemental syllables and sounds: "Oomb, allwombing tomb" (48:41/48:8); "ooeeehah" (49:1/48:9); "wayawayawayawayawayaway" (49:2/48:10); "seesoo, hrss, rsseeiss, ooos" (50:21/49:30).

Stephen's concern with time also introduces a special kind of change, the inevitable and progressive change caused by time's passing. The midwives remind him that he himself was once a baby (38:40/37:40). The "sun's flaming sword" moves "to the west" to "evening lands" (48:28/47:35). Thus evening follows a regular succession of "Blue dusk, nightfall, deep blue night" (45:17/44:19). And a woman follows the inevitable path of "Bridebed, childbed, bed of death, ghostcandled" (48:33/47:40). He too is walking through life and time, "a stride at a time" (38:13/37:13).

In addition to change (the discussion of which, above, has covered Gilbert's "triad of directive themes"), there are other threads running through the Proteus episode. One, of course, is Aristotle's discussion of the nature of sight and reality with which the chapter opens ("Ineluctable modality of the visible"—38:1/37:1) and to which Stephen's thoughts return later ("My soul walks with me, form of forms"—45:24/44:26; "Endless, would it be mine, form of my form?"—49:13/48:22).

Another is the history of the Catholic church, and more particularly the story of its heresies. Thus the chapter is sprinkled with comments about church leaders and heresiarchs: Arius (39:16/38:16); Joachim Abbas (40:37/39:37); Dan Occam (41:12/40:13); Columbanus, Fiacre, and Scotus (43:6/42:8); Saint Canice (45:1/44:4); Saint Ambrose (50:29/49:39). Fragments of Ireland's past also appear throughout the chapter. There is mention of Mananaan MacLir, half-mythical, half-historical founder of the Manx nation, and, as lord of the sea, a symbol of flux and change (39:24/38:24). Stephen remembers the stories of the Irish revolutionists told to him by Kevin Egan in Paris (44/43); Egan's remarks about Saint Canice, who founded a monastery in Kilkenny, and Richard Fitzgerald, who had a castle on the Nore (45:1/44:4); and Egan's singing of "The Boys of Kilkenny" (45:4/44:6). And Stephen pictures to himself the Danes invading Ireland (46:7/45:10) and the time that the Dubliners caught a school of whales stranded in the shallow waters of the bay (46:10/45:13).

Stephen's own past also figures in his thoughts. He thinks of his birth (38:40/37:40); his schooldays at Clongowes (40:34/40:31; 46:36/45:39); his adolescent sexual urges (41:20/40:21); his youthful plans for writing and hopes for success (41:31/40:33); his meetings with the Egans, Kevin (*père*—44/43) and Patrice (*fils*—42/41); his stay in Paris (42-44/41-43; 50:12/49:21); and his impecunious return (43:8/42:12); Mulligan's taking the key to the Martello tower (one of the surprisingly few thoughts about the immediate past—45:20/44:22); a dream he had the night before (47:39/47:4); and a woman he saw on Monday (49:29/48:38). He is reminded also of his lack of courage and of his dead mother by a drowned man who bobs in the stream of his thoughts (46:32/45:35; 50:36/50:4; 51:6/50:16).

As one might expect of a man with a "true scholastic stink," Stephen's thoughts abound with words and phrases from foreign languages, ancient and modern: Greek, Latin, French, German, Italian, and Spanish.[23] And they are full of echoes of famous authors and their works: Aristotle, Matthew Arnold, Blake, Dryden, Gray, Milton, Shakespeare, Swift, Swinburne, Tennyson, Traherne, Wilde, Yeats, and the anthologist Richard Head.[24] To this list should be added the names of some Continental authors and journalists, largely French: Drumont (44:10/43:12), Gautier

(45:33/44:36), Millevoye (44:12/43:14), Pico della Mirandola (41:36/40:37), Taxil (42:19/41:22), and Veuillot (45:33/44:36). Such additional odd bits of information and subject matter as a short discussion of pretenders to the British throne (46:22/ 45:25) and a mention of the Indian mahamanvantara (41:36/ 40:37) attest further to the catholicity and intellectuality of Stephen's thoughts and interests.

As might be expected, Shakespearian allusions occur frequently in Stephen's stream of consciousness. In the fourteen pages of Proteus there are at least fifteen quotations and echoes from Shakespeare's plays. These allusions, however, are not presented as quotations. Most of them are blended deftly into the flow of Stephen's thoughts. For example, in Telemachus, Haines self-consciously quotes from Shakespeare: "I mean to say, Haines explained to Stephen as they followed, this tower and these cliffs here remind me somehow of Elsinore *That beetles o'er his base into the sea,* isn't it?" (20:3/18:23).[25] The same reference, when it appears in Stephen's thoughts in Proteus, is inconspicuously woven into the fabric of what he is preoccupied with at the moment: "Open your eyes. No. Jesus! If I fell over a cliff that beetles o'er his base, fell through the *nebeneinander* ineluctably" (38:15/37:15). Shakespearian allusions, then, which appear in Stephen's thoughts tend not to be references to Shakespeare. That is, they tend not to point at Stephen's thinking of a particular Shakespearian play or character, but rather to use Shakespeare to express what is in Stephen's mind. They are bits of precise thought, appeals to a proven master of communication and self-expression, used to help Stephen (and Joyce) crystallize his thoughts in the clearest possible way. Thus when Stephen thinks, "Where is poor dear Arius to try conclusions?" (39:16/38:16), he is thinking of a phrase supplied by Shakespeare, but the phrase is so unobtrusive, so integral a part of the thought and structure of the sentence which contains it, that Stephen seems to have made it truly his own.[26] Stephen, then, knows Shakespeare's plays so well that he uses quotations from them quite naturally in his thinking, much as members of various trades and professions draw on their technical jargon to express what they have to say, or as a bilingual person can slip quite unconsciously from one language to another to borrow words or phrases to express most clearly what he wants to say. Indeed, although he certainly would recognize them if they were brought to his attention, Stephen may not even be aware that some of the phrases he uses are borrowings.

It should also be noted that although some of the references to the works of Shakespeare are to well-known passages (for example, Ariel's song, Ophelia's song, and Polonius' "Very like a whale"), others are from relatively unimportant and certainly less well-known passages of the plays: "that on the unnumbered pebbles beats" (41:41/41:1) is a distinct echo of "that on the unnumb'red pebbles chafes" (*King Lear,* act 4, sc. 6, line 21); and "the wet sign" (48:32/47:39) is an echo of Horatio's "moist star" (*Hamlet,* act 1, sc. 1, line 118). Here again is evidence that Stephen knew his Shakespeare well. Perhaps his using Shakespeare in the library episode to advertise his own erudition can be thought of less harshly in the light of the evidence in Proteus that at least he knows whereof he speaks and that he does not always drag Shakespeare out only as a showpiece for the advancement of his own interests.[27]

B. Bloom (in Lestrygonians)

Bloom is concerned with many of the same matters that Stephen is, but with a significant difference: Bloom's concerns are generally on a much less sophisticated level of understanding. For example, triggered by the blind boy's inability to see, Bloom's thoughts roam quite unwittingly over the same catalogue of the senses discussed by Aristotle in *De Anima* as Stephen's did earlier. Bloom wonders whether blind people "See things in their foreheads perhaps. Kind of sense of volume" (178:42/181:26). He also thinks about smells (179:14/181:40) and tastes (179:16/181:42), the "voice temperature" (179:22/182:6), and touch (179:23/182.7). Like Stephen, Bloom even tries a little experiment. The two experiments, however, point up an important difference in the two men: Stephen knows his Aristotle and is thinking of him while he does his experiment; Bloom not only knows little of Aristotle but is not thinking of him while he does his experiment. Bloom's experiment is to see if he can tell by his sense of touch first the color of his hair (179:30/182:15) and then the color of his stomach (179:36/182:21). So, like Stephen, he closes his eyes and tries. But Bloom's experiment is much more naive than Stephen's, for as Aristotle points out, color is the "special object" of sight: "I call by the name of special object of this or that sense that which cannot be perceived by any other sense than that one and in respect of which no error is possible; in this sense colour is the special object of sight, sound of hearing, flavour of taste."[28]

In other instances, Bloom unknowingly approximates some Aristotelian concepts. Imagining the blind boy's making love to a girl, Bloom thinks, "Must be strange not to see her. Kind of a form in his mind's eye" (179:21/182:5). That statement is reminiscent of Aristotle's "the mind is the form of forms," although Aristotle is talking about men with normal sight, whereas Bloom is not. A little earlier, in another experiment, Bloom drops his eyelids over his irises so that his view of a distant bank clock is just obscured and thinks: "Can't see it. If you imagine it's there you can almost see it. Can't see it" (164:16/166:31). Thus like Stephen (38/37), Bloom concerns himself with the idealist concept of whether the world exists outside of man's mind; but unlike Stephen, Bloom is apparently not aware that he is dealing with an age-old philosophic problem. Bloom, in his uninformed, unscientific way, even discovers for himself a fact about which Aristotle wrote some two thousand years earlier. Near the beginning of Lestrygonians, Bloom's thoughts turn to objects that shine in the night: "Phosophorous it must be done with. If you leave a bit of codfish for instance. I could see the bluey silver over it. Night I went down to the pantry in the kitchen" (149:25/151:25). Aristotle, in his discussion of the visible, says: "Some objects of sight which in light are invisible, in darkness stimulate the sense; that is, things that appear fiery or shining. This class of objects has no simple common name, but instances of it are fungi, flesh, heads, scales, and eyes of fish."[29] The point of interest here is not so much Bloom's discovery, because countless people have made that for themselves, but rather that, along with the other examples given, it indicates a striking difference between the thoughts of Stephen and Bloom: Stephen's thoughts here stemming from the academic, are abstract and often unworldly—but sophisticated; Bloom's thoughts, stemming from the mundane, are practical but often unaware and misinformed—and generally naive.

There are many other appeals to the senses in Lestrygonians, quite a few of which deal with food and taste. A good many, of course, come as a result of Bloom's eating lunch (169-72/171-74): after ordering his lunch (169/171), he "smellsipped the cordial juice" (170:30/173:7), "ate his strips of sandwich, fresh clean bread, with relish of disgust, pungent mustard, the feety savour of green cheese" (171:12/173:31), and tasted "Wine soaked and softened rolled pith of bread mustard a moment mawkish cheese" (172:6/174:25). But there are also references to taste before and after the luncheon episode: Bloom thinks of the taste of pastry (155:18/157:25); of spicy fruits from Jaffa (116:16/168:34); of the flavor of garlic, onions, mushrooms, and truffles (168:28/171:5); of "smoking hot, thick sugary" blood (168:40/171:17); of all sorts of food (172/174, 173/175, and 174/176); of the taste of Molly's seedcake (173:32/176:11) and her lips (173:33/176:13) on Howth hill; and he thinks "Tastes all different" for the blind stripling (178:29/181:13).

There are also references to the other senses throughout the chapter. Bloom is aware of the smells of soup and jampuffs as they pour out of Harrison's (155:17/157:24; 156:19/158:29) and of the smell of food at Burton's (166:33/169:9). The sights and sounds of "Grafton Street gay with housed awnings" (165:34/168:10), entice him ("Muslin prints silk, dames and dowagers, jingle of harnesses"—165:35/168:11), as do the colorful windows of Brown Thomas, silk mercers (165:41/168:17; 166:12/168:30). He responds also to thoughts of the color and warmth of the East (166:15-20/168:33-38) and thinks of lovers, "Perfumed bodies, warm full" (166:24/168:42). And he remembers the warmth of Molly's stays (154:20/156:27). By comparison with Lestrygonians, Proteus (and thus Stephen), concerned with the senses merely in an academic way, seems ascetic.

Bloom, like Stephen, is also concerned with science. But in keeping with the pattern described above, where Stephen is concerned with the philosophy of science, and of early science at that, Bloom is interested in the practical aspects of modern science. And where Stephen's thoughts indicate a trained mind, Bloom's indicate the mind of the man on the street, full of half-truths, folklore, and misinformation. Bloom thinks about Röntgen rays (176:41/179:22) and how they work, about what sunspots are (164:23/166:39) and of the total eclipse that is coming (164:24/166:41). He also thinks about the effects of different types of food on people (163:37/166:9) and of how the digestive system works. He indicates an awareness of acceleration (150:26/152:28) and of the various stages that planets go through (164:39/167:13). But most of these thoughts indicate Bloom's ignorance and suggest the dim memory of Sunday supplement articles on science rather than any real knowledge. For example, Bloom thinks that in order to follow food through the digestive system with x rays, a green tracer is necessary (176:40/179:21). His comment that "I never exactly understood [parallax]" is such an understatement that it is funny (152:3/154:6). His ideas of biochemistry and diet are derived more from old wives' tales than from discoveries in the laboratory; his understanding of the digestive tract is largely in terms of an analogy with a plumbing system (177:19/180:1); and his concept of acceleration is thoroughly confused (150:26/152:28). Of sunspots and eclipses he does not say enough for the reader to tell whether he understands them or not.

Bloom is also interested in the same two aspects of change that appear in Stephen's thoughts. First there is protean change. Even candy goes through a transformation: the king sits on his throne "sucking red jujubes white" (149:5/151:5). Bloom knows that the physical world changes: "Same old dingdong always. Gas, then solid, then world, then cold, then dead shell drifting around, frozen rock like that pineapple rock" (164:40/167:14). So does what we eat: "And we stuffing food in one hole and out behind: food, chyle, blood, dung, earth, food: have to feed it like stoking an engine" (174:12/176:35). He is interested, too, in transmigration of the soul, metempsychosis (180:3/182:30)— or "met him pikehoses" as Molly calls it (64:10/64:18; 152:4/154:8).

And, like Stephen, Bloom is concerned with the changes wrought by time. Water flowing under the bridge reminds him of "the stream of life we trace. Because life is a stream" (151:27/153:30). The same thought returns later (153:37/155:40). Remembering an anti-English riot that he once got mixed up in (160/162), Bloom thinks wryly of what time does to young hotheads: "Few years time half of them magistrates and civil servants. War comes on: into the army helterskelter: same fellows used to whether on the scaffold high" (161:1/163:14).[30] Thinking about the early days of his marriage, Bloom realizes, "Can't bring back time. Like holding water in

your hand" (165:30/168:5). And remembering his exciting
courting of Molly on Howth hill, he thinks heartbrokenly, "Me.
And me now" (173:42/176:22). Thinking of Dignam's burial and
Mrs. Purefoy's being about to give birth, he remarks how
"Things go on same; day after day" (162:3/174:17); that is,
people are being born and others are dying "every second." And
he thinks of the effect of time on civilizations, how, although
as people of one city pass away, more come, cities themselves
disappear: "Piled up in cities, worn away age after age.
Pyramids in sand. Built on bread and onions. Slaves Chinese
wall. Babylon. Big stones left. Round towers. Rest rubble,
sprawling suburbs, jerrybuilt, Kerwan's mushroom houses, built
of breeze. Shelter for the night" (162:18/164:32). The big
difference between Stephen's and Bloom's thoughts on this
concept seems to be that Bloom tends to be aware of the more
commonly discussed aspects of change and tends to think of
them in terms of the trite image and the tired phrase. Stephen's
awareness of time and change is more original in conception
and expression than Bloom's.

Again like Stephen, Bloom is concerned with Ireland's past,
historic and immediate. He thinks of Cormac, an Irish king of
the third century A.D. (167:6/169:24). But most of his references
are to men who figured more recently in Irish affairs: Joe
Chamberlain (160:27/162:40), Parnell (161:28/163:42;
162:42/165:14), Griffith (161:28/163:42), David Sheehy
(163:5/165:19). He also thinks of a student riot in which he
took part (160/162), and of the invincibles (161:6/163:20) and
Sinn Fein (161:24/163:38). Thus where Stephen tends to be
interested in ancient Ireland, Bloom's interest is largely in the
Ireland of his own lifetime. Furthermore, as will be seen below,
Bloom's knowledge of old Ireland is confused.

Like Stephen, too, Bloom is interested in the Roman Catholic
church, but again with an important difference. Whereas
Stephen is interested in the history of the church and its
philosophical and theological disputes, Bloom is interested in the
everyday life of church people and the effects of the church
and its teachings on the lives of its communicants. He thinks
of the violence often done in the name of religion: "God wants
blood victim. Birth, hymen, martyr, war, foundation of a
building, sacrifice, kidney burntoffering, druid's altars"
(149:13/151:13).[31] He comments unsympathetically on the effect

of Catholicism on the size of families: "Fifteen children he had. Birth every year almost. That's in their theology or the priest won't give the poor woman the confession, the absolution. Increase and multiply. Did you ever hear such an idea? Eat you out of house and home" (149:35/151:36). He also thinks about the soft life of a priest (149:40/151:41): "Living on the fat of the land. . . . Does himself well. . . . Mum's the word." And although he is more sympathetic toward the nuns, he is still critical of them: "They like buttering themselves in an out" (153:8/155:13). And he also thinks of an ad that he saw for a luminous crucifix (149:22/151:22).

Another parallel with the Proteus episode is found in the bits of foreign languages that appear in Bloom's stream of consciousness. But again there is an important difference between the two. Where there are twenty-eight different foreign words and phrases from six different languages, ancient and modern, in the fourteen pages of Proteus, there are only nine instances of foreign words and phrases in the fifty-three pages of Lestrygonians, and those in only two languages, French and Italian, both modern. And where Stephen's references to foreign languages and his use of them are adept and are woven firmly into the pattern of his thought, Bloom's foreign language quotations are either clichés, restaurant terms, or echoes of operas, none of them requiring any great knowledge or appreciable understanding of languages: "*cherchez la femme*" (165:15/167:31); "*élite. Créme de la créme*" (172:39/175:17); "*table d'hôte*" (168:24/170:42); "*chef*" (173:2/175:22); "*à la duchesse de Parme*" (173:3/175:23); "*La cause é santa!*" (166:2/168:20), from Meyerbeer's *The Huguenots;* and "*Don Giovanni, a cenar teco/M'invitasti*" (177:11/179:36; 177:23,24/180:6,7). Bloom's linguistic ignorance and lack of facility with languages is further pointed up by his wondering what *teco* means (177:24/180:7), just as elsewhere he wonders how to pronounce *voglio* (63:40/64:5; 434:6/441:12; 606:19/622:16).

Bloom's allusions to the literary arts are also fewer and less sophisticated than Stephen's. Bloom cannot even get straight a bawdy limerick about the unfortunate Reverend MacTrigger (169:19/171:38; 170:10,16/172:30,35). His references to literature are relatively few and undistinguished. His information about "That last pagan king of Ireland Cormac" is derived from a "schoolpoem" (167:6/169:23). And, characteristically, he remembers the poem incorrectly, to the confusion of history. In the poem, "The Burial of King Cormac," by Sir Samuel Ferguson, Cormac says, "'twas at Ross that I first knew / One, Unseen, who is God alone."[32] Bloom, however, attributes Cormac's conversion to Saint Patrick (167:8/169:26). The poem does not attribute the conversion to anyone, however, and Patrick, born about 373 A.D., was not supposed to have landed at Wicklow to begin his preaching until 432.[33] The fifth-century saint could not have converted an Irish king of the third century.[34]

Some of Bloom's other misquotations, however, may be conscious and purposeful. Remembering Professor Goodwin's innumerable "farewell concerts," he thinks wryly, "May be for months and may be for never" (154:11/156:17). The reference is to a line in "Kathleen Mavourneen," by Mrs. Julia Crawford: "It may be for years, and it may be forever!"[35] Later, seeing a squad of apparently well-fed constables, his mental comment is, "Policeman's lot is oft a happy one" (160:9/162:22), a complete perversion of the line from *The Pirates of Penzance*, which reads, "A policeman's lot is not a happy one."

Bloom's allusions to Shakespeare are particularly interesting when compared to Stephen's. Of the four Shakespearian echoes in Bloom's stream of consciousness, two, although they may have originally come into use from Shakespeare, probably got to Bloom first through someone's everyday conversation. Bloom might know that they appeared in Shakespeare if they were held up for his inspection. But it is significant that, even if he did pick them up from his own inspection of *Hamlet*, he chose passages which had become clichés:

> Method in his madness. (158:36/161:6)
> *Pol.* [*aside*] Though this be madness, yet there is method in't.
> (Act 2, sc. 2, lines 208-09)

> Jack Power could a tale unfold. (160:23/162:36)
> *Ghost.* Pity me not, but lend thy serious hearing
> To what I shall unfold.
> (Act 1, sc. 5, line 6)

Bloom quotes the third. He is thinking of the techniques of poetry and of Shakespeare, and he recites to himself a bit of the ghost's speech to Hamlet:

> *Hamlet, I am thy father's spirit*
> *Doomed for a certain time to walk the earth* (150:36/152:41)

> *Ghost.* I am thy father's spirit,
> Doomed for a certain time to walk the night.
> (Act 1, sc. 5, lines 9–10)

Again, of course, Bloom misquotes. The fourth reference to
Shakespeare is, like the ghost's speech, a well-known line from
a well-known scene in a well-known play, the scene where
Hamlet upbraids his mother for betraying his father:

> Look on this picture then on that. (167:18/169:36)

> *Ham.* Look here upon this picture, and on this,
> The counterfeit presentment of two brothers.
> (Act 3, sc. 4, lines 53–54)

Bloom's references to Shakespeare, then, are all from
Shakespeare's best-known play, *Hamlet;* they are from speeches
which are highlights rather than from lesser-known speeches;
and one of the four, at least (assuming, of course, that all four
came to Bloom directly from Shakespeare), is a conscious
quotation. Thus, although Bloom has "applied to the works of
William Shakespeare more than once for the solution of difficult
problems in imaginary or real life" (661:28/677:28), he has not
absorbed much beyond the most obvious. Indeed, the picture of
Bloom groping through Shakespeare for passages that would
apply to his own problems is pathetic, partly because he would
have to grope, and partly because it is so naive. The further
irony is that if he did find a solution to any of his difficulties
in Shakespeare, he would be powerless to act on it, or acting
on it, could do so only ineffectually.

Another important difference between Stephen's thoughts and
Bloom's in these two chapters is that Stephen's seem to turn
to himself much more often than Bloom's turn to himself. The
sight of the midwives on Sandymount strand makes Stephen
think of how he walked the same route and of his own birth.
Thinking of all the cords of life that "link back" to heaven
as a sort of telephone line, he sees himself at the earthly station
trying to call Eden. A brief thought about Adam and Eve and
the concept of original sin makes him think immediately of his
own conception and his predestination. Almost immediately
thereafter he reminds himself of his errand for Mr. Deasy and

his promised visit to The Ship, a pub. And then he ponders paying a visit to his Aunt Sara's and in his mind plays over the scene of his possible visit. All of these instances occur on the first two pages of Proteus. And the rest of the section proceeds much the same way. Stephen's thoughts always quickly return to himself and his own problems.

On the other hand, Bloom in Lestrygonians seems much less concerned with himself than Stephen is and much more concerned with the world around him. He is of course reminded from time to time of Molly's infidelity, but even the pressure of that unhappiness does not turn his thoughts inward as often as Stephen's are turned inward. In his envisioning of past or imaginary episodes, Bloom is concerned not so often as Stephen is with his own part in them but more with the actions of the other people involved. His worries about his own problems are likely to be more acute and more painful than Stephen's; they occur like a stab: as we saw, he worries that Boylan might infect Molly (151:36/153:39); remembering Molly flirting with Boylan a fortnight before, he urges himself rather desperately, "Stop. Stop. If it was it was. Must" (165:9/167:25); reminded of the approaching meeting of Boylan and Molly by a comment by Nosey Flynn, he experiences a lurch in the midriff (170:27/173:4); dreaming of making love to Molly in the days of their courtship, he brings the scene in his mind to a quick close with "Mc. And me now" (173:42/176:22); wondering whether he should buy Molly a silk petticoat to match her garters, he is again reminded of the assignation and checks himself with "Today. Today. Not think" (177:35/180:18); and seeing Boylan, he gets all upset (180:29/183:14).[36] But Bloom manages to put the problem from his mind quickly. As a result there is not, either in these passages or in Lestrygonians as a whole, the brooding quality that the reader feels in Stephen's stream of consciousness in Proteus.

It might be argued that on Sandymount strand Stephen has much less to distract his thoughts than does Bloom in Lestrygonians, who is in a busy section of Dublin. But we must recognize here the psychologists' description of

the *individuality* of response to stimuli and the *selective* nature of attention. . . . Individuality is also apparent in our observations. When two people look out of the same window, one sees a passing car, the other looks at the trees. What the person "selects" to attend to varies with the attitude and experience of the attending person. . . . The way the subject organizes his material, then, is determined much more by his own personality characteristics than by the nature of the stimulus. This permits the examiner to make inferences about the subject's internal life—about his motivations, wishes, fantasies, and modes of structuring situations.[37]

Thus, on Sandymount strand, there are people and things on the beach that can and do attract Stephen's attention: the midwives, the cocklepickers, the dog, the sea, the refuse. But as has been pointed out above, Stephen's thoughts continue to turn quickly from these to himself. Secondly, later in the day Bloom appears on Sandymount strand, but instead of wandering off where he will be by himself, he stays where he can watch Gerty, Cissy, and the children. It would seem, therefore, that Stephen's being where he could think about himself is not a matter of accident but a matter of his own choice. Thus his choosing of the relatively deserted portion of Sandymount strand serves to emphasize his aloofness and his concern with himself rather than to vitiate the evidence that supports the thesis of his egocentricity. Stephen's decision not to return to the Martello tower (45:20/44:22) is further evidence that the wedge being driven between him and his friends is largely of his own making.

Bloom's stream of consciousness, then, jumps from advertising to bicycle races, from lost-and-found offices to sunspots. And it manifests the warmth of generous concern for hungry seagulls, the public welfare, and a blind stripling. Lestrygonians thus presents a striking contrast to Proteus, with its heavy burden of philosophy and mysticism and its chill of self-concern.

Another (rather odd) parallel between the two chapters is that the blind stripling whom Bloom aids at the end of Lestrygonians is much like Stephen.[38] Quite obviously the blind stripling is a young man who has lost his way, just as Stephen has. His blindness may be compared to Stephen's inability to see his own faults and the world as it really exists. Bloom, of course, helps both young men in their difficulty. And just as Stephen does not immediately accept Bloom's proffered aid (574:11/589:19) and does not immediately respond to what Bloom says (599:33/615:32), so the stripling does not answer Bloom's first

question, which is really an offer of aid (178:15/180:40). As
Stephen is dirty, because he does not like water (17:26/15:41;
656:6/672:7), the stripling is dirty, because he drops food on
his coat (178:29/181:13).

Similarities between Proteus and the episode of the stripling
in Lestrygonians are even more striking. To match the
stripling's cane (178:8/180:35), Stephen has an ashplant, of
which he says, "Tap with it: they do"[39] (38:18/37:18). And in
Lestrygonians the stripling taps the curbstone with his cane
(178:8/180:35), as Stephen taps Sandymount strand with his.
As a parallel to Stephen's remembering his dream of Haroun
al Raschid the night before (47:40/47:5), Bloom wonders what
dreams the stripling would have (179:42/182:2). And wondering
about the stripling leads Bloom to make an experiment
(179:30/182:14) something like the one that Stephen attempts
at the opening of Proteus.

Finally, Lestrygonians (Bloom's stream of consciousness and
actions) has a whole series of minor parallels to Proteus
(Stephen's stream of consciousness and actions). Both:

1. think of pregnancy and birth[40]
    (S 38:34/37:34)   the two midwives
    (B 159:30/161:1)   two pregnant women—Molly and
                        Mrs. Moisel
    (B 156:34/159:3; 158:41/161:11)   Mina Purefoy
    (S 38:40/37:40)   Stephen thinks of his own birth
    (B 159:10/161:27)   Bloom thinks of the difficulty
                        of birth
2. are concerned with a letter
    (S 39:25/38:25)   taking Mr. Deasy's letter to the
                        press
    (B 165:33/168:8)   answering Martha's letter
3. are concerned with hoof-and-mouth disease
    (S 39:25/38:25)   Mr. Deasy's letter
    (B 151:17/153:19)   thinks that gulls spread it
4. think of a woman with lifted skirts
    (S 41:21/40:22)   the "fubsy widow" in Serpentine
                        Avenue
    (B 154:13/156:20)   Molly
    (B 158:25/160:37)   remembers the "pugnosed
    driver" who drove a tramcar between him and a

        woman with lifted skirts outside the Grosvenor,
        preventing his seeing (73:26/74:28).

5. think of writing they did not do—and probably will
   not do
     (S 41:30/40:31)   books with letters for titles;
                       epiphanies on green oval leaves
     (B 156:27/158:38)   stories like Matcham's
                       masterpieces

6. are disgusted by the eating habits of their fellow men
     (S 42:31/41:32)   belching cabmen
     (B 166-67/169-70)   "dirty eaters"

7. eye a dog warily
     (S 46:19/45:22)
     (B 177:3/179:27)

8. think of the East
     (S 47:40/47:5)   dream of Haroun al Raschid
     (S 39:4,6/38:4,6; 41:35,36/40:36,37)   Edenville,
      Eve, Alexandria, mahamanvantara
     (B 166:17/168:35)   Agendath Netaim

9. look in shop windows
     (S 49:29/48:38)   Hodges Figgis's window—in
                       memory
     (B 165:42/168:18; 166:12/168:30)

10. comment unfavorably on woman's clothing
     (S 49:34/49:1)   suspenders and yellow stockings
     (S 48:14/47:21)   rancid rags
     (B 156:11/158:20)   Mrs. Breen's clothes

11. comment on their own bad teeth
     (S 51:23/50:34)
     (B 168:27/171:3)

12. write a poem and think about poetics
     (S 49:5/48:13; 38:27/37:27)
     (B 150:31/152:34; 164:1/166:15)

13. search their pockets at the end of the episode
     (S 51:30/50:41)   for a handkerchief—unsuccessfully
     (B 181:7/183:34)   for a cake of soap—successfully
   In both instances, the objects searched for are directly
     related to the character's chief antagonist:
     Stephen's handkerchief is thrown to him by
     Mulligan (18:24/16:41) and subsequently mislaid;

> Bloom buys his soap while leaving a prescription for Molly (84:4/85:15).

14. are looking back over their shoulder at the end of the episode

> (S 51:35/51:4)   "rere regardant," looking at the *Rosevean*
>
> (B 181/183)   looking back to see if Boylan saw him

15. do not think much either about yesterday or the immediate past

Some of the parallels are, of course, strained (items five and nine, for example), and others are, perhaps, trivial (items ten and thirteen). But most of them are neither. And in total, whether purposeful or not, they are impressive. Moreover, some of them fit into the pattern we have already established for Stephen and Bloom. For example, in item one, Stephen is thinking about his own birth and his own problems, whereas Bloom is thinking about the difficulties of other people, in this case women, in childbirth. And whereas Stephen expected his unwritten writings to be worthy of the shelves of "all the great libraries of the world" (41:34/40:35), Bloom is thinking of writing fluff for a cheap magazine, *Tidbits* (item five). And finally (item eight):

> Where Stephen goes to the Fathers of the Church, the heresiarchs, Eve, and Buddha in terms of Spain, Averroes, Moses Maimonides coming out to the sea which is both all-mothering and Old Father Ocean, Bloom goes East for warmth and oranges and ease in terms of Spain, Moorish eyes, and Moses Montefiore coming out on the dead sea that could bear no more.[41]

There are threads, of course, in Bloom's stream of consciousness that are peculiarly his own. As an advertising man, he thinks of ads and newspapers (158:8/160:20), phrases an idea like an ad ("Handyman wants job. Small wages. Will eat anything"—177:40/180:24), remembers an advertising scheme that he at one time proposed for selling stationery (152:27/154:38), and thinks of the Keyes ad, on which he is working (159:6/161:18; 180:23/183:8). Molly and his marital difficulties provide the focus for another theme: he remembers

making love to Molly on Howth hill during their courtship
(173:21/175:42); he thinks with nostalgia of the relatively happy
early years of their marriage (153:14/155:19; 154:20/156:27;
165:27/168:2; 172:4/174:23); and he worries about Molly's
assignation with Boylan (151:36/153:39; 170:23/173:1;
177:35/180:17; 181:6/183:33). He also thinks of the flirtation
he is currently carrying on by mail (157:40-158:3/160:10-
160:15). His Jewish background evidences itself briefly in a
reference to Yom Kippur, the Jewish Day of Atonement
(149:41/151:42); in his use of *meshuggah,* a Jewish word, to
characterize Denis Breen (157:27/159:38);[42] in his comment that
a chef's hat looks like a rabbi's hat (173:2/175:22); and in the
self-consciousness of his evaluation of Reuben J. Dodd ("Now
he's really what they call a dirty jew"—180:17/183:2). These
few references do not suggest, however, much of a concern,
understanding, or even awareness of the Jewish religion or of
Jewish problems.[43]

There are also in this chapter, as Gilbert and Budgen
explained early, parallels with the Lestrygonian episode of the
Odyssey. Budgen says that Joyce told him: "I am now writing
the *Lestrygonians* episode, which corresponds to the adventure
of *Ulysses* with the cannibals. My hero is going to lunch. But
there is a seduction motive in the *Odyssey,* the cannibal king's
daughter. Seduction appears in my book as women's silk
petticoats hanging in a shop window."[44] Certainly there is much
made of food and eating in the chapter, and of colorful, although
not necessarily seductive, sights. But I question the usefulness
of the echoes from the *Odyssey.* Gilbert tells us, for example:
"The descent of the gulls, pouncing on prey, recalls the
onslaught of the Lestrygonians, swooping down from their cliffs
upon the unexpected quarry, and the soup pot may be likened
to the ring of the harbour, where the crews of all the Achaean
ships save that of Odysseus (who had prudently moored without)
were drowned or harpooned by the cannibals."[45] Finding such
parallels is interesting in the same way that solving a puzzle
is interesting. But paralleling the pouncing of the gulls with
the swooping of the Lestrygonians makes neither the pouncing
nor the swooping more meaningful. There may be, perhaps, some
ironic comment in the comparison of Bloom, who hates "dirty
eaters" (167:42/170:18), with the Lestrygonians, who ate

Odysseus' men with little ceremony. But the connection is too tenuous to be effective even as irony.

The many parallels that occur between Proteus and Lestrygonians would seem to suggest that in a number of important ways Bloom is merely a weak, materialistic, and sometimes comic echo of Stephen. That each man is ineffectual in his own sphere, critics have long pointed out. But that each concerns himself with the same problems on different levels of philosophic profundity has not generally been recognized.

We have here an interesting pair of examples of how an author's statement of intention can affect the reading of a text. Joyce called the third chapter of *Ulysses* Proteus and saw to it, through Budgen, Gilbert, and others, that the world was informed of the designation. Critics, therefore, regularly point out the protean aspects of the chapter. Lestrygonians, however, is just as protean as Proteus; but there has been no general critical recognition of that fact.

Similarly, Joyce built into Lestrygonians many other parallels to Proteus and echoes of that earlier chapter. But since he did not point them out (indeed, he may not have been aware of them himself), they have not generally been recognized. For too many years, Joyce criticism has been led—and misled—by what Joyce said about his works. Too frequently critics have been influenced by Joyce's pronouncements about his work and have not shown the necessary independence of judgment and autonomy. The primary document is the text, not an author's statement about it.

Joyce may have intended these parallels. That possibility is suggested by the fact that he added many of the items that built up the paralleling motifs in Lestrygonians after the final manuscript of *Ulysses* (that is, the Rosenbach manuscript) had been typed. For example, many of the references to the senses were added or enlarged upon either just before the type was set or in the galleys. References to the taste of pastry (155:18/157:25), spicy fruits from Jaffa (166:16/168:34), the taste of Molly's seedcake (173:32/176:11), the fact that tastes are different for the blind stripling (178:29/181:13), and the color and warmth of the East (166:15-17/168:33-35) were all such late additions; and the references to the flavor of certain vegetables (168:28/171:5) and of blood (168:39/171:16) and to the colorful windows of Brown Thomas (165:42/168:18) were considerably enlarged upon at the same time.

Other themes in Lestrygonians were also expanded to the point where they became significant parallels with similar themes in Proteus. In the protean theme itself, for example: "sucking red jujubes white" (149:5/151:5) was originally just "sucking red jujubes," and thus without any connotation of change; the protean cycle of "food, chyle, blood, dung, earth, food" (174:14/176:36) was a late addition; and the passage about the gradual crumbling of cities ("Piled up in cities"— 162:18-22/164:32-36) was expanded after the manuscript was typed. Similarly, of the nine appearances of foreign languages in Lestrygonians, all but three, the echoes of *Don Giovanni*, were added in the galleys. Thus, if *Ulysses* had been printed exactly as it was in typescript, there would have been no language parallel between Proteus and Lestrygonians. Further, five of the six language additions were clichés and restaurant terms, making the language parallel a point of distinction between Bloom and Stephen, whose use of foreign languages was not only much more extensive than Bloom's but also more sophisticated. Three of the four echoes of Shakespeare were also late additions, building up in the same way a parallel between the two chapters and a further distinction between the two characters that would not otherwise have existed. Other of the major parallels between the chapters and seven of the fifteen minor parallels noted were either similarly added or enlarged upon.

The other possibility, of course, is that Joyce himself did not see the parallels and that they are simply reflections of his own interest or that they express different aspects of his personality. If, for example, we merely run down the items listed under "Joyce, James" in the index of Budgen's *James Joyce and the Making of "Ulysses,"* we see that Budgen ascribes to Joyce, among other things, a fear of dogs, an interest in time, opinions on music and Shakespeare, and a preference for Proteus (and thus an interest in protean change?).[46] All these characteristics are also evidenced in parallels showing up both in Proteus and Lestrygonians. Whether Joyce intended these parallels or not, however, they function in the novel—both to link Stephen and Bloom and to discriminate between them.

C. Molly (in Penelope)

The best indication of the relation of Molly's thoughts to Stephen's or Bloom's is what she does to Aristotle's name. Where Stephen (in Proteus) is conversant with Aristotle and ponders and tests his ideas, and where Bloom (in Lestrygonians) is interested (probably unwittingly, but nevertheless interested) in many of the same matters that concerned Aristotle, Molly knows (and probably cares) so little about him that she turns his name into Aristocrat (757:39-41/772:37-39).[47]

As Joseph Prescott points out, an "important aspect of Molly is her limited intellectual equipment. Her ignorance transpires chiefly in her beliefs and in her language. Again and again her mind throws out popular superstitions." Prescott then demonstrates how Joyce reinforced this aspect of Molly by adding, in the proofs, evidences of superstition, grammatical mistakes, and limited command of the idiom. And he shows that Joyce even gave

> Molly an awareness of her intellectual limitations when she thinks about her daughter: "such an idea for him to send the girl down there to learn to take photographs only hed do a thing like that." After "photographs" Joyce adds "on account of his grandfather instead of sending her to Skerry's academy where shed have to learn not like me." Later, after "me" he inserts "getting all ls at school."[48]

The rest of the matters of major interest in Proteus and Lestrygonians appear equally diluted in Penelope. Molly seems to have absolutely no knowledge of science. She evidently does not even understand, for example, the functioning of the female reproductive system (754:26/769:23) or anything else about her own physiology (755/770). Nor does she seem much concerned with change. She thinks a lot about the past and a little of tomorrow's meal (749:19/764:18) and of a possible future as Stephen's mistress (761/776); but she seems to have little or no awareness of progression or change due to time. Unlike Stephen and Bloom, however, she is concerned with the immediate, for Boylan keeps appearing in her thoughts.

Bloom's interest in politics does not find an echo in Molly's thoughts either. She comments, "I hate the mention of politics" (733:39/748:42); and she refers to the "Sinner Fein"

(733:34/748:37; 757:26/772:24), home rule (756:20/771:18), and the land league (756:21/771:19) with scorn.

Unlike Stephen, who is interested in theology and religious philosophy, and Bloom, who is interested in the everyday effects of religion, Molly's religious interests are largely on the level of superstition. She hates confession (725:42/741:1), says a Hail Mary to protect herself against thunderbolts (726:36/741:38), and lights candles for luck (726:40/741:42). Superstitions abound in her thoughts. She reads the cards to tell her fortune (760:2/774:41; 761:15/776:11; 763:13/778:8), arranges and handles knives in a certain way to avoid bad luck (753:13/768:10; 764:32/779:27), and thinks that "Fridays an unlucky day" (766:33/781:29).

Molly's interests in the arts are also different from Stephen's and Bloom's and in keeping with the other aspects of her personality. Although she has been exposed to such novels as *The Moonstone, East Lynne, Eugene Aram,* and *Moll Flanders* (741/756), she seems to prefer erotic literature like *Sweets of Sin* (750:12/765:10). And although she claims, "I always liked poetry when I was a girl" (760:13/775:10) and once received a present of Byron's poems from Bloom (728:10/743:11), she does not recognize the opening line of Keats's *Endymion,* which Bloom once quoted to her in a letter during their courtship. In her thoughts, it becomes "a thing of beauty and of joy for ever something he got out of some nonsensical book that he had" (756:8/771:6).[49] References to Shakespeare, so prominent in Stephen's thoughts, and at least present in Bloom's, do not appear in Molly's at all. Phrases and titles of songs do, however, appear everywhere in her thoughts, as one might expect of a singer.[50] As a result of her profession and her early life in Gibraltar, she also knows some phrases in Spanish and Italian.[51]

Some of the incidental parallels between Proteus and Lestrygonians also find echoes in Penelope. Like Stephen and Bloom, Molly thinks of pregnancy and birth (727:23/742:22); of letters (Attorney Dillon's—743:36/758:38; Mulvey's—744:3/759:5; and Bloom's—743:8/758:10; 756:8/771:6); of an annoying dog (723:17/738:17); and of the East (Gibraltar, the Jews and the Arabs—767/782). And Molly, too, is "rere regardant" at the end of the chapter (figuratively); for on the last pages she is thinking of the days of her youth, before her marriage (767-68/782-83).

Thus, Molly's soliloquy is mostly rumination about the past: about Boylan, her earlier meetings with him and her liaison with him that afternoon; about Bloom, his courtship of her and his relations with other women; about Mulvey, her first suitor; about Milly, her daughter; about Rudy, her dead son; about a variety of other men in her past; and about Gibraltar, where she spent her girlhood. Probably largely because she is lying in bed in a darkened room, her awareness of the present moment is not very strong. Some matters of the moment do, of course, intrude on her thoughts: a train whistle; her period. Only occasionally does she think about the future: the concert tour she is to make with Boylan; Boylan's promised visit on Monday; a possible affair with Stephen; Bloom's breakfast the next morning.[52]

6
Paragraph and Sentence Structure

Not only the ideas, but also the ways in which the words which express those ideas are grouped into sentences and paragraphs serve to differentiate the streams of consciousness of the three characters. Much has been made, for example, of the lack of punctuation in Molly's soliloquy, a stylistic device which has often been referred to as a characterizing feature of Penelope, and thus of Molly. It is of interest in this study, therefore, to examine the paragraph and sentence structure of the streams of consciousness of the three main characters to determine to what extent, if any, they are significantly different.[1] We shall first examine Proteus and Lestrygonians. An examination of Penelope, which poses special problems, will then follow.

A. Omniscient Author's Sentences in Proteus and Lestrygonians

Proteus and Lestrygonians, as has been pointed out earlier, are considered good examples of the stream-of-consciousness technique. And yet the careful reader notices that throughout both chapters many of the sentences are obviously statements by the author, with no attempt made to make them appear as if they were flashing through a character's mind. For example, although the first paragraph in Proteus is entirely a stream-of-consciousness passage ("Ineluctable modality of the visible. . . . Shut your eyes and see"—38:1-10/37:1-10), the second paragraph begins "Stephen closed his eyes to hear his boots crush crackling wrack and shells" (38:11/37:11). An examination of Proteus and Lestrygonians shows that although such sentences, which hereafter will be referred to as omniscient author's sentences, appear in both, each chapter seems to have

92

them arranged differently within its paragraphs. We shall summarize these differences in a moment.

As we have seen, the reader is introduced to *Ulysses* by long passages of omniscient author's sentences and dialogue, flavored with increasingly longer passages of stream of consciousness. As the stream-of-consciousness passages become longer, the frequency of omniscient author's sentences abates. But the reader may not realize that in Proteus and Lestrygonians the process is *not* carried to its possible conclusion: the complete disappearance of omniscient author's sentences.

Before summarizing their arrangements, we might also examine several paragraphs as examples to see the different ways in which omniscient author's sentences may be placed:

1. He walked along the curbstone. [s] (153:36/155:41)
2. He stood at Fleet street crossing. [a1] Luncheon interval a six penny at Rowe's? Must look up that ad in the national library. An eightpenny in the Burton. Better. On my way. (159:5-7/161:17-19)
3. He had come nearer the edge of the sea and wet sand slapped his boots. [a1] The new air greeted him, harping in wild nerves, wind of wild air of seeds of brightness. [a2] Here, I am not walking out to the Kish lightship, am I? He stood suddenly, his feet beginning to sink slowly in the quaking soil. [b] Turn back. (45:8-12/44:10-14)

The first example is a paragraph made up of a single omniscient author's sentence (s). In the second example, the paragraph is introduced by an omniscient author's sentence (a1); and in the third example, the paragraph is introduced by two omniscient author's sentences (a1 and a2), with a third omniscient author's sentence (b) buried in the stream-of-consciousness portion of the paragraph. In some instances (for example, 167:31-36/170:7-12; 41:39-42:5/40:41-41:7), as many as four or five omniscient author's sentences are to be found at the beginning of a paragraph.[2] Using these definitions and explanations, table 1 compares the arrangement of omniscient author's sentences in Proteus and Lestrygonians.

Some of the percentages derived from table 1 and reported below have been calculated in two ways: first on the basis of the total number of paragraphs in each chapter (p), including

TABLE 1
Arrangement of Omniscient Author's Sentences in Proteus and Lestrygonians

Proteus (Stephen)		
Introductory sentences (a1, a2, a3, a4, a5)	35	
Single-sentence paragraphs (s)	0	
Buried sentences (b)	27	
Total omniscient author's sentences		62
Paragraphs of conversation		
real (c)	1	
imagined (c1)	18	
Total paragraphs in chapter (p)		100
Total paragraphs with omniscient author's sentences (po)		28
Total paragraphs in chapter excluding conversation (p−c)		81
Lestrygonians (Bloom)		
Introductory sentences (a1, a2, a3, a4)	95	
Single-sentence paragraphs (s)	31	
Buried sentences (b)	18	
Total omniscient author's sentences		144
Many-sentence paragraphs* (s+)	4	
Paragraphs of conversation		
real (c)	132	
imagined (c1)	13	
Total paragraphs in chapter (p)		385
Total paragraphs with omniscient author's sentences (po)		112
Total paragraphs in chapter excluding conversation (p−c)		240

*I.e., many-sentence paragraphs composed entirely of omniscient author's sentences.

paragraphs entirely of conversation (c); and second on the basis of the number of paragraphs in each chapter *not* including paragraphs of conversation (p−c). A strong argument can be made for the greater validity of the second set of figures (that is, those calculated without considering each conversational statement as a paragraph): first, it is the stream-of-consciousness

passages of each character that we are examining and not
dialogue; second, more than two full pages of conversation in
Lestrygonians, totaling fifty-three paragraphs (174:22-176:29/
177:3-178:3), have nothing to do with Bloom's stream of
consciousness at all since he is out of the room while the
conversation is going on; third, since Stephen did not meet and
talk to anyone in Proteus and Bloom did in Lestrygonians,
comparing the number of paragraphs in each chapter without
any adjustment for the differing situations would give a
distorted picture; and, fourth, as Joyce arranged his dialogue
on the page, an omniscient author's sentence could not possibly
appear in a conversational paragraph. However, both sets of
figures will be given.

The differences now begin to appear. In Proteus, of the
paragraphs that could possibly include omniscient author's
sentences (that is, $p - c$), only 34.6 percent do, whereas in
Lestrygonians 46.7 percent do.[3] Thus a larger percentage of the
paragraphs in Bloom's stream of consciousness have omniscient
author's sentences than do paragraphs in Stephen's. In addition,
where in Proteus 56.5 percent of the omniscient author's
sentences are introductory and 43.5 percent are buried sentences,
in Lestrygonians 87.7 percent of the omniscient author's
sentences are introductory and only 12.3 percent are buried
sentences.[4] Thus Lestrygonians shows a strong pattern of
omniscient author's sentences appearing at the beginning of
paragraphs[5] or as paragraphs in themselves, operating much like
stage directions in a play, to orient the reader.[6] This
comparatively regular appearance provides a skeleton or
framework on which passages of stream of consciousness can
be hung. The result is that the reader is surer of the actions
and position of the main character in Lestrygonians than he
is of the main character in Proteus. The reader never has to
puzzle over where Bloom is or what he is doing. The reader
is not so well informed, however, about Stephen. It is easy to
read the last pages of Proteus without realizing, for example,
that Stephen writes a poem (48:32-36/47:39-48:3) or that he
urinates (50:16-24/49:25-34; 51:1-3/50:11-13).

The comparatively regular appearance and placement of
omniscient author's sentences in Lestrygonians is most likely the
result of Joyce's need to keep Bloom's whereabouts clear. It is
appropriate to Bloom's personality, however, and probably helps

to establish the impression of that personality for the reader. For, compared to Stephen, Bloom is a plodder. Similarly, the attempt to create the impression of Stephen as an artist, typically given to flights of fancy, less earthbound than Bloom, is served better by the less regular placement of omniscient author's sentences in Proteus. With a large proportion of the omniscient author's sentences in Proteus buried inside the paragraphs (43.5 percent compared with only 12.3 percent in Lestrygonians), one is less aware of them in Proteus than he is in Lestrygonians. The result is that in Proteus the flight of thought is more emphasized than in Lestrygonians because the reader is not as aware of being pulled back for orientation regularly. The greater number and regularity of omniscient author's sentences in Lestrygonians further helps to project a difference in personality between Stephen and Bloom, for in Lestrygonians the reader is reminded of external reality more frequently and more regularly than in Proteus, in keeping with the more plodding, materialistic, and conventional Bloom. Conversely, with fewer omniscient author's sentences in Proteus and with their less regular appearance, Proteus gives the effect of a more fluid mind: the ideas and actions in Proteus are less clearly outlined and more inclined to blur one into the other. In a word, because of its construction, Proteus is— appropriately—more protean.

B. Characteristic Sentence Patterns in Proteus and Lestrygonians

As a further difference, the streams of consciousness of Stephen and Bloom each contain different types of characteristic sentences. For example, Lestrygonians has many examples of a type of sentence that one usually associates with the Irish, in which part of the predicate of the sentence comes at the beginning rather than at the end of the sentence. Forty-one instances of this type of sentence appear in Lestrygonians:

Phosphorous it must be done with. (149:25/151:25)
Underfed she looks too. (150:7/152:8)
It's after they feel it. (150:8/152:9)
The flow of the language it is. (150:34/152:37)
Live on fishy flesh they have to (151:10/153:12)

Good idea that. (151:25/153:28)

Powerful man he was at storing away number one Bass. (152:15/154:18)

Like that priest they are this morning (152:19/154:23)

Well out of that ruck I am. (152:39/155:2)

Devil of a job it was collecting accounts of those convents. (152:39/155:2)

Rabbit pie we had that day. (153:28/155:34)

Snug little room that was (153:30/155:35)

Funny she looked soaped all over. (153:33/155:38)

Pleasure or pain is it? (155:21/157:29)

Philip Beaufoy I was thinking. (156:27/158:37)

Wrote it for a lark in the Scotch house, I bet anything. (157:34/160:4)

Strong as a brood mare some of those horsey women. (158:21/160:33)

Stonewall or fivebarred gate put her mount to it. (158:24/160:36)

Didn't take a feather out of her my handling them. (158:28/160:40)

Mayonnaise I poured on the plums thinking it was custard. (158:32/161:2)

Hardy annuals he presents her with. (158:41/161:11)

Three days imagine groaning on a bed with a vinegared handkerchief round her forehead (159:10/161:22)

Dreadful simply! (159:12/161:24)

Kill me that would. (159:14/161:26)

Nine she had. (159:17/161:29)

Funny sight two of them together, their bellies out. (159:30/162:1)

Mackerel they called me. (160:5/162:18)

Pupil of Michael Balfe's wasn't she? (160:20/162:34)

That horse policeman the day Joe Chamberlain was given his degree in Trinity he got a run for his money. (160:26/162:40)

Those literary ethereal people they are all. (163:36/166:8)

Terrific explosions they are. (164:23/166:40)

Thick feet that woman has in the white stockings. (165:36/168:12)

Great chorus that. (166:3/168:21)

Hot fresh blood they prescribe for decline. (168:39/171:16)

Hygiene that was what they call now. (169:23/172:1)
Pillowed on my coat she had her hair (173:25/176:5)
Ravished over her I lay (173:29/176:8)
Flowers her eyes were (173:34/176:13)
Weight would he feel it if something was removed.
(179:1/181:27)
Queer idea of Dublin he must have, tapping his way round
by the stones. (179:2/181:28)
Power those judges have. (180:17/183:3)

This type of sentence is not reserved solely for Bloom, of
course. Lenehan uses it, for example:

Val Dillon it was (230:33/234:5)
Lashings of stuff we put up (231:3/234:16)
Fast and furious it was. (231:4/234:18)
He's a cultured allroundman, Bloom is (231:42/235:15)

And so does Kernan:

Good drop of gin, that was. (237:6/240:25)
Damn good gin that was. (237:32/241:9)
Fine poem that is: Ingram. (237:36/241:13)

This Irish type of sentence is to be expected of Bloom, who
was educated in regular Irish schools, who mixed in everyday
Irish circles, and who was seldom subjected to accents other than
the Irish. Although the reader may not be aware of it, this
type of sentence in Bloom's stream of consciousness provides a
distinguishing characteristic. The Irish flavor that it imparts is
one of the many features which go to make up in the reader's
mind the pattern that is Bloom.

The thoughts of Stephen, who had a more formal education,
who had teachers and acquaintances who were English, who had
read considerably in English literature, who travelled generally
in educated circles, who spoke of his nationality and language
as nets he would "try to fly by," and who had been abroad—
Stephen's thoughts show, as might be expected, few sentences
of such a construction—in fact, only three in the whole of
Proteus:

Bald he was and a millionaire (38:7/37:7)
About the nature of women he read in Michelet.
(42:18/41:20)

Morose delectation Aquinas tunbelly calls this (48:20/47:27)

Another characteristic of the structure of a good many sentences in Bloom's stream of consciousness is what may be described as condensation. Each of the sentences below, all of the examples of this type found in Lestrygonians, reads as if it were composed of the main elements of ideas which would normally be expressed in several sentences; in each of these condensations, however, these elements have all been rolled together awkwardly into a single sentence:

> Where was that ad some Birmingham firm the luminous crucifix? (149:21/151:21)
> Elijah thirty-two feet per sec is com. (150:25/152:28)
> Windy night that was I went to fetch her there was that lodge meeting on about those lottery tickets after Goodwin's concert in the supper room or oakroom of the mansion house. (154:4/156:10)
> Whole thing quite painless out of all the taxes give every child born five quid at compound interest up to twenty-one, five per cent is a hundred shillings and five tiresome pounds, multiply by twenty decimal system, encourage people to put by money save hundred and ten and a bit twenty-one years want to work it out on paper come to a tidy sum, more than you think. (159:22/161:34)
> I wouldn't be surprised if it was that kind of food you see produces the like waves of the brain the poetical. (163:37/166:9)
> The full moon was the night we were Sunday fortnight exactly there is a new moon. (165:3/167:19)
> John Howard Parnell example the provost of Trinity every mother's son don't talk of your provosts and provost of Trinity women and children, cabmen, priests, parsons, fieldmarshals, archbishops. (168:11/170:29)
> After all there's a lot in that vegetarian fine flavour of things from the earth garlic, of course, it stinks Italian organgrinders crisp of onions, mushrooms truffles. (168:28/171:5)
> Wine soaked and softened rolled pith of bread mustard a moment mawkish cheese. (172:6/174:25)
> Glowing wine on his palate lingered swallowed. (173:19/175:40)

Seems to a secret touch telling me memory. (173:20/175:41)

Touched his sense moistened remembered. (173:21/175:42)

Pillowed on my coat she had her hair, earwigs in the
heather scrub my hand under her nape, you'll toss me
all. (173:25/176:5)

Lovely forms of woman sculped Junonian. (174:12/176:34)

Bend down let something fall see if she. (174:16/176:38)

They could: and watch it all the way down, swallow a pin
sometimes come out of the ribs years after, tour round
the body, changing biliary duct, spleen squirting liver,
gastric juice coils of intestines like pipes. (177:17/179:41)

The voice temperature when he touches her with fingers
must almost see the lines, the curves. (179:22/182:6)

All those women and children excursion beanfeast burned
and drowned in New York. (180:1/182:28)

Karma they call that transmigration for sins you did in
a past life the reincarnation met him pikehoses.
(180:3/182:30)

Sir Thomas Deane was the Greek architecture.
(180:42/183:27)

He thrust back quickly Agendath. (181:5/183:32)

His hand looking for the where did I put found in his hip
pocket soap lotion have to call tepid paper stuck.
(181:11/183:38)

Much the same effect is given by sentences from which some
of the words seem to be missing and seem, therefore, also to
be condensations. Lestrygonians has five examples of this type
of condensation:

A housekeeper of one of those fellows if you could pick
it out of her. (150:1/152:3)

She didn't like it because I sprained my ankle first day
she wore choir picnic at the Sugarloaf. (153:23/155:29)

Suppose that communal kitchen years to come perhaps.
(168:9/170:27)

Will I tell him that horse Lenehan? (171:41/174:18)

Perhaps he young flesh in bed. (172:26/175:4)

The awkwardness and the confusion of the condensation have
even infected the omniscient author's sentences in Lestrygonians
in four instances:

> His eyes sought answer from the river and saw a rowboat
> rock at anchor on the treacly swells lazily its plastered
> board. (151:20/153:23)
> Mr Bloom smiled O rocks at two windows of the ballast
> office. (152:7/154:10)
> With a keep quiet relief, his eyes took note: this is street
> here middle of the day Bob Doran's bottle shoulders.
> (165:12/167:28)
> A man and ready he drained his glass to the lees and
> walked, to men too they gave themselves, manly
> conscious, lay with men lovers, a youth enjoyed her, to
> the yard. (174:19/176:41)

All of Proteus shows only two examples of condensation (as
opposed to the twenty-nine in Lestrygonians):

> Hunger toothache. (42:41/42:1)
> Thanking you for hospitality tear the blank end off.
> (49:3/48:11)

The difference in the frequency of this type of sentence in the
two chapters again indicates for the reader a difference between
Stephen and Bloom. It creates the effect of much more muddled
thinking by Bloom.

A third type of sentence found often in Bloom's stream of
consciousness, somewhat similar in effect to the condensed
sentence but recognizably different in construction, is the
accumulating sentence. Many of this type are merely a listing
of perceptions, items, or ideas, generally with, but sometimes
without, punctuation. The following are all the examples of the
accumulating sentence in Lestrygonians:

> Houses, lines of houses, streets, miles of pavements, piledup
> bricks, stones. (162:13/164:27)
> Piled up in cities, worn away age after age. Pyramids in
> sand. Built on bread and onions. Slaves Chinese wall.
> Babylon. Big stones left. Round towers. Rest rubble,
> sprawling suburbs, jerrybuilt, Kerwan's mushroom
> houses, built of breeze. (162:18/164:32)
> Muslin prints silk, dames and dowagers, jingle of
> harnesses, hoofthuds lowringing in the baking causeway.
> (165:35/168:11)
> Perched on high stools by the bar, hats shoved back, at

the tables calling for more bread no charge, swilling,
  wolfing gobfuls of sloppy food, their eyes bulging, wiping
  wetted moustaches. (166:36/169:12)
Spaton sawdust, sweetish warmish cigarette smoke, reek of
  plug, spilt beer, men's beery piss, the stale of ferment.
  (167:12/169:30)
Corner of Harcourt road remember that gust?
  (154:13/156:19)
Pungent mockturtle oxtail mulligatawny. (156:19/158:28)
She was twenty-three when we left Lombard street west
  something changed. (165:28/168:3)
Cauls mouldy tripes windpipes faked and minced up.
  (169:21/171:41)
Just as well to write it on the bill of fare so you can
  know what you've eaten too many drugs spoil the broth.
  (173:4/175:24)
Keep his cane clear of the horse's legs tired drudge get
  his doze. (178:32/181:16)
Police chargesheets crammed with cases get their
  percentage manufacturing crime. (180:31/182:41)

Some of these sentences are accumulations of visual perceptions:
162:13/164:27; 162:18/164:32. Others are accumulations of
several types of perception (that is, visual, auditory, olfactory):
165:35/168:11; 166:36/169:12; 167:12/169:30. Of the sentences
without punctuation, some seem to be a cross in effect between
condensations and accumulations, single sentences which could
properly be written as two sentences if portions of them were
set off by terminal punctuation; for example:

She was twenty-three. When we left Lombard street west
  something changed. (165:28/168:3)

Or:

She was twenty-three when we left Lombard street west.
  Something changed.

There are also omniscient author's sentences in Bloom's
stream of consciousness in which words have been wrenched out
of their normal order, but which seem to fall into no discernable
pattern:

Perfume of embraces all him assailed. (166:19/168:37)

With hungered flesh obscurely, he mutely craved to adore. (166:19/168:37)

His midriff yearned then upward, sank within him, yearned more longly, longingly. (170:27/173:4)

Was the oyster old fish at table. (172:26/175:3)

Dribbling a quiet message from his bladder came to go to do not to do there to do. (174:19/176:40)

Where the accumulating sentences in Bloom's stream of consciousness are composed of items jumbled together without any apparent pattern, the accumulating sentences in Stephen's stream of consciousness are composed of parallel items in series—usually in threes—a characteristic of formal prose. Once again, then, the sentence structure aids in giving the reader different impressions of the personalities of Stephen and Bloom. Where the jumbled accumulating sentences of Bloom's stream of consciousness create the impression of muddled thinking, the nicely balanced parallels of Stephen's accumulating sentences give the impression of a person who thinks more carefully and more coolly. The parallel construction also suggests a more trained mind. Following are all the examples of accumulating sentences in Proteus:

Signatures of all things I am here to read, seaspawn and seawrack, the nearing tide, that rusty boot. Snotgreen, bluesilver, rust: coloured signs. (38:4/37:4)

Belly without blemish, bulging big, a buckler of taut vellum. (39:7/38:7)

With beaded mitre and with crozier, stalled upon his throne, widower of a widowed see, with upstiffed omophorion, with clotted hinderparts. (39:19/38:19)

The whitemaned seahorses, champing, brightwindbridled, the steeds of Mananaan. (39:23/38:23)

Houses of decay, mine, his and all. (40:33/39:23)

The oval equine faces, Temple, Buck Mulligan, Foxy Campbell. (40:40/39:40)

A choir gives back menace and echo, assisting about the altar's horns, the snorted Latin of jackpriests moving burly in their albs, tonsured and oiled and gelded, fat with the fat of kidneys of wheat. (41:4/40:4)

And at the same instant perhaps a priest round the corner is elevating it Dringdring! And two streets off another locking it into a pyx. Dringadring! And in a ladychapel another taking housel all to his own cheek. Dringdring! Down, up, forward, back.[7] (41:8/40:9)

His boots trod again a damp crackling mast, razorshells, squeaking pebbles, that on the unnumbered pebbles beats, wood sieved by the shipworm, lost Armada. (41:39/40:41)

Broken hoops on the shore; at the land a maze of dark cunning nets; farther away chalkscrawled backdoors and on the higher beach a dryingline with two crucified shirts. (42:4/41:6)

Gold light on sea, on sand, on boulders. (43:23/42:25)

The sun is there, the slender trees, the lemon houses. (43:24/42:26)

Moist pith of farls of bread, the froggreen wormwood, her matin incense, court the air. (43:26/42:28)

Maud Gonne, beautiful woman, *La Patrie*, M. Millevoye, Felix Faure, know how he died? (44:12/43:14)

Got up as a young bride, man, veil, orangeblossoms, drove out the road to Malahide. (44:23/43:25)

Disguises, clutched at, gone, not here. (44:26/43:28)

Loveless, landless, wifeless. (44:36/43:38)

Peachy cheeks, a zebra skirt, frisky as a young thing's. (44:38/43:41)

Blue dusk, nightfall, deep blue night. (45:17/44:20)

My people, with flayers' knives, running, scaling, hacking in green blubbery whalemeat. Famine, plague and slaughter. (46:13/45:15)

The dog's bark ran towards him, stopped, ran back. (46:18/45:21)

I just simply stood pale, silent, bayed about. (46:19/45:22)

The Bruce's brother, Thomas Fitzgerald, silken knight, Perkin Warbeck, York's false scion, in breeches of silk of whiterose ivory, wonder of a day, and Lambert Simnel, with a tail of nans and sutlers, a scullion crowned. (46:22/45:25)

Waters: bitter death: lost. (46:42/46:4)

He turned, bounded back, came nearer, trotted on twinkling shanks. On a field tenney a buck, trippant, proper,

    unattired. (47:6/46:11)
Bridebed, childbed, bed of death, ghostcandled.
    (48:33/47:42)
She, she, she. (49:28/48:37)
Vehement breath of waters amid seasnakes, rearing horses,
    rocks. (50:21/49:30)
Day by day: night by night: lifted, flooded and let fall.
    (50:27/49:38)
To no end gathered: vainly then released, forth flowing,
    wending back: loom of the moon. (50:31/49:42)
Driving before it a loose drift of rubble, fanshoals of fishes,
    silly shells. (50:37/50:5)
God becomes man becomes fish becomes barnacle goose
    becomes featherbed mountain. (51:3/50:13)
My cockle hat and staff and his my sandal shoon.
    (51:14/50:25)
Moving through the air high spars of a threemaster, her
    sails brailed up on the crosstrees, homing, upstream,
    silently moving, a silent ship. (51:35/51:04)

Proteus begins and ends with these balanced accumulating
sentences.

    One other type of sentence is typical of Stephen's stream of
consciousness—the appositive. Something like Bloom's Irish
sentence in that it rises, pauses, and then falls, it is distinctly
different in that the relative shortness of the appositive and
the quick falling off tend to make the pause in Stephen's
sentence much more abrupt. Where Bloom's Irish sentence goes
⌣⌢⌣ , Stephen's appositive sentence tends instead to go
⌣⌢ . Lestrygonians has only one such appositive sentence
("Nectar, imagine it drinking electricity; god's food"—174:11/
176:33) as opposed to the following twelve instances found in
Proteus:

    Snotgreen, bluesilver, rust: coloured signs. (38:4/37:4)
    Bald he was and a millionaire, *maestro di color che sanno.*
        (38:7/37:7)
    They came down the steps from Leahy's terrace prudently,
        Frauenzimmer (38:33/37:34)
    Spouse and helpmate of Adam Kadmon: Heva, naked Eve.
        (39:6/38:6)

In a Greek watercloset he breathed his last: euthanasia.
(39:18/38:18)
They are coming, waves. (39:22/38:22)
The oval equine faces, Temple, Buck Milligan, Foxy
Campbell. (40:40/39:40)
Then from the starving cagework city a horde of jerkined
dwarfs, my people (46:11/45:14)
Something he buried there, his grandmother. (47:34/46:41)
With woman steps she followed: the ruffian and his
strolling mort. (48:5/47:12)
The foot that beat the ground in tripudium, foot I dislove.
(50:10/49:19)
Weary too in sight of lovers, lascivious men, a naked
woman shining in her courts, she draws a toil of waters.
(50:33/50:1)

The steady rise and rapid fall of Stephen's appositive sentence
helps further to characterize Stephen. It supports the suggestion
of an ordered and efficient mind that the reader gets from the
accumulating sentence, for it shows a mind that gathers in a
group of people and characterizes them precisely and efficiently
(38:33/37:34), a mind that views a scene or remembers an action
and comments on it neatly "in a formulated phrase" (38:4/37:4;
50:10/49:19).

Joyce's use of the colon in the two chapters adds to the
impression that one gets from the appositive sentences that
Stephen's mind tends to observe or gather information and then
comment, characterize, or expand. In the fourteen pages of
Proteus, Joyce uses a total of fifty-eight colons, or slightly more
than four to a page. In the thirty-two and a half pages of
Lestrygonians, however, he used only seventy-five colons, or
about two and a quarter colons to a page.[8] Thus, although Joyce
seems to use the colon relatively heavily in both chapters, he
uses it much more heavily for Stephen's stream of consciousness
than he does for Bloom's.[9]

The colon provides a pause of anticipation much like the pause
in the appositive sentence described above. Indeed, three of the
appositive sentences in the list above contain colons to indicate
the point of pause.

There are other examples of unusual usage, or sentence
construction, in both chapters:

Bloom

womaneyes (155:7/157:15)
quick breathing (165:10/167:26)
a keep quiet relief (165:12/167:28)
sheepsnouts bloodypapered snivelling nosejam on sawdust
    (168:35/171:13)
windpipes faked (169:22/171:41)
smellsipped (170:30/173:7)

Stephen

Then he was aware of them bodies before of them coloured.
    (38:5/37:5)
Wombed in sin darkness (39:10/38:10)
contransmagnificandjewbangtantiality (39:17/38:17)
brightwindbridled (39:23/38:23)
see him me clambering down (41:2/40:2)
loudlatinlaughing (43:7/42:9)
His snout lifted barked (47:9/46:15)
wavenoise (47:10/46:16)
seamorse (47:10/46:16)
pissed quick short (47:32/46:38)
I am almosting it (47:41/47:6)
Our souls, shamewounded (49:23/48:32)
his my sandal shoon (51:15/50:26)
fourworded wavespeech (50:20/49:29

and of reversals in the usual word order:

Bloom

His eyes unhungrily saw shelves of tins (172:31/174:31)

Stephen

Proudly walking (42:38/41:40)
Paris rawly waking (43:25/42:28)
her hand gentle (49:26/48:35)

Thus in fewer than half the number of pages, Stephen's stream
of consciousness contains more than twice the number of
unusual usages as Bloom's. The comparison again indicates a
difference between the two men. To the careful reader, Stephen's
playing with words suggests a man interested in language, a
suggestion reinforced by other aspects of Stephen's stream of
consciousness. Even the casual reader must pause long enough

at such combinations as *contransmagnificandjewbangtantiality* and *loudlatinlaughing* to realize that here is a mind with interests different from Bloom's—and possibly from his own.

From the lists and discussions above, it is obvious that the streams of consciousness of Bloom and Stephen have different patterns. Over Bloom's Irish sentences, which serve as the underlying framework of Bloom's speech and thoughts, giving them some base, Joyce has poured jumbled sentences, sentences into which words and phrases seem to have been tumbled helter-skelter (condensations and accumulations) and sentences in which the normal word order seems purposely to have been violated (wrenched sentences). Therefore, although Lestrygonians has, in the arrangement of its omniscient author's sentences (which keep the reader oriented) and in Bloom's Irish sentences, a basic framework, its immediate impact on the reader is one of disorder and sometimes even confusion. The sentences characteristic of Stephen's stream of consciousness, however, have a very definite—and usually measured—pattern: the *a*, *b*, and *c* type parallel construction, usually in triads. Above this basic pattern, other minor patterns appear. Some sentences have a measured balance of rise and fall: "Their blood is in me, their lusts my waves" (46:15/45:17). Others have a more involved form, rising, pausing, falling, and continuing on to rise and fall again: "He rooted in the sand, dabbling, delving and stopped to listen to the air, scraped up the sand again with a fury of his claws, soon ceasing, a pard, a panther, got in spousebreach, vulturing the dead" (47:35/46:41). The effect of the carefully planned complexity of these sentences, reminiscent, appropriately, of the classical languages, is broken on occasion by the rapid fall of the end of an appositive sentence: "They are coming, waves" (39:22/38:22). But even here, though the break is sharp, it is orderly and not at all like the shifts in Bloom's stream of consciousness, which often herald sharp changes in direction or mere lumping together of ideas. Thus, what little pattern there is in Bloom's stream of consciousness (the Irish sentence) is a folk pattern, whereas the pattern in Stephen's stream of consciousness is an indication of training and education.

Further added to the major difference in effect between the two streams of consciousness—the relative awkwardness of the structure of the sentences representing Bloom's thoughts as compared with the balanced flow of Stephen's—is the fact that Bloom's sentences are shorter and thus give the effect of being more elementary. The mean number of words per sentence in Lestrygonians is only 6.63 as compared with 8.14 for Proteus.[10]

What the critics have long indicated about the differentiating rhythms or styles of Stephen's and Bloom's streams of consciousness (but have not documented), this analysis thus finds evidence for. The total effect of Proteus on the reader *is* different from the total effect of Lestrygonians. And this analysis shows that the difference is partly a result of the difference in distinguishing or typical sentence patterns—what the critics seem to be referring to when they speak of different rhythms or styles.

The myriad changes in the Rosenbach manuscript and in the galley proofs at the Houghton Library show that, whether Joyce was conscious of it or not, his revisions strengthened the distinctive elements of Bloom's stream of consciousness, sentence patterns found typically in Lestrygonians but not in Proteus. Thus, of the forty-one instances of the Irish sentence culled from Lestrygonians, seventeen were added either in the Rosenbach manuscript or later.[11] Had Joyce not added these sentences in revision or had he removed sentences of this pattern instead of adding them, Lestrygonians would have been much less distinguishable from Proteus than it is. By that much, therefore, Bloom would have been less distinguishable from Stephen. Six of the condensations and accumulating sentences were also added between the time of the writing of the final handwritten draft and going to press.[12] Once again, therefore, Joyce's revisions served to strengthen two typical patterns of Lestrygonians. There is considerably less rewriting of Proteus in the manuscript and galleys, but even in that chapter, some of the sentences listed above as typical of Stephen's stream of consciousness were adjusted and revised.[13]

Perhaps a few striking examples of addition and revision would be helpful here:

Irish sentences
The flow of language it is [added in first galley].
  (150:34/152:38)
Mackerel they called me [added in second galley].
  (160:5/162:18)

Weight. Would he feel it if something was removed.
[Rosenbach manuscript reads: "Weight a line if
something blackened man in dark. Wonder if he'd feel
it if. . . ."] (179:9/181:27)

Condensations

Pillowed on my coat she had her hair, earwigs in the
heather scrub my hand under her nape, you'll toss me
all [not in Rosenbach manuscript, but in first galley].
(173:25/176:5)

Lovely forms of woman sculped Junonian [read originally:
"Lovely form of woman bodies." "Junonian" substituted
for "bodies" in Rosenbach manuscript; "sculped" added in
second galley]. (174:12/176:34)

Other

Nectar, imagine it drinking electricity: god's food.
[sometime between the Rosenbach manuscript and the
first galley, the word "like" was deleted from between
"it" and "drinking"]. (174:11/176:33)

Wombed in sin darkness I was too . . . [changed in first
galley from: "Wombed in darkness sin . . ."].
(39:10/38:10)

The point of this discussion is not merely that Joyce added
and revised endlessly, but that he made many and significant
additions and revisions of sentences and paragraphs which now
seem to be characteristic of the stream of consciousness of Bloom
and that these additions and revisions strengthened the patterns
typical of Lestrygonians rather than weakening them.

Another aspect of Joyce's revisions that should be mentioned
here is that they sometimes obscure the meaning of the
particular passage, making the deciphering of *Ulysses* more
difficult. For example, in the passage, "Live on fishy flesh they
have to, all sea birds, gulls, seagoose. Swans from Anna Liffey
swim down here sometimes to preen themselves. No accounting
for tastes. Wonder what kind is swanmeat. Robinson Crusoe had
to live on them" (151:10/153:12), all the words from "Swans
from Anna Liffey" to "swanmeat" were interpolated during the
revision of the galleys, causing the reader of the published
version to have to dig for what it was that Robinson Crusoe
had to live on. There is even the possibility that the

interpolation might cause the reader to misinterpret the passage: knowing that Bloom might easily use a pronoun for which there is no antecedent, or for which the antecedent is remote, he might think that "them" refers to "Swans" or even to "Swans from Anna Liffey." In another instance (161:4-27/163:18-41), about fourteen lines of text (from "Drop him like a hot potato"—161:8/163:22—to "Tobacco shopgirls. / James"— 161:21-22/163:35-36) were interjected into the middle of a passage on the invincibles and Sinn Fein. The reader, led off into a short discussion on the love life of maids (161:14/163:28), is returned rather abruptly a few lines later to the ramblings about the Irish nationalist underground (161:22/163:36).[14]

Special attention ought also to be given to two particular passages in these chapters. In one section of Lestrygonians (174:22-176:38/177:3-179:19), a chapter which is otherwise all stream of consciousness, after twenty-five pages of being in Bloom's mind watching the thoughts go by and the perceptions enter, the reader is suddenly dislodged and deposited unceremoniously on the floor of Davy Byrne's pub in the midst of a conversation as Bloom leaves for the men's room. For more than two pages (174:22-176:29/176:3-179:10), then, the reader listens to some Dubliners discussing Bloom. The sentences are perfectly conventional in that they read much the way sentences from a conversational passage in any modern novel would read. The only sentence that is in any way unusual is: "Davy Byrne smiledyawnednodded all in one: / —Iiiiiichaaaaaaach!" (175:16-17/177:38-39). Bloom's return (176:30/179:11) intrudes on the conversation, forcing it down to a mere whisper (176:33/179:14), so that even for a few lines after Bloom reappears the reader does not resume his position in Bloom's mind but sees Bloom conventionally from the outside. Finally, several lines later, after an omniscient author's sentence (176:39/179:18), the reader is reinstalled in Bloom's mind and remains there for the rest of the chapter. The reason for this lapse may well have been that Joyce, having so many Dubliners so conveniently together, felt that this would be a good place to give the reader some outside views of Bloom. Since the presentation of such views would be difficult with Bloom present, Joyce marched him off. That Bloom should receive "a message from his bladder" after having drunk and eaten is, of course, not unusual. But that Joyce should violate the technique of an entire chapter because it was convenient, when he might easily have accomplished the same thing in another chapter (e.g., Cyclops) without any change in technique is noteworthy.

There is also a passage in Proteus that merits pointing out because it is a noticeable change in the density of omniscient author's sentences. On page 47/46 is a long passage, a total of thirty-six out of the forty-two lines on the page (47:2-25, 27-39/46:7-31, 33-42; 47:3), composed mainly of omniscient author's sentences. In this passage of almost a page, 70.4 percent of the sentences are omniscient author's sentences, as compared with only 7.8 percent of omniscient author's sentences for the chapter as a whole.[15] Thus 30.6 percent of the total number of omniscient author's sentences in this chapter of fourteen pages appear in one passage of less than a page.

The concentration of omniscient author's sentences is probably the result here of Stephen's concentration on the scene before him, the only time in the chapter that Stephen focuses more intently for any period of time on the world before his eyes than on his own thoughts. Many of the sentences, of course, are written in Stephen's idiom and show the patterns described above as typical of Stephen. Stephen's acute awareness of the dog's activities stems from his fear of the dog.[16] Coming immediately after a stream-of-consciousness passage which simulates some of Stephen's concern, however, the omniscient author's passage seems curiously unemotional.

C. Paragraph and Sentence Structure in Penelope

In a letter to Budgen, Joyce says of the last chapter in *Ulysses:*

> *Penelope* is the clou of the book. The first sentence contains 2500 words. There are eight sentences in the episode. It begins and ends with the female word *yes*. It turns like the huge earth ball slowly surely and evenly round and round spinning, its 4 cardinal points being the female breasts, arse, womb and cunt expressed by the words *because, bottom* (in all sense bottom button, bottom of the class, bottom of the sea, bottom of his heart), *woman, yes.*[17]

Most Joyce critics, although they often refer to the lack of punctuation, shy away from calling each of the eight paragraphs of Penelope a sentence as Joyce does. But their characterization of the rhythm of the episode is much like Joyce's, although they may not use the same imagery. To Budgen, Molly's thoughts are "an oleaginous, slow-moving stream, turning in every direction to find the lowest level."[18] Tindall feels that "if syntax is the shape of thought and punctuation is a sign of it, Mrs. Bloom's thought, devoid of punctuation and syntactically liberal, is almost thoughtless. Compared with Stephen's clear well-banked stream and Mr. Bloom's wider, muddier, but still well-banked stream, her enormous flow is less stream than flood."[19] Wilson speaks of "the deep embedded pulse" of the flight of Molly's mind, and says that it is represented "by a long, unbroken rhythm of brogue, like the swell of some profound sea."[20]

The truth about Penelope's being one sentence or eight sentences was stated early by Rebecca West: "Most of the wildness of the chapter is typographical cheating, a surface effect which is created by the lack of punctuation, and would instantly disappear and show a groundwork of ordinary ecstatic prose if a few commas and full stops and dashes and exclamation points were inserted." Miss West, however, agrees with the other critics that Penelope has a "strong, tremendous pattern and rhythm."[21]

If Penelope is not written in eight long sentences, there is evidence that Joyce tried to create the *impression* that it is, and the degree to which critics have talked about Molly's soliloquy as an "unbroken rhythm" and an "oleaginous stream" is at least a partial measure of his success. Applying the needed punctuation to the first page of Penelope, one finds that the chapter does in fact begin with a long sentence, a sentence of ninety-eight words:

> Yes, because he never did a thing like that before as ask to get his breakfast in bed with a couple of eggs since the *City Arms* hotel when he used to be pretending to be laid up with a sick voice doing his highness to make himself interesting to that old faggot Mrs Riordan that he thought he had a great leg of, and she never left us a farthing, all for masses for herself and her soul, greatest miser ever was, actually afraid to lay out 4d for her methylated spirits, telling me all her ailments.
> (723:1-8/738:1-8)

The interesting thing about this passage is not only the length
of the sentence, but also the fact that after the opening "Yes"
it goes on for sixty-three words without a pause ("because . . .
a great leg of"—723:1-6/738:1-6). Here, then, begins the
impression of steady flow and the ever forward-moving current.
When the first sentence does begin to slow down, it merely
hesitates and changes direction ("and she"); it does not stop.
There are four more pauses before the sentence actually
concludes.

It should also be noted that the introductory pauseless passage
is not merely a series of statements joined, Malory- and
Caxton-like, by *and*s. The organization here is much tighter
than a mere stringing together with coordinating conjunctions.
Rather the elements of these five lines are closely related in
idea and connected by subordinating conjunctions (*because, as,
since, when, that*). Perhaps a comparison with a sentence from
Le Morte Darthur would show the difference in effect:

> Thenne Syr Bedwere departed and wente to the swerde and
> lyghtly took hit up and wente to the water syde and there he
> bounde the gyrdyl about the hyltes and thenne he threwe the
> swerde as farre in to the water as he myght; & there cam an
> arme and an hande above the water and mette it & caught it
> and so shoke it thryse and braundysshed and then vanysshed
> awaye the hande wyth the swerde in the water.[22]

Whereas the sentence from *Le Morte Darthur* bumps along from
and to *and* in a pedestrian fashion, the sentence from Molly's
soliloquy moves forward rapidly, seemingly without pause. The
forward-moving quality in the opening passage of Penelope
cannot be laid simply to the lack of punctuation because the
similar lack of punctuation (save for the semicolon and the final
period) in the passage from Malory and Caxton does not create
the same effect. Molly's passage seems to press forward much
more than does the other. The difference then must be the one
pointed out above: the tying of the elements of the passage
together with subordinating conjunctions rather than stringing
them together with coordinating conjunctions.

The manuscript versions of *Ulysses* indicate that Joyce
probably intended this impression of continuing flow from the
first writing. In an early draft of Penelope (that is, the
Rosenbach manuscript), the passage that is now the first page

of that chapter in the two Random House editions (723/738) reads like this:

> Yes because he never did a thing like that before as ask to get his breakfast in bed with a couple of eggs since the City Arms hotel when he used to be pretending to be laid up with a sick voice doing his highness to make himself interesting for that old faggot Mrs Riordan ∂ (that) never left us a farthing all for masses for herself ℕ and her talk about Mr Riordan here and Mr Riordan there I suppose he was glad to get shut of her and her dog smelling my fur and always edging to get up under my petticoats ℚ if ever he got anything really serious the matter with him it's much better for them to go into a hospital where everything is clean F yes because they're weak and puling when they're sick A father was the same besides I hate bandaging and dosing when he cut his toe with a razor paring his corns afraid he'd get blood poisoning yes he came somewhere I'm sure by his appetite anyway love it's not or he'd be off his feed thinking of her so either it was one of those night women if it was down there he was really

In that same manuscript the following additions were made, in the places indicated by the symbols (Joyce's own):

∂ that he thought he had a great leg of and she

      greatest   ↗   ever was actually

ℕ and her soul ∧ miser ∧afraid to lay out fourpence for her methylated spirit telling me all her ailments she was a well educated woman

ℚ still I like that in him polite to old women like that

                T dring
F but I suppose I'd have to (drive) T it in to him for a month

A and that dyinglook one when he sprained his foot at the choir party at lough Bray the day I wore that dress Miss Stack bringing him flowers the worst she could find at the bottom of the basket though he looked more like a man with his beard a bit grown in the bed

It is clear, then, that, from the early stages of writing, the opening sentence of Penelope was intended to be long and, as we shall see in a moment, flowing. In its original form it contained 77 words, as compared with 28 words for the longest sentence in Proteus and 43 words for the longest sentence in Lestrygonians. Even though Joyce did later whittle the first sentence of Penelope down from the 115 words to which he had lengthened it in the Rosenbach manuscript, in final form it is 98 words long: longer than the original and more than twice as long as the longest sentences in Proteus and Lestrygonians. And most significant of all, of the six additions that Joyce made in this passage in the Rosenbach manuscript, all save one ("still I like that in him") were additions to existing sentences, lengthening the originals, rather than new sentences which would halt the flow. The one sentence ("still I like that in him") does break the flow; but one would gather that the break was a purposeful one, because it introduces a sharp change in direction of thought and even a reversal of opinion. Thus Joyce would seem to have wanted a long introductory sentence for Penelope and an opening page composed of long sentences (although not as long as the first one).[23]

The opening page of Penelope also has examples of three connecting devices that Joyce uses throughout the chapter to tie Molly's thoughts together and give the impression of an undulating flow rather than a series of discrete statements: a large number of coordinating conjunctions (chiefly *and* and *but*); the conjunctionlike *yes*; and the narrative *then*. In the fourteen lines following the pauseless sixty-three words of the opening sentence, there are thirteen coordinating conjunctions: eleven instances of *and* and two of *but*. This number compares with five coordinating conjunctions in the first half page (twenty-one lines) of Proteus, four *and*s and one *but*, and only two (both *and*s) in the first half page (twenty-one lines) of Lestrygonians. Joyce also uses *yes* and *then* as transitional elements in Penelope, particularly at the very beginning and end. Because there is no punctuation in the chapter, *yes* poises between sentences, adhering equally to the sentence preceding and following. The reader, coming to it, finds that it can go with the next sentence as well as with the one he has just read, and goes on. In a few pages the convention is established and the reader accepts *yes* as a transitional element. Similarly, *then*, sometimes with a coordinating conjunction but often without it, effects a transition to decrease the gap between otherwise separate elements. Because *then* obviously belongs to one sentence or another, however, regardless of whether punctuation has been left out or not, it does not maintain quite the tension between two sentences that *yes* does in this chapter. The first page of Penelope provides examples of all of these devices:

> its much better for them go into a hospital where everything is
> clean but I suppose Id have to dring it into him for a month
> yes and then wed have a hospital nurse next thing on the carpet
> (723:21/738:22)

> besides I hate bandaging and dosing when he cut his toe with
> the razor paring his corns afraid hed get blood poisoning but if
> it was a thing I was sick then wed see what attention only of
> course the woman hides it not to give all the trouble they do
> yes he came somewhere Im sure by his appetite anyway love its
> not or hed be off his feed thinking of her[24] (723:36/738:37)

Other transitional elements (*only*, 723:29/738:30; *anyway*, 723:41/738:42) are also apparent here.

Compared with the opening passages of Proteus and Lestrygonians, then, the opening passage of Penelope, with its lack of punctuation, its ninety-eight word sentence, its initial sixty-three words without a pause, and its many transitional elements certainly does give the feeling of continuing flow.

Joyce also worked over the end of the chapter so that the reader would finish it having the same feeling of continued flow that he had at the beginning. In the last fifty lines (slightly under a page and a half), what would otherwise be separate sentences are similarly woven together by transitional elements. In that passage there are three *thens*, twenty-one *yeses*, and sixty-four *ands*. The final sentence in Penelope is 387 words long, thirty-two and a third lines of text: (767:28-768:18/782:25-783:14). Of these 387 words, 245 (63.3 percent of the sentence) were added during the revision of the galleys, including nine of the twelve instances of *yes* in the sentence. This lengthening of the final sentence in revision, like the lengthening of the opening one, is again in the direction of Joyce's statement that Penelope is composed of eight sentences, although it certainly is not a fulfillment of it.

One other point that should be noted here is that the final passage of Penelope is not like the opening five lines of that chapter. Whereas the opening passage relies entirely on subordinating conjunctions to hold it together and to move the reader along, the closing passage relies heavily on coordinating conjunctions. It is still not as naively constructed, however, as the passage quoted above from *Le Morte Darthur*. The last

thirty-odd lines of Penelope do contain some subordinating
conjunctions (*where, when*); and they have, in addition, the
twelve conjunctionlike *yeses* and other interpolations in the form
of lines from songs, probably from Molly's repertoire.

The six sample passages of Penelope indicate that the average
length of the sentences in that chapter is 19.13 words. If one
discards the first and last of the six sample passages as atypical
because they contain unusually long sentences, even for
Penelope, the mean sentence length is 15.04 words, still
significantly longer than the 8.14 for Proteus and the 6.63 for
Lestrygonians.[25] Since the initial step to determining mean
sentence length for Penelope was, of course, supplying the
missing punctuation, I include here as an example one of the
six sample passages as I punctuated it:

> How could he have the face to any woman after his company
> manners, making it so awkward. After when we met asking me
> have I offended you, with my eyelids down. Of course he saw
> I wasn't. He had a few brains, not like that other fool, Henny
> Doyle. He was always breaking or tearing something in the
> charades. I hate an unlucky man, and if I knew what it meant.
> Of course I had to say no for form sake. "Don't understand you,"
> I said, "and wasn't it natural?" So it is, of course. It used to
> be written up with a picture of a woman's on that wall in
> Gibraltar with that word I couldn't find anywhere. Only for
> children seeing it too young. Then writing a letter every morning,
> sometimes twice a day. I liked the way he made love then. He
> knew the way to take a woman. When he sent me the 8 big
> poppies because mine was the 8th. Then I wrote the night he
> kissed my heart at Dolphin's barn. I couldn't describe it. Simply
> it makes you feel like nothing on earth. But he never knew how
> to embrace well like Gardner. I hope he'll come on Monday as
> he said, at the same time, four. I hate people who come at all
> hours. Answer the door, you think it's the vegetables, then it's
> somebody, and you all undressed; or the door of the filthy sloppy
> kitchen blows open the day old frostyface Goodwin called about
> the concert in Lombard street, and I just after dinner all flushed
> and tossed with boiling old stew. (731:42-732:21/747:1-747:23)

No two people, of course, would agree on how this passage
should be punctuated. I attempted to supply the marks of
punctuation according to the meaning of the passage and
according to the way Joyce used punctuation in Proteus and
Lestrygonians. Any disagreement, however, will probably

suggest that this passage was overpunctuated rather than underpunctuated. Thus the rectifying of any error in determining sentence length in Penelope would show that the sentences are even longer than indicated here, increasing the difference between Penelope on the one hand and Proteus and Lestrygonians on the other.

Thus we see how Joyce managed to give the impression of continuous flow in Penelope. He began the chapter with a long, initially pauseless sentence with many transitional elements. The lack of punctuation, the comparatively long sentences, and the use of transitional words maintain the impression of continued flow in the body of the chapter. And the very long final sentence reinforces that impression and leaves the reader with the feeling that he has indeed read a passage of "long, unbroken rhythm."

D. Rhetorical Gestures in Omniscient Author's Sentences

Now that we have considered both omniscient author's sentences and characteristic sentence patterns in Proteus and Lestrygonians, we can examine David Hayman's analysis of "*the* persona behind the action of the first eleven chapters*" and that "*narrator's particular brand of exuberance." As Hayman points out, what I have labeled omniscient author's sentences frequently contain "rhetorical gestures which add point, interest and humor to what might otherwise be bland descriptive passages connecting bits of dialogue or monologue."[26]

Thus, on the first page of Proteus, omniscient author's sentences declare Stephen's boots to be "crush crackling wrack and shells" (38:11/37:11) and one of the midwives to be swinging her bag "lourdily" (38:37/37:37). And the next two pages have omniscient author's sentences which contain echoes of Shakespeare: "Airs romped around him, *nipping and eager airs*" (39:22/38:22); "His boots trod again a damp crackling mast, razorshells, squeaking pebbles, *that on the unnumbered pebbles beats*, wood sieved by the shipworm, lost Armada" (41:39/41:1). Later omniscient author's sentences contain alliteration, unusual words, or both: "then his forepaws *dabbled and delved* (47:33/46:40); "the *ruffian* and his *strolling mort*"

(48:05/47:13); "He turned his face over a shoulder, *rere regardant*" (51:35/51:4).

Similarly, in Lestrygonians some of the omniscient author's sentences contain rhetorical gestures: "Mr Bloom smiled *O rocks* at two windows of the ballast office" (152:7/154:10); "Perfume of embraces *all him assailed*" (166:19/168:37); "Dribbling a quiet message from his bladder *came to go to do not to do there to do*" (174:18/176:40).

Clearly these are not the standard stage directions of the omniscient author. They do indeed show evidence of rhetorical gesture. But consider:

1. In the first eleven chapters, there is no sign of a narrator other than the rhetorical gestures. On the other hand, later, in Cyclops, when Joyce intends a narrator, he provides clear evidence of one:

> I was just passing the time of day with old Troy of the D.M.P. at the corner of Arbour Hill there and be damned but a bloody sweep came along and he near drove his gear into my eye. I turned around to let him have the weight of my tongue when who should I see dodging along Stony Batter only Joe Hynes.
> —Lo, Joe, says I (287:1/292:1)

2. As we have seen, Joyce moves carefully in the first part of the book away from the standard omniscient author's presentation to the stream-of-consciousness technique, in keeping with his earlier stricture that "the artist, like the God of Creation, remains within or behind or beyond or above his handwork, invisible, refined out of existence, paring his fingernails."[27]

3. The omniscient author's sentences in Proteus echo lines from Shakespeare that have not become common coin or clichés for the multitude ("nipping and eager airs," "that on the unnumbered pebbles beats"), little-known seventeenth-century canting language ("the ruffian and his strolling mort"), and alliteration; whereas the omniscient author's sentences in Lestrygonians echo the sentence structure typical of Bloom's stream of consciousness (what I have designated earlier as condensations). We do not find in the omniscient author's sentences of Proteus any phrasing as clumsy as "came to go to do not to do there to do"; nor do we find in the omniscient

author's sentences of Lestrygonians any language as exotic as "lourdily" or "rere." And we certainly would not expect to find as one of the omniscient author's sentences of Lestrygonians anything like: "Under the upswelling tide he saw the writhing weeds lift languidly and sway reluctant arms, hising, up their petticoats, in whispering water swaying and upturning coy silver fronds" (50:25/49:35).

The rhetorical gestures found in the omniscient author's sentences of Proteus, therefore, are not the same as those found in the omniscient author's sentences of Lestrygonians, and thus the omniscient author's sentences in the two chapters would seem not to be the utterances of a single persona.[28] I would suggest, rather, that in effacing himself, in attempting to become "invisible," Joyce tried to make his omniscient author's sentences less obtrusive by flavoring them with the characteristics of the stream of consciousness of the character with which he was dealing at the time. If the flavoring was not conscious, I would assume that while working on a particular section he fell into the personality and rhythm of the character he was portraying at the time and wrote omniscient author's sentences that tended to echo the stream of consciousness that he employed for that character.

Because Joyce chose to give Molly a stream of consciousness which was entirely monologue, he did not need omniscient author's sentences for the last chapter. The difference between the sentence patterns in Penelope on the one hand and in Proteus and Lestrygonians on the other is more a difference in kind rather than of mix or degree.

7
Patterns of Association

As we have seen, the principle of association is important in the direction and organization of the stream of consciousness. The psychologist's traditional methods of examining associations, however, are not available to the student of literature. One cannot give Stephen a stimulus word and ask him for a response. Analyses and characterizations of associations, too, have been done by means of this single-word, stimulus-response method. The resultant typologies are sometimes interesting to a literary critic, of course. It is, perhaps, helpful to know that Joyce's adding "clack" to "Bits all khrrrrklak in place back" (43:2/42:4) was probably suggested by a phenomenon known as the clang reaction and that such a response is not peculiar to Joyce. And the concepts of similarity, contiguity, and recency by which psychologists tend to explain associations are also useful in explaining the flow of thought of a particular character. But they are not useful in comparing the streams of thought of different characters, in determining whether the thoughts of different characters pattern differently.

Recent research, however, indicates that associative relationships can be defined as psychological *structures*

> in terms of a network theory of the psychic apparatus. . . .
> Associative relationships [are] defined as psychological structures
> which transmit energy from one mental representation to another.
> As a consequence of the activity of associative relationship
> structures, associations of a primed stimulus are in a state of
> readiness and may become contents of awareness under certain
> conditions.[1]

Other research indicates that, although one's associative behavior may vary, "under normal circumstances, subjects will adopt one characteristic set. This typical response set, or cognitive style, represents one of a small number of such sets which it is possible to adopt, and it appears to be a characteristic of the individual which is stable over time."[2] James Deese's statement that "all nominal concepts are organized as groups" suggested a method of examining passages of stream of consciousness for typical response sets, which might reflect idiosyncratic cognitive styles: an examination of how the nouns in a particular passage relate to one another.[3]

Such a methodology seems appropriate to use on *Ulysses*, because by 1913, before Joyce began serious work on that novel, he was using associative strings and clusters of nouns to store his ideas. In the notes for *Exiles*, for example, we find:

> N. (B.)—12 Nov. 1913
> > Garter: precious, Prezioso, Bodkin, music, palegreen, bracelet, cream sweets, lily of the valley, convent garden (Galway), sea.
> > Rat: Sickness, disgust, poverty, cheese, woman's ear (child's ear?)
> > Dagger: heart, death, soldier, war, band, judgment, king.
>
> > Blister—amber—silver—oranges—apples—Sugarstick—hair—spongecake—ivy—roses—ribbon
>
> > Snow:
> > > frost, moon, pictures, holly and ivy, current-cake, lemonade, Emily Lyons, piano, window sill,
> > tears:
> > > ship, sunshine, garden, sadness, pinafore, buttoned boots, bread and butter, a big fire.[4]

Accompanying each of the last two clusters (that is, "Blister—amber . . ." and "Snow . . . tears . . .") in the notes are Joyce's careful analyses of how the ideas symbolized by those nouns relate to one another. About the last cluster, for example, Joyce wrote:

> In the first the flow of ideas is tardy. It is Christmas in Galway, a moonlit Christmas eve with snow. She is carrying picture almanacs to her grandmother's house to be ornamented with holly and ivy. The evenings are spent in the house of a friend where they give her lemonade. Lemonade and currant cake are also her grandmother's Christmas fare for her. She thumps the piano and sits with her dark-complexioned gipsy looking friend Emily Lyons on the window sill.

In the second the ideas are more rapid. It is the quay of Galway harbour on a bright morning. The emigrant ship is going away and Emily, her dark friend, stands on the deck going out to America. They kiss and cry bitterly. But she believes that some day her friend will come back as she promises. She cries for the pain of separation and for the dangers of the sea that threaten the girl who is going away. The girl is older than she and has no lover. She too has no lover. Her sadness is brief. She is alone, friendless, in her grandmother's garden and can see the garden, lonely now, in which the day before she played with her friend. Her grandmother consoles her, gives her a new clean pinafore to wear and buttoned shoes, a present from her uncle, and nice bread and butter to eat and a big fire to sit down to.[5]

Walton Litz finds that "Joyce used the associational technique which governs [such passages] in two ways: (1) to order the impressions and memories of his characters, and (2) to organize the heterogeneous raw materials of his art."[6]

In discussing the last set of associations (that is, "Snow . . . tears . . ."), Joyce actually organized them into clusters of structures in much the way I propose: "A persistent and delicate sensuality (visual: pictures, adorned with holly and ivy; gustatious: currant cake, bread and butter, lemonade; tactual: sunshine in the garden, a big fire, the kisses of her friend and grandmother) runs through both series of images."[7]

Joyce continued to use such associative clusters in planning and writing *Ulysses*. For example, in his notes for the Eumaeus episode is one cluster: "Dilly's Kitchen: oatmeal water, cat devours charred fishheads & eggshells heaped on brown paper, shell cocoa in sootcoated kettle."[8] Litz points out that these notes appear in *Ulysses* as follows:

There was no response forthcoming to the suggestion, however, such as it was, Stephen's mind's eye being too busily engaged in repicturing his family hearth the last time he saw it, with his sister, Dilly, sitting by the ingle, her hair hanging down, waiting for some weak Trinidad shell cocoa that was in the sootcoated kettle to be done so that she and he could drink it with the oatmeal water for milk after the Friday herrings they had eaten at two a penny, with an egg apiece for Maggy, Boody and Katey, the cat meanwhile under the mangle devouring a mess of eggshells and charred fish heads and bones on a square of brown paper in accordance with the third precept of the church to fast and abstain on the days commanded, it being quarter tense or, if not, ember days or something like that. (604/620)

Robert M. Adams demonstrates that Joyce did some of his original preparing for *Ulysses* on notesheets

> of small free-association patterns, episodes in a state of radical compression, and phrases or words which were ultimately scattered freely through the book. When Joyce thought of a property useful for his novel, he did not generally indicate (or, probably, know) its ultimate dimensions or even its ultimate function. He threw it into the note-sheets, to grow and seek its attachment as it would.[9]

In the three chapters under examination, there are passages in which Stephen, Bloom, and Molly think of pregnancy and birth—one each in Proteus and Penelope, and two in Lestrygonians. For each of those passages, I first listed all of the nouns.[10] Then I grouped them according to their meaning and looked for relationships among the groups. The procedure is much like the examination of the images in a poem to see to what extent they cluster around a central image—that is, whether the images present a coherent whole or whether they are disparate. The reader probably should compare the analyses before reading the following discussion. (See figures 1, 2, 3, 4.)

In the episode from Proteus, the sight of the midwives triggers in Stephen's mind some thoughts about birth, for our purposes conveniently set off in a paragraph (38:33/37:33; see figure 1). The central cluster of associations seems to be Creation-life-flesh-misbirth. The cluster relict-sister-mother relates to it, at least through *mother,* and probably as a group. The ocean-related cluster (shore-sand-beach) also associates with it because in our (and most other) mythology, creation of the world occurred from a primeval watery abyss: "And God said, Let the waters under the heaven be gathered together unto one place, and let the dry land appear: and it was so" (Genesis i, 9). Furthermore, Mulligan plays on Swinburne's reference to the sea as a mother (7:1-9/5:5-13), and Stephen's thoughts echo the same idea (38:36/37:36).

The pair omphalos-navelcord clearly relates to the central cluster; and the individual words below *Creation* seem to connect to it in different ways: one—primal; nothing—creation out of chaos; gods—create, and monks worship gods; day—created during Creation.

For the rest, women carry gamps and bags; and terraces,

according to the dictionary, are frequently associated with rivers, lakes, or seas. Only *liberties* resists association with one of the established clusters.

A paragraph near the beginning of Lestrygonians contains Bloom's first thoughts about birth (A—149:31-150:6/151:32-152:7; figure 2). The cluster about religion (Birth-theology . . .) is the important structure, but not clearly the central structure. The people cluster (woman-mother . . .) ties in with it, but in the food cluster, only *Crossbuns* does. The corner-walk pair and the individual words *idea, L.s.d.,* and *water* are isolates.

A second paragraph devoted to birth occurs ten pages later

FIGURE 1
Associative Structures: Birth
Proteus

38:33/37:33	steps	terrace		
34/	*Frauenzimmer*	shore		
35/	feet	sand		
36/	mother	one		
37/	bag	gamp	beach	
38/	liberties	day		
39/	relict			
40/	sisterhood	life		
41/	Creation	nothing	bag	misbirth
39:1/38:1	navelcord	wool	cords	
2/	link	cable	flesh	
39:3/38:3	monks	gods	omphalos	

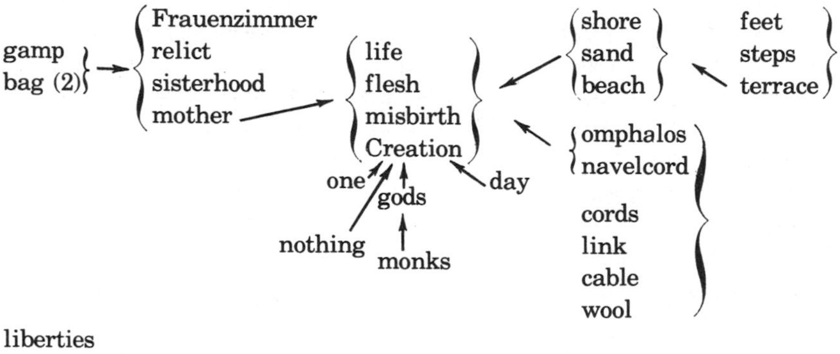

liberties

(B—159:30-41/162:1-12; figure 3). The paragraph immediately above starts out about birth, but halfway through wanders off in a different direction. This time the important cluster is the one about people: the parts-of-the-body cluster relates to it, as

FIGURE 2
Associative Structures: Birth
Lestrygonians A

149:31/151:32	corner			
32/	walk			
33/	auctionrooms	furniture		
34/	eyes	father		
35/	Home	mother	children	
36/	Birth	theology		
37/	priest	woman	confession	absolution
38/	idea			
39/	house	home	families	
40/	fat	land	butteries	larders
149:41/152:1	fast	Crossbuns		
150:1/	meal	collation	altar	housekeeper
2/	fellows			
3/	L.s.d.			
4/	guests	one	water	
5/	bread	butter	reverence	
150:6/152:7	word			

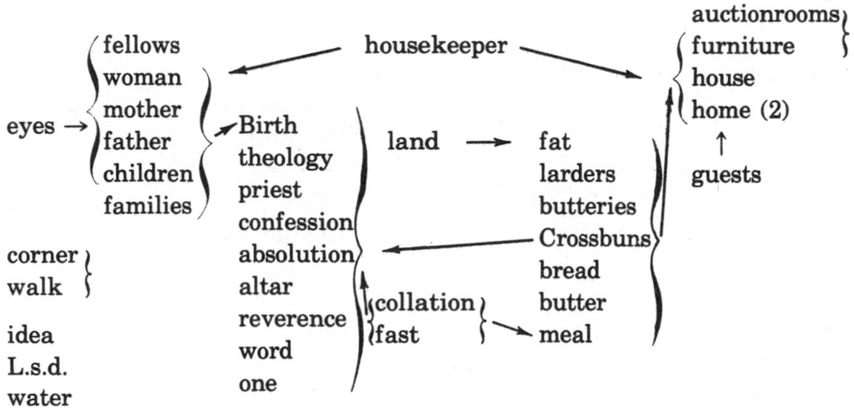

does some of the illness cluster. And again, there is an isolated cluster and this time four isolated words.

The passage about birth from Penelope (figure 4) shows a main cluster, child(ren)-twins-husband; but since there are two isolated clusters and three isolated words, it cannot be called central.

From the analysis of these four passages, we can set up a

FIGURE 3
Associative Structures: Birth
Lestrygonians B

159:30/162:1	sight	two	bellies	
31/	meeting	Phthisis	time	
32/	sudden			
33/	eyes	weight	minds	
34/	soul	babies	spoon	pap
35/	mouth			
36/	hand	son	bow	public
37/	head	pumpkin	Murren	people
38/	hours	doctor	wife	throes
39/	months	fee	attendance	
159:40/162:12	wife	gratitude	people	doctors

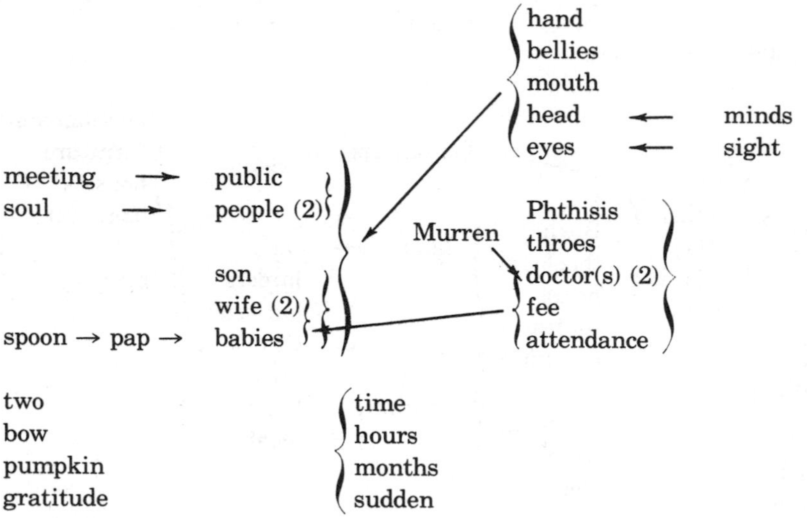

hypothesis about nominal clusters or structures which we can test by analysis of additional passages: the associations in Proteus are organized coherently around a clear central image which reflects the central idea of the passage from which they came; the associations in Lestrygonians are organized and show one cluster more important than the others, but all the other clusters do not center on it; and the associations in Penelope

FIGURE 4
Associative Structures: Birth
Penelope

727:20/742:21	touch			
21/	teeth			
22/	husband	swing	whiskers	
23/	child	twins	year	clock
24/	smell	children		
25/	nigger	shock	hair	
26/	child	black	time	squad
27/				
28/	ears			
29/	elephants			
30/				
31/	child			
727:32/742:33	spunk			

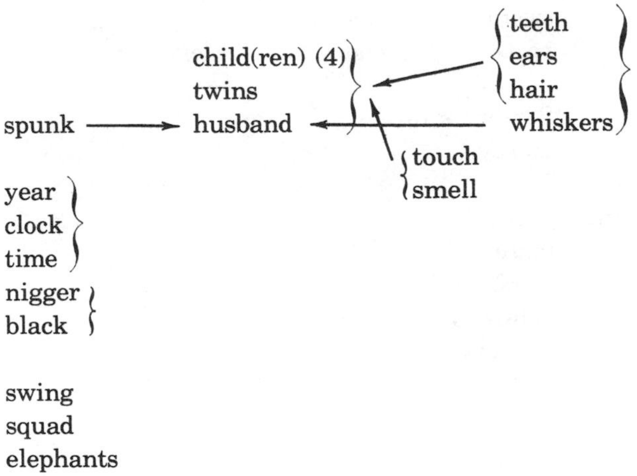

show an organization somewhat similar to that in Lestrygonians, but a little more loosely structured.

Similar experiments by Stephen and Bloom with the senses provide another pair of passages for comparison: Proteus

FIGURE 5
Associative Structures: Experiment with Senses
Proteus

38:1/37:1	modality	visible			
2/	more	thought	eyes	signatures	things
3/	seaspawn	seawrack	tide		
4/	boot	Snotgreen	bluesilver	rust	signs limit
5/	diaphane	bodies			
6/	bodies	sconce			
7/	millionaire				
8/	*maestro*	limit	diaphane		
38:9/37:9	Diaphane	adiaphane	fingers		
10/	gate	door	eyes		
11/	Stephen	eyes	boots		
12/	wrack	shells			
13/	stride	time	space	time	
14/	times	space	*nacheinander*		
15/	modality	audible			
16/	eyes	cliff	base		
17/	*nebeneinander*				
38:18/37:18	dark	sword	side		
19/	feet	boots	end	legs	
20/	mallet				
21/	eternity	Sandymount			
22/	strand	money			
23/	Deasy				
24/	Sandymount				
38:25/37:25	Madeline	mare			
26/	Rhythm	tetrameter			
27/	lambs	deline	mare		
28/	eyes	moment			
29/	adiaphane				
30/					
31/	time				
38:32/37:32	world	end			

FIGURE 5—*Continued*

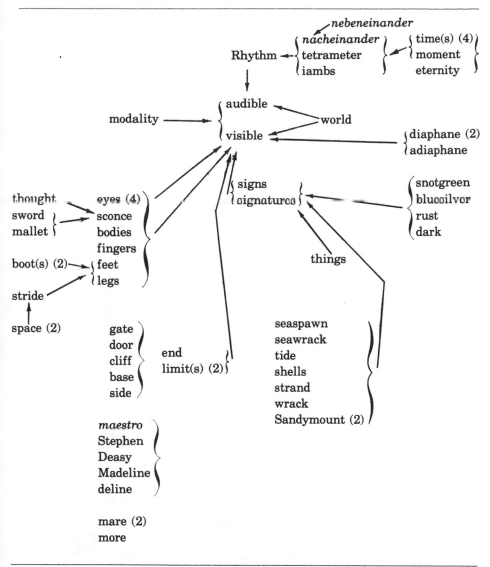

38:1-32/37:1-32; Lestrygonians 178:40-179:42/181:24-182:27.
Unfortunately, there is no comparable passage in Penelope. (See
figures 5 and 6.)

Once again, the passage from Proteus shows a central image
as an organizing core: the modality of the audible and the

(Continued on page 136)

FIGURE 6
Associative Structures: Experiment with Senses
Lestrygonians

178:40/181:24	Bloom	feet	suit		
41/	tweed	fellow	earth		
42/	van	things			
179:1/181:27	foreheads	Kind	sense	volume	weight
2/	gap	idea			
3/	way	stones			
4/	beeline	came	face		
5/	fellow	priest			
6/	Penrose	name			
179:7/181:33	things	things			
8/	fingers	pianos	brains		
9/	person	hunchback			
10/	senses				
11/	baskets	People			
12/	basket	birthday	sewing		
13/	objection	men			
179:14/181:40	sense	smell	smells	sides	
15/	person	spring	summer		
16/	smells	Tastes	wines		
17/	eyes	cold	head	dark	
18/	pleasure				
19/	woman	seeing			
20/	girl	institution	head	air	

179:21/182:5	Kind		temperature	
22/	form	eye	curves	
23/	fingers	lines		
24/	hands	hair		
25/	skin			
26/	feel	Feeling		
27/	Postoffice	order		
179:28/182:12	shillings	crown	present	Stationer's
29/				
30/	finger	hair	straw	
31/	ears	Fibres		
32/	finger	skin	cheek	hair
33/	belly			
34/	street			
35/	academy	piano	braces	
179:36/182:21	house	hand		
37/	waistcoat	trousers	shirt	
38/	fold	belly		
39/	dark			
40/	hand	dress		
41/	fellow	boy		
179:42/182:27	dreams	Life	dream	

FIGURE 6—*Continued*

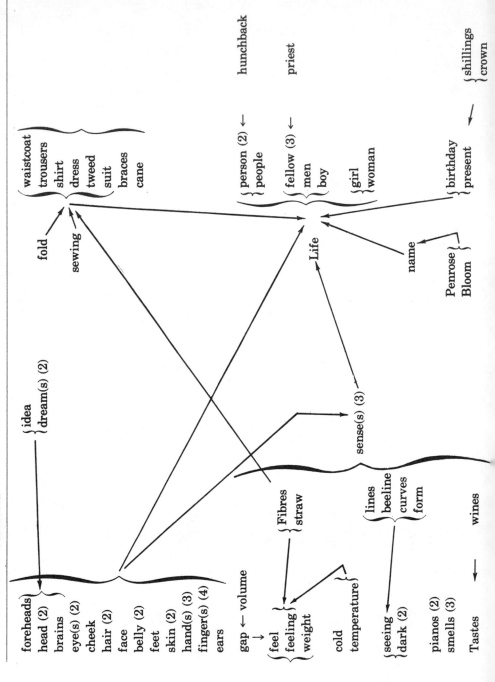

Dublin
Stationer's
(Stewart) institution
(Frederick) street
(Levenston's) academy
(Doran's public) house
Postoffice

spring
summer
earth
air

stones →

things (2)
basket(s) (2)
Kind (2)
van
objection
sides
pleasure
order
way

visible. There are some isolates: the proper noun cluster, *more,* and *mare.* Each might conceivably be related to existing clusters: the people cluster to the parts-of-the-body cluster; *more* to either the rhythm cluster or the time cluster—in the sense that it is a measure; and *mare* to the sea cluster—as an echo of both the Latin *mare* and the French *mer* and *mère.* (I would hesitate to suggest the *mare* association with most other authors, but not with Joyce.)

The nouns in the Lestrygonians passage tend to focus around the people cluster; but in this analysis again the most important cluster is not as central as is the one in the Proteus passage. The passage from Lestrygonians shows two isolated clusters (the nature and the city-place clusters) and many isolated words.

The analysis also suggests that Bloom is a more sensuous person than Stephen. Stephen's experiment involves only two senses: sight (heavily) and sound (to a lesser extent). Bloom's association structure of sense nominals includes those two and also touch, taste, and, by inference, hearing (pianos).

We might stop here for a moment to note the need for close analysis of the text to provide useful tests of generalizations by critics. In *The Art of James Joyce,* Litz says:

> In *Ulysses* the communication of setting through sound is intensified. There is very little conventional description, the novel is composed mainly of conversation and interior monologues; yet when we reach the end of *Ulysses* we know Dublin in visual terms. By this ingenious use of techniques which are primarily aural Joyce has made the City a concrete reality to all the senses. Stephen Dedalus suggests the secret of this method in the opening pages of *Proteus,* where he broods on the interrelation of temporal and spatial sequences, the *nacheinander* and the *nebeneinander.* "Shut your eyes and see" (U38).[11]

The analysis of the nouns in that episode from Proteus, however, has shown that reference to the visual outweighs reference to the audible many times. A return to the text for nonnominal references to sound yields only these additions, hardly enough to change the proportions:

> to hear his boots crush crackling wrack and shells
> (38:11/37:11)
> Sounds solid (38:20/37:20)
> Crush, crack, crik, crick (38:22/37:22)

The analysis of the parallel episode in Lestrygonians shows that in the cataloguing of the senses there, hearing is the only one of the five not alluded to directly and that the references are primarily visual and tactile. The addition of nonnominal references to sound are even less impressive here. In forty-five lines of text, over a page, there are only three:

tapping (179:3/180:29)
Tune (used as a verb—179:8/181:34)
voice (used as an adjective—179:22/182:6)

An examination of all the other associative structures shows the same heavy emphasis on the visual.

In fact, following Bloom around in Lestrygonians, we see a lot, but hear very little. On the very first page (149/151), for example, we see a girl in Graham Lemon's sweet shop dispensing candies to a Christian brother, a YMCA young man placing a throwaway in Bloom's hand, Butler's monument house corner, Bachelor's walk, and Stephen's sister standing outside Dillon's auction rooms. The only thing we are meant to hear is the jingle about Dowie's coming (149:18/151:17); and even that is more likely intended as an auditory image in Bloom's mind than something that he actually sings. The other images in Bloom's consciousness are all visual.

On the next page (150/152), the images and perceptions are overwhelmingly visual. Later we see the timeball, Wisdom Hely's sandwichboard men, the vapor and steam rolling out of Harrison's, Mrs. Breen, Farrell, Denis Breen, a flock of pigeons before the Irish House of Parliament, a squad of constables. But aside from Mrs. Breen's conversation, which hardly helps us to "know Dublin in visual terms," we hear very little.

The same is true of the images in Bloom's daydreams. There are occasional references to songs and a singer's voice, to people talking or shouting, and to a band; but most of the images are visual.

Elsewhere in *Ulysses*, Joyce does undertake some interesting experiments in sound, as Prescott's documentation demonstrates:

Grossbooted draymen rolled barrels dullthudding out of
   Prince's stores and bumped them up on the brewery float
   (115:23/116:23)

(Continued on page 140)

FIGURE 7

Associative Structures: Perception-Triggered Stream of Thought

Proteus

45:13/44:15	shore	feet			darkness
14/	sockets				
15/	room	tower			
16/	barbicans	shafts	light		
17/	feet				
18/	floor	dusk	nightfall	night	
19/	dome	chairs			
45:20/44:21	valise	board	platters		
21/	key	night			
22/	door	tower	bodies		
23/	panthersahib	pointer	answer		
24/	feet	suck	mole	boulders	
25/	soul	form	forms		
26/	midwatches	path	rocks		
45:27/44:28	sable	flood			

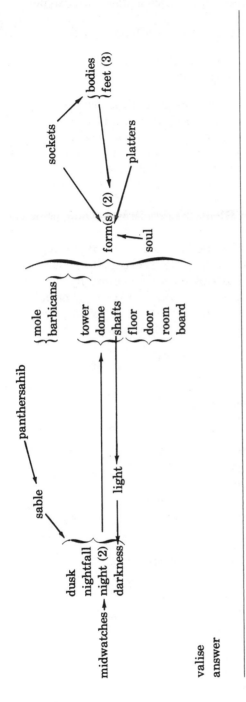

valise
answer

A black crack of noise in the street here, alack, bawled,
  back (388:14/394:31)
Mkgnao! . . . Mrkgnao! . . . Mrkrgnao! (55/55)
Iiiiiichaaaaaaach (175:17/177:39)[12]

The reader can hear the sound of the dullthudding barrels, the
crack of the thunder, the cat's increasing meow, and the
expanding yawn in those onomatopoeic renditions. And then
"wavyavyeavyheavyeavyevyevy" (273:16/277:31) is an auditory
as well as visual analogue to the hair being described.

  In recording "simultaneously, what a man says, sees, thinks,"
Joyce gave us more than strings of words spoken either aloud
or as internal soliloquy. When Bloom passes Brown Thomas in
Grafton Street, we read "Cascades of ribbons. Flimsy China
silks" (165:42/168:18). Those phrases are not internal soliloquy,
but simulations of perceptions. Furthermore, except for the
special instances where Joyce calls attention to sound by
onomatopoeia, the reader reads silently. So that even when a
passage does represent internal soliloquy, Joyce is not
communicating by sound. Except for the unfortunate person who

FIGURE 8
Associative Structures:
Perception-Triggered Stream of Thought
Lestrygonians

165:12/167:28	relief	eyes	note	street
13/	middle	day	shoulders	
14/	bend	M'Coy		
15/	*femme*	Coombe	chummies	
16/	streetwalkers	rest	year	judge
17/	Empire	soda		
18/	Kinsella	theatre		
165:19/167:36	Whitbread	Queen's	Broth	boy
20/	business	face	bonnet	
21/	Maids	School	time	
22/	pantaloons	skirts	Drinkers	
23/	drink	breath		
24/	power	Pat	fun	drunkards
25/	hat	eyes		
165:26/168:1	Beggar	harp		

FIGURE 8—*Continued*

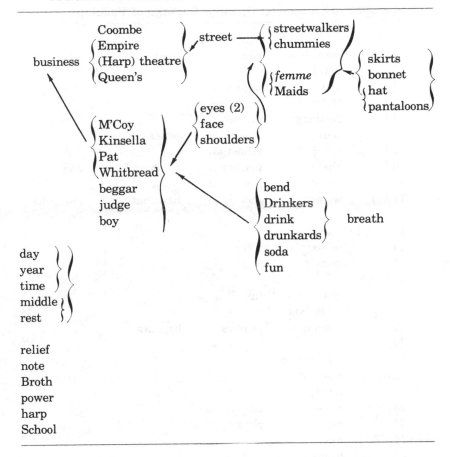

has not learned to read properly, few readers will sound aloud in their minds, for example, "Come out of them, Stephen. Beauty is not there." (40:35/39:35)

When we reach the end of *Ulysses* we know Dublin in visual terms because Joyce presented it visually. Joyce does use aural techniques quite effectively, and as Prescott points out, "Although this kind of experiment is not entirely original, it has seldom if ever been carried out on so extensive a scale."[13] In Joyce the aural does not begin to rival the visual until *Finnegans Wake*, where, as Litz says, Joyce turns "the verbal unit into a polysemantic vehicle capable of producing polyphonic effects."[14] We will examine that shift in a later chapter.

It is interesting to note here that when Joyce discussed the

FIGURE 9
Associative Structures: Opening Passage of Penelope

723:1/738:1				
2/	breakfast	bed	eggs	
3/	hotel			
4/	voice	highness		
5/	faggot	leg		
6/	farthing	masses		
7/	soul	miser	pence	
8/	spirit	ailments		
9/	chat	politics	earthquakes	end
10/	world	fun	world	
11/	women	sort	bathingsuits	lownecks
12/				
723:13/738:13	man			
14/	wonder	faces		
15/	woman	talk		
16/				
17/	dog	fur		
18/	petticoats			
19/	women	waiters	beggars	
20/				
21/	matter			
22/	hospital			
23/	month			
24/	nurse	carpet		
25/	nun	photo		
723:26/738:27	nun			
27/	woman			
28/	bleeds	foot		
29/	circular			
30/	party	Mountain	day	dress
31/	flowers			
32/	bottom	basket		
33/	bedroom	voice		
34/	face			
35/	beard	bed		
36/	father			
37/	toe	razor	corns	
38/	poisoning			
39/	attention	woman		
723:40/738:41	trouble			

FIGURE 9—*Continued*

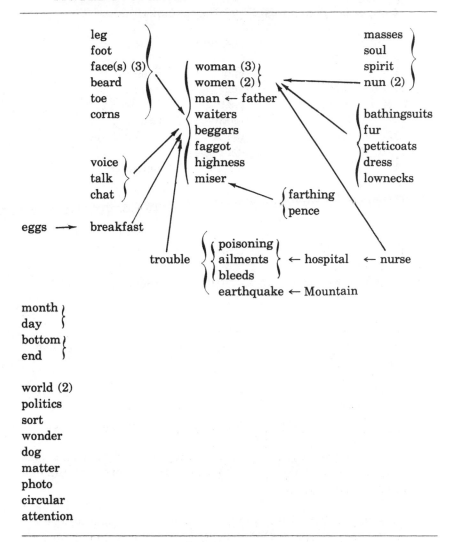

fourth set of associations in his notes from *Exiles* quoted above
(that is, "Snow . . . tears . . .), he organized them into three
categories of sensuality: "visual," "gustatious," and "tactual."[15]
There was only one item in the list with clear aural
associations—"piano." In his analysis, Joyce specifically said,
"She thumped the piano." For some people, there might even
be a second aural association: a roaring sound with "a big fire."

FIGURE 10
Associative Structures: Final Passage of Proteus

51:17/50:28 hilt	ashplant			
18/ evening				
19/ days	end	Tuesday		
20/ day	year	mother		
21/ Tennyson	poet			
22/ hag	teeth	Drumont		
23/ journalist	teeth			
51:24/50:35 shells	dentist			
25/ money	Kinch	superman		
26/				
27/				
28/ handkerchief				
29/				
30/ hand	pockets			
51:31/50:42				
51:32/51:1 snot	nostril	ledge		
33/ rock	rest			
34/				
35/ face	shoulder	rere		
36/ air	spars	threemaster	sails	
37/ crosstrees				
51:38/51:7 ship				

In this instance, at least, Joyce seems not to have been much concerned with or aware of the aural.

Joyce may have been influenced in this matter by Aristotle, who considered sight the most important of the senses,[16] and by Aquinas, who agreed:

> It is clear that [Aristotle] gives two reasons why sight is superior to the other senses in knowing. The first is that it knows in a more perfect way; and this belongs to it because it is the most spiritual of all the senses. . . .
> The other reason . . . is that it gives us more information about the nature of things.[17]

Aristotle and Aquinas do not seem to agree on the next most important sense, however. Aristotle suggests hearing; Aquinas seems to think it is touch.[18]

Another comparison can be made between passages in Proteus

FIGURE 10—*Continued*

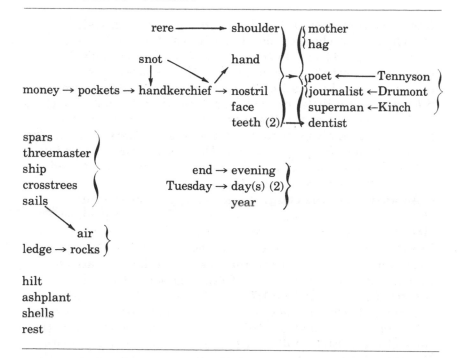

and Lestrygonians. At the beginning of each of these passages a look around starts each character on a stream of thought: Proteus 45:13-27/44:15-28; Lestrygonians 165:12-26/167:28-168:1. (See figures 7 and 8.) Again, unfortunately, there is no comparable passage in Penelope.

Once again the hypothesis holds: the nominal concepts in the passage from Stephen's thoughts are more centrally structured than those in the passage from Bloom's thoughts. A good test for the degree of coherence is to attempt to build a phrase which will comprehend each of the two sets of associations. "Dark architectural form" does rather well for Stephen's. Although Bloom's associations are related, they are too sprawling to be subsumed under or described by any kind of neat statement. And once again the analysis yields more isolates for the passage from Lestrygonians than for the passage from Proteus.

It is more difficult to tell for Molly where particular concerns or interests begin and end. Standard paragraphs, which usually serve as markers for such breaks, are, of course, not available in Penelope. I went, therefore, to the beginning of each of the first three sentences in Penelope and followed each train of thought until it changed significantly: 723:1-40/738:1-41; 729:9-730:14/744:41-745:16; and 738:4-42/753:7-754:3. The analyses support the hypothesis that Molly's associative structures would be noticeably less well organized than would Stephen's and a little less well organized than Bloom's. I include here the analysis of the first passage. (See figure 9.) In the layout of the analysis of that passage, four clusters focus on the largest cluster, the people cluster. However, three clusters focus not on the whole people cluster but on small parts of it; and two clusters and nine words are isolates.

An analysis of the closing passages of each of the three chapters shows no change in the pattern for Lestrygonians (180:26-181:14/183:11-41) or Penelope (767:40-768:18/782:36-783:14). The analysis of the closing passage of Proteus, however, shows an associative pattern that does not echo the pattern demonstrated by the analyses of other passages from that chapter: 51:17-38/50:28-51:7. (See figure 10.) There is much less coherence of nominal concepts and little centrality of structure.

Several of the isolated words could, perhaps, be tied in with some of the clusters: hilt → ashplant → hand; shells → teeth. But that still leaves two words and three clusters isolated. The loosening of the structure would seem to reflect the relaxation of Stephen's thoughts as he concludes "reading the book of himself" (185:8/187:11) and turns to leave.

The associative structures of the nouns Stephen, Bloom, and Molly use do show different patterns. Although it would probably be unwarranted to refer to the characteristic associative pattern of a single character as his cognitive style, such a pattern would certainly seem to be an important aspect of that style.

8
Words

Students of language and of psychology have long agreed that since language is a function (or projection) of personality, one can discover much about a person by examining his language: "There are many indications that language is a vehicle of personality as well as thought, for when the person speaks, he tells us not only about the world but also, through both form and content, about himself."[1] The purpose of this chapter, therefore, is to determine to what extent Joyce differentiated his three main characters by providing their streams of consciousness with different vocabularies. Where these analyses lend themselves to quantitative measurement, such measurement is undertaken. In other instances, a more subjective treatment is employed. These two approaches are not to be considered as opposite or in any sense conflicting, but rather complementary, each approach being used where it is more suitable for bringing into focus the particular aspect of language and thought under scrutiny.

> There is . . . a reasonable argument, reinforced by some empirical evidence, that a quantitative analysis of written expression can discover individuality. It may well be, however, that there are subtle aspects of uniqueness in style which cannot be uncovered by analytical procedures. It is reasonable to expect that the sensitive observer can appreciate relationships and coexistences which escape objective analysis. The brain is a more subtle instrument than the calculating machine.[2]

When quantitative analysis is possible, however, it should be undertaken; for, as I shall show, it can be very revealing. As Osgood explains:

> Any language includes both obligatory and variable features at all levels of analysis, phonemic, morphemic, and syntactical. The

147

study of style concerns the *variable features* of the code. However, the variability need not be completely "free" (i.e., chance, unpredictable); rather, the student of style is interested in the *statistical properties of choices* where there is some degree of freedom in selection. The choices made in speaking and writing can also be characterized as either lexical or structural. Stylistics is generally more concerned with *structural choices* than with lexical choices, that is, in *how* a person talks about something rather than *what* he talks about. Finally, the student of style is usually interested in *deviations from norms* rather than the norms themselves, although the norms have to be determined before deviations from them can be noted and interpreted.[3]

In his study, Osgood defines *style* as "an individual's deviations from norms for the situations in which he is encoding, these deviations being in the statistical properties of those structural features for which there exists some degree of choice in his code."[4]

In this study, we are interested not in deviations from norms, but rather in differences between and among the streams of consciousness of the three main characters: Stephen Dedalus, Leopold Bloom, and Molly Bloom. Many of those differences can be demonstrated by simple (and sometimes tedious) counting. Some readers will be impatient with the lists, tables, and figures in this study. I can only reply that, unfortunately, they are necessary. A critic develops a hypothesis about style or about characterization in a text by careful, sympathetic, and sensitive reading; but he must support that hypothesis by detailed evidence. Too frequently critics settle for the insight or for enthusiasm and neglect the evidence. Joyce scholarship is particularly vulnerable to this charge.[5]

Students of stylistics have much to learn from psychologists,

TABLE 2
Length of Words in Proteus, Lestrygonians,
and Penelope (by Percentage)

	One-Syllable Words	Two-Syllable Words	Three-Syllable Words	Four- and Five-Syllable Words
Stephen	70.80%	21.87%	5.62%	1.72%
Bloom	71.27	21.28	5.71	1.75
Molly	76.50	18.62	3.96	0.87

linguists, psycholinguists, and even, as I shall show, from
psychiatrists. Many of their techniques are applicable to the
analysis of literary texts. We can learn, too, from their respect
for evidence and from how they marshal it. Like them, we must
insist on the presentation of evidence in full detail in support
of hypotheses and generalizations. When it is spread in such
detail, we must pay it the respect of careful examination. Only
then can we judge the evaluations for which they are offered
as support.

A. Length of Words

In our concern here, the analysis and comparison of the
language in Proteus, Lestrygonians, and Penelope, the most
obvious place to begin is with the individual words. An analysis
of the length of words (by syllables) in the sample passages
in the three chapters yields the results shown in table 2. As
might be expected, Molly uses more short words and fewer long
words than do Stephen and Bloom. What might not be expected
is the similarity of length of words for Stephen and Bloom and
the fact that, although the margin is very slight, too slight to
be statistically significant, Bloom seems to use slightly more
words of three, four, and five syllables than Stephen does.[6]

B. Derivation of Words

An analysis of the samples of the three vocabularies for
derivation of words yields somewhat similar results, as shown
in table 3. Here we find that Bloom's vocabulary is slightly

TABLE 3
Derivations of Words in Proteus, Lestrygonians,
and Penelope *(by Percentage)*

	Words Derived from Greek, Latin, and the Romance Languages	Words Derived from the Germanic Languages	Words Not Countable
Stephen	17.10%	76.67%	6.23%
Bloom	19.17	75.81	5.02
Molly	11.10	84.65	4.25

more Latinate than Stephen's, although not enough more to indicate a statistically significant difference. The vocabularies of both Stephen and Bloom, however, have a significantly higher percentage of words derived from Greek, Latin, and the Romance languages than does Molly's.[7]

C. Levels of Abstraction

Thus, in comparison with Bloom's vocabulary, Stephen's does not show the difference that one might expect of a man with a classical education, that is, longer words and a more Latinate vocabulary. Stephen's education does, however, show in other ways. For example, the sample passages in Proteus contain the following highly abstract words and phrases: "Ineluctable modality of the visible" (38:1/37:1), "diaphane" (38:5/37:5), "eternity" (38:21/37:21), "ineluctable modality of the audible" (38:15/37:15), "My soul walks with me, form of forms" (45:24/44:23), "Morose delectation" (48:20/47:27).[8] These are abstractions that one might expect of a student of philosophy. And again as one might expect, the words echo, by derivation, the Greek and Latin sources of much of Stephen's thinking.

The six samples of Bloom's stream of consciousness, however, show few examples of high-level abstractions: "Christianity" (167:6/169:26), "memory" (173:21/175:42), "Kind of a form in his mind's eye" (179:21-22/182:5-6). Bloom's language remains rather close to the world of objects even when he is thinking about matters that invite highly abstract thoughts and language. For example, when his mind turns to man's relationship with God, he thinks: "Birth, hymen, martyr, war, foundation of a building, sacrifice, kidney burntoffering, druid's altars" (149:14/151:14). Except "sacrifice," these words are all relatively low-level abstractions: they stand for objects which can be touched or pointed to (hymen, martyr, foundation, kidney, altar) or for not unusual occurrences whose obvious results can be touched or pointed to (birth, war).

The samples of Molly's stream of consciousness show abstractions which, although they are of a high level, are nevertheless common. Indeed, for a woman of Molly's interest in her particular society (that is, Catholic Dublin), they are clichés: "soul" (732:11/738:7), "pious" (723:12/738:12), [for] form [sake] (732:6/747:8), "Love" (732:11/747:13), "idiotics"

(759:2/773:42), "goodlooking" (759:10/774:7), "flirtyfying" (759:20/774:17).

D. Level of Usage

An examination of the language in the samples for level of usage shows further differences among the characters. We have already noted that Molly's language is simpler than Stephen's and Bloom's. Thus her language is less formal than theirs. A reading of the samples for evidence of slang, dialectal words, and the trite expressions one expects of vulgate speech not only supports this difference, but indicates also a difference between the language of Stephen's stream of consciousness and that of Bloom's.[9] In the six samples in Proteus, I found only these examples of slang, dialect, and trite expressions:

Jesus! (38:16/37:16)
Come out of them, Stephen. (40:35/39:35)
Shoot him to bloody bits (42:42/42:2)
O, that's all right. (43:2,3/42:4,5)
O, that's only all right. (43:4/42:6)
Mind you don't get one bang on the ear. (45:37/44:41)
Buss. (48:12/47:19)
hising up their petticoats (50:26/49:36)

strolling mort (48:6/47:13)
bing awast, to Romeville (48:9/47:16)
wap in rogue's rum lingo (48:12/47:19)
O, my dimber wapping dell. (48:13/47:20)

White thy fambles, red thy gan
And thy quarrons dainty is.
Couch a hogshead with me then.
In the darkmans clip and kiss. (48:16-19/47:23-26)

The second group of words and the quatrain are seventeenth-century cant, according to Richard Head, who wrote *The Canting Academy,* published in London in 1673, "a way of speaking, commonly known by the name of Canting, a speech as confused, as the Professors thereof are disorderly dispos'd; and . . . much . . . in use among some Persons, I mean, the more debauched and looser sort of people."[10] Most of the cant that Stephen uses comes from two verses of a canting song quoted by Head:

The Rogue's delight in praise
of his Stroling Mort

2. White thy fambles, red thy gan,
    And they quarrons dainty is,
Couch a hogshead with me than,
    In the Darkmans clip and kiss.

7. Bing awast to Rome-vile then
    O my dimber wapping Dell,
Wee'l heave a booth and dock agen
    Then trining scape and all is well.

Head translates thus:

2. Thy hand is white and red thy lip,
    Thy dainty body I will clip,
    Let's down to sleep ourselves then lay,
    Hug in the dark and kiss and play.

7. Therefore to *London* let us hie
    O thou my sweet bewitching eye,
    There wee'l rob and kiss pell-mell
    Escaping Tyburn all is well.[11]

Head did not translate exactly. Note the following definitions supplied by Eric Partridge, who identifies all the words below as cant of the sixteenth or seventeenth century:[12]

bing awast—to go[13]
couch a hogshead—to lie down and sleep
darkmans—at night
dell—a young wanton
dimber—pretty, neat
dock—to deflower (a woman); hence to 'have' a woman
famble—hand
gan—mouth
heave a booth—to rob a house
mort—woman, harlot
quarrons—the body
rogue—beggar or vagrant
Romeville—London
rum—excellent; fine, good
strolling mort—a female tramp
wap—to copulate
wapping-dell—a whore

Stephen uses and quotes these cant expressions quite consciously, much the way he would use quotations from literature. He probably came across the canting song in the library. His use of this slang, therefore, is literary.

In the samples from Lestrygonians, however, there is evidence of a mind which slips more easily into the level of language classified as vulgate:

> Some school treat (149:2/151:2)
> Bad for their tummies (149:3/151:3)
> Paying game. (149:20/151:20)
> His wife will put the stopper on that. (149:20/151:19)
> ad [for advertisement] (149:21/151:21)
> rolypoly poured (155:15/157:24)
> helterskelter (161:13/163:16)
> Corny Kelleher he has Harvey Duff in his eye.
>   (161:4/163:17)
> blew the gaff (161:6/163:19)
> Drop him like a hot potato. (161:8/163:22)
> slaveys [maids] (161:9/163:24)
> twig a man (161:10/163:24)
> the next thing on the menu [the next piece of business]
>   (161:11/163:25)
> Chump chop (167:2/169:26)
> booser's (167:2/169:21)
> Bitten off more than he can chew. (167:3/169:22)
> galoptious (167:8/169:26)
> piss (167:14/169:32)
> old chap picking his tootles (167:16/169:34)
> chewing the cud (167:17/169:35)
> Scoffing up stewgravy (167:18/169:36)
> Geese stuffed silly (173:6/175:27)
> a swell hotel (173:8/175:28)
> Tips [gratuities] (173:8/175:29)
> bedad (173:10/175:31)
> making money, hand over fist (173:13/175:34)

Thus Lestrygonians shows more slang, dialectal words and phrases, and trite expressions than does Proteus, and, further, these words and phrases are what one would expect of a member of the lower middle class of early twentieth-century Dublin: they are neither imaginative nor original, and are certainly not in any sense literary.

Penelope evidences even more vulgate:

Doing his highness (723:4/738:4)
he had a great leg of (723:5/738:5)
she never left us a farthing (723:6/738:6)
old chat (723:9/738:9)
gabby talk (723:15/738:16)
he was glad to get shut of her (723:16/738:17)
hes not proud out of nothing (723:20/738:20)
how could he have the face to any woman (731:42/747:1)
it simply it makes you feel like nothing on earth
    (732:14/747:16)
filthy sloppy kitchen (732:19/747:21)
old frostyface Goodwin (732:19/747:21)
boiling old stew (732:21/747:23)
whats this else (741:2/756:5)
so as he see I wasnt without (741:19/756:22)
it came on to get rough the old thing crookeding about
    (749:40/764:39)
its a mercy (750:2/764:43)
black and blue (750:6/765:4)
all the good in the world (750:6/765:4)
chap (750:7/765:5)
that other beauty Burke (750:8/765:6)
on the slip (750:9/765:7)
no love lost (750:11/765:9)
feather all blowy (750:16/765:15)
get my husband again into their clutches (758:42/773:39)
making fun of him then behind his back (759:1/773:40)
his idiotics (759:2/773:42)
teetotum (759:7/774:3)
awfully becoming (759:9/774:6)
Dolly face (759:14/774:11)
childs botty (759:14/774:11)
balmy ballocks (759:15/774:12)
the preserved seats (759:16/774:13)
half screwed (759:17/774:14)
flirtyfying (759:20/774:17)

Here is the language of a mind that reaches usually for the common word, the obvious phrase, and the worn-out image.[14]

E. The Type-Token Ratio

Another measure of difference between language samples is the type-token ratio (TTR), described by John B. Carroll:

> The word-frequency distribution, however it is analyzed, reflects a relationship between the number of types (different words) in a sample and the number of tokens (total words). . . . Sometimes the type-token ratio (the number of different words divided by the number of total words) is used as a measure of the diversity or richness of vocabulary in a sample.[15]

The higher the TTR (that is, the more *different* words per total number of words), the more diverse or the richer the vocabulary.

Before comparing the TTRs for the samples from Proteus, Lestrygonians, and Penelope, I must say a few words about methodology. First, what is a word? Is *Buck Mulligan* one word or two? What of *City Arms*, the hotel? Are *think* and *thinks* to be counted as the same word or different words? And *a* and *an*, *cheek* and *cheeks*? How does one deal with homonyms? There is wide disagreement among people using the type-token ratio.

For several reasons, I have defined a word as a letter or group of letters with a space before and after. The most obvious reason for such a decision is that it is the easiest way to undertake the analysis. There would be little disagreement, for example, with a decision that *you* (s.), *you* (pl.), *your*, and *yours* were all variants of the same word. Thus the type-token ratio of "The aunt thinks you killed your mother" (43:14/42:16) would be considered 5/7 rather than 6/7. But how does one count *yourself* (750:3/765:1): the same type as *you*, which occurs in the same sample; two words, *you* and *self*, neither to be counted as a type if there is an earlier instance of it in the sample; or as a word different from *you* or from *you* and *self* and thus a distinct type? Is *chewchewchew* (167:1/169:19) the same word as *chew*, which occurs in the same sample, or a different word? The fact that there will be disagreement however the decisions are made argues for the choice of the simpler way of tallying.

Furthermore, the numbers involved do not make a major

difference. If one counts the plural of a word as the same word (and thus the same type) as the singular, it would mean an average of one and a half words fewer in each of the six 175-word samples in Proteus, and an average of one word fewer in each of the six 175-word samples in Lestrygonians. In Penelope, only one (the last) of the six 175-word samples had such an instance. Thus, not only are the numbers involved not very large, but even where they differ from one set of sample passages to the next they do not affect the differences in the proportions very much, since all passages are analyzed according to the same criteria.

There are other, perhaps more cogent reasons arguing for the use of the simpler tallying method. TTRs have seldom, if ever, been used in analysis of literature. If they are to be used, they will be much more meaningful if they are tallied according to the same criteria and thus be susceptible of comparison. As I have indicated, if one chooses a set of criteria other than the simple criterion employed in this study, there will be inevitable disagreement. I suspect that that simple criterion will be most acceptable to people using the TTR and thus allow most easily for comparison between studies.

Furthermore, as Frederick Mosteller and David L. Wallace point out, "Distinguishing between words of the same spelling cannot be done . . . yet by a high-speed computer (except in experimental programs)."[16] Word counts like this will surely be undertaken more often by those with such high-speed aids than by others. This again argues for the single, simple criterion.

Finally, the Hanley word count of *Ulysses* uses that simple criterion.[17] Using any other criteria, therefore, would make comparisons with that study impossible.

Type-token ratios must be based on samples of the same size:

> TTR's for samples of different magnitudes are not directly comparable because of the tendency for the TTR to vary inversely with size of sample. . . . TTR's for samples of different magnitude can be made comparable by dividing each sample into like-sized segments of, say, 100 words each, computing the TTR for each segment and then averaging the segmented TTR's for each sample.[18]

Because all of the eighteen samples employed in this study save two had 175 or more words, I used the first 175 words of each.

(For two of the six samples in Lestrygonians which had fewer than 175, I added the necessary words following from the text, eleven in one instance and ten in the other.)

To see how the TTR of each of the three stream-of-consciousness chapters compared with that of the early part of the novel, before the stream-of-consciousness technique was introduced, I also did an analysis of the first 175 words for each of the first three pages of the first chapter, Telemachus.

The results of the analysis are shown in table 4, Type-Token Ratios.

The figures suggest strongly that, according to the measure provided by the TTR at least ("a measure of the diversity or

TABLE 4
Type-Token Ratios

	Type-Token Ratios by Sample						
	1	2	3	4	5	6	Average
Telemachus	66.3	70.3	61.1				65.9
Proteus	61.1	69.1	72.0	70.0	78.3	77.1	71.3
Lestrygonians	70.9	76.0	76.0	78.3	77.1	70.9	74.9
Penelope	65.7	65.1	57.7	69.1	74.3	59.4	65.2

NOTE: The observed significance level for the difference between the TTR for Lestrygonians and that of Penelope is .01 and thus highly significant (standard error 5.3384); and the observed significance level for the difference between the TTR for Lestrygonians and that of Telemachus is .05 and thus significant (standard error 5.3384). The observed significance between Telemachus and Lestrygonians is .05 (standard error 6.5421). The differences between Telemachus and Proteus and Penelope are not statistically significant. The difference between the TTR for Proteus and for Penelope, is significant at the .10 level (standard error 5.3384), generally not considered significant. However, William H. Kruskal says:

> Probably the most common significance levels are .05 and .01. . . . But special circumstances may dictate tighter or looser levels. . . . In exploratory work, it might be quite reasonable to use levels of .10 and .15 in order to increase the power. What is of central importance is to know what one is doing and, in particular, to know the properties of the test that is used ("Test of Significance" [see *Significance*], *International Encyclopedia of the Social Sciences*, ed. David L. Sills, vol. 14 [N.Y.: Macmillan Co. and Free Press, 1968], p. 246).

Given the similarity of the figures for Proteus and Lestrygonians and of those for Telemachus and Penelope and the stated significance levels, we may speak of the difference between the two sets with some confidence.

richness of vocabulary," as Carroll characterized it), Penelope is more closely related to Telemachus than it is to Proteus or Lestrygonians. Telemachus is not written in the stream-of-consciousness technique. Certainly the first 175 words of each of the first three pages of *Ulysses* do not contain any stream-of-consciousness passages.

We also find in these figures a suggestion that Bloom's language is more diversified than Stephen's: the TTR for Lestrygonians is slightly higher than that for Proteus. That difference is not statistically significant; but as slight as it is, it is not one that we would expect.

F. Content Words and Function Words

Linguists also compare language samples by examining them for relative proportions of content and function words. Gustav Herdan proposes that "the simplest, and the crudest, way in which to assess the grammar load of a particular language would be to count in a given sample of linguistic utterance (be it spoken or written language) the number of grammatical forms, as far as they are words, and express that number as a percentage of all words."[19] He lists as "grammatical forms" pronouns, prepositions, conjunctions, auxiliary verbs, and sentence types. Since he characterizes the last class as negligible, I shall disregard them. To Herdan's list, however, we must obviously add articles: as noun determiners they are clearly grammatical forms. Pronouns, prepositions, conjunctions, auxiliary verbs, and articles, then, carry more grammatical meaning than lexical meaning. Furthermore, nouns, verbs, adjectives, and adverbs carry a heavier load of lexical meaning than do the grammatical forms. Linguists sometimes, therefore, call them "content words" and refer to Herdan's grammar forms as "function words."[20]

An interesting variation of the analysis that Herdan suggests would be to compare the proportion of content words in each of the three sets of samples. In undertaking this comparison, in order to see how the proportion of content words in each of the three stream-of-consciousness chapters compared with that of the early part of the novel, before the stream-of-consciousness technique was introduced, I also analyzed the first three pages of Telemachus. The results of the analysis appear in table 5.

TABLE 5
Percentage of Content Words

| | *Percentage of Content Words to Total by Sample* | | | | | | |
	1	2	3	4	5	6	*Average*
Telemachus	62.8%	59.2%	55.0%				59.0%
Proteus	51.6	57.7	62.3	57.6%	63.4%	68.0%	60.1
Lestrygonians	67.7	63.3	60.7	64.1	63.6	57.9	62.9
Penelope	53.0	53.7	48.8	55.6	56.9	50.7	53.1

Clearly the proportion of content words in the sample from Penelope is much lower than the proportion of content words in the samples from the other chapters.[21] Penelope—and thus Molly's interior monologue—can therefore be said to communicate less lexical meaning per given number of words than do Proteus (Stephen), Lestrygonians (Bloom), and Telemachus (the omniscient author).

And once again, although the difference is not statistically significant, Lestrygonians shows a slightly higher percentage of content words than Proteus. Again the difference is in a direction we would not have expected.

G. Word Agglutinations

William A. Evans has called attention to word agglutinations in *Ulysses*:

> *Ulysses* contains 260,430 words, and of these 29,899 are different words. Significantly, more than seven percent (more precisely, 2,279) of these different words are agglutinations. Occasionally these agglutinations are portmanteau creations in the manner of Lewis Carroll, but in the main they are not merely the arbitrary splicing of words (as in *slithy*, produced from *slimy* and *lithe*). Rather, the agglutinations in *Ulysses* are the weldings of two or more single words to produce units with special meanings (for example, *gigglegold*).[22]

The agglutinations culled from the eighteen sample passages are found in table 6.

TABLE 6
Agglutinations by Sample

1	2	3	4	5	6
			Proteus		
bluesilver	bigdrumming	creepystools	bladderwrack	creamfruit	fanshoals
seaspawn	hundredheaded	loudlatinlaughing	panthersahib	shefiends	foampool
seawrack		pintpots	stoneheaps	shellgrit	
snotgreen				turnedup	
				windraw	
			Lestrygonians		
burntoffering	heartscalded	backdoor	chewchewchew	halfnaked	
sugarsticky	newbaked	helterskelter*	halfmasticated	whitehatted	
	noonreek	hotblooded	schoolpoem		
	womaneyes	squarepushing	stewgravy		
			spaton		
			Penelope		
bathingsuits			longnosed	barreltone	deepdown
lownecks				goodfornothing	figtrees
				goodlooking	rosegardens
				wellwhipped	wineshops

*Contemporary dictionaries generally give "helter-skelter" as hyphenated.

There are interesting—and typical—differences to be observed. First, the analysis of Proteus shows agglutinations in each of the six samples, of Lestrygonians in only five of the six samples, and in Penelope in only four of the six samples. In addition, the totals and the relation of those totals to the total number of words in each of the six subsets of three samples differs:

Proteus: 19 agglutinations out of a total of 1,208 words—that is, one agglutination for every 64 words

Lestrygonians: 17 agglutinations out of a total of 1,201 words—that is, one agglutination for every 71 words

Penelope: 11 agglutinations out of a total of 1,681 words—that is, one agglutination for every 153 words

Furthermore, there is a difference in the quality of the agglutinations. William Evans points out that the noun-noun combinations usually tend to be the most poetic and the most significant: "The noun-noun combinations are largely metaphoric and image-producing; these qualities frequently lead by association to endless thematic clusterings of the images."[23] Of the agglutinations in Proteus, 10 of the 19 (more than half) are noun-noun: seaspawn, seawrack, pintpots, bladderwrack, panthersahib, stoneheaps, creamfruit, shellgrit, fanshoals, and foampool. In Lestrygonians, 4 of the 17 are noun-noun: noonreek, womaneyes, schoolpoem, and stewgravy; and in Penelope, 4 of the 11: barreltone, figtrees, rosegardens, wineshops.

Finally, most of the agglutinations from the Proteus samples are unusual combinations of words, as are some of the agglutionation of the Lestrygonians samples; but only one of the agglutinations in the Penelope samples is an unusual combination (barreltone). Similarly, of the three three-word agglutinations, the one from Proteus (loudlatinlaughing) and the one from Lestrygonians (chewchewchew) are creative—and even poetic—combinations; however, the one from Penelope (goodfornothing) is just a standard phrase with the words run together.

9

Expressive Behavior

In recent years, psychiatrists have been examining more complex language patterns for revelations of personality. Thus Maria Lorenz writes:

> Expressive behavior is broadly defined as a reflection of the structure of personality in its relatively stable traits and dispositions, insofar as these are shown by external behavior such as movement. Certain aspects of movement have, in addition to an adaptive and purposeful function, the function of expressing characteristics of the agent. . . . Habitual and unself-conscious activity, such as that exhibited in gait, posture, handwritings, speech, and facial expression, lends itself to this approach. . . . The expressive component of such activities is manifested in the spontaneous, unself-conscious tendency of the person to organize and integrate even his purposeful behavior along lines determined by his basic psychological nature. Language behavior, which has communication as its conscious purpose, also includes these components of spontaneity and unconsciously determined organization and integration.[1]

Psychiatrists doing research on this matter agree that "while to a great extent man's pattern of speech is determined by grammar and rhetoric of the language he speaks, it is reasonable to assume that within this framework the individual's choice of words, themes, and style of speech may reveal something of his personality dynamics and his current emotional state." Some of them point out that "indeed, psychiatrists make this assumption daily in their interpretation of what the patient is saying in therapeutic sessions, but the cues he uses are for the most part subjective and unsystemized."[2]

Laymen make such an assumption, too, of course, and act on it—sometimes consciously and sometimes unconsciously. So, of course, do readers and literary critics—and authors. Joyce, for example, made much of Molly's repetition of "yes."[3] So does Tindall.[4]

Thus Louis Gottschalk, Goldine Gleser, and Gove Hambidge, Jr., searched for the tested "content and form variables in speech that may be particularly relevant to personality adjustment." Among the categories which they found significant were:

1. "words indicating a sense of belonging to a group (first person plural pronouns, such as 'we' and 'us')"
2. "words referring to the self"
3. "words indicating negation"[5]

Albert Gilman and Roger Brown have undertaken somewhat similar analyses of belles lettres. Pairing passages by Thoreau and Emerson, they determined, among other things, that

1. "of the 25 pairs of passages usable for pronoun analysis [I, me, my], Thoreau exceeded Emerson 19 times and Emerson exceeded Thoreau 6 times."
2. "in the 24 pairs Thoreau had the greater proportion of negatives, whereas Emerson had the greater proportion in only 8 pairs."

Thoreau also seems to have led Emerson in the "conjunction of a first-personal singular pronoun and a negative. There were 16 untied cases and Thoreau led Emerson in 14 of them."[6]

Such analyses, then, can be used to distinguish between personality types and between authors. Will they distinguish among Stephen, Bloom, and Molly? Analysis of the eighteen samples, six each for Proteus, Lestrygonians, and Penelope, shows some interesting differences.

There are differences, for example, in references to self. Stephen and Bloom refer to themselves in two ways:

1. The way people generally refer to themselves, by pronouns of the first person—
   "*My* ash sword hangs at my side." (38:18/37:18)
   "Houses of decay, *mine,* his and all." (40:33/39:33)
   "Heart trouble, *I* believe." (155:1/157:8)
2. As if they were talking about or to someone else, by pronouns of the second person, by direct address, and by name—

"*You* are walking through it howsomever." (38:12/37:12)
"*Go* easy." (38:7/37:7)
"Come out of them, *Stephen*." (40:34/39:35)
"*Look* at all the things they can learn to do."
(179:7/181:33)

References to self, therefore, were tabulated under those two categories. (See table 7.)

The tabulations suggest some interesting differences, primarily of Molly's overwhelming egocentricity, which shows up in several ways. She refers to herself almost twice as often per

TABLE 7
References to Self

Sample	Proteus			Lestrygonians			Penelope		
	First Person Singular Pronoun	*Second Person or Own Name*	*Total*	*First Person Singular Pronoun*	*Second Person or Own Name*	*Total*	*First Person Singular Pronoun*	*Second Person or Own Name*	*Total*
1	9	8	17	1	0	1	8	0	8
2	1	5	6	1	0	1	16	0	16
3	2	6	8	0	0	0	27	0	27
4	8	4	12	1	1	2	13	0	13
5	0	0	0	7	0	7	5	0	5
6	0	0	0	1	1	2	17	0	17
Totals	20	23	43	11	2	13	86	0	86

NOTE: The analyses in this table did not lend themselves to tests for statistical significance. If anyone is concerned that the differences shown by the samples do not adequately reflect differences in the three chapters, he should analyze an equal number of passages chosen by another sampling method.

page as does Stephen and more than six times as often as does
Bloom; furthermore, she refers to herself regularly. In table 7,
two of Stephen's sample passages show no references to self;
and one of Bloom's shows no references to self and two others
show only a single self-reference; but all of Molly's show
self-references. Five of the six sample passages from Molly's
soliloquy show more self-references than the highest number of
self-references in any single sample passage from Bloom's
stream of consciousness.

Another interesting difference is that Stephen makes more
than half of his self-references in the six sample passages *to*
or *at* himself rather than *about* himself. Such reference to self
by second person or by name suggests a self-consciousness and
an objectivity about oneself, an ability to stand aside and look
at oneself that is necessary for self-criticism. These analyses
suggest that Stephen clearly has that capacity, that Bloom has
it in modest amounts, but that Molly has little of it.

Another difference shows up in references to self and others
in the use of the group pronouns of the first person plural:
we, us, our. Table 8 offers dramatic support for the often-made
statement of Stephen's aloofness and even alienation: not a
single use of a pronoun which suggests membership in any
group. Although it is not as complete as Stephen's, Bloom's
aloofness or alienation, also frequently referred to, is likewise
evident.

I would also argue that the analysis of references to self and

TABLE 8
References to Self and Others

Sample	Proteus	Lestrygonians	Penelope
1	0	1	4
2	0	1	1
3	0	0	5
4	0	2	2
5	0	0	0
6	0	3	1
Totals	0	7	13

others in Penelope shows that Molly sees herself as a relative loner, too. In the total of 1,681 words in six passages of a monologue devoted largely to reminiscences of the past, with some thoughts of the future, thirteen references to group membership do not seem to be very many—particularly when held alongside eighty-six references to self alone.

Still another difference shows up in the use of negatives: no, not, nothing, never, and so on. These figures are given in table 9. Molly's great affirmation shows here—in the last sample,

TABLE 9
Negatives

Sample	Proteus	Lestrygonians	Penelope
1	3	1	9
2	2	1	9
3	2	1	4
4	2	3	7
5	0	2	6
6	1	5	0
Totals	10	13	35

which is the last half page of her soliloquy. But what also shows is how negative she is compared with Stephen and Bloom: four of the samples from Penelope contain more negatives than any of the twelve samples from Proteus and Lestrygonians; indeed, each of the first two samples from Penelope contains almost as many as do all of the samples from Proteus. Clearly that sixth sample seems atypical; and random checking through the chapter proves that it is.

In their analysis of sex differences in verbal behavior related to adjustive mechanisms, H. Aronson and Walter Weintraub used negation as one of their categories:

> Negation.—All negatives, e.g., "not," "no," "never," etc., are scored. We believe this category reflects a tendency to negate and deny.[7]

They expected no significant difference in negation between men and women—and found none; but in other studies, negation did discriminate between other groups.[8] In analyzing all the evidence later, we shall return to this matter, since it promises to shed some light on a continuing disagreement in *Ulysses* scholarship.

Aronson and Weintraub used a total of twelve categories in their extensive studies of verbal behavior as a manifestation of idiosyncratic psychological defense mechanisms. I have already referred to their concept of negation. Other of their discriminators are relevant to this study:

> *Qualification.*—Three principal maneuvers are scored: (1) Uncertainty, e.g., "I *suppose* he is all right." (2) Modifiers which detract force without adding information, e.g., "It's *more or less* a nice day." (3) The suggestion that a word or phrase is used loosely, e.g., "I did *what you might call* a loop-de-loop." The scoring for this category was chosen to reflect what psychoanalysts consider "undoing before the fact."

> *Retraction.*—A "retractor" is a word, phrase, or clause, which takes back what has been thought or stated. The statement "I believe in freedom of the press. Still, there are some books which must be kept from the public" is an example of retracting. Also, words such as "although," "but," "on the other hand," "except," etc., are so frequently used to refute other material that they are scored automatically. The maneuver focused upon here is similar to what analysts call "undoing."[9]

The pattern of instances of qualification and retraction (that is, of "undoings") is much like the pattern of instances of negation (see table 10).

There is almost no evidence of "undoing" for Stephen. Like his feet, Stephen's ideas in Proteus may simply stand, coast warily, or march in sudden proud rhythm; but they seldom reverse themselves. Bloom's mind shows a few more "undoings" than Stephen's; but not with any regularity. In addition to being regularly negative, however, Molly's ideas are much more frequently—and more regularly—"undoings"; except, once again for the last half page of her soliloquy.

Another of the Aronson and Weintraub categories is:

> *Explaining.*—This category is scored when the speaker uses a word, phrase or clause which (1) states a causal relationship, e.g., "because," "due to," "as a result of," etc., (2) gives a reason for an action, thought or attitude, e.g., "The purpose of the trip is

TABLE 10
Instances of Qualification and Retraction

Sample		Proteus	Lestrygonians	Penelope
1	Qual.			I suppose (723:12/738:12) but (723:16/738:17) I suppose (723:16/738:17) still (723:18/738:19) but (723:20/738:21)
	Retr.	But (38:5/37:5)		
2	Qual.		I believe (155:1/157:8)	
	Retr.			but (732:15/747:16)
3	Qual.			
	Retr.			but (741:14/756:17)
4	Qual.			I suppose (750:13/765:21)
	Retr.			
5	Qual.		I expect (173:11/175:31)	in a way (759:5/774:2)
	Retr.			all the same (759:5/774:2) unless (759:6/774:3) though (759:10/774:6)
6	Qual.		perhaps (179:1/181:27) kind of sense of volume (179:1/181:27)	
	Retr.		of course (179:10/181:36)	
Totals		1	5	12

to . . . ," or (3) contains a participial phrase which provides justification, e.g., "Having been there, I can speak with authority." We believe this category is a measure of the use of rationalization.[10]

The following are all the explanatory statements from the eighteen samples. Only the ones marked with an asterisk, however, qualify as "explaining" in the sense that Aronson and Weintraub use the term (that is, causal or explanatory statements about an action of the speaker or someone with whom the speaker is involved).

Proteus
How? By knocking his sconce against them, sure. (38:6/37:6)
If you can put your five fingers through it, it is a gate, if not a door. (38:9/37:9)
that is the ineluctable modality of the audible. (38:15/37:15)
*That's why she won't. (43:14/42:16)
*And I'll tell you the reason why. (43:17/42:19)

Lestrygonians
Like that Peter (161:5/163:19)
Sun's heat it is. (173:20/175:41)
See things in their foreheads, perhaps. (178:42/181:26)
Kind of sense of volume. (179:1/181:27)
*Why we think (179:9/181:35)

Penelope
*because he never did a thing like that before (723:1/738:1)
*because no man would look at her twice (723:13/738:13)
*after his company manners (731:42/747:2)
*for form sake (732:6/747:8)
*because mine was the 8th (732:12/747:14)
*it wouldn't have been nice on account of her (741:14/756:14)
*so as he see I wasnt without (741:19/756:22)
*Molly bawn she gave me . . . on account of the name (741:20/756:23)
*because the smell of the sea excited me (750:18/765:16)
*because he has sense enough (759:2/773:42)
*I thought well as well him as another (768:13/783:9)

Most of the explanations found in the samples from Proteus and Lestrygonians are explanations of natural phenomena. Few of them can be categorized as "explaining" as Aronson and Weintraub define that concept. Most—and I would say all—of Molly's eleven explanations can be so categorized, however. Not only are there many more of such occurrences in the samples from Penelope than in those from Proteus and Lestrygonians; but whereas they occur only in one sample passage from Proteus and in four from Lestrygonians, they occur in all of the sample passages from Penelope. Since Aronson and Weintraub employ this category as "a measure of the use of rationalization," we can say that Molly rationalizes much more than do Stephen and Bloom.

Still another Aronson and Weintraub discriminator is the frequency of expression of personal feelings:

> *Feelings*.—All clauses are scored in which the speaker describes himself as experiencing or having experienced: attraction-aversion, like-dislike, satisfaction-dissatisfaction, pleasure-displeasure, hope, fear, enjoyment, shock, etc. We have no analytic name for this maneuver. It appeared, clinically, that some people avoid facts by concentrating on emotion while others reverse this process. The category was included in the hope that either extreme would be reflected.[11]

In their manual they elaborated on the meaning of this category in describing how to score "feelings": "Score only phrases in which the speaker, using the first person, singular or plural, describes a feeling as being his own. The emphasis must be placed upon the feeling tone rather than the aspect which gave rise to the feeling."[12]

There are no "feelings" to be scored in the six sample passages from Proteus. Indeed, in all twenty pages of the chapter there are at the most four instances scorable by the Aronson and Weintraub criteria:

I am lonely here (49:37/49:4)
foot I dislove (50:11/49:20)

For that are you pining (46:21/45:24)
you were delighted (50:11/49:20)

In the last two instances, Stephen is speaking to himself and thus they do not quite fit the category. The second instance is a curiously self-conscious statement of dislike by indirection. I have not counted a possible fifth instance which occurs while Stephen works on his poem, since it seems to be a general philosophic—or poetic—statement rather than one Stephen is making about himself: "Our souls, shamewounded by our sins, cling to us yet more" (49:23/48:32).

At times there seems in Proteus to be a deliberate attempt to deny statements of feeling: "The dog's bark ran towards him, stopped, ran back. Dog of my enemy. I just simply stood pale, silent, bayed about. *Terribilia meditans.* For that are you pining, the bark of their applause?" (46:18/45:20). Not only is there not an expression of fear. There seems to be a disdain for even recognizing such an emotion—or any emotion.

In the six sample passages from Lestrygonians, there is only a single scorable instance of feeling: "we are surprised they have any brains" (179:8/181:34). The entire chapter, however, provides considerably more instances:

> Happy. Happier then. (153:30/155:35)
> Happy. Happy. (154:23/156:30)
> I'm sorry to hear that. (156:40/159:9)
> hate this hour. Feel sad as if I had been eaten and spewed.
>   (162:25/164:39)
> I detest that. (163:35/166:7)
> I was happier then. (165:27/168:2)
> I hate dirty eaters. (167:42/170:18)

Bloom also experiences other feelings: sympathy and compassion for Stephen's poorly clothed and underfed sister (150:7/152:8), for hungry birds (151:3/163:5), for Mrs. Purefoy in labor (159:10/161:22), for animals waiting to be slaughtered (168:31/171:8), for the blind stripling (178/180), and for the women and children who were burned and drowned in a maritime tragedy (180:1/182:28); unhappiness and embarrassment over Boylan and his liaison with Molly (151:31/153:39; 165:9/167:25; 170:22/172:42; 177:37/180:18; 180-81/183); sexual excitement (166:18-32/168:36-169:8; 173:21-41/175:42-176:21) and deflation (173:42/176:22). One of those last passages, 173:21-41/175:42-176:21, is an exact parallel of Molly's final paean of affirmation, to which the critics so frequently refer.

In Penelope, scorable instances of feeling are plentiful in the six samples alone. Whereas the samples from Proteus contain no instances and the samples from Lestrygonians only one, the samples from Penelope contain:

> I hope Ill never be like her (723:13/738:14)
> I like that in him (723:18/738:19)
> I wasnt [offended] (732:2/747:4)
> I hate an unlucky man (732:5/747:6)
> I liked the way he made love then (732:11/747:12)
> I hope hell come on Monday (732:16/747:17)
> I hate people who come at all hours (732:17/747:18)
> I felt something go through me like all needles
> (741:9/756:13)
> I dont like books with a Molly in them (741:21/756:24)
> how annoying and provoking (750:17/765:15)
> the smell of the sea excited me (750:18/765:16)
> Im sorry in a way for him (759:5/774:2)

Almost half of these are statements of dislike ("I hate," "how annoying"), some of which are expressed negatively ("I hope Ill never," "I dont like"). The following five examples, two of which are either negative or expressed in negative terms, probably should be added to the list:

> I couldnt describe it it simply makes you feel like nothing
> on earth (732:14/747:15)
> We were fighting in the morning with the pillow what fun
> (741:6/756:8)
> I had a splendid skin from the sun and the excitement
> (741:12/756:15)
> there was no love lost between us thats 1 consolation
> (750:10/765:9)

And, of course, the frequently quoted last few lines of the sixth sample (the end of Penelope, which was discussed above) are memories of a scene of intense feeling:

> and then I asked him with my eyes to ask again yes and then
> he asked me would I say yes to say yes my mountain flower
> and first I put my arms around him yes and drew him down
> to me so he could feel my breasts all perfume yes and his heart
> was going like mad and yes I said yes I will Yes (768/783)

For Molly, there is no need to score instances through the entire chapter. The six sample passages provide evidence enough.

The last of the Aronson and Weintraub discriminators is also useful in the comparison of the three streams of consciousness:

> *Evaluation.*—The expression of value judgments is scored in the following areas: goodness-badness (e.g., "He's an *excellent* student."), useful-useless, right-wrong, propriety-impropriety, and pleasant-unpleasant. This category was added as an indicator of the defensive use of opinions and preoccupation with what is proper and right. A high score may reflect a strong or precociously developed superego.[13]

Again, a note from the scoring manual is especially helpful in understanding the category: "In scoring this category, remember that it is not the speaker's expression of feelings which is being scored but his indication that there exists a universal standard by which anyone would arrive at a similar judgment."[14] Here are Stephen's evaluations from the six sample passages from Proteus:

> I am getting on nicely in the dark. (38:17/37:17)
> His tuneful whistle sounds again, finely shaded
>   (40:30/39:30)
> You were going to do wonders, what? (43:5/42:7)
> lascivious men (50:33/50:2)

Here, for separate comparison, are the evaluations that the Aronson and Weintraub category specifically excludes: the speaker's expressions of feelings:

> Houses of decay, mine, his and all. (40:33/39:33)
> the stagnant bay of Marsh's library (40:36/39:36)
> The hundredheaded rabble of the cathedral close.
>   (40:38//39:37)
> The oval equine faces. . . . Lantern jaws. (40:40/39:41)
> The slimy pier at Newhaven. (43:9/42:11)
> Rich booty you brought back (43:10/42:12)
> A shut door of a silent tower entombing their blind bodies,
>   the panthersahib and his pointer. (45:21/44:24)

They are not as direct expressions of feeling, however, as are the comparable collection from Lestrygonians and Penelope.

Bloom's stream of consciousness in the sample passages from Lestrygonians contains the following Aronson-Weintraub type of evaluation:

> Bad for their tummies. (149:3/151:3)
> [He died quite suddenly,] poor fellow. (155:1/157:8)
> Want to make good pastry (155:18/157:25)
> Pleasure or pain is it? (155:21/157:29)
> a swell hotel (173:8/175:28)
> ignorant as a kish of brogues (173:16/175:37)
> Queer idea of Dublin he must have (179:2/181:28)

The passages also contain some instances of evaluation which express largely Bloom's personal feelings:

> Paying game. (149:20/151:20)
> Dosing it with Edward's dessicated soup. (173:6/175:26)
> Bloodless pious face (179:4/181:30)

The six samples from Penelope contain many instances of both types of evaluation. The type positing universal standards:

> she had too much old chat in her (723:8/738:9)
> let us have a bit of fun first (723:10/738:10)[15]
> God help the world if all the women were her sort (723:10/738:10)
> no man would look at her twice (723:13/738:13)
> she was a welleducated woman certainly (723:13/738:13)
> its much better for them to go into the hospital (723:21/738:22)
> making it so awkward (732:1/747:3)
> embrace well like Gardner (732:15/747:17)
> It wouldnt have been nice (741:14/756:17)
> my new white shoes all ruined with saltwater (750:15/765:13)
> he has sense enough not to squander every penny piece he earns (759:2/773:42)
> theyre awfully becoming (759:9/774:6)
> if youre goodlooking (759:10/774:7)
> he was always turning up half screwed (759:17/774:14)
> he had a delicious glorious voice (759:21/774:18)
> those handsome Moors (767:41/782:38)
> the glorious sunsets (768:7/783:3)

And the type expressing largely Molly's personal feelings:

> that old faggot Mrs Riordan (723:5/738:5)
> greatest miser ever was (723:7/738:7)

I hope Ill never be like her (723:13/738:14)
her gabby talk (723:15/738:16)
he was glad to get shut of her (723:16/738:17)
hes not proud out of nothing (723:20/738:20)
he had a few brains not like that other fool Henny Doyle
   (732:3/747:5)
the filthy sloppy kitchen (732:19/747:21)
old frostyface Goodwin (732:19/747:21)
the one from Flanders a whore (741:22/756:25)
you vomit a better face (750:10/765:8)
their clutches (758:42/773:40)
his idiotics (759:2/773:42)
goodfornothings (759:4/774:1)
didnt he look a balmy ballocks (759:14/774:11)
that must have been a spectacle (759:15/774:12)

Thus Stephen's stream of consciousness shows few instances
of evaluations which suggest universal standards, Bloom's shows
a few more, and Molly's shows many more.

The instances of evaluations which reflect personal feeling
rather than universal standards reinforce the results of the
analysis of the Aronson-Weintraub category of feelings: Stephen
shows little direct evidence of feeling. Every search for evidence
of emotion or feeling in Stephen's stream of consciousness in
Proteus seems to yield the same result: he is sometimes scornful,
of himself as well as others, but typically coldly scornful; and
beyond that, austerity. Bloom is clearly more relaxed about his
feelings—or more subject to feelings, depending upon one's point
of view; even though this particular subcategory does not show
many instances of expression of feeling. "Bloodless pious face,"
however, is more openly a statement of feeling than "oval
equine faces" or "the panthersahib and his pointer." In
comparison with Stephen and Bloom, of course, Molly wallows
in feelings; and in expressing them she almost never has a good
word to say for anyone or anything—except in the last half
page of her soliloquy.

10
Poetic Devices

Throughout *Ulysses* Stephen is presented variously as a real or would-be poet, novelist, and literary critic. Mulligan refers to him as "the bard" (6:39/5:1; 8:20/6:26; 211:40/214:27), as does Lenehan (258:27/262:31), Molly calls him a poet (761:41/776:36), and he actually starts to write a poem on Sandymount strand (48-49/47-49);[1] he reminds himself of books he was going to write (41:30/40:31); and he propounds at some length his own theory of *Hamlet* (185-211/187-213), in the hope, perhaps, that John Eglinton will commission him to do a piece for *Dana*. Many of the earlier critics, Levin, for example, call Stephen an artist.[2] Kain refers to him as a man "possessing a literary gift which is doomed to neglect."[3] Tindall says: "During Stephen's walk along the beach, his monologue is that of a poet and philosopher. Imagination, intellect, and memory combine with the senses to create brightness and innocence."[4] Later critics, however, tend to write of "Stephen's *potentialities* as an artist," and his poem is considered by many as being "less than great art."[5]

We have seen, and will see again, that Stephen's stream of consciousness presents to the reader a man interested in philosophy. Does it also present a poet?

A. Sound Correspondences

1. *Proteus*

Proteus does actually reveal considerable use of poetic devices: rhyme, assonance, alliteration, coliteration; rhythm; and imagery. The following list gives all the examples of sound correspondences found in the six samples of Stephen's stream of consciousness:

38:3/37:3	seaspawn and seawrack '--'-	(s, w)†
38:9/37:9	five fingers "-	(f)
38:11/37:11	crush crackling wrack and shells "-'-'	(k, r, l) * (*)
38:16/37:16	beetles o'er his base '-'-'	(b) *
38:20/37:20	made by the mallet of *Los Demiurgos* '--'--'-'-	(m, l) * (*)
40:34/39:34	an uncle a judge and an uncle a general -'--'--'--'--	(uncle, j-g) * (*)
40:37/39:37	hundredheaded '-'-	(h, d) * (*)
40:38/39:38	cathedral close -'-'	(k, l) * (*)
40:39/39:39	the wood of madness, his mane foaming in the moon -'-'- -"---'	(m, n) * (*)
40:40/39:40	Houyhnhnm, horsenostrilled '-- '--	(h, n) * (*)
42:42/42:2	bloody bits '-'	(b) *
43:1/42:3	brass buttons "-	(b, s)
43:2/42:4	khrrrrklak in place clack back "-'"	(k, l, ack)
43:7/42:9	loudlatinlaughing "-'-	(l) *
45:21/44:24	A shut door of a silent tower -"--'-'-	(sh-s, d-t)

---

†The letters within the parentheses represent the sound correspondences in
the phrase quoted. An asterisk—*—indicates a phrase all of which or a
significant portion of which has a rhythmic pattern. An asterisk within
parentheses—(*)—indicates a phrase which has both more than one sound
correspondence and a rhythmic pattern. A fuller discussion of these matters
follows the lists.

45:21/44:24	blind bodies ''_	(b, d)
45:22/44:25	the panthersahib and his pointer _'_'_'_'_	(panther- pointer) * (*)
45:24/44:27	form of forms '_'	(form) *
45:25/44:28	moon's midwatches '_'_	(m, s) * (*)
45:26/44:28	sable silvered '_'_	(s, l) * (*)
45:27/44:30	flood is following '_'__	(f, l)
45:29/44:31	the sedge and eely oarweeds _'_'_'_	(ee, s, d) * (*)
45:29/44:32	sat on a stool '__'	(s, t)
45:32/44:35	sunk in sand '_'	(s, n) * (*)
45:35/44:38	a warren of weasel rats _'__'_'	(w, r)
45:36/44:39	Sands and stones '_'	(s, n) * (*)
45:38/44:41	bloody well boulders '_''_	(b, l, d)
45:39/45:1	bones for my steppingstones '__'_'	(ones, st)
45:39/45:1	feefawfum '''	(f) * (*)
45:41/45:3	the sweep of sand _'_'	(s) *
47:42/47:7	smiled: creamfruit smell ''_'	(sm, l)
48:4/47:11	turnedup trousers '_'_	(t, r) * (*)
48:4/47:11	slapped the clammy sand '_'_'	(s, a, l) * (*)
48:6/47:13	spoils slung ''	(s, l) * (*)

48:8/47:15	Behind her lord his helpmate _'_'_'_	(h, r, l) * (*)
48:14/47:21	rancid rags '_'	(r, s) * (*)
48:21/47:29	rode and not rutted '__'_	(r, t)
50:22/49:31	In cups of rocks it slops: flop, slop, slap _'_'_' '''	(s, op, p, l) * (*)
50:23/49:32	bounded in barrels '__'_	(b)
50:23/49:32	spent, its speech ceases '_''_	(sp, ea, s)

50:23/49:32	It flows purling, widely
	    flowing, floating foampool,
	    flower unfurling
	_''_'_'_'_'_''_'_
		(fl, url, f,
		ow-oa)
		* (*)

50:25/49:35	writhing weeds '_'	(w) *
50:25/49:35	lift languidly ''__	(l)
50:27/49:37	whispering water swaying '__'_'_	(w, s) * (*)
50:28/49:38	lifted, flooded, and let fall '_'___'	(f, l, t-d) * (*)
50:32/49:42	forth flowing ''_	(f)
50:33/50:1	loom of the moon '__'	(oo)
50:36/50:4	five fathoms ''_	(f)
50:36/50:4	full fathom five _'_'	(f) *
50:37/50:5	found drowned ''	(ou-ow, d) * (*)
50:38/50:6	fanshoals of fishes '__'_	(f, sh)
50:38/50:6	silly shells '_'	(s, l) * (*)
50:40/50:8	a pace a pace a porpoise _'_'_'_	(a, p) * (*)

These should be compared with the following, all the sound
correspondences found in the same number of samples from
Bloom's stream of consciousness and from Molly's.

2. Lestrygonians

149:1/151:1	sugarsticky ′-′-	(s) *	
149:2/151:2	shovelling scoopfuls ′--′-	(s, l)	
149:2/151:3	some school treat ′′′	(s) *	
149:11/151:11	Blood of the Lamb ′--′	(l)	
155:5/157:12	*Diddlediddle* *dumdum/Diddlediddle* ′-′- ″ ′-′-	(d, l, dum) *	(*)
155:14/157:23	the law of libel -′-′-	(l) *	(*)
155:16/157:25	rolypoly poured ′-′-′	(oly, p) *	(*)
155:17/157:26	tickled the top ′--′	(t)	
155:21/157:30	Pleasure or pain ′--′	(p)	
161:1/163:14	The Butter exchange band -′--″	(b)	
161:3/163:16	helterskelter ′-′-	(elter) *	
161:8/163:22	secret service ′-′-	(s, r) *	(*)
161:14/163:28	Decoy duck ′-′	(d, k) *	(*)
167:2/169:20	Chump chop ″	(ch, p) *	(*)
167:3/169:22	See ourselves as others see us ′-′-′-′-	(s, r) *	(*)
167:4/169:22	Hungry man is an angry man ′-′--′-′	(ngry, man) *	(*)

Reference	Text	Codes
167:12/169:30	Spaton sawdust ˈ_ˈ_	(s, t) * (*)
167:12/169:30	sweetish warmish cigarette smoke ˈ_ˈ___ˈ_ˈˈ	(s, w, sh, m)
173:3/175:23	Curly cabbage ˈ_ˈ_	(k) *
173:6/175:26	Dosing it with Edward's desiccated soup ˈ___ˈ_ˈ___ˈ	(s)
173:6/175:27	Geese stuffed silly ˈˈˈ_	(s) *
173:7/175:27	Lobsters boiled alive ˈ_ˈˈ	(l)
173:7/175:27	Do ptake some ptarmigan ˈˈ_ˈ__	(pt)
173:9/175:30	filleted lemon sole _ˈˈ_ˈ	(l)
173:10/175:30	Dubedat . . . do bedad . . . did bedad ˈ__ ˈ__ ˈ__	(d, b, e, a)
173:14/175:35	finger in fishes' gills ˈ__ˈ_ˈ	(f, s, i)
173:19/175:40	Glowing wine on his palate lingered swallowed ˈ_ˈ__ˈ_ˈ_ˈ_	(l) *
173:20/175:41	Seems to a secret touch telling me ˈ__ˈ_ˈˈ__	(s, t)
179:14/181:40	Sense of smell ˈ_ˈ	(s) *
179:14/181:40	Smells on all sides ˈ__ˈ	(s)
179:15/181:41	Then the spring, the summer: smells ˈ_ˈ_ˈ_ˈ	(s, m) * (*)

3. Penelope

Reference	Text	Codes
723:2/738:2	breakfast in bed ˈ__ˈ	(b, ea-e)

723:10/738:10	fun first	(f)	
	"	*	(*)
731:42/747:1	how could he have	(h)	
	_'__		
732:5/747:8	for form sake	(f, r)	
	_"		
732:16/747:17	hope hell come	(h)	
	'''	*	
732:19/747:21	frostyface	(f, s)	
	'_'	*	
741:7/756:10	Alameda esplanade	(l)	
	'_'_'_'	*	
741:10/756:13	all needles	(l)	
	"_		
741:12/756:15	splendid skin	(s, n)	
	'_'	*	
741:15/756:18	stopped it in time	(t)	
	'__'		
741:19/756:22	Lord Lytton	(l)	
	"_		
749:42/764:41	the right reins	(r)	
	_"		
750:6/765:4	black and blue	(bl)	
	'_'	*	
750:8/765:6	that other beauty Burke	(b)	
	_'_'_'	*	
750:9/765:7	where he wasnt wanted	(w, n, t)	
	__'_'_	*	(*)
750:11/765:9	love lost	(lo)	
	"	*	(*)
750:12/765:10	Sweets of Sin	(s)	
	'_'	*	
750:17/765:16	the smell of the sea	(s)	
	_'__'		
759:3/773:43	penny piece	(p)	
	'_'	*	
759:4/774:1	poor Paddy	(p)	
	"_		
759:8/774:5	Bill Bailey	(b, l)	
	"_		

759:9/774:5	widows weeds ˈ_ˈ	(w, d, s) ∗ (∗)
759:11/774:8	base barreltone ˈˈ_ˈ	(b)
759:13/774:10	squeezed and squashed ˈ_ˈ	(squ, d) ∗
759:14/774:11	wellwhipped ˈˈ	(w) ∗ (∗)
759:15/774:12	balmy ballocks ˈ_ˈ_	(b, l) ∗ (∗)
759:19/774:16	so sweetly sang the maiden _ˈ_ˈ_ˈ_	(s) ∗
768:6/783:2	the sea the sea crimson sometimes _ˈ_ˈˈ___	(sea, s)
768:7/783:2	glorious sunsets ˈ__ˈ_	(s)

4. Comparison and Discussion

An explanation of the terms "sound correspondence" and "rhythmic patterns" used above are in order here. In her chapter on tone patterns, Edith Rickert identifies the following principal sound patterns that one should look for in "the study of tone color":

A. Repetition (of words and groups of words)
B. Rhyme (repetition of syllables and groups of syllables)
C. Alliteration (repetition of letters beginning words or syllables)
D. Assonance (repetition of vowels surrounded by different consonants)
E. Consonance (repetition of consonants surrounded by different vowels)[7]

Examples of all these patterns can be found in the lists above:

A. Repetition: "an uncle a judge and an uncle a general" (40:34/39:34)
"do bedad . . . did bedad" (173:10/175:30)
B. Rhyme: "bones for my steppingstones" (45:39/45:1)
"rolypoly" (155:16/157:25)

C. Alliteration: "law of libel" (155:14/157:23)
                   "Decoy duck" (161:14/163:28)
D. Assonance: "eely oarweeds" (45:29/44:31)
                  "spent, its speech ceases" (50:23/49:32)
E. Consonance: "sable silvered" [1] (45:26/44:28)
                  "Dosing it with Edward's desiccated soup"
                  (173:6/175:26)

Each of the patterns indicated by Rickert is a repetition of a
sound or of a complex of sounds; I have called them *sound
correspondences*. Where such correspondences were discernable in
the lists above, they were indicated.

Poetry also has rhythmic patterns. The most common are:

A. Iambic $\cup\;'\;\cup$
B. Trochaic $'\;\cup\;'$
C. Anapestic $\cup\cup\;'\;\cup\cup$
D. Dactylic $'\;\cup\cup\;'\;\cup\cup$

We are not concerned here with identifying rhythms, but simply
with discovering rhythmic patterns; for such patterns are a
poetic device. Where rhythmic patterns were discernable in the
lists above, they were indicated.

It takes no more than a reading of these lists, of course, to
note the greater richness in sound and rhythm of Stephen's
stream of consciousness. Table 11, however, helps to make the

TABLE 11
Sound Correspondences and Rhythmic Patterns
in Proteus, Lestrygonians, and Penelope

	Proteus	*Lestrygonians*	*Penelope*
Phrases of sound correspondence	53	31	29
Phrases with two or more sound correspondences	38	14	10
Phrases of sound correspondence with a rhythmic pattern	35	19	20
Phrases with two or more sound correspondences and a rhythmic pattern	24	9	2

differences even clearer. There are many more instances of sound correspondence in the samples from Proteus than there are in the samples from Lestrygonians or Penelope. By comparison, many more of the phrases quoted above from Stephen's stream of consciousness contain repetitions of more than one sound. Many more of the phrases showing sound correspondence in Stephen's stream of consciousness evidence an obvious rhythm than do those of Bloom or Molly. And finally, whereas 24 of the 53 phrases quoted above from Proteus have both more than one sound correspondence and an obvious rhythm, in Lestrygonians only 9 out of 31 and in Penelope only 2 out of 29 show both. Proteus, therefore, by all odds, evidences not only a more frequent use of poetic devices, but also a considerably more complex use of them.

The two sounds most frequently repeated in all three lists above are the same for each character: first s and then l. These two would seem to be Joyce's own favorites, for they also appear as the most frequent sound correspondences in his poems (and prominently in the name Ulysses). Both Stephen's and Molly's samples, however, also evidence a relatively high frequency of repetitions of b. Stephen's alone show a fondness for the repetition of f and r. These differences again show the greater complexity of the poetic devices employed in Stephen's stream of consciousness: whereas Bloom's stream of consciousness shows a noticeably high frequency for only two sound correspondences (s, l) and Molly's for three (s, l, b), Stephen's shows a noticeably high frequency for five sound correspondences (s, l, f, r, b) and in every instance save one (b) a greater frequency for any particular sound correspondence (see table 12).

TABLE 12
Frequency of Dominant Sound Correspondences
in Proteus, Lestrygonians, and Penelope

	s	l	f	r	b
Stephen	15	16	9	7	6
Bloom	14	7	1	2	2
Molly	8	7	3	2	6

B. Poetic Images

Less easy to define than sound correspondences and thus less easy to discuss and compare are poetic images. I prefer the definition of the image that Ezra Pound gave in connection with his explanation of the imagist poets: "An 'Image' is that which presents an intellectual and emotional complex in an instant of time."[7] Pound's *image* is a French word, and as the imagists used it it is a little broader than the English word *image*. One of its meanings however is the equivalent of the English *image*, and I have therefore used Pound's definition in extracting the poetic images from the three sets of six samples.

1. Proteus

38:2/37:2	thought through my eyes	ph*
38:2/37:2	Signatures of all things	ph
38:3/37:3	seaspawn and seawrack	d
38:16/37:16	a cliff that beetles o'er his base	gr
38:17/37:17	fell through the *nebeneinander*	ph
38:18/37:18	ash sword [walking stick]	
38:19/37:19	My two feet . . . at the end of his legs	
38:20/37:20	[the earth] made by the mallet of *Los Demiurgos*	
38:21/37:21	walking into eternity	ph
40:30/39:30	tuneful whistle . . . finely shaded	
40:30/39:30	rushes of the air	
40:31/39:31	bigdrumming on his padded kness	
40:32/39:32	This wind is sweeter	
40:33/39:33	Houses of decay	d
40:36/39:36	the stagnant bay of Marsh's library	d
40:36/39:37	the fading prophecies of Joachim Abbas	d
40:37/39:37	The hundredheaded rabble	gr
40:39/39:39	the wood of madness	gr
40:39/39:39	his mane foaming in the moon	gr
40:39/39:40	his eyeballs stars	gr

---

* In this list *ph* indicates an image arising from or expressing Stephen's philosophic interests; *d* indicates an image of death or decay; *gr* indicates a grotesque image; and *th* indicates a threatening image, an image which suggests danger or dark mystery.

40:40/39:40	horsenostrilled	gr
40:40/39:41	oval equine faces	gr
40:41/39:42	Lantern jaws	gr
40:42/39:42	what offence laid fire to their brains	gr
43:6/42:8	fiery Columbanus	gr
43:6/42:8	creepystools	gr
43:7/42:9	loudlatinlaughing	
43:20/42:23	sudden proud rhythm	
43:22/42:25	piled stone mammoth skulls	d
45:21/44:24	A shut door of a silent tower	th
45:21/44:24	entombing their blind bodies	d
45:22/44:25	the panthersahib and his pointer	gr
45:23/44:26	[He lifted his feet up from] the suck	th
45:24/44:27	My soul walks with me, form of forms	ph
45:25/44:28	the moon's midwatches [Echoes of ghost scene in *Hamlet*]	th
45:26/44:29	sable silvered	th
45:26/44:29	Elsinore's tempting flood	th
45:27/44:30	The flood is following me	th
45:29/44:32	the sedge and eely oarweeds	th
45:32/44:35	*Un coche ensablé* [Gautier's prose]	gr
45:33/44:36	These heavy sands are language tide and wind have silted here	
45:35/44:38	a warren of weasel rats	gr
45:36/44:39	[Sand and stones] Heavy of the past	
45:37/44:40	Sir Lout's toys	gr
45:38/44:41	boulders bones for my steppingstones	gr
45:39/45:1	I zmells de bloodz oldz an Iridzman	gr
45:40/45:3	A point, live dog, grew into sight	
45:41/45:3	the sweep of sand	
47:42/47:8	creamfruit smell	
48:4/47:11	blued feet . . . slapped the clammy sand	gr
48:5/47:12	a dull brick muffler strangling his unshaven neck	gr
48:5/47:12	woman steps	
48:8/47:15	her windraw face	gr
48:9/47:16	night hides her body's flaws	th
48:13/47:20	A shefiend's whiteness	gr
48:20/47:28	Morose delectation	ph
48:20/47:28	Aquinas tunbelly	

48:21/47:29	Unfallen Adam rode and not rutted
50:21-35/	Vehement breath of waters amid
49:30-50:3	seasnakes, rearing horses, rocks. In cups of rocks it slops: flop, slop, slap: bounded in barrels. And, spent, its speech ceases. It flows purling, widely flowing, floating foampool, flower unfurling.
	Under the upswelling tide he saw the writhing weeds lift languidly and sway reluctant arms, hising up their petticoats, in whispering water swaying and upturning coy silver fronds. Day by day: night by night: lifted, flooded and let fall. Lord, they are weary: and, whispered to, they sigh. Saint Ambrose heard it, sigh of leaves and waves, waiting, awaiting the fullness of their times, *diebus ac noctibus iniurias patiens ingemiscit.* To no end gathered: vainly then released, forth flowing, wending back: loom of the moon. Weary too in sight of lovers, lascivious men, a naked woman shining in her courts, she draws a toil of waters.[8]
50:37/50:5	[High water] Driving before it a loose drift of rubble d
50:38/50:6	fanshoals of fishes
50:38/50:6	silly shells
50:39/50:7	A corpse rising saltwhite d
50:40/50:8	a pace a pace a porpoise
50:41/50:9	the watery floor

Excluding the long passage (50:21-35/49:30-50:3), in which the images are impossible to separate (and which thus defies analysis by individual images), the list above contains sixty-four images. Of these, six are philosophical (*ph*), arising out of

Stephen's philosophic interests. They are echoes of Stephen's interest in Aristotelian physics and metaphysics and in theology.

Eight of the sixty-five images are images of death and decay (d). Of these eight, however, seven are also the only protean images (images of change) to be found in the list.[9] Critics have pointed out decay as one aspect of the protean character of Stephen's thoughts in the third chapter, but have not indicated that it was such an important aspect. To see the world in a constant state of change is one thing. To see the world as a place where change means largely decay is something else again. "God becomes man becomes fish becomes barnacle goose becomes featherbed mountain" (51:3/50:13). But each metamorphosis involves death and decay, so that the living breathe "Dead breaths . . . tread dead dust, devour a urinous offal from all dead" (51:4/50:14). In discussing Nestor, Kristian Smidt points out that to Stephen "time . . . was a destroyer. Time was a limitation of possibilities, a tie on his creative godhead, and an unwelcome reminder of another God."[10] The same remark could be made of Proteus. For to Stephen, as he comments in Scylla and Charybdis, "this vegetable world is but a shadow [of eternity]" (184:18/186:18). Small wonder, therefore, that he feels that he must "*Hold to the now, the here*, through which all future plunges to the past" (184:18/186:19).[11]

Twenty-one other images, almost a third of the total of sixty-four, are grotesque (gr). And seven others still, if they are not quite grotesque, are threatening or uneasy (th). The people are a "hundredheaded rabble" (40:37/39:37); men of genius go grotesquely mad (40:38-40/39:38-40); Stephen's friends have "oval equine faces" and "Lantern jaws" (40:40-41/39:41-42); Sir Lout yearns for an Irishman's blood (45:39/45:1); a woman's body has a "shefiend's whiteness" (48:13/47:20). Nature is equally hostile. A pile of stones is a pile of "mammoth skulls" (43:22/42:25); the sea "tempts" Stephen and then "follows" him (45:26-27/44:29-30); the waters have a "vehement" breath (50:21/49:30); oarweeds are "eely" (45:29/44:32); the sand is not wet but "clammy" (48:4/47:11), and it sucks at Stephen's feet (45:23/44:26). Of the sixty-four images found in the six sample passages in Proteus, then, thirty-seven (57.8 percent) are images of a hostile world: images of death and decay and of a life in which man and nature alike are grotesque and threatening.

2. *Lestrygonians*

The following, all the images in the samples of Bloom's stream of consciousness, show a very different type of person:

149:1/151:1	a sugarsticky girl	f*
149:9/151:9	Heart to heart talks	
149:11/151:11	Blood of the Lamb	b
149:13/151:13	washed in the blood of the lamb	b
149:13/151:13	blood victim	b
149:20/151:21	Paying game	
149:20/151:21	His wife will put the stopper on that	
155:7/157:15	Mrs Breen's womaneyes said melancholily	
155:10/157:18	your lord and master? [Mrs. Breen's husband]	
155:16/157:25	vapour and steam . . . rolypoly poured	
155:17/157:25	The heavy noonreek tickled the top of Mr Bloom's gullet	pl
155:21/157:30	Deaden the gnaw of hunger	pl
161:2/163:15	into the army helterskelter	
161:3/163:16	same fellows used to whether on the scaffold high	
161:4/163:18	Corny Kelleher he has Harvey Duff in his eye	
161:6/163:20	blew the gaff on the invincibles	
161:7/163:21	Egging raw youths on to get in the know	f
161:8/163:22	Drop him like a hot potato	f
161:10/163:24	Easily twig a man used to uniform	
161:10/163:24	Squarepushing up against a backdoor	
161:14/163:28	Decoy duck	f
161:14/163:28	Hotblooded young student	b
167:2/169:20	Chump chop from the grill	f
167:2/169:20	Bolting to get it over	pl
167:2/169:20	Sad booser's eyes	pl
167:3/169:21	Bitten off more than he can chew	pl
167:4/169:23	Working tooth and jaw	pl

---

* In this list, *f* indicates images involving food and drink; *b*, blood images; *pl*, physiological reactions; *s*, smell; and *ph*, philosophy, as in the list for Proteus.

167:12/169:30	His gorge rose	pl
167:12/169:30	Spaton sawdust	
167:13/169:31	reek of plug	s
167:13/169:31	men's beery piss	
167:14/169:32	the stale of ferment	s
167:17/169:35	chewing the cud	pl
167:18/169:36	Scoffing up stewgravy with sopping sippets of bread	f
167:21/169:39	the stooled and tabled eaters	f
167:21/169:39	tightening the wings of his nose	f
173:2/175:22	Whitehatted *chef* like a rabbi	f
173:3/175:23	Combustible duck	f
173:3/175:26	Curly cabbage *à la duchesse de Parme*	f
173:6/175:26	Dosing it with Edward's desiccated soup	f
173:6/175:27	Geese stuffed silly	f
173:14/175:34	making money hand over fist	
173:15/175:35	think he was painting the landscape with his mouth twisted	
173:16/175:37	Ignorant as a kish of brogues	
173:19/175:40	Glowing wine	f
173:20/175:41	Sun's heat it is [the wine]	f
173:20/175:41	Seems to a secret touch telling me memory	pl
173:21/175:42	Touched his sense moistened remembered	pl
179:2/181:28	Feel a gap	ph
179:4/181:30	walk in a beeline	
179:4/181:30	Bloodless pious face like a fellow going in to be a priest	b
179:13/181:39	Dark men they call them	
179:14/181:40	Smells on all sides bunched together	s
179:21/182:5	Kind of a form in her mind's eye	ph

While the poetic images in Bloom's stream of consciousness are not all pleasant, they are not as threatening as Stephen's. Bloom may find his fellowmen melancholy (155:7/157:15) or even disgusting (167:2-21/169:20-39), but not violent. And although the images show an occasional comment on the way life takes its toll ("blood victim"—149:13/151:13; "Paying game"—149:20/151:21), they also show an occasional chuckle ("Geese stuffed silly"—173:6/175:27) and a yielding to the warmth of wine

("Glowing wine—173:19/175:40; "Touched his sense moistened remembered"—173:21/175:42).

A summary of the major categories into which the poetic images from the six samples of Lestrygonians fall shows a very sensuous man. For twenty-seven of the fifty-six images listed above (almost half) have to do with food and drink (f—14), smell (s—3), or the physiological reactions to food, drink, or smell ($p1$—10).

Of the other images, whereas the samples of Stephen's stream of consciousness show six images mirroring his philosophic interests, Bloom's show only two (ph). The samples of Lestrygonians also show six blood images (b), whereas only one, one of the grotesque images, appears in Stephen's. All of Bloom's blood images, however, are not grotesque. That Bloom is more aware of blood (and the lack of it) than is Stephen is in keeping with his greater sensuality, noted above.

The reader of this study may feel that in comparing the thoughts of a man at lunchtime with the thoughts of a man earlier in the day, one should not be surprised to find the former more concerned with food and drink. There are several answers to this objection. In the first place, when Stephen walks along Sandymount strand, it is 11:00 a.m. or after, certainly not very far from lunchtime and certainly time for one who breakfasted only on bread, butter, honey, and milk (13:41/12:10; 17:1/15:15) some three hours earlier to be getting hungry again.[12] But Stephen is absorbed with matters other than food. Bloom is also everywhere more aware of his body and its functions than Stephen is, and thus makes the reader more aware of them. When Stephen urinates (50:16-24/49:25-34; 51:1-3/50:11-13), for example, the reader may not realize it, so ambiguous are the references. When Bloom relieves himself (68:32/69:3), however, the reader certainly knows it. Furthermore, as we have seen, "what the person 'selects' to attend to varies with the attitude and experience of the attending person. . . . The way the subject organizes his material, then, is determined much more by his own personality characteristics than by the nature of the stimulus."[13] It is thoroughly appropriate, therefore, to compare Stephen and Bloom by the stimuli to which they respond. Finally, Joyce chose to show Bloom looking for food, eating, and responding to food and smells and did not choose to show Stephen so. The stress on Bloom's sensuousness, then, is a result of what Joyce wrote into *Ulysses* and not a result of arbitrary comparisons.

3. *Penelope*

The following is the list of images found in the sample passages for Molly:

723:4/738:4	doing his highness	a*
723:5/738:5	that old faggot Mrs Riordan that he thought he had a leg of	r
723:8/738:8	she had too much old chat in her	
723:16/738:17	he was glad to get shut of her	a
732:14/747:16	it simply it makes you feel like nothing on earth	M
732:19/747:21	old frostyface Goodwin	l
732:20/747:22	I . . . all flushed and tossed	M
741:9/756:12	I felt something go through me like all needles	M
741:10/756:13	my eyes were dancing	M
741:12/756:15	splendid skin . . . like a rose	M
741:13/756:16	a wink of sleep	M
749:42/764:41	the tide all swamping in floods	
750:3/765:1	keep yourself calm in his flannel trousers	a
750:4/765:2	Id like to have tattered them down	M
750:9/765:7	[Burke] spying around . . . on the slip	l
750:10/765:8	you vomit a better face	l
750:16/765:14	that feather all blowy and tossed on me	M
758:42/773:39	get my husband . . . into their clutches	a
759:2/773:42	his idiotics	a
759:3/773:42	squander every penny piece . . . down their gullets	a
759:6/774:3	comical little teetotum always stuck up in some pub corner	l
759:11/774:8	Ben Dollard base barreltone	v
759:13/774:10	squeezed and squashed into them	l

*In this list M indicates images about Molly; a, specific actions about specific men; l, the appearance of specific men in specific situations; v, specific men's voices; and r, the relationship between Bloom and Mrs. Riordan.

759:13/774:10	grinning all over his big Dolly face like a wellwhipped childs botty	l
759:14/774:11	didn't he look a balmy ballocks	l
759:16/774:13	preserved seats	
759:17/774:14	turning up half screwed	a
759:21/774:18	he had a delicious glorious voice	v
767:41/782:38	handsome Moors all in white and turbans like kings	l
768:2/782:41	glancing eyes a lattice hid	
768:5/782:43	the watchman going about serene with his lamp	a
768:5/783:1	O that awful deepdown torrent O	
768:6/783:2	the sea the sea crimson sometimes like fire	
768:10/783:6	I was a Flower of the mountain	M
768:14/783:10	I asked him with my eyes	M
768:16/783:11	my mountain flower [Molly]	M
768:18/783:14	his heart was going like mad	a

Of the thirty-seven images listed above, eleven are about Molly (M): four concern her appearance (732:21/747:22; 741:10/756:13; 741:12/756:15; 750:16/765:14); two concern her visceral sensations (732:14/747:16; 741:9/756:12); three concern her actions (741:13/756:16; 750:4/765:2; 768:14/783:10); and two are from her memory of phrases Bloom applied to her during their courting days (768:10/783:6; 768:16/783:11). Twenty others describe men in some way: nine deal with specific actions of specific men (a); eight deal with the appearance of specific men in specific situations (l); two deal with specific men's voices (v); and one deals with the relationship between Bloom and Mrs. Riordan (r). Actually, all save one of the images about Molly (M) are also concerned about men (768:10/783:6), and sixteen are Bloom's descriptive phrases of Molly; Bloom is involved in 750:14/765:12, and 732:14/747:16 is Molly's memory of her reaction to a kiss from Bloom; 741:9/756:12, 10/13, 12/15, and 13/16 are a result of glances from Captain Grove at Gibraltar; and 732:21/747:22 describes Molly when she opened the door for Professor Goodwin. The eleventh image about Molly also relates to a man indirectly: it is Molly's memory of how she looked as a result of a rowing excursion with Bloom (750:16/765:14). Thus twenty of the thirty-seven images in the sample passages of Molly's stream of consciousness are about men directly and eleven more concern men.

4. Discussion of Methodology

This characterization by dominant image has the support of both literary criticism and psychology. Caroline Spurgeon, for example, did much the same sort of thing for Shakespeare's tragedies:

> Recurrent images play a part in raising, developing, sustaining, and repeating emotion in the tragedies, which is somewhat analogous to the action of a recurrent theme or 'motif' in a musical fugue or sonata, or in one of Wagner's operas.
>
> Certain groups of images . . . stick out in each particular play and immediately attract attention because they are peculiar either in subject or quantity, or both.[4]

Miss Spurgeon feels that the peculiar mood and impact of each play are due to a considerable extent to these recurrent images:

> This method of working by way of suggestion, springing from a succession of vivid pictures and concrete details, is, of course, of the very essence of "romantic" art; and, in the case of Shakespeare, the poet's mind, unlike the dyer's hand, subdues to itself what it works in, and colours with its dominating emotion all the varied material which comes his way, colours it so subtly and so delicately that for the most part we are unconscious of what is happening, and know only the total result of the effect on our imaginative sensibility.[15]

The same thesis is applicable to the analysis made above of the images in the three streams of consciousness. For example, whether the reader realizes it or not, the preponderance of images of decay and the grotesque in Stephen's stream of consciousness communicates to him Stephen's own uneasiness and fears and helps build for him Stephen's personality.

The psychologists' concept of projection, to which I have referred several times, also sanctions such an interpretation: "[Projection] may be defined as a type of self-deception by which a person ascribes his own secret thoughts, wishes, and shortcomings to another person. If one can castigate others, one is thereby saved from the painful duty of castigating oneself." Projection also has another form:

There is likewise a complementary form of projection whereby
a person does not attribute his own frame of mind to others but
rather one that explains and justifies his own frame of mind to
himself. Thus the over-timid child thinks that others have
aggressive intentions toward him, and the paranoiac believes that
others are plotting his destruction. Through such complementary
projection one's personal quirks of temperament and traits receive
"rational" explanation and do not appear as unfounded and foolish
as they are.[16]

According to this psychological concept, Stephen's seeing nature
as decaying and grotesque could be either his compensating for
his lack of success (that is, how can a young man possibly be
expected to succeed in such a baleful world?) or his ascribing
his own concealed aggression, the result of his personal
frustration, to the people and things about him. The dominance
of particular types of images in the streams of consciousness
of Bloom and Molly is similarly an expression of their needs
and thus a projection of their personalities.

11
Synthesis: Stephen, Bloom, and Molly

Having analyzed carefully the streams of consciousness of Stephen, Bloom, and Molly in three chapters in *Ulysses,* we can now assemble the results. In the process, we will see to what extent our close analyses of the text can help to unravel some of the controversies in Joyce scholarship.

A. Stephen

There is disagreement among the critics not only about such matters as whether the Stephen of *Ulysses* is more mature than the Stephen of *A Portrait* and about the meaning of the relationship established between Stephen and Bloom in the Circe, Eumaeus, and Ithaca chapters, but also about Stephen's personality, his state of mind, and the way he views the world. Frank Budgen said of Stephen in Proteus, "There is nothing in him sullen, listless, bitter, resigned, weary" and suggested that if Stephen is not already a poet he is at least "a magician's apprentice";[1] and as we have seen a later critic called Stephen a "poet and philosopher" in whom "imagination, intellect and memory combine with the senses to create brightness and innocence."[2] A more recent critic, however, finds Stephen "beset by anxiety, guilt, self-contempt and even practical worries."[3] While one critic argues that Stephen shows "potentialities as an artist," another feels that the poem he writes in Proteus is "less than great art" and still another that he is "a sterile aesthete."[4] Some critics feel that, either because of what happens to Stephen during Bloomsday or for some other reason (frequently the proposition that Stephen is the young Joyce), he will mature into an author who will write a *Ulysses.*[5]

Whether because he had developed Stephen so fully in *A Portrait,* because Stephen was largely a reflection of his own youth, or because he simply grew too tired of him to develop him further, all the evidence is that Joyce, at least, had a relatively clear and stable image of Stephen and that he had few questions in his own mind about how to portray him.[6] There are fewer changes in manuscript versions or proofs of the first three chapters than of later chapters, and, similarly, Joyce's letters say much less about those opening chapters than they do about later chapters.[7]

What picture of Stephen do our analyses of Proteus give us, and is it consistent with what we know of him from other chapters? He is interested in philosophy and literature, clearly. His thoughts contain references to and echoes of Aristotle, Aquinas, Berkeley, Boehme, Blake, Shakespeare, and other authors and their works. Moreover, he does not allude to them self-consciously or grandiosely but uses them easily as counters in his thinking, as symbols for ideas, as shorthand devices of thought. He uses foreign languages in the same easy, unselfconscious way. He is also very familiar with Irish history and with the intricacies of the history and doctrine of Roman Catholicism. Stephen is obviously a highly—and traditionally— educated young man.

His interest in mysticism might seem unusual, but given his preoccupation with Catholic theology and aesthetics, his involvement with Aristotle is appropriate. From Aristotle to Berkeley and then to Boehme and Blake are easy steps. Furthermore, as a would-be poet growing up in Dublin in the late nineteenth and early twentieth centuries, Stephen would have heard much about the occult from Yeats, George Russell (A.E.), and their circle—about Mme Blavatsky, theosophy, and Rosicrucianism, particularly.[8]

Stephen is also interested in time and in change. Now out on his own, he sees time slipping through his fingers while he accomplishes nothing. His interest in change stems partly from his concern with death, particularly his mother's, partly from his theological bent, and partly from his interest in language, motifs which run all through Ulysses.

Aristotle's ideas on the nature of sight and reality, which form a major theme in Proteus, also appear in Stephen's thoughts in other places in the book: "It must be a movement then, an actuality of the possible as possible. Aristotle's phrase formed itself within the gabbled verses" (26:35/25:35); "Touch lightly

with two index fingers. Aristotle's experiment" (190:8/192:16).
Aristotle the man also appears (183:26/185:24; 184:5/186:4;
184:10/186:10; 671:34/687:26). Once again, then, one of the
primary themes in Proteus is a theme which is of concern to
Stephen throughout *Ulysses.*

Stephen's interests in Proteus in Irish history, in languages,
and in literature—particularly in Shakespeare—are also
manifest throughout *Ulysses.* All of these interests show the
same marked intellectual bent and the same active mind
evidenced by Stephen in other chapters. Intellectually, then,
Proteus is of a piece with the views of Stephen that one gets
in other chapters of the novel and with what the reader knows
of Stephen's background and training.

Similarly, Proteus helps to project other aspects of Stephen's
personality than the intellectual that are also evident elsewhere
in *Ulysses.* The Stephen in Proteus shows a syndrome of
unpleasant characteristics: he is proud, egocentric, vain,
sardonic, and aloof.

There is considerable evidence of vanity in Proteus, not only
that Stephen was vain in the past but that, although he mocks
many of his former dreams, he continues to be vain. Not too
many years before the current episode on Sandymount strand,
he saw himself as the author of a world-famous series of
epiphanies, "copies to be sent . . . to all the great libraries
of the world, including Alexandria" (41:33/40:34). He even
practiced taking bows (41:28/40:29). When he was at Clongowes,
his need for impressing his fellow students with his importance
was so great that he told them, untruthfully, that he "had an
uncle a judge and an uncle a general in the army" (40:34/
39:34). And at another time he saw himself as a "Missionary to
Europe" (43:5/42:7), destined, perhaps, to bring truth and
culture to the Continent, as early Irish missionaries had done.
True, he mocks his earlier fantasies; but he also mocks his
failure to achieve the importance that he dreamed he would
attain, the importance he achieved in his adolescent daydreams.
Furthermore, he gives evidence that his defiant pride has not
abated much. As he remembers Mulligan's earlier insult he
marches "in sudden proud rhythm" (43:20/42:22). He sneers at
a poet laureate of England: "Lawn Tennyson, gentleman poet"
(51:21/50:32). And even though there is probably no one around
to see him, there is defiance in his gesture as he lays "the

dry snot picked from his nostril on a ledge of rock, carefully. For the rest let look who will" (51:32/51:1). Thus, although Stephen in Proteus turns his cynicism and scorn largely against himself, he maintains a cold, proud attitude toward the world around him even when there is no one to observe it—an attitude also much in evidence elsewhere in *Ulysses.*

Stephen is obviously a young man with many personal problems. He is estranged not only from friends but from family; and he feels guilty about his dead mother. Joyce emphasizes this aspect of Stephen in a variety of ways. First of all, of course, Stephen ponders his personal problems. He thinks about his birth, his school days, his adolescence, his writing plans, his stay in Paris, his mother's death, his relations with Mulligan. Even when his thoughts turn to other matters, his personal concerns soon come to the fore: for example, when he performs his experiment to test Aristotle's theories, he is aware that his two feet are in Mulligan's shoes (38:19/37:19); two midwives remind him of his own birth (38:40/37:40); Eve's "Womb of sin" (39:9/38:9) reminds him of his own begetting.

Furthermore, Stephen's view of the world is an uneasy and unhappy one: his interest in church history runs to heretics, and in his mind, a choir "gives back menace and echo" (41:11/40:4); his thoughts about Irish history concern unsuccessful revolutions (44/43) and "Pretenders" (46:22/45:25) and he pictures the early Dubliners as "jerkined dwarfs" (46:12/45:15) subject to "Famine, plague, and slaughter" (46:14/45:17); the dog (46/45) and the man and women on the beach (48/47) are menacing figures; contemporary Dublin is made up of "Houses of decay, mine, his and all" (40:33/39:33); and his imagination runs to such threatening figures as Sir Lout, "the bloody well gigant" (45:38/44:42), Haroun al Raschid in an open hallway in the street of harlots (47:40/47:5), a "pale vampire . . . his bat sails bloodying the sea" (48:35/48:2), and "A corpse rising saltwhite from the undertow" (50:39/50:7). As we have seen in the analysis of poetic images, running through all of Stephen's thoughts are images of a hostile world—images of death and decay and of a life in which man and nature are grotesque and threatening.

Sheldon R. Brivic offers a psychoanalytic interpretation of Stephen which helps to explain the threatening imagery in

Stephen's thoughts. He sees him in Proteus (and elsewhere) "preoccupied with the idea of God as '*dio boia,* hangman god' [210:38/213:23]. The *dio boia,* essentially a paternal castration threat, is a monster or vampire who destroys life through the media of time and circumstance": "The conception of the mother's death as a sexual violation by the father appears forcefully in 'Proteus,' where Stephen broods upon the sexual relationship of his parents: 'Wombed in sin darkness I was. . . . They clasped and sundered and did the coupler's will' [39:10-13/38:10-13]." Brivic quotes Stephen's attempt at poetry as further evidence of his claim—"He comes, pale vampire, through storm his eyes, his bat sails bloodying the sea, mouth to her mouth's kiss" [48:34/48:1]. He sees these lines as reflecting the threat of the castrating father and of the *dio boia*: "We recall that the idea of kissing the mother had heavy sexual connotations in *Portrait.* This image cluster . . . haunts Stephen throughout *Ulysses.* It is a version of the *Portrait's* combination of a longing for the mother and an accompanying fear of castration, now transformed by the injury of the mother's death."[9] Thus there is a reason for all of the threatening, hostile images that Stephen projects upon his world.

Joyce also helps to emphasize the heavily internal nature of Stephen's stream of consciousness by using relatively few omniscient author's sentences in Proteus and by burying many of those he uses inside paragraphs instead of using them to open paragraphs. Thus they are neither frequent nor obvious. This helps to focus the reader on Stephen's inner thoughts rather than on the physical world outside of him.

Stephen's frequent references to himself but his absolute avoidance of pronouns which refer to the self and others (we, us, our, etc.) not only reinforces the sense of self-concern but emphasizes also his aloofness. The fact that more than half of the self-references occur in some form of self-address (you, Stephen) also emphasizes his alienation. He is not even comfortable with himself: he chides himself, is at least as scornful of himself as he is of others.

The fact that there are only a very few instances of the Aronson-Weintraub category of "feelings" in Proteus is further evidence of Stephen's withdrawal. He is not even willing to admit to himself that he has feelings. Where some people avoid facts by concentrating on feelings, Stephen seems to avoid feelings by concentrating on facts; and he almost never qualifies or retracts.

Isolated and aloof, sometimes perhaps misguided, Stephen is not, however, a whiner. The analyses show few negatives in his thoughts, little rationalizing ("explainings"), few instances of defensiveness or preoccupation with violations of propriety ("evaluations"). He is, rather, cold and rational.

Here, too, the analyses demonstrate how that impression is reinforced. As we have noticed, he eschews feelings. In addition, his language is more abstract and formal than that of the other characters in the novel. His appositive and accumulating sentences are clear and efficient: the first characterize ideas neatly and quickly; the second, by their use of parallel construction, order thoughts well and show the interrelationship of often highly sophisticated ideas clearly. Analysis of his associations also demonstrates coherence and a tendency to centrally organized and related structures.

Stephen's lack of warmth and his rationality do not bring with them, however, any narrowness or sterility of imagination. On the contrary, his mind soars and ranges. It plays not only with ideas and with ideas which are often irreverent, but with language. His agglutinations are imaginative. His thoughts are enriched by poetic imagery, sound correspondences, and rhythms.

Is Stephen a poet? The analyses of poetic images, sound correspondences, and rhythms suggest that he has the technical competence to write poetry. And he meets some of the other criteria established by one modern critic and poet, C. Day Lewis: that his view of the world should come "from the perception of a unity underlying all phenomena" and that his mind be bent to poetry's task of "the perpetual discovery, through its imaging, metaphor making faculty, of new relationships within this pattern, and the rediscovery and renovation of old ones."[10] The analyses of Stephen's poetic images and of his associations demonstrate not only capacity to meet those criteria, but actual successful performance.

On the other hand, as Robert M. Adams demonstrates, the poem that Stephen writes "is less than great art, perhaps even less original than creation." It suffers from the same "hothouse atmosphere of Dowson-cum-Swinburne" as the villanelle of *A Portrait*, and it owes too much to one of Douglas Hyde's *Love*

Songs of Connacht to sustain a claim for originality.[11]

A reader may thus come to any of a variety of conclusions. If Stephen is a poet, he is a poor one. If he should not yet be considered a poet, he may well become one. How strongly one feels about this matter probably depends upon how closely one identifies Stephen with the young James Joyce.

The Homeric parallel gives us little extra information. In the *Odyssey*, Menelaos wrestles with Proteus in order to learn how to get back to Lacedaemon. By overcoming Proteus, he earns the required information; then he performs the necessary rites and is rewarded by the gods with a fair wind which speeds him home. In the Proteus episode of Joyce's *Ulysses*, however, the emphasis is on the wrestling and not on the knowledge gained. At the end of the chapter, the present is ominous: "Clouding over" (51:12/50:23); and directions for the future are only dimly suggested. Stephen is not even looking to the future; he is "rere regardant" (51:35/51:4).

Furthermore, the dimly seen future is not very promising: "Come. . . . Where? To evening lands. Evening will find itself. . . . Yes, evening will find itself in me, without me. All days make their end" (51:12-19/50:23-30). Sultan says of Stephen at the end of Proteus: "He has run the gamut from the arrogance of the morning star to the resignation of 'evening will find itself in me, without me,' from 'Welcome, O life!' at the end of the *Portrait* to the acceptance of a journey 'to the west, trekking to evening lands' [48:28/47:35]. The answer he derives from his Protean inquiry is nothing more promising than a life that is like death, until the release of death itself."[12]

The chapter does not end in despair, however. Sultan sees the crosstrees of the threemaster (51:37/51:6) as a sign of divine grace and thus a promise of salvation;[13] and Goldberg sees the ship as a sign that Stephen "too is silently moving homeward."[14] But the more important point is that Stephen's spirit is not broken. After he thinks briefly on evening lands, he refers disparagingly to "Lawn Tennyson" as a "gentleman poet" (51:21/50:32) and to Monsieur Drumont as a "gentleman journalist" (51:23/50:34), he pokes fun at himself as "Toothless Kinch, the superman" (51:25/50:36), and in a characteristic gesture of defiance, when he lays "the dry snot picked from his nostril on a ledge, carefully," his attitude is "For the rest let look who will" (51:33/51:2).

Proteus, then, sets the basic pattern for Stephen in *Ulysses*. He has a clear, cold, rational, wide-ranging mind, a good education, and an excellent command of language. Ambitious, he has not yet met either his own or the world's criteria for the accolade of poet. Beset by several personal problems, he characterizes man and nature as hostile, even threatening. Although self-conscious, he is not self-righteous. If he has not yet performed, he shows the ability, the restless energy, and the desire to perform.

As Goldberg says: "His potentiality of growth is perhaps here most clearly visible. The humorless and priggish aesthete appears much less certain about his poses; he has after all, we discover, some sense of the ridiculous and some glimmerings of maturer values."[15] That is probably why, as cold and priggish as Stephen is, the reader still has some sympathy for him. For although in Proteus and elsewhere throughout *Ulysses* we see aspects of Stephen that are less than admirable, in Proteus we also see his vulnerability, his basic integrity, and his potential.

B. Bloom

Because the reader of *Ulysses* learns about Stephen in considerable detail at the beginning of the novel, when he meets Bloom he is led to compare him with Stephen. In the critical literature, that tendency is reinforced by the fact that Stephen and Bloom are frequently considered to reflect two different aspects of Joyce's personality or to be reciprocally related in some way: Stephen intellectual, introverted, the son; Bloom materialistic, extroverted, the father.

In making those comparisons, however, the critics frequently disagree. For example, Adams finds that "there are a number of instances in the novel where Bloom and Stephen think along vaguely parallel lines. . . . But, looked at a second time, these seem to be tangential and fleeting similarities, growing out of the fact that Stephen and Bloom have lived for the last twenty-two years in the same medium-sized city, at about the same social level."[16] Goldberg, however, discovers that "the similarities between Bloom and Stephen appear more significant than the differences."[17] Sultan contrasts Stephen's rejection with Bloom's "benighted submission" and decides that the "contrast between them is not to Bloom's advantage." He thus rejects the idea that "the man who will not assent to the conditions of life is damned."[18] Goldberg would seem to reject both of the interpretations. He sees Bloom as "not merely passive but active, not merely involved but free, not merely representative of, but crucified by his world, the scapegoat and redeemer, tied all the while by close analogy and parallel with Stephen."[19] Sultan feels that each character must learn from the other: "The actual case presented in *Ulysses*, its basic conceptual principle, is that both of its subjects are headed for catastrophe and that each must adopt as a model for correction the wrong conduct of the other."[20] Goldberg thinks, however, that "Bloom's ambiguous position, his example, his love, his freedom, if only he could understand them, are what Stephen must come to."[21] But then Brivic thinks that "movement from Stephen to Bloom is movement from hopeless conflict to a reconciliation based on delusion."[22]

As we have seen, the parallels between the thoughts of Stephen in Proteus and those of Bloom in Lestrygonians are not only many, but significant. Bloom's thoughts indicate a man of more materialistic interests than Stephen, a man with considerably less training and intellectual ability. Whereas Stephen is concerned with the philosophic aspects of the senses and of science and his knowledge about them is precise and sure, Bloom is interested in their mundane manifestations and applications and his knowledge about them is hazy and frequently wrong. Stephen's knowledge of history is markedly wide-ranging and accurate; Bloom's interest in history is largely contemporary, his knowledge of ancient history confused. Bloom's thoughts of Catholicism do not concern the philosophical and theological matters that interest Stephen, but rather the effect of religion on everyday life. Unlike Stephen, he knows only the commonest phrases from foreign languages and from literature. Whereas Stephen dreams of writing epiphanies that people would read "after a few thousand years" (41:35/40:37), Bloom thinks often about various ways of making money, particularly by advertising, which is his business.

These differences suggest that in a number of important ways, Bloom is merely a weak, materialistic, and sometimes comic echo of Stephen. In fact, the feeling of pathos that Bloom arouses in the reader in this chapter as elsewhere stems partly from his being so poorly informed and so desirous of success;

for he is obviously interested in a wide variety of ideas and eager to understand them. But in almost every area his lack of understanding and, sometimes, his failure to realize that he does not understand, as well as his frequent ineptitude, cause the reader to feel sorry for him.

The parallels also show that Bloom is much more compassionate than Stephen. Stephen's experiment with the senses is triggered by his interest in Aristotle (38/37), Bloom's by his sympathy for the blind stripling (178-79/180-82). Stephen is concerned about himself, Bloom about the hungry seagulls, a woman in the pangs of childbirth, and another woman with a distraught—or mad—husband. Stephen's interest in change tends to be expressed in terms of a dog which becomes a hare, a buck, a wolf, and a calf (47/46) or in terms of the day moving to sunset and the subtle shift in meaning among synonyms: "the sun's flaming sword, to the west, trekking to evening lands. She trudges, schlepps, trains, drags, trascines her load" (48:29/47:35). Bloom's interest in change extends not only to change in the physical world, but also to change in people: how young radicals become civil servants (161:4/163:15), how his marriage has deteriorated (173:42/176:22), how a Paddy Dignam dies when a Mina Purefoy gives birth (162/164). Bloom is also warmer than Stephen in other ways. He is more sensuous. He does not withdraw to an empty beach, but remains within sight of people. The fact that Bloom is more interested in other people's problems and that he does not bathe in self-concern also gives the reader cause to feel that here is a man who is being poorly used.

Bloom, as we have seen, does not measure up to Stephen in intelligence or in potential as a poet, and he uses the trite image and the tired phrase much more frequently. But he is by no means stupid or even simply routine. He would do very well, for example, on the Plot Titles Test, which examines for " 'originality' . . . adaptive flexibility with semantic material, where there must be a shifting of meanings":

> The examinee must produce the shifts or changes in meaning and so come up with novel, unusual, clever, or farfetched ideas. The Plot Titles Test presents a short story, the examinee being told to list as many appropriate titles as he can to head the story. One story is about a missionary who has been captured by cannibals in Africa. He is in the pot and about to be boiled when

a princess of the tribe obtains a promise for his release if he
will become her mate. He refuses and is boiled to death.

In scoring the test, we separate the responses into two
categories, clever and nonclever. Examples of nonclever responses
are: African Death, Defeat of a Princess . . . , and Boiled by
Savages. These titles are appropriate but commonplace. The
number of such responses serves as a score for ideational fluency.
Examples of clever responses are: Pot's Luck . . . , Goil or Boil,
a Mate worse than Death, He left a Dish for a Pot, Chaste in
Haste, and A Hot Price for Freedom.[23]

Bloom would make a high score on both originality and ideational
fluency for just his quips in Lestrygonians:

Do ptake some ptarmigan. (173:7/175:27)

May I tempt you to a little more filleted lemon sole, miss
Dubedat? Yes, do bedad. And she did bedad.
(173:9/175:29)

The harp that once did starve us all [an echo of "The harp
that once through Tara's halls"]. (165:26/168:1)

a urinal: meeting of the waters. (160:17/162:30)

Poached eyes on ghost. (162:39/165:11)

Nutarians. Fruitarians [on the model of vegetarians].
(163:31/166:4)

As Lenehan says seriously: "He's not one of your common or
garden . . . you know . . . There's a touch of the artist about
old Bloom" (232:1/235:16).

As even a casual reader of *Ulysses* would expect, however,
much of Bloom's language is less interesting than Stephen's and
shows less education. It has fewer interesting words, fewer
words that are highly abstract, fewer and less metaphoric and
image-producing agglutinations, fewer poetic images, and fewer
examples of sound correspondences and of sound correspondences
undergirded by rhythmic patterns. Bloom's language contains
more slang, more dialectal words and phrases, and more trite
expressions.

Similarly, Bloom's language is less well structured than
Stephen's. His associations, for example, are less coherent. And
the sentences which I have labeled condensations and wrenched
sentences as well as his jumbled accumulating sentences give
an impression of awkwardness and sometimes even of disorder
or confusion. Thus Bloom's ineptitude with people is frequently
reflected in the patterning of his language.

It is surprising to find, therefore, that in five separate analyses Bloom's use of language compares with Stephen's in a way that one would not expect: Bloom uses slightly more long (three, four and five syllable) words than Stephen, a higher percentage of words of Latin, Greek, and Romance-language origin, and a higher proportion of content to form words; his language has a higher type-token ratio, which is a measure of language richness or diversity; and his sentences are longer. None of these differences is great enough to be statistically significant, but in sum they make an impressive difference in a direction one would not expect.

Quite frankly, I was not prepared for these results; and I am still not quite sure what to make of them. The relatively mature uses of language may contribute to the reader's acceptance of Lenehan's finding "a touch of the artist about old Bloom." Perhaps they account for some of the feeling that readers and critics have that Bloom is a better person than some of his fellow Dubliners will admit. Perhaps, too, they make it easier for the critics to see Bloom as a reflection of one aspect of Joyce's personality: Bloom is sometimes inept, as all of us are—even geniuses who write great novels; but the way he uses words and the breadth of his language, added to his originality and ideational fluency, suggest a basic competence.

The other analyses of Bloom's language give us additional information about him and demonstrate some of the ways in which Joyce projected Bloom's personality for the reader. The six sample passages in Lestrygonians show many fewer references to self than do the sample passages in Proteus, only one-quarter as many, in fact. Here is not only confirmation of little egocentricity, but also a demonstration of how Joyce gave that impression of Bloom. Although the passages contain references to the self and others (we, us, our, etc.)—seven for Bloom compared with none for Stephen—the references are so few that they are a demonstration of Bloom's sense of not belonging. Like Stephen, he does not use many negatives and thus shows little tendency to negate and deny.[24] Similarly, he shows little evidence of "undoing" (qualification and retraction). This analysis underlines his ability to face facts squarely and to be forthright, even with himself. The paucity of instances of rationalizing ("explaining") provides further evidence of that ability. And the relatively few instances of "evaluation" indicate little defensive use of opinions or preoccupation with the right and the proper.

Bloom does show more "feeling" than Stephen, however. He cannot be accused, as Stephen can, of avoiding emotion by concentrating on facts. This finding supports other analyses summarized earlier.

Another contrast with Stephen is in religion. All of the critics make much of the fact that Bloom is Jewish. In this, of course, they are following Joyce's many remarks to that effect and the comments of Joyce's friends.[25] There is not much evidence of Bloom's Jewishness in Lestrygonians, however. There are two references to Old Testament stories: "Manna" (151:10/153:12) and "Pillar of salt" (152:32/154:37), the first to the exodus from Egypt, the second to Lot's wife. But knowing them certainly does not mark anyone as Jewish. Bloom remarks to himself that Denis Breen is "Meshuggah" and then provides a slang equivalent in English: "Off his chump" (157:27/159:38). He reminds himself that "Kosher" means "No meat and milk together. Hygiene that was what they call now" (169:23-24/ 171:42-172:1). That is the kind of remark that a Jew might make to a non-Jew by way of explanation, but hardly to himself.

His remarks in Lestrygonians about Yom Kippur, the Jewish Day of Atonement, are curious, too. He says, "I'd like to see them do the black fast Yom Kippur" (149:41/152:1); and later, "Yom Kippur fast spring cleaning of inside" (169:24/172:1). Bloom was, of course, born of a Jewish father, but his father had been converted to Protestantism in 1865, the year before Bloom was born (701:12/716:24). And Bloom's mother was a Protestant. Bloom himself had thus been born and baptised a Protestant, and then later, in preparation for his marriage to Molly, was baptised a Catholic (666:21/682:18). What, then, is the meaning of the reference to the Yom Kippur fast? He certainly never undertook one. And "spring cleaning" is an odd remark to make about the fast, even as a metaphor, because Yom Kippur always takes place in September or October.

Bloom evidences little interest in his father's having been Jewish. Nor does he show any signs of a sense of fellowship with Dublin Jews. His comment that the Protestant missionaries "used to give pauper children soup to change to protestants in the time of the potato blight" reminds him of the "Society over the way papa went to for the conversion of poor jews," which in turn brings the mildly sarcastic comment "Same bait"; but he shows no sign of resentment (178:4-6/180:27-30). He considers a story about the money-pinching of Reuben J. Dodd, a Jewish Dubliner, "droll" (150:22/152:25) and later thinks about Dodd, "Now he's really what they call a dirty jew" (180:17/183:2).

Elsewhere in the novel Bloom does say once that he belongs "to a race that is hated and persecuted" (326:38/332:32) and defends the Jews by mention of Mendelssohn, Marx, and Spinoza (and Christ) (336/342), but he specifically says that he does not consider himself a Jew (627:12/643:4). He feels remorse not because he did not follow the traditional Jewish beliefs and practices, but because in his immaturity he treated them with disrespect (708:36/724:5). And, even under the influence of the twinge of remorse, he finds the traditions of Judaism "Not more rational than they had then appeared, not less rational than other beliefs and practices now appeared" (709:9/724:19). Furthermore, as Joseph Prescott has shown, Bloom is quite confused about many of those beliefs and practices. For example, "only vaguely familiar with Jewish customs, [Bloom] indicates his remoteness from them by the expression 'those mazzoth' [79:41/81:3] and conflates the unleavened bread of Passover (Exodus 12:8) with the showbread of the Tabernacle (Exodus 25:30; Leviticus 24:5-9)."[26] He also refers to "those jews" (107:13/108:31) in the ballad of little Harry Hughes (674-76/690-91). The use of "those" with "mazzoth" and "jews" suggests distance, not membership.

There is a suggestion that Bloom's father read the story of Passover to him from the Haggadah (121/122; 708/723); but Bloom thinks of it as "All that long business" (121:20/122:21). Nor does he remember any of it very well.[27] In thinking of Passover, he thinks also of the *Sh'ma*, the central prayer of Judaism, sometimes called "the watchword" of the faith; but he leaves out what is probably its most important part. He remembers only *"Shema Israel Adonai Elohenu"* and forgets *"Adonai Echod."* What he remembers, therefore, means roughly, "Hear, O Israel, the Lord our God." But the whole prayer is, "Hear, O Israel, the Lord our God the Lord is One." He thus leaves out the very important affirmation of monotheism. The Circumcised do not make this error in Circe; they repeat the entire prayer properly (532/544). Thus Bloom's significant

misreading must be attributed to him and not to Joyce's lack
of knowledge. The suggestion, therefore, that Bloom knows some
Hebrew (672-73/688-89) or that he can write even a few letters
of the Hebrew alphabet (672:23/688:15) is not very convincing.[28]

Bloom is frequently referred to as a Jew, of course. Mulligan
calls him "The wandering jew" (215:4/217:34); but that happens
not long after he refers to Stephen as "you inquisitional drunken
jew jesuit" (213:34/216:22). Martin Cunningham, curiously, calls
Bloom "a perverted jew" (331:28/337:32). And the narrator of
Ithaca refers to Bloom as "a jew" (675:2/691:6), as do others.
But Father Farley also calls him "an episcopalian, an agnostic,
an anythingarian" (481:2/490:23). Rudolph Virag charges that
Leopold "left the god of his fathers Abraham and Jacob"
(430:23/437:27), an echo of another oft-repeated Jewish prayer
which begins, "Our God and God of our fathers, God of Abraham
and God of Jacob." Since Bloom was never committed to the
God of Israel either by birth or conviction, however, the charge
does not make much sense.

Joyce even makes mocking reference to the state of Bloom's
Judaism in a long passage on page 713/728, in which some
of Bloom's actions during the day are compared to various
Jewish rites and holidays. Bloom's visit to the "jakes" to relieve
himself (68/69), for example, is compared to one of the most
sober and awe-inspiring moments of an ancient practice of the
Jewish religion: the moment on the Day of Atonement when
the High Priest of Israel moved aside an otherwise inviolable
curtain, and, stepping into a bare room (the Holy of Holies)
behind the altar in the Temple in Jerusalem, called upon God
by His name (713:26/738:36). Similarly, Bloom's bookhunt along
Bedford Row, which resulted in his purchase of the pornographic
Sweets of Sin (232/235), is compared to Simchath Torah, the
joyous holiday on which the Jews celebrate the recurrent
reading of their Book of Law, the first five volumes of the Old
Testament (713:31/729:3).

According to Jewish law a person can be Jewish by birth only
if he is born of a Jewish mother. Bloom was not.[29] Nor was
he raised as a Jew—nor did he convert to Judaism. And, as
we have just seen, he does not consider himself a Jew, know
much about Judaism, or demonstrate any affinity for Jews or
things Jewish.

Indeed, all of this helps to make Bloom the pathetic figure

that he is. Labeled a Jew, he does not consider himself one. Never having been a Jew, he is accused of rejecting Judaism. Born an Irishman, he is not considered one. Born a Protestant and cut off by his actions and convictions from Judaism, he is in turn barred by the community he desires to be a part of because it considers him Jewish. His isolation is thus complete.

There is an interesting lesson here in taking too seriously what Joyce said about his writings. If Joyce really intended Bloom to be a Jew becaus he saw many parallels between the Jews and the Irish, he could have presented Bloom as more convincingly Jewish.[30] As Bloom is given to the reader, about the only thing that makes him Jewish is that his fellow Dubliners (and Joyce, as some readers may learn) think him Jewish. "In fact, Bloom is a magic-lantern Jew, as he is a cut-out Hungarian."[31] That characterization suggests the stage Jew, partner of the stage Irishman. But Bloom is not a stage Jew either. Reuben J. Dodd fits that description much better.[32] Had Joyce made Bloom truly Jewish, either by commitment to the Jewish religion, or to a sense of a Jewish culture pattern, or to a Jewish community, Bloom would have been an entirely different character because he would have had a feeling of belonging and thus something to sustain him. But, as Prescott points out, Bloom's "thought and his feeling . . . are shot through with the disturbing awareness that he is everywhere neither fish nor fowl; and the attitude of his fellow-Dubliners toward him bears him out."[33] Bloom cannot even be called a Jew in the sense that Stephen can be called a Catholic. Perhaps it is just as well. For if Bloom were a Jew by virtue of any criterion other than that the people of Dublin call him one, *Ulysses* would be a very different novel.

There are some other aspects of Bloom's personality in Lestrygonians for which there are no parallels in Stephen's in Proteus. For example, Bloom thinks about Molly's warm stays (154:19-20/156:26-27), records an imaginative exchange between a maid and a young man of the household about a female undergarment (161:16-17/163:30-32), notices and makes a remark to himself that he detests loose stockings on a woman (163:35/166:7), is attracted by petticoats and silk stockings in a store window (166:12/168:30), thinks of buying a petticoat "for

Molly, colour of her new garters" (177:33/180:16), and sees the
erect stance of a young woman passing by as saying, "Look at
me. I have them all on" (179:20/182:5). Throughout the novel,
Bloom is preoccupied with the naughty in sex. Thus women's
undergarments sometimes seem to have an unusual interest for
him. Of this tendency, Sigmund Freud says: "There are others
yet to whom even a part of the body is meaningless, while a
particle of clothing, a shoe or a piece of underclothing, will
gratify all their desires; these are the fetichists."[34] Bloom may
not be far enough along in this tendency to be classed a pervert
(as Freud labels fetishists), but his inclination in that direction
is unmistakable. The pattern of his bizarre requests of Molly
before they were married and since Rudy's death, as it emerges
from her soliloquy, adds merely the final evidence here. His
flirtations (with Martha, by mail; and with Gerty along
Sandymount strand) are enough to make him feel romantic and
daring, but he does not seem interested in attempting to carry
them to any sort of regular consummation. Where Molly is
concerned with sex, Bloom is concerned with the trappings of
sex. Where Molly is excited by the memory and anticipation
of actual love-making, Bloom is excited by a glimpse of a
woman's underwear and the little details of everyday life that
might suggest sex.[35]

The key to understanding this characteristic, which sometimes
seems to border on perversion, is Bloom's masochism. Many
critics mention it. But it should be more than mentioned, for
although it is not much in evidence in Lestrygonians, it is
central to Bloom's personality. Freud says of masochism:

> It comes under our observation in three shapes: as a condition
> under which sexual excitation may be roused; as an expression
> of feminine nature; and as a norm of behaviour. According to
> this one may distinguish an *erotogenic*, a *feminine*, and a *moral*
> type of masochism. The first, the erotogenic masochism, the lust
> of pain, is also to be found at bottom in the other forms; the
> concept of it can be supported on biological and constitutional
> grounds. . . . The third, in certain respects the most important
> form in which masochism appears, has only lately, as a sense
> of guilt that is for the most part unconscious, been properly
> appreciated by psychoanalysis. . . . Feminine masochism, on the
> other hand, is the form most accessible to observation, least
> mysterious, and is comprehensible in all its relations.[36]

This passage was quoted at length because all three categories fit Bloom so well. His erotogenic masochism is plainly exhibited all through the Circe episode, but particularly in his excited grovelling before Bella Cohen (passim) and in his watching through the keyhole the love-making of Molly and Boylan (533/567)[37] A Freudian would also say that only a man who is trying to hurt himself would get himself into as many painful circumstances as Bloom does, forcing himself into situations where he must know he will be ignored, or snubbed, or even attacked.[38] Bloom's feminine masochism is shown in the Circe episode by his turning into a woman (524/536), by his confessing to trying on Molly's clothes (524/536), and by his being assigned tasks of housekeeping (527/539)—a reflection of his similar tasks in actual life: his shopping, his bringing breakfast to Molly. Of moral masochists, Freud says that "the persons in question, by their behavior . . . make the impression of being morally inhibited to an excessive degree, of being dominated by an especially sensitive conscience, although they are not at all conscious of any such ultra-morality."[39] Bloom fits the pattern here too. He disapproves strongly of gambling (171:41/174:18), he drinks sparingly and only at what he considers to be appropriate times of the day (175:25/178:6; 599:26/615:25), he magnifies the importance and the extent of his mild flirtations (360:36/367:10), and yet he seems to think of himself as a daring fellow (707:14/722:26; 707:21/722:33).

There are many other instances in which Bloom fits the Freudian pattern of the masochists. For example, Freud says: "Their phantasies either terminate in an onanistic act or else themselves constitute the sexual gratifications."[40] Bloom, watching Gerty, correspondingly relieves his sexual excitement (363-64/370-71)—to the accompaniment of very appropriately Freudian rockets and roman candles (360/367). Again, Freud says that "the designation masochism comprises all passive attitudes to the sexual life and to the sexual object; in the most extreme form the gratification is connected with suffering of physical or mental pain at the hands of the sexual object."[41] Certainly this description of masochism describes accurately Bloom's relationship to Molly, a relationship which will be gone into more fully later in this chapter.

In Lestrygonians, however, Bloom's fetishism and his masochism are not as apparent as they are later. The half dozen instances of Bloom's interest in female undergarments listed above will seem to some readers to be more than outweighed in the chapter by other evidence of his more normal interest in heterosexual relations. The "Hotblooded young student" (161:14/163:28) in Bloom's thoughts is interested in more than what Mary is ironing. Bloom's little fantasy on love-making "in deep summer fields, tangled pressed grass, in trickling hallways of tenements, along sofas, creaking beds" (166:23/169:1) sends "His heart astir" (166:32/169:8). If there is a touch of voyeurism to those two incidents, Bloom's memory of making love to Molly on Howth (173/175-76) is direct and honest.

There is even less evidence of masochism. In the twenty-two pages of Lestrygonians he thinks of Molly's impending assignation with Boylan only half a dozen times and then generally quite briefly; and his typical reaction is to turn the thought away quickly with "Think no more about that" (152:1/154:3). Several of the references, in fact, are only a few words: "Me. And me now" (173:42/176:22); "Today. Today. Not think" (177:36/180:18). He gives no evidence in Lestrygonians of the kind abundantly available in Circe that he enjoys being cuckolded.

Brivic would probably not support my findings of differences between Stephen and Bloom in the matter of personality pattern. He feels that

> Joyce's attempt to differentiate the two protagonists founders on the fact that they have essentially identical psychological complexes. Both men are centrally preoccupied by the idea of the father taking the mother away from them and castrating or violating her (God taking May Dedalus, Blazes taking Molly). Both consider the mother to have betrayed them; both view sex as a castrating violence; both are horrified at the thought of the woman's castrated genitals and tend to associate themselves with the mother; both feel strongly threatened and tempted by father figures; both are inclined toward fetishism and other strategies of perversion, although only Bloom has submitted to the authoritarian mother so as to placate the threat of the father.[42]

Brivic's analysis indicates, however, that Stephen's fetishism is more clearly seen in *A Portrait* than in *Ulysses* and that in the second novel "his masochism is played down" and appears largely in Scylla and Charybdis, in Stephen's references to Shakespeare, with whom, of course, he identifies. In addition,

Brivic feels that "in certain respects Stephen is a healthier character than Bloom, for Stephen realizes that the essential conflict is with the father and he refuses to live, as Bloom does, in a world of delusion and subterfuge."[43] Finally, as we have seen, the reader's awareness of Bloom's fetishism and masochism grows as he reads. The muting of these aspects in Stephen's personality while one's awareness of them in Bloom's grows, therefore, and Stephen's confronting the threat compared with Bloom's submitting to it do in fact provide important personality differences that help to distinguish the two characters.

What, then, finally, should be said of Bloom? Most of the recent critics, even the most perceptive ones, think well of him. Goldberg says of him, for example:

> Bloom's personal virtues . . . are not to be reduced to a mere good-will which is continually and inevitably frustrated by the ignoble world in which he lives. The good-will is there . . . ; but with it go other, more unusual qualities—tolerance, sympathy, generosity, prudence, fortitude, moderation and humour, and self-knowledge. . . . In all his virtues lies an unselfconscious love of and reverence for life. . . . If his limitations are partly those of his time and place, they are also those of ordinary humanity itself.[44]

A little more enthusiastically, after warning that "Bloom is capable of disgusting acts, and has many petty faults," Sultan concludes:

> He is a unique spirit disguised even from himself within a common, an indistinguishable, externality. It is as though he were a living example of the tension between natural endowment and environmental influence. To the extent that a culture and a set of attitudes and values can impose themselves on a man, modern bourgeois industrial civilization has molded Bloom. But his claim upon our interest and sympathy comes from his showing again and again an innate superiority to the Everyman his environment would have him be.[45]

And Leslie Fiedler proclaims: "Bloom is not merely mythic, much less an ironic commentary on a dying myth. He is a true, a full myth, a new and living myth. . . . Bloom is Ulysses resurrected and transfigured, not merely recalled or commented on or explained."[46]

One can go most of the way with Goldberg, can go much
of the way with Sultan, and can understand Fiedler's
enthusiasm but stop short of Bloom as myth. If Bloom is
superior to Everyman in many ways, he is also inferior to
Everyman in many ways. To the extent that he represents
modern bourgeois culture and its values, he cannot rise above
it. To make him superior to Everyman is to strip him of his
pathos. Furthermore, to mythicize him is to see him as a new
archtype. One can conceive of a modern Everyman as
well-intentioned bumbler, but as fetishist and masochist? One
must honor all of Bloom's virtues; but one must also recognize
his shortcomings and his vices. If he is sometimes endearing,
he is also sometimes exasperating; if worldly, also naive; if
warm, also repelling; if honorable, also devious; if original, also
trite; if clever, also obtuse. He not only helps blind striplings
(178/180) and makes telling social comment like "Flapdoodle
to feed fools on" (159:21/161:33); but he considers seriously the
idea that a vegetarian diet "produces the like waves of the brain
the poetical" (163:38/166:10) and he calls Reuben J. Dodd "a
dirty jew" (180:17/183:2). For Bloom is the man with the "firm
full masculine feminine passive active hand" (658:34/674:33),
whose singing reveals "the ecstasy of catastrophe" (674:10/
689:33), and who "From infancy to maturity . . . resembled
his maternal procreatrix" and "From maturity to senility . . .
would increasingly resemble his paternal creator" (692:30/
708:8).

In the light of this picture of Bloom, it is interesting to
examine Joyce's own pronouncements about him. Early in the
writing of *Ulysses*, Joyce told Budgen of "his Ulysses" (that is,
Bloom): "He is both ["all-round three dimensional" as well as
"ideal"]. . . . But he is a complete man as well—a good man.
At any rate, that is what I intend he shall be"[47] Some of these
claims are open to question. Bloom is frequently a good man,
and he can be considered a complete man in the sense that
he has both virtues and vices; but he is not a complete man
in the sense that Joyce said the original Ulysses was a complete
man: "Ulysses is son to Laertes, but he is father to Telemachus,
husband to Penelope, lover of Calypso, companion in arms of
the Greek warriors around Troy and King of Ithaca."[48] Certainly
this is not a picture of Bloom, for he is an ineffectual son and
a failure in his attempt to be a father to Stephen-Telemachus;

he is cuckolded by Molly-Penelope and kept at a distance by Molly-Calypso; and, a companion to no one, he is the butt of the jokes of the men of Dublin and servant in his own household. Indeed, much of the irony of *Ulysses* stems from Bloom's complete inability to measure up to Ulysses in so many ways. Thus, Bloom as a twentieth-century Ulysses is an ironic commentary on our times.

C. Molly

Critics disagree even more widely about Molly than they do about Stephen and Bloom. Since Philip F. Herring has recently examined that disagreement, I shall summarize his findings. He feels that J. Mitchell Morse and I "are perhaps the severest of Molly's critics," and that Hugh Kenner, S. L. Goldberg, Mary Colum, and Harry Levin "are similarly hostile." C. G. Jung "was more complimentary." "Critics such as Frank Budgen, Stuart Gilbert, Richard Ellmann, Richard Kain, Joseph Prescott and William Y. Tindall find Molly in varying degrees attractive."[49]*

In his overview, Herring finds that Robert M. Adams "is essentially in agreement with Morse" and supports this contention with appropriate—and full—quotations from Adams's two books on Joyce.[50]* Here, however, the controversy becomes unalterably confused; for in *Surface and Symbol* Adams disagreed vigorously with the evaluation of Molly that Morse and I espoused in separate articles.[51]

The degree of Molly's infidelity is only one of many specific matters of disagreement. In Ithaca, a list of twenty-five men who have presumably entered Molly's bed is given (716/731). Herring evidently accepts the list, because he says, "Molly seems to have an insatiable appetite for adultery."[52]* In a more recent article in *Approaches to "Ulysses,"* David Hayman agrees with Sultan that in her relationship with Boylan Molly is engaging "in her first affair" (but he finds naive Sultan's view "that Molly's relative fidelity and her return in spirit to a consideration of Bloom bodes well for the couple's relations").[53] In the very next article in the same volume, however, Darcy O'Brien proposes that there are "obvious exaggerations in

---

Modern Fiction Studies, © 1969, by Purdue Research Foundation, Lafayette, Indiana.

Bloom's list of Molly's twenty-five lovers. . . . But not only is the list at least partially accurate; it is likely that there are lovers unknown to Bloom."[54]

Herring offers several reasons for such wide disagreements about Molly:

> The hostility of many critics to the characterization of Molly Bloom seems to polarize around the following views: they are either revolted by the ugliness of Joyce's mind, the ugliness of Molly's mind (or both), or they see little verisimilitude. If it is primarily the first view, the critics see her as a product of bitterness; this would be the position of Adams. If it is primarily the second view, the hostility springs from an inability to accept Molly's vulgarity as natural, essential or desirable; this view, espoused by Morse and Steinberg, constitutes a rejection of Molly on the basis of personal taste and in addition seems to imply a moral judgment.

> Another objection to the characterization of Molly springs from the disparity between her symbolic and her realistic functions. If on the former level she represents the essence of *Weiblichkeit*, her sensuality is necessarily exaggerated and it is pointless to protest the lack of verisimilitude. On the real level her inadequacies are merely ironic.[55]*

Without necessarily rejecting all of Herring's three reasons, I prefer two others.

I can give them best by quoting first from Goldberg and then from Adams. Goldberg finds Penelope unimpressive: Molly is "self-consciously conceived," the language is "rather weary," and "the mere lack of punctuation does not produce an unbroken rhythm at all." However, he says:

> There is one passage . . . where the coyly ambiguous syntax and the absence of punctuation, unsuccessfully masquerading as the flux of consciousness, do not distract the reader's attention and he is not slightly bored by the sheer monotony of Molly's mind. This is the passage in which Joyce's conception is most clearly realized (and from which most critics quote): the last two pages or so, beginning with Molly's praise of Nature (mountains, sea, fields, cattle, "and all kinds of things") and ending with the final "yes." Whereas the rest of the monologue has an effect rather like that ascribed to Milton—you have to read it once (supplying

_____

Modern Fiction Studies, © 1969, by Purdue Research Foundation, Lafayette, Indiana.

punctuation) for the sense and a second time (taking the
punctuation out again) for the sound—the last pages do flow more
easily.[56]

In objecting to an analysis of Molly by two other critics, Adams
says, "It is odd that precisely on this point of Molly's being
the earth—planetary, uninterrupted, and common as dirt
underfoot—Joyce has left most explicit evidence of his
intentions."[57]

I would not argue, as some do, that an author's intention
before he writes a work of literature or while he is writing
it must be disregarded. Nor do I feel that his statements about
the work after he completed it are irrelevant. Such statements
of intention or accomplishment are generally at least interesting,
sometimes helpful, and on occasion provide necessary clues for
the proper understanding of a work. Sometimes, too, the
argument over whether to consider an author's statement is
hairsplitting. Even if we could somehow manage to destroy all
of Joyce's remarks about the parallels with the *Odyssey* that
he intended in his second novel, we would still have its title,
Ulysses, to tell us of that intention.[58]

The problem, then, is not whether to disregard what the
author said. It is perfectly legitimate for a critic to consider
what Joyce said about the parallels between the *Odyssey* and
Ulysses and the effect he intended; but then the critic must
evaluate not only the intention but how successfully it was
carried out. In evaluating the intention, the critic must be
explicit about his own philosophy of literature and the particular
genre concerned. In evaluating its success, he must draw his
evidence from the whole text and take care that he does not
either project on that text what he wishes to see there or draw
his evidence only from that portion of the text which would
tend to support the author's statement of intentions or the
critic's own purposes.

To suggest that a particular critical interpretation is
inadequate because Joyce intended something else, therefore, or
to characterize Molly on the basis of only the last 5 percent
of Penelope and to disregard the other 95 percent is simply
wrong. What Joyce said about her is interesting and potentially
helpful; what the other characters in the novel say and think
about her is more directly relevant; but her own thoughts, given

to us at some length, are the primary evidence by which we must judge her. Then, if we wish, we can judge how well Joyce accomplished what he said he tried to do.[59]

What then does one learn about Molly from a thorough examination of the text of Penelope? First, she is largely "rere regardant"—not only at the end of the chapter, as Stephen is in Proteus and Bloom in Lestrygonians, but throughout. She thinks mostly about herself: about her girlhood, about Bloom, Boylan, and the other men in her life, about past singing performances, about her living daughter and her dead son. Occasionally she thinks about what may or will come: the concert tour, possible future liaisons, Bloom's breakfast. She shows herself to be of limited intellectual capacity and education; and she is superstitious.[60]

The fact that Molly's silent soliloquy has no omniscient author's sentences makes an important difference between Penelope on the one hand and Proteus and Lestrygonians on the other. The reader of this study may also have noticed in this connection that none of the examples in the section on simulating the psychological stream of consciousness were drawn from Penelope (Molly). One may note the reason by turning to any page of Penelope and examining the text: nowhere will he find the simulations or analogues of sensations, mental images, or perceptions described earlier in this study and found throughout Proteus and Lestrygonians. Rather he will find the words of a woman talking (not necessarily aloud) to herself:

> Frseeeeeeeefronnnng—train somewhere, whistling. The strength those engines have in them, like big giants; and the water rolling all over and out of them all sides, like the end of Love's Old Sweet Sonnnng. The poor men that have to be out all the night from their wives and families in those roasting engines. Stifling it was today! I'm glad I burned the half of those old Freemans and Photo Bits—leaving things like that lying around. He's getting very careless and threw the rest of them up in the W. C. I'll get him to cut them tomorrow for me instead of having them there for the next year to get a few pence for them. (739:34/754:38)[61]

The effect of Molly's inner monologue is less staccato, more flowing, than the streams of consciousness of either Stephen or Bloom because of the impression created by the carefully constructed opening and closing passages of the chapter, by the relatively longer sentences, and by the lack of punctuation. Like Goldberg, however, I find "the coyly ambiguous syntax and the absence of punctuation" unsuccessful as an attempt to simulate "the flux of [Molly's] consciousness."[62] This, of course, is a matter of taste.

In keeping with and a contributor to the impression of flow of Molly's interior monologue is the fact that her thoughts are less well organized than either Stephen's or Bloom's—indeed, so little organized that by almost any standard they can be called unstructured. No one as yet seems to have been able to find an organizing principle behind the eight so-called sentences in Penelope; and the associative pattern of her nominal concepts is less well organized than Bloom's and considerably less well organized than Stephen's.

The words she uses give an impression of the "rather weary language of the English lower middle class."[63] Compared with Bloom (and, of course, Stephen), she tends significantly toward the monosyllabic. Again in comparison, she uses significantly more words of Germanic origin and significantly fewer of Latin, Greek, and Romance origin. She uses only the most common high-level abstractions and tends to reach for the common word, the obvious phrase, and the worn-out image.

Other measures confirm the comparative thinness of Molly's vocabulary and thought content. Test by type-token ratio, a measure of language diversity or richness, shows that Molly uses fewer different words than Stephen does in Proteus and significantly fewer than Bloom does in Lestrygonians. Similarly, the ratio of content words to form words in her stream of thought is significantly lower than the ratio for Stephen and for Bloom.

Although, as one might expect, the ratio of content to form words is significantly lower for Penelope than for Telemachus, the opening chapter of *Ulysses*, oddly, the type-token ratio for Telemachus and Penelope is about the same. Given the relatively sophisticated discussion and language of the sample of Telemachus used (the opening three pages), one would expect a higher type-token ratio for that chapter than for Penelope. The reason that expectation is not born out is largely that Telemachus is narrated by an omniscient author. As a result there is a greater repetition of some nouns and verbs and thus a drop in the type-token ratio. For example, on the first page of the novel, Joyce tells us that Buck "came . . . bearing a bowl," that "He held the bowl aloft," and that he "covered the bowl," using the word *bowl* three times in less than half a page.

Similarly, on the third page Joyce uses the word *said* five times. There are also more repetitions in the omniscient author presentation of a conversation of the names of the characters (Buck, Mulligan, Stephen, Dedalus) than there are in the presentation of a stream of consciousness or inner monologue. Finally, when two people talk, they tend to repeat a single word more frequently than does a person thinking to himself, perhaps partly because two people tend to stay with a topic longer than a person thinking to himself would, but certainly to prevent confusion of reference. Thus the third page of the novel has six uses of the word *mother* and four uses of the word *sea*.

These results indicate that type-token ratios are only useful when comparing passages of similar kinds. One can compare meaningfully type-token ratios for chapters all of which simulate what is happening in a character's mind, but not for a chapter of stream of consciousness and a chapter of omniscient author presentation.

Molly's language is comparatively less interesting in other ways. She uses fewer agglutinations, 1 for every 153 words compared with 1 for every 64 for Stephen and 1 for every 71 for Bloom; and those she does use are less imaginative. Similarly, her thoughts include far fewer poetic images than do the thoughts of Stephen and Bloom and fewer sound correspondences; and her sound correspondences are much less likely to show rhythmic patterns.

The techniques for analysis of expressive behavior developed by Aronson and Weintraub and others are particularly useful in examining Molly's interior monologue. She is clearly much more egocentric than the other two major characters: the sample passages show 86 references to self compared with 43 for Stephen and 13 for Bloom. Furthermore, she evidences no capacity to stand aside and look at herself: whereas the sample passages show 23 examples of direct address for Stephen and 2 for Bloom, the references to self for Molly, more than half again as many for Stephen and Bloom combined, do not show a single example of direct address.

Hayman points out that "in 1904 [Molly] has no women

friends at all and few kind things to say about her sex, whose membership she distrusts individually and en masse."[64] The same is true of her attitude toward men. Thus, although the sample passages from Penelope show 13 examples of references to self and others, almost twice as many as for Bloom and Stephen (7 for Lestrygonians and none for Proteus), the total does not suggest much feeling of group membership of any kind.

The number of negatives found in the sample passages is particularly revealing: 35 for Molly compared with 10 for Stephen and 13 for Bloom, about three times as many as for either of the other two. That finding leads one to question the characterization of Molly's interior monologue as "an affirmation of pure spiritual joy" or as saying "Yes to what happens to herself, Yes to variation and repetition, gestation and parturition, Yes Yes, Yes to Yes."[65]

TABLE 13
**Comparison of *Yes* and Negatives
in Penelope**

Sample	Yes	Negatives
1	1	9
2	0	9
3	0	4
4	0*	7
5	1	6
6	11*	0
Totals	13*	35

*In samples 4 and 6, the word immediately preceding the first word in the sample is *yes*. The total, therefore, could be considered 15 rather than 13; but it would not change the pattern.

Table 13 compares the occurrences of *yes* with the occurrences of negatives in the samples from Penelope. The only two examples of *yes* in the first five sample passages of Penelope are associated with negatives: "Yes because he never did a thing like that before" (723:1/738:1); "what man wasnt he yes he was at the Glencree dinner" (759:10/774:7). Similarly, in the first five sample passages almost all the statements that could in any way be considered affirmative are associated with negatives

or are carefully qualified: "hes not proud out of nothing"
(723:20/738:20); "I couldnt describe it simply it makes you feel
like nothing on earth but he never knew how to embrace well
like Gardner" (732:14/747:15); "how annoying and provoking
because the smell of the sea excited me" (750:17/765:15); "all
the same Im sorry in a way for him" (759:5/774:1); "didnt he
look a balmy ballocks sure enough that must have been a
spectacle on the stage" (759:14/774:11).

A check of the rest of Penelope shows that many of the few
yeses in the rest of the chapter are associated with—and
sometimes bracketed by—negatives: "you couldnt call him a
husband yes its some little bitch hes got in with" (758:18/
773:15); "didnt I dream something too yes there was something
about poetry in it I hope he hasnt" (760:9/775:6); "didnt he
kiss our halldoor yes he did what a madman" (762:27/777:23).

The pattern is very clear. Penelope is heavily negative. Most
of the affirmation comes at the very end of the chapter. In
addition, if one looks at those last lines, it is also clear that
Molly is not affirming the present or the future, but simply
responding to her memory of the physical excitement of Bloom
making love to her on Howth some sixteen years before. And
even then, at the height of her passionate response, her feeling
was "I thought well as well him as another" (768:13/783:9).

Furthermore, in remembering that same episode six hundred
pages earlier (173:21-41/176:1-21), Bloom has reminded us of
all that has happened since and what the current situation is:
"Me. And me now" (173:42/176:22). Whether Molly decides to
give Bloom his breakfast in bed the next morning or not, there
is nothing to indicate that their life together will change, let
alone that the earlier physical passion will be revived.

In this connection it is interesting to review the writing of
Penelope to see how late Joyce himself came to the decision
to make the end of it "affirmative." He began work on the
handwritten draft of the chapter early in 1921, in January or
February. At the end of February, he wrote to Frank Budgen,
"The last word (human, all too human) is left to Penelope"; but
there is no sign of what that last word would be, and later
developments suggest that Joyce did not know at that time.[66]

Ellmann reports that

> one day in July [Joyce] visited [some American friends, Mr. and
> Mrs. Richard Wallace] at their small country house at Chatillon,

and happened to overhear a conversation between Mrs. Wallace and a young painter. The conversation went on and on, Mrs. Wallace repeating the word 'yes' over and over in different tones of voice. Joyce suddenly realized he had found the word he needed to begin and end *Ulysses*, as many years later he would discover with the same excitement that the final word of *Finnegans Wake* would be *the*. He wrote at once to Larbaud, "*Vous m'avez demandez une fois quelle serait la derniere parole d'Ulysse. La voila*: yes." ["You asked me one time what the last word of *Ulysses* would be. Here it is: *yes*."][67]

The letter to Larbaud is dated summer 1921. At about the same time he wrote his often-quoted letter to Frank Budgen (dated 16 August 1921) about Penelope in which he described *yes* as one of the four words expressing the "4 cardinal points" of the chapter and concluded, "though probably more obscene than any preceding episode it seems to me to be perfectly sane full amoral fertilisable untrustworthy engaging shrewd limited prudent indifferent *Weib. Ich bin der Fleisch der stets bejaht*" ["I am the flesh that is constantly affirming"; note that *be jah-en* is translated "answer in the affirmative, assent to, accept, give consent to."][68]

Even at that stage, however, the end of the chapter was not nearly as affirmative as it was to be in the published text. The holograph manuscript of *Ulysses* at the State University of New York at Buffalo, which Peter Spielberg dates August-October 1921, concludes: "and first I put my arms around him and drew him down to me so he could feel my breasts all perfume and I said I will yes.—Trieste—Zurich—Paris 1914-1921." (The fact that Joyce put down the names of the three cities and the dates suggests a sense of conclusion, however momentary.) Ellmann reports that as late as October, Joyce was still "testing out the last words."[70] And an examination of the galley proofs at Harvard shows that nine of the eleven final instances of *yes* were added at that stage and the final manuscript "*yes*" changed to "*Yes*."[71] Since Joyce had not received the proofs of Penelope on 29 October 1921, and was still revising them on 23 January 1922, and since *Ulysses* was published on 2 February 1922, these changes were late indeed.[72]

I would conclude, therefore, that 95 percent of Penelope is negative, that the very late decision to make the ending of the chapter affirmative can be considered as making Penelope affirmative only by disregarding 95 percent of the chapter, and that what affirmation there is is not of the present or the future but of a romantic episode in the past which was flawed at the time ("I thought well as well him as another"), went bad when Rudy died a little more than five years later (720:39-721:1/736:12), and deteriorated gradually but steadily during the eleven years following. Joyce's original written version of Penelope was negative, and the overwhelmingly negative aspects of Molly's personality remain quite clear in the chapter. Unfortunately, Joyce's comments about Penelope as a result of an epiphany he experienced during the summer of 1921 have caused some critics to focus on the last page and a half of the chapter instead of the whole forty-six pages; and, as a result of Joyce's remarks, some of the critics misread even that page and a half.

There is one final bit of evidence in Joyce's comments on the conclusion of Penelope that provides a further warning against accepting an author's evaluation of what he wrote without testing it against the text. Louis Gillet reported that Joyce told him once: "In *Ulysses*, in order to convey the mumbling of a woman falling asleep, I wanted to finish with the faintest word that I could possibly discover. I found the word *yes*, which is barely pronounced, which implies consent, abandonment, relaxation, the end of all resistance."[73] Joyce seems to be the only one, however, who interprets the conclusion of Penelope that way. Hugh Kenner, for example, considers "her 'yes' . . . confidant and exultant." Sultan sees it as an "enthusiastic response." Goldberg writes of the "rhetorical power" of the conclusion. Darcy O'Brien speaks of the conclusion as "a sustained lyrical burst." And Siobhan McKenna's reading of it is firm and full—not in any sense passive or mumbling.[74]

The Aronson-Weintraub pattern of "undoing" ("qualification" and "retraction") is also more in evidence in Molly's thoughts: twelve examples in the samples from Penelope compared with one from the samples from Proteus and five from those from Lestrygonians. Even in the privacy of her own thoughts, therefore, Molly is less forthright or less certain. She tends to qualify with an advance "I suppose" or a following "but." There is also much more evidence of "explaining," a certain measure of rationalization, in Penelope. Both the "undoings" and the rationalizations set up little eddies and side currents in the stream of Molly's thoughts and probably help give it the feeling of being heavy and slow moving compared with the thoughts of Stephen and Bloom.

As any reader might expect, Molly's interior monologue contains many more instances of feeling than do the streams of thought of Stephen and Bloom. Almost half of the expressions found in the first five samples from Penelope are negative, deprecatory, or expressed in negative terms, adding further to the negative aspect of Molly's personality. The statements from the last sample are, as we would expect, positive.

Molly's interior monologue contains even more instances of evaluation. In fact, it is difficult for Molly to think of anyone without passing judgment—and most of the judgments she makes are negative: "That old faggot," "that other fool Henny Doyle," "old frostyface," "his idiotics," "goodfornothings." Aronson and Weintraub describe this category "as an indicator of the defensive use of opinions and preoccupation with what is proper and right."[75]

The picture that develops of Molly from the first 95 percent of the chapter is quite clear. She is very self-centered; her thoughts are not very well organized (understandable, perhaps, for a person in bed in a dark room); her vocabulary is thin and uninteresting; she tends to qualify, retract, and rationalize; she is often negative in her expression of feeling; and she is defensive and often negative in her very frequent evaluations.

In the last page and a half of Penelope, however, remembering an episode that occurred sixteen years before, Molly is warm, affirmative, and even exultant.

If Molly's stream of consciousness fares so poorly when it is compared with Stephen's and Bloom's, perhaps she ought to be examined in other frames of reference. What, for example, can be made of Joyce's having her recline "in the attitude of Gea-Tellus" (721:36/737:8)? An examination of what this goddess meant to the Greeks and Romans suggests the same kind of ironic contrast afforded by the paralleling of Molly and Penelope. Let us first look at the Greek Gaea:

> The surnames and epithets given to her have more or less reference to her character as the all-producing and all-nourishing mother.[76]

> In Athens in particular, she was worshipped as . . . the nourisher
> of children, and at the same time as the goddess of death, who
> summons all her creatures back to her and hides them in her
> bosom. She was honoured also as the primeval prophetess,
> especially in Delphi, the oracle of which was at first in her
> possession as the power who sent forth the vapours which inspired
> the seer.[77]

The very same characteristics appertain to Tellus, her Roman
correlative: "One and the same earth has a twin force, both
a masculine, in that it puts forth seeds, and a feminine, in
that it receives and nourishes them. Hence Tellus is named from
the feminine force, Tellumo from the masculine."[78] All-producing
and all-nourishing mother, nourisher of children, receiver and
nourisher of seeds, sanctuary of the dead, prophetess—certainly
this is the antithesis of Molly, who agrees to sending her
daughter away so as to have more freedom to indulge in her
own physical pleasures (751:18/766:16), who is interested in
receiving the seed neither of her husband nor of her current
lover (727/742), who sneers at a woman who does produce and
nourish many children (727:22/742:21), who denies the memory
of her own dead son a place in her heart (763:39/778:34), and
whose dreams of the future are not prophecies of civic or human
importance, but rather erotic daydreams about being the
celebrated mistress of a famous young poet (761/776). Thus to
the extent that one should consider her Gea-Tellus, her question
"why dont they go and create something" (767:8/782:4) would
be as appropriate a measure of her as of the men for whom
she intended it.

An anthropological yardstick throws further light on Molly as
earth-mother. Here again we see that she can be Gea-Tellus
only in the same sense that she is Penelope:

> Let us briefly summarize and characterize these social
> codeterminants of motherhood in our own society. Maternity is
> a moral, religious and even artistic ideal of civilization, a pregnant
> woman is protected by law and custom, and should be regarded
> as a sacred object, while she herself ought to feel proud and
> happy in her condition. That this is an ideal which can be realized
> is vouched for by historical and ethnographical data. Even in
> modern Europe, the orthodox Jewish communities of Poland keep
> it up in practice, and amongst them a pregnant woman is an
> object of real veneration, and feels proud of her condition. In the

Christian Aryan societies, however, pregnancy among the lower
classes is made a burden, and regarded as a nuisance; among
the well-to-do people it is a source of embarrassment, discomfort,
and temporary ostracism from ordinary social life.[79]

Certainly Molly's mental shrinking at the thought of Milly's
birth and Mina Purefoy's large brood (727:20/742:19) are
representative of the Christian Aryan society and not of the
older tradition of mother as sacred object. Molly thus represents
a sterile society which is the very antithesis of the Melanesian
society described by Malinowski, where

> to the biological adjustment of instinct there are added the social
> forces of custom, morals and manners, all working in the same
> direction of binding mother and child to each other, of giving
> them full scope for the passionate intimacy of motherhood. This
> harmony between social and biological forces ensures full
> satisfaction and the highest bliss.[80]

Molly, however, caught between contradictory rather than
mutually reinforcing social and biological forces, can only repeat
endlessly with different men the routine of love-making. But
that meaningless routine provides for her merely temporary
satisfaction which she must always seek to renew, and for
society, nothing.

A psychoanalytic frame of reference shows Molly to no better
advantage. Indeed, she falls so far short of fitting Helen
Deutsch's picture of "the normal woman in our society" that
in many ways she represents the unhealthy woman in our
society. For example, Deutsch says, "A psychically integrated
woman can gratify both sexuality and motherhood through the
mediation of one man." Almost every page of Molly's soliloquy
offers evidence of her inadequacy by this standard. Molly fails
by other tests too. If a "woman's love for her child is normally
greater than her self-love," Molly's rejection of her live daughter
and her dead son point up further the weakness of her maternal
instincts and the strength of her self-love. For Molly's concern
is largely with compensating for her own personal insecurity:
"In narcissistic women who are physically vain and belong to
the courtesan type . . . , the concern with beauty and sexual
attraction becomes . . . a motive for rejection of the maternal
function. In our own civilization . . . , such motives are only

a superficial rationalization of the woman's deep-lying fear that her ego will be destroyed."[81] Thus the twentieth-century earth-goddess!

Another fictional personage with whom Molly invites comparison, as some critics have remarked, is Chaucer's Wife of Bath.[82] But what a different character emerges from the Wife of Bath's Prologue than from Molly's soliloquy! Where the Wife of Bath thinks of husbands as antagonists to be bested in a never-ending game, Molly thinks of her husband as someone whom she can humiliate.[83] And where the good wife confesses strong admiration for her fifth husband, who subdued her, Molly, in her maturity, admires no man, with the exception perhaps of Stephen, and finds reason for degrading almost every one of whom she thinks. Her pleasant thoughts of youthful admirers are memories of puppy love in the days before she became a woman. She seems to approve of Stephen, but largely as a means of self-gratification and self-glorification. And as yet, Stephen has no claims on her. Should the unlikely liaison develop, Molly would quite obviously try to dominate the situation, and, failing, would probably resort to her typical depreciation and humiliation.

Neither does Molly share the Wife of Bath's scruples about extramarital activities. One could hardly imagine the unfaithful Molly saying, "I wol bistowe the flour of al myn age / In the actes and in fruyt of mariage."[84] The Wife of Bath may flirt to get even with her husband for playing with other women, but she will not cuckold him:

> I seye, I hadde in herte greet despit
> That he of any oother had delit.
> But he was quit, by God and by Seint Joce!
> I made hym of the same wode a croce;
> Nat of my body, in no foul manere,
> But certainly, I made folk swich cheere
> That in his owene grece I made him frye
> For angre, and for verray jalousye.[85]

Molly, of course, has taken at least one lover, makes no attempt to hide the fact from her husband, and even considers, with evident satisfaction, a scene in which she might taunt him with the knowledge (765:27/780:22).

Little things also show the Wife of Bath to be a much more

expansive character. For example, where Molly disapproves of drinking ("couldnt they drink water"—749:8/764:7), Dame Alisoun begins the story of her five husbands with "As evere moote I drynken wyn or ale."[86]

Molly is also lazy. She lies abed long after her husband has not only arisen but shopped. She has her husband bring her mail (61/60) and her breakfast (62-63/62-63) to her in bed, and the reader would gather that this is an everyday occurrence. She finds it much simpler to wait until he can tell her what *metempsychosis* means than to look it up (64:1/64:8). She sends him to have the prescription for her skin lotion filled (83/84) and for books for her to read (64:30/64:39). At twenty past eleven, Bloom comments to himself that Molly must be "Up" (92:18/93:24). But although she is up, at three in the afternoon she does not have a dress on (222:34-36/225:39-41). When she ate in bed, she left not only crumbs but also "some flakes of potted meat, recooked" (716:7/731:16), Plumtree's no doubt (73:41/75:2). That she does not do her own housework is indicated by Bloom's "Mrs. Fleming is in to clean" (92:18/93:24). Even David Hayman, suggesting as a reason for Molly's laziness that there is nothing for her to do, concludes: "A passive woman to whom life must come if it is to be greeted, she clearly lacks the resources of her husband. Consequently, boredom is a condition of her existence and a motive for her behavior."[87]

Has Molly no redeeming features? One can credit her for her frank earthiness, her recognition of Bloom's good qualities, and the fact that her warmest memory is of a passionate episode she shared with Bloom; and as Hayman has pointed out, she sometimes displays "a shrewd eye for character traits, and a gift for epigrammatic description."[88] One can also sympathize with the fact that the bloom of her youth is probably gone and that her husband has failed her in many ways.

By all standards, however, ancient, medieval, and modern, Molly falls far short not only of being an earth-goddess, but even of being an adequate woman. Her stream of consciousness depicts for the reader a shallow mind working over the mulch of everyday existence.

D. Their Relationships

Analysis of the relationships of the three main characters has been as often confused as helped by the analogies to the

Odyssey. Too many of these alleged parallels have been taken literally, the critics not realizing that Joyce often developed characters and relationships in *Ulysses* which, by contrast with characters and relationships in the *Odyssey*, enable him to make ironic comment. Kenner's remark on this subject is extremely well made:

> Homer is employed constantly in a critical mode. He provides a measure of what Joyce's characters *don't* do. The new Penelope, it is obvious, isn't faithful, Telamachus doesn't refuse to cast out his mother for fear of being haunted by her curses, Nausicaa's father isn't a king but a drunkard, she doesn't take Ulysses home with her, and so on.[89]

An understanding of this function of the Homeric parallels is vital to the understanding of the relationships of the three main characters.

Gilbert, amid a good bit of metaphysical and mystical discussion, discovers Stephen to be "the son striving to be atoned with the father."[90] Following Gilbert, the critics have seen Stephen as Telemachus in search of Ulysses. Levin concludes his section on the *Portrait* with "the labyrinth leads towards a father," and quotes the lapwing passage in the library scene from *Ulysses* (208:11/210:35) in support of his thesis. He feels that Stephen, seeking a father, is drawn to Bloom, just as Bloom, seeking a son, is drawn to Stephen, although "the attraction of opposites is not enough to produce a synthesis." Again in referring to the library scene, Levin interprets certain passages (203:15/205:34) to mean that "Bloom . . . is a worthier object of Stephen's filial love than Simon Dedalus."[92] (Many of the critics rely heavily on this scene for their interpretation of the Bloom-Stephen relationship because it is here that Stephen, discussing *Hamlet*, outlines also the theory of a father-son relationship.) Tindall, of course, carries this line of reasoning considerably further. To him, "Bloom is not the disappointment of a quest, but the father found." And "the encounter with Bloom has changed Stephen's inhumanity to humanity." For Tindall, "the drinking of . . . [the] cocoa, Stephen's communion with man, is the climax of the hunt for the father."[93]

Some of the recent critics deny the possibility of a meaningful communion between Stephen and Bloom. Staley, for example, sees Stephen rejecting the "contemporary reenactment of the good Samaritan parable."[94] Many, however, do not. Sultan finds

that "Bloom and Stephen turn from error to the right path,"
that "*Ulysses* is a comic novel in the sense that it depicts a
reconciliation rather than an irrevocable rupture between man
and life: Bloom and Stephen correct and adjust to their
situations," and that "finally Bloom and Stephen are regenerated.
. . . Their story has a 'happy ending.' "[95]

Goldberg would seem to be less hopeful about the fulfillment
of the Telemachus-Odysseus relationship. Although he describes
the similarities and the kinship between Stephen and Bloom in
considerable detail, he recognizes that future meetings of
Stephen and Bloom are "problematic," and that "neither is
capable of that imaginative insight whereby past, present, and
future may all be contemplated together, and which alone could
reveal them to themselves." But, though "they know quite well
that their futures lie apart, they do not know that *in another
sense they do not*," and if self-revelation "is only a possibility
in Stephen's future, *for the artist, for us, it is already present
at this moment*"; and he goes on to find that "from our position
the similarities and parallels appear more significant than the
differences."[96] If true communion and salvation may not occur
for Bloom and Stephen, in other words, their *possibility* is
enough for them to be fact for the author and the reader. As
I read Goldberg, therefore, he feels that in some real sense
salvation occurs.

But claims for a meaningful relationship between
Stephen-Telemachus and Bloom-Odysseus will not stand up
when judged by the text. Gilbert's discussion, since it may well
have been the signpost which indicated the direction for those
who followed, is the most important. The quotation about the
son striving for atonement with the father comes from Haines,
not from Stephen, and is said of Hamlet, not of Stephen
(20:17/18:37). Gilbert's decision to apply this reference to
Stephen, however, seems to be based on the mystical writings
of Mme Blavatsky and her followers rather than on *Ulysses*.[97]
Joyce specifically says that the act of atonement is made by
Bloom (714:2/729:13). There is no reason to ascribe it also to
Stephen. Levin's reference to Stephen's comparing himself to
Icarus (in the lapwing passage), who in his distress called for
his father (Pater, ait) is again no support for this thesis, because
Icarus was calling to Dedalus, his "consubstantial" father. But
just as Icarus is beyond help from his father because he ignored

his instructions, so is Stephen beyond help from his father
because he has refused to follow in his footsteps and has ignored
his advice. If Stephen is a lapwing, "the emblematic bird that
safeguards its children by crying away from its nest," then he
is helpless, because he, as a child, is without parents.[98] Although
it is certainly true, as Levin and all the critics say, that Bloom
is drawn to Stephen, there is no evidence to indicate that
Stephen is drawn to Bloom. And there is much evidence to the
contrary.[99]

Little can be said, either, for any evidence offered from the
library scene.[100] In that "theolologicophilolological" tangle,
Shakespeare is Ulysses, the ghost in *Hamlet*, and Hamlet.[101]
And in that same discourse Stephen is Hamlet, Shakespeare and
the ghost, and Oscar Wilde (or at least Wildean).[102] Thus,
setting up the various equations and substituting in them, one
finds that

Stephen	=	Shakespeare
Shakespeare	=	Ulysses
But, Ulysses	=	Bloom

Therefore,

Stephen	=	Bloom

Or

Wilde	=	the mocker (196:22/198:38 and 196:37/199:13)
Stephen	=	the mocker (200:39/203:16)
Mulligan	=	the mocker (195:13/197:28)
Joyce	=	the mocker[103]

Therefore,

Wilde = Stephen = Mulligan = Joyce

And by further substitutions it can easily be shown that Stephen
is himself his own father and the ghost of his own father, as
Mulligan says that Stephen can show (19:34/18:12;
205:42/208:23). There is also considerable internal evidence that
Stephen is merely giving a display of intellectual gymnastics
in order to impress his audience and is not sure himself how
much of his analysis he really believes.[104] Since what he
says of paternity is an integral part of his exposition of the

Shakespeare-Hamlet relationship, if he is not serious about the latter, the reader might well beware of the former. If, then, it cannot be assumed that even Stephen believes the thesis, how seriously can we accept it as the outline of a concept of paternity which Joyce believed and which he wanted the reader to remember in his understanding of the relationship between Stephen and Bloom. What can be said of the library scene with its puns, shifting cross-references, and myriad possible equations is that it is a brilliant tour de force reminiscent of the schizophrenic conversations in which intellectual undergraduates delight to outdo one another.[105]

Thus the old tale of the *Odyssey* is given a new twist. Stephen (Telemachus) is not looking for a father; he is looking for himself. (Mallarmé's description of Hamlet is equally valid as a description of Stephen on Sandymount strand: *"il se promène, lisant au livre de lui-même"*—185:7/187:10). Having denied his own father, having cut himself off from his family, his country, his religion, his immediate livelihood (Mr. Deasy's school), and his immediate home (the Martello tower), he is lost. In this new version of the old story, Ulysses searches for Telemachus. Instead of Telemachus ordering that Ulysses be fed, we now have Ulysses feeding Telemachus. Instead of Telemachus making arangements for Ulysses (unknown) to have a place to sleep, Telemachus (known but unknowing) refuses Ulysses' offer of a place to sleep. And so Ulysses returns home to an unfaithful wife and Telemachus continues his odyssey.

All that can be said of Molly and Bloom is that she will probably continue to make a fool of him unless he overcomes his embarrassment and his tendencies toward procrastination and masochism enough to take some action.[106] Molly may give Bloom his breakfast in the morning, but as soon as he interferes with her activities or makes any serious demands on her, two things that he must do if he is to reestablish his own manhood, she will put him in his place. Since Bloom probably does not have enough courage to complete his isolation by forcing a showdown with Molly and since in a sense he is enjoying his subjugation, there remains for him only the other alternative: continuance in a state of complete emasculation.

E. Psychological Typologies

It would have been interesting if some of the typologies established by research in daydreaming and in mental imagery were reflected in Proteus, Lestrygonians, and Penelope, but there was not much evidence of them. Singer, for example, found a pattern of daydreaming "reflecting broad and wishful fantasy activity" and "another predominantly associated with fearful daydreams or fantasies preoccupied with the body." He also identified a "dimension of inner experience" at one end of which "one finds the person given to extremely fantastic, fanciful daydreams, while at the other end the pattern suggests a considerably controlled, orderly, objective type of daydreaming."[107] There is nothing in the three chapters that can properly be considered fantastic and surprisingly little that can be considered fanciful in the sense in which Singer uses the terms.

Stephen remembers with some self-mockery a former fantasy of himself as a great author (41:28-38/40:29-40), and in his imagination he shoots a post office employee "to bloody bits" (42:42/42:2) and engages in some erotic play with a "virgin" he brings from "beyond the veil" (49:26-39/48:25-49:6). One might also consider the "pale vampire" of his poem (48:34/48:1) a "fearful daydream." Bloom has a short erotic fantasy triggered by thoughts of Agendath Netaim (166:15-31/166:33-167:7) and imagines himself briefly as a hotel waiter serving "halfnaked ladies" (173:8-11/175:28-32). And Molly has short fantasies about being taken by Boylan (733:15/748:17; 739:20/754:24) and a "blackguardlooking fellow" (762:40/777:36); and she dreams of taking Stephen as a lover (760:38-761:23/775:35-776:19). But there are no surrenders to Messianic fantasies or to daydreams of orgies or heroic achievement; and what fanciful daydreaming there is is relatively short.[108] The fantasies in *Ulysses* are reserved largely for the *Walpurgisnacht* of Circe, where their unreality and their nightmare characteristics are emphasized.

One of the personality patterns associated with types of mental imagery that Richardson summarized is reflected in Penelope. As we have seen, Molly is a verbalizer—her stream of consciousness is a monologue, not a train of visual images or a mixture of images and words. According to Richardson, verbalizers tend to be passive, dependent, submissive, slow, calm,

and even-tempered. These adjectives certainly do apply much
more to Molly than they would to Stephen or Bloom. Richardson
also reports that visualizers tend to be active, independent, and
hypersensitive and that people who both visualize and verbalize
tend to be impatient, aggressive, and intolerant.[109] Both Stephen
and Bloom visualize and verbalize, but it is difficult to tell
whether the mix of visualization and verbalization for either
one differs significantly from the mix for the other; and the
individual personality patterns associated with visualizers and
with visualizer-verbalizers do not fit either Stephen or Bloom
very well. Stephen, for example, is independent, hypersensitive,
and intolerant; and Bloom is active and independent, but not
hypersensitive.

There is no necessity, of course, for the three streams of
consciousness to reflect the typologies and attendant personality
patterns described by psychological research. Psychologists
describe the patterns as tendencies, not types to which everyone
can be assigned. It is interesting to note, however, that for all
his imagination, Joyce did not write into the streams of
consciousness in Proteus, Lestrygonians, or Penelope the often
complex and bizarre fantasies that psychologists tell us are
typical of many people. Had he chosen to do so for one of the
three characters, he would have differentiated that character
even more from the other two than he did. Perhaps his not
having done so is a reflection of the moral standards of his
day and of the problems he had with censors of various kinds.

That does not mean, however, that the daydreaming of all
three characters is at the "controlled, orderly, objective" end of
Singer's continuum. As we have seen, Stephen's stream of
consciousness shows quite a bit of control and order, and even
of objectivity, whereas Molly's shows little; and the degree and
kind of control in Bloom's stream of consciousness is different
from that shown in the streams of consciousness of the other
two characters. Another difference is the degree of sensuality
of the erotic daydreams of the three characters. Stephen's erotic
fantasy evokes echoes of a cool, ethereal, almost sexless maiden:
"Touch me. Soft eyes. Soft soft soft hand. I am lonely here.
O, touch me soon, now" (49:37/49:4). Bloom's erotic fantasy is
much more sensual: "A warm human plumpness settled down
on his brain. . . . All kissed, yielded: in deep summer fields,
tangled pressed grass, in trickling hallways of tenaments, along

sofas, creaking beds. . . . His heart astir" (166:18/168:33). Molly, of course, daydreams of orgasm (739:20/754:24).

F. Unsolvable Problems

The final paragraph of this chapter's section on relationships begins, "All that can be said of Molly and Bloom is that she will *probably . . . unless he. . . .*" Those words typify the problem of the critic or scholar who writes about Joyce, for frequently Joyce does not give enough evidence on which to base secure conclusions. The reader of *Ulysses* is frequently not even sure about important aspects of the past in the Bloom household, let alone of its future.

Let us take, for example, the matter of Molly's lovers. As we have seen, despite the list of Molly's so-called lovers on page 716/731, David Hayman says that "on June 16, 1904, she is beginning, after ten years of virtual abstinence, her first adulterous affair." In support of this contention, he argues:

> First, she has only Bloom to measure against Boylan as a sexual partner. Second, she makes too much of her newly acquired status. Third, the wording ("Assuming Mulvey to be the first term of his series"—731)[110] indicates that this is a subjective list or at least a projection arranged by an objective voice in chronological order. If Bloom is the true author, we must ask what the sources of his information are and why they are not more reliable. Perhaps the list is best seen as a product of the narrator's playfulness; a whimsical pandering to Bloom's apprehensions, Molly's aspirations and the reader's expectations.[111]

Let us examine the points one by one. Darcy O'Brien contends, "When Molly says of Boylan, 'I never in all my life felt anyone had one the size of that' (742), she obviously implies a good deal of experience."[112] One could add an additional item of evidence from Molly's soliloquy: "theyre all mad to get in there where they come out of youd think they could never get far enough up and then theyre done with you" (745:30/760:31). Does that mean that Molly must have had lovers before Boylan? Certainly not. But it does make Hayman's first point untenable.

To Hayman's second point, that Molly "makes too much of her newly acquired status," I would reply that she is much less defensive and self-justificatory than one would expect of a woman in her first adulterous affair. Nowhere in Penelope is there a statement like "does he expect me to do without because he wont" or "how many years does he expect me to wait before I find someone to do what he should." Instead, we find the relatively mild and uninformative "well he can think what he likes now" (727:34/742:35) and "O thanks be to the great God I got somebody to give me what I badly wanted to put some heart up into me" (743:25/758:27). Not "I *finally* got" or "*after all these years* I got"; just "I got." Once again, the evidence does not prove that Molly had lovers before her affair with Boylan; but it is at least an adequate counterargument to Hayman's second point.

Hayman's third point brings us to the crux of the problem: Is Bloom the true author? "Perhaps the list is best seen as a product of the narrator's playfulness." There is no way of telling who made the list; and therefore there is no way of evaluating it. Thus by blurring the matter in Ithaca with stylistic experimentation ("I am writing *Ithaca* in the form of a mathematical catechism")[113] and by not providing in Molly's thoughts the evidence that the reader might well expect to find there, Joyce prevents any solution of the question.

I cannot claim that Joyce did this purposely. Nor can I insist that it is an unfortunate lapse. I am quite aware that one can argue that the reader should not expect to know more about Molly than her fellow Dubliners do; that if there is no evidence that Bloom knows, why should the reader; or that *that* is the way life is (do we ever really know in real life?). There is, after all, the example of Pirandello's writings. The point is not whether Joyce left the question unanswered deliberately or by inadvertence or even whether his having obscured the answer to the question makes *Ulysses* a better or a poorer novel (although in candor I find that I must express my personal dissatisfaction). Rather it is that there is no profit in discussing the matter any further. The text does not provide enough information for a satisfactory answer. And appealing to Irish sexual patterns or to Joyce's personal life for clues, as some critics do, is not helpful.[114] (Even if it were, many would argue that it is not appropriate.)

This and many other unanswered questions about *Ulysses*, therefore, never will be answered. Did Stephen and Bloom achieve some sort of communion? Will Stephen return and recognize and emulate Bloom's virtues; and will Bloom thus find a son? Does Bloom reassert his manhood? Will Molly give their marriage another chance? Will she even give Bloom his breakfast in the morning? And, finally, will a poor boy from an Irish slum find fame and fortune as a writer? Joyce does not give us enough information in *Ulysses* to answer these questions. And precisely because we cannot tune in again next week, we will never know.

PART III
The Stream-of-Consciousness
Technique and Beyond

12
The
Stream-of-Consciousness
Technique Defined

In discussing James Joyce's *Ulysses,* critics frequently use interchangeably a whole series of terms: stream of consciousness, stream of thought, *monologue intérieur,* internal monologue, interior monologue, soliloquy, silent soliloquy. Are they all appropriate? Certainly *monologue* and *soliloquy,* even when qualified by such adjectives as *interior* and *silent,* are odd terms to apply to thought and consciousness, which, while they may contain words, have many other components.

Jacques Souvage raises the problem again in his careful survey of what the critics have said about the dramatized novel in his *Introduction to the Study of the Novel*:

> Mr Edel makes an attempt at clearing up the confusion which has arisen round the terms "stream of consciousness" and "internal monologue." He finally draws the following tentative distinction between the two terms: "The term 'internal monlogue' becomes merely a useful designation for certain works of fiction of sustained subjectivity, written from a single point of view, in which the writer narrows down the stream of consciousness and places us largely at the 'centre' of the character's thoughts—that centre where thought often uses words rather than images." May I, by way of qualifying Mr Edel's statement, propose that the terms "internal (or interior) monologue" and "stream of consciousness" be reserved for, respectively, the cases where the inner flux is being released and those where sensory experience is superimposed upon the inner flux in process of releasement.[1]

We must go on from Edel's definition, however, as, in fact, he himself does, because, as I shall show below, the problem is not only one of "where thought often uses words rather than images," but also where consciousness often uses images rather than—or in addition to—words.

What is needed to distinguish usefully among these terms so

245

that they themselves will distinguish what various authors are attempting is a valid psychological or semantic framework. Such a framework would help differentiate not only the levels of speech involved but also the prespeech levels of consciousness. One could then meaningfully sort out the various terms and assign them according to their literal meaning (rather than the meaning arbitrarily assigned to them by a critic) and the level of speech or prespeech which they can most adequately define. An adequate framework for such a purpose is, in fact, available.

At this point it will be useful to examine again what the stream-of-consciousness novelists and some other critics claim the stream-of-consciousness technique to be. Placing Joyce's stream-of-consciousness technique in such a context will help to show more clearly what it is and may help to sharpen the term *stream-of-consciousness technique* and the other terms associated with it.

Dujardin, regarded by many as the innovator of the technique, writes:

> Le monologue intérieur est, dans l'ordre de la poésie, le discours sans auditeur et non prononcé, par lequel un personnage exprime sa pensée la plus intime, la plus proche de l'inconscient, antérieurement à toute organisation logique, c'est-à-dire en son état naissant, par le moyen de phrases directes réduites au minimum syntaxial, de façon à donner l'impression "tout venant".[2]

And Dujardin quotes Valery Larbaud, an early enthusiast of the stream-of-consciousness technique, as saying that the *monologue intérieur* is the expression "des pensées les plus intimes, les plus spontanées, celles qui paraissent se former a l'insu de la conscience et qui semblent antérieures au discours organisé."[3] Budgen says that Joyce told him, "I try to give the unspoken, unacted thoughts of people in the way they occur"; and Djuna Barnes notes that Joyce said, "I have recorded, simultaneously, what a man says, sees, thinks, and what such seeing, thinking, saying does, to what you Freudians call the subconscious."[4] Virginia Woolf, herself acclaimed a successful stream-of-consciousness novelist by the critics, discusses at some length what modern novelists should try to do:

> Examine for a moment an ordinary mind on an ordinary day. The mind receives a myriad impressions—trivial, fantastic, evanescent, or engraved with the sharpness of steel. From all

sides they come, an incessant shower of innumerable atoms; and as they fall, as they shape themselves into the life of Monday or Tuesday, the accent falls differently from of old.

The task of the novelist, then, as she sees it, is "to convey this varying, this unknown and uncircumscribed spirit, whatever aberration or complexity it may display with as little mixture of the alien and external as possible." She gives what well may be a credo for stream-of-consciousness writers: "Let us record the atoms as they fall upon the mind in the order in which they fall, let us trace the pattern, however disconnected and incoherent in appearance, which each sight or incident scores upon the consciousness." Of *Ulysses*, she says:

> Mr. Joyce . . . is concerned at all costs to reveal the flickerings of that innermost flame which flashes its messages through the brain, and in order to preserve it he disregards with complete courage whatever seems to him adventitious, whether it be probability, or coherence or any other of these signposts which for generations have served to support the imagination of a reader when called upon to imagine what he can neither touch nor see.[5]

She made this analysis on the basis of chapters of *Ulysses* which were then (April 1919) appearing in the *Little Review*.

More recent critics have also attempted definitions. Lawrence E. Bowling writes:

> . . . The stream of consciousness technique may be defined as that narrative method by which the author attempts to give *a direct quotation of the mind*—not merely of the language area but of the whole consciousness. . . . The only criterion is that it introduce us directly into the interior life of the character, without any intervention by way of comment or explanation on the part of the author.[6]

And Robert Humphrey finds that "we may define stream-of-consciousness fiction as a type of fiction in which the basic emphasis is placed on exploration of the prespeech levels of consciousness for the purpose, primarily, of revealing the psychic being of the characters."[7]

These statements agree on several important points. First, they suggest that the stream-of-consciousness writer must not intervene "by way of comment or explanation"; he must provide "as little mixture of the external and alien as possible." Other statements by some of the authors quoted above support this contention. For example, Dujardin says that the *monologue intérieur* "est un discours du personnage mis en scène et a pour objet de nous introduire directement dans la vie intérieure de ce personnage, sans que l'auteur intervienne par des explications ou des commentaires."[8] An oft-quoted statement of Joyce holds that "the artist, like the God of creation, remains within or behind or beyond or above his handiwork, invisible, refined out of existence, indifferent, paring his fingernails."[9] The intrusive author of old, then, must disappear.

Second, the statements agree that the stream-of-consciousness technique is not soliloquy, either spoken or unspoken; and third, they agree that the stream-of-consciousness technique expresses, or explores, or simulates, or is concerned with a prespeech level of consciousness: "sa pensée . . . la plus proche de l'inconscient, anterieurement à toute organisation logique"; "des pensées . . . qui paraissent se former à l'insu de la conscience et qui semblent antérieures au discours organisé"; "unspoken, unacted thoughts"; "the atoms as they fall upon the mind"; "*a direct quotation of the mind*—not merely of the language area but of the whole consciousness"; "the prespeech levels of consciousness."

Before we can decide, therefore, just exactly what we mean by the stream-of-consciousness technique, we must first decide what the prespeech levels of consciousness are. Alfred Korzybski has included them in his outline of the four basic levels of abstraction: "(1) the event, or scientific object, or the submicroscopic physico-chemical processes, (2) the ordinary object manufactured from the event by our lower nervous centres, (3) the psychological centres, and (4) the verbal definition of the term."[10] According to the stream-of-consciousness novelists and to the critics quoted, the stream-of-consciousness technique deals with the levels below, or at least before, Korzybski's fourth or verbal level. Furthermore, it cannot possibly be concerned with Korzybski's first level, the physicochemical level; for as Phyllis Bentley says, "James Joyce records the swift succession of thought association, but even he does not detail the physical nerve processes of which they are a result."[11]

Miss Bentley might have said that a novelist cannot (rather than does not) detail the physical nerve processes, for contemporary science is still not sure of what they are and how they operate. And even if the processes were thoroughly understood, they would be so far removed from our organization of them into what we know as reality and so numerous that the author could not possibly present them in such a way that the reader could collect them into meaningful patterns of any sort. Instead of being confronted by a simulation of the stream of consciousness, the reader would be confronted by William James's "booming, buzzing confusion." It might be further argued that, psychologically at least, Korzybski's first level is not a level of consciousness.

The stream-of-consciousness technique, therefore, is concerned with the second and third levels of abstraction set up by Korzybski. It is at these levels that one finds psychological images, sensations, and perceptions. And, as we have already seen, it is precisely these two levels of consciousness that Joyce simulates in Proteus and Lestrygonians. We have already seen that all the examples of Joyce's presentation of sensations, images, and perceptions used in the discussion of simulating the psychological stream of consciousness came from Proteus and Lestrygonians. There are no such examples in Penelope, for in that chapter Joyce was doing something else. I would prefer, therefore, to use the term *stream-of-consciousness technique* for what Joyce attempts in Proteus and Lestrygonians and to apply another term to Penelope.

Penelope, Molly's monologue, represents Korzybski's fourth, or verbal, level. At this next higher level, an author presents the ruminations of a character who has organized his thoughts into language, translating the matters of paramount importance in his stream of consciousness into language patterns. At this level, the character is speaking silently to himself. *Interior monologue* or *silent soliloquy* would therefore be a very apt characterization of what the author is attempting. As Edel points out, the term *monologue* (or *soliloquy*) "because of its associations with the theatre, has distinct literary and dramatic connotations that do not convey the idea of flux." They indicate a character speaking in some coherent, organized way, even if silently. Thus *interior monologue* and *silent soliloquy* are more adequately suited to the characterization of a level of abstraction higher than the stream of consciousness.[12] Penelope, then, would be a good example of silent soliloquy. As Humphrey says, soliloquy in the stream-of-consciousness novel "tacitly" assumes an audience, and "respects the audience's expectation of mental wandering."[13]

We can continue to employ Korzybski's concept of abstraction to describe still higher levels of abstraction in writing. The next level would be the *spoken* monologue or soliloquy, which is seldom used in the novel. Edel says: "In the traditional monologue—in its original Greek sense it was a 'speaking alone'—the character gives the audience logical and reasoned thoughts. These are 'structured' even while they represent inner reflection or reverie, and are rendered without relation to external stimuli." The great soliloquies of Shakespeare, Edel points out, "are *structured* monologues in which the mind presents reasoned and ordered thought, the 'end-product' of the stream of consciousness, not the disordered stream itself."[14]

Much of the Cyclops episode in *Ulysses* is a variety of spoken monologue:

> I was just passing the time of day with old Troy of the D.M.P.
> at the corner of Arbour hill there and be damned but a bloody
> sweep came along and he near drove his gear into my eye. I
> turned around to let him have the weight of my tongue when
> who should I see dodging along Stony Batter only Joe Hynes.
> —Lo, Joe, says I. How are you blowing? Did you see that bloody
> chimneysweep near shove my eye out with his brush?
> (287:1/292:1)

Gilbert characterizes the chapter nicely: "The story, here, is told by a simple and bibulous Dubliner, a nondescript, in the highly coloured idiom of the profane vulgar, and his simple periods are punctuated by Our Lady's adjective."[15]

At the next level we have *erlebte Rede,* or narrated monologue, a term not used in discussions of *Ulysses.* Dorrit Cohn defines *erlebte Rede* as

> the renderings of a character's thoughts in his own idiom, while
> maintaining the third-person form of narration. Its transposition
> into present tense and first person . . . yields an interior
> monologue. It would appear . . . that these two techniques for
> rendering a character's psyche differ only by simple grammatical
> details. But when we see *erlebte Rede* in a surrounding epic
> context, its distinctiveness becomes clear: by maintaining the
> person and tense of authorial narration, it enables the author
> to recount the character's silent thoughts without a break in the
> narrative thread.

She offers the following example from Kate Leslie's thoughts in D. H. Lawrence's *The Plumed Serpent*:

Yet she could not be purely this, this thing of sheer reciprocity. Surely, though her woman's nature was reciprocal to his male, surely it was more than that! Surely he and she were not two potent and reciprocal currents between which the Morning Star flashed like a spark out of nowhere. Surely this was not it? Surely she had one tiny Morning Star inside her, which was herself, her very own soul and star-self![16]

Mrs. Cohn finds a version of *erlebte Rede* in *A Portrait*:

The slide was shot suddenly. The penitent came out. He was next. He stood up in terror and walked blindly to the box.

At last it had come. He knelt in the silent gloom and raised his eyes to the white crucifix suspended above him. *God would see that he was sorry. He would tell all his sins. His confession would be long, long. Everybody in the chapel would know then what a sinner he had been. Let them know. It was true. But God had promised to forgive him if he was sorry. He was sorry.* He clasped his hands and raised them toward the white form, praying with his darkened eyes, praying with all his trembling body, swaying his head to and fro like a lost creature, praying with whimpering lips.[17]

About this passage she makes the comment: "Unlike Kate's thoughts, Stephen's—which are not italicized in the original—are presented in alternation with outer happenings, including his own actions. He waits, stands up, kneels, raises his eyes, clasps and raises his hands, and so forth. At the same time he thinks his thoughts of fervent penitence in *erlebte Rede* (past tense and third person)."[18]

At the next level, the author summarizes in omniscient author's sentences what his characters think, feel, and do. A passage from Dorothy Richardson's *Pilgrimage* quoted by Edel exemplifies this level very well:

She glanced through the pages of its opening chapter, the chapter that was now part of her own experience; set down at last alive, so that the few pages stood in her mind, growing as a single day will grow, in memory, deep and wide, wider than the year to which it belongs. She was surprised to find, coming back after the interval of disturbed days, how little she had read.[19]

As we have seen, Joyce uses omniscient author's sentences in Proteus and Lestrygonians.

The highest level of abstraction would be the one in which

the author quite obviously intrudes, as does Trollope in the
following passage:

> But let the gentle-hearted reader be under no apprehension
> whatsoever. It is not destined that Eleanor shall marry Mr. Slope
> or Bertie Stanhope. And here, perhaps, it may be allowed to the
> novelist to explain his views on a very important point in the
> art of telling tales. He ventures to reprobate that system which
> goes so far to violate all proper confidence between the author
> and his readers. . . . Our doctrine is, that the author and the
> reader should move along together in full confidence with each
> other.[20]

Joyce gives a satiric sample of such writing in *Ulysses* in Oxen
of the Sun: "Did heart leap to heart? Nay, fair reader. In a
breath 'twas done but—hold! Back! It must not be! In terror
the poor girl flees away through the murk. She is the bride
of darkness, a daughter of night. She dare not bear the
sunnygolden babe of day" (406:37/413:36).

The six levels described above should be thought of as points
on a vertical continuum rather than as steps on a ladder.
Similar continua can be made of points which fall between those
specified above. For example, Dickens characterizes a waterman
at the beginning of chapter two of *The Pickwick Papers* as "a
strange specimen of the human race, in a sackcloth coat, and
apron of the same, who with a brass label and number round
his neck, looked as if he were catalogued in some collection
of rarities." Because Dickens says that the man is "a strange
specimen of the human race" instead of supplying the reader
with the necessary details by which he can form the same
conclusion for himself, the statement is a higher level of
abstraction than the quotation from Dorothy Richardson cited
above. It is not as high a level of abstraction as the quotation
cited from Trollope, however, because it does present some
detail; thus Dickens is less intrusive than Trollope in the
passages quoted.

Similarly the omniscient author's sentences in *Ulysses* are not
quite as high a level of abstraction as the passage quoted from
Dorothy Richardson, for Joyce would never say that one of his
characters "*was surprised to find* . . . how little she had read."[21]
Yet they are certainly higher than the example from the
Penelope chapter of *Ulysses* which was labeled above as silent
soliloquy. For example:

Stephen, an elbow rested on the jagged granite, leaned his palm against his brow and gazed at the fraying edge of his shiny black coatsleeve. Pain, that was not yet the pain of love, fretted his heart. Silently, in a dream she had come to him after her death, her wasted body within its loose brown graveclothes giving off an odour of wax and rosewood, her breath, that had bent upon him, mute reproachful, a faint odour of wetted ashes. (7:25/5:29)

The omniscient author is apparent here, much more so than in soliloquy.

Any single paragraph or passage may draw from several levels of abstraction, as does this passage from *Ulysses*, which includes an omniscient author's sentence and silent soliloquy: "Stephen bent forward and peered at the mirror held out to him, cleft by a crooked crack, hair on end. As he and others see me. Who chose this face for me? This dogsbody to rid of vermin. It asks me too" (8:21/6:27). Or this one, which contains stream of consciousness, silent soliloquy, and omniscient author's statement: "He passed, dallying, the windows of Brown Thomas, silk mercers. Cascades of ribbons. Flimsy China silks. A tilted urn poured from its mouth a flood of bloodhued poplin: lustrous blood. The huguenots brought that here. *La causa è santa!* Tara, tara. Great chorus that. Tara. Must be washed in rainwater. Meyerbeer. Tara: bom bom bom" (165:41/168:17).

Finally, we must recognize that none of the sections from *Ulysses* are what could be called pure stream of consciousness. Proteus and Lestrygonians contain silent soliloquy and omniscient author's sentences. And, as I have already indicated, Penelope is interior monologue or silent soliloquy; so, it cannot be pure stream of consciousness either. Indeed, pure stream of consciousness would be difficult, if not impossible, to read; for it would be a mass of psychological images, sensations, and perceptions which would provide little or no orientation or method of organization for the reader. Furthermore, it would be much too inefficient. As Phyllis Bentley points out, summary is particularly useful and efficient in dispatching unimportant matters on which the author does not wish to dwell.[22] Attempts to locate a character in time and space by means of a device of a lower level of abstraction than omniscient author's statements also lead to the same sort of self-conscious writing so typical of Dujardin's *Les Lauriers sont coupés*. Here is a typical passage from the opening pages:

The hour is striking, six, the hour I waited for. Here is the house I have to enter, where I shall meet someone; the house; the hall; let's go in. Evening has come; good the air is now; something cheerful in the air. The stairs; the first steps. Supposing he has left early; he sometimes does; but I have got to tell him the story of my day. The first landing; wide, bright staircase; windows.[23]

Dujardin might have done better if his opening sentence in the paragraph above stated simply, "Prince entered the house, walked through the hall, and began to mount the first set of steps." His character oriented, hc could then have focused on Prince's thoughts, pausing only now and then to maintain the orientation with a phrase or two. As the passage stands, most of it is taken up with really unimportant matters. Joyce regularly locates or moves his characters in both Proteus and Lestrygonians by means of omniscient author's sentences, which, as summaries, take less time to inform the reader than do the simulated raw data of the stream of consciousness. Frequently, however, because he presents these sentences in the idiom and style of the character's stream of consciousness, they are not as obtrusive as they otherwise would be.

We have thus characterized Proteus, Lestrygonians, and Penelope by means of the vertical continuum which we have built up:

- statement by an obviously intrusive author
- summary statement by an omniscient author
- narrated monologue (*erlebte Rede*)
- spoken soliloquy or monologue
- silent, internal, or interior soliloquy or monologue (*monologue intérieur*)
- (simulated) stream of consciousness[24]

The lowest level of abstraction is the one to which I would limit the term *stream of consciousness*. Proteus and Lestrygonians would thus be stream-of-consciousness chapters. Again according to my definition, silent, internal, or interior soliloquy or monologue occurs when a character speaks silently to himself, in his own mind; the character can hear himself in his mind's ear, but no one else can hear him or need even be aware that he is thinking. Penelope would thus be classified as internal monologue or silent soliloquy. Simple summary statement appears in Proteus and Lestrygonians as the omniscient author's sentences which help to orient the reader.

Neither spoken soliloquy nor statement by an obviously
intrusive author appears in Proteus, Lestrygonians, or Penelope.
The characters in those three chapters sometimes speak to
themselves (for example, "Here. Am I going to Aunt Sara's or
not?"—39:28/38:38), but there is nothing to suggest that they
do so aloud. The obviously intrusive author, of course, would
have no place in either passages of stream of consciousness or
of silent monologue. In the light of Joyce's statement about the
desirability of the author's being "invisible," one would not
expect him to intrude in his works. (Critics generally agree that
the Oxen of the Sun chapter, from which an example of the
intrusive author was given above, is a series of parodies. Joyce
does intrude, however, particularly in the second half of *Ulysses*.
We shall examine this intrusion and the possible reasons for
it in chapter fourteen.)

Discrimination between the different levels of abstraction is
useful for several reasons. First, the technique Joyce used in
Proteus and Lestrygonians is different from the one he used
in Penelope. It should not, therefore, be given the same label.
Second, the series of terms that the critics tend to use
indiscriminately (stream of consciousness, stream of thought,
monologue intérieur, internal monologue, soliloquy, silent
soliloquy, *erlebte Rede*) have different connotations, which causes
critical confusion. I have, therefore, attempted to assign them
to the different levels of abstraction according to the meanings
of the words which make up those terms so that the terms
would be meaningful critically and psychologically.

What, then, may finally be said about Joyce's stream-
of-consciousness technique? First of all, it certainly does not
provide an "exact reproduction" of thought or "the total contents
of thought" as some critics have claimed; it *simulates* the
psychological stream of consciousness. From the evidence
provided by the analyses in this study and from the evidence
of the extensive revisions that Joyce made in the various
manuscripts during the various stages of *Ulysses,* it is also
apparent that any charges that his stream-of-consciousness
technique was simply automatic writing or that it presented
gibberish or confusion must be discarded. Careful planning and
extensive revising on the one hand and automatic writing on
the other are mutually exclusive. And the fact that from the
streams of consciousness of Stephen and Bloom and from the
internal monologue of Molly the reader sees three distinctly

different personalities is ample evidence that while Joyce's technique may give the appearance of confusion (an appearance carefully cultivated by the author, it should be noted), it is actually highly selective and very carefully organized.

The analyses indicate, finally, that the stream-of-consciousness technique provides the novelist with an additional means of projecting the personality of his characters beyond what is available to the traditional author. A novelist generally develops the personality of a character by having him do and say certain things, by having other characters say certain things about him, and by omniscient author's descriptions and comments. These devices are all available to the modern novelist; as we have seen, even Joyce, who thought that an author should be "invisible, like God," did not forgo entirely the use of omniscient author's sentences in Proteus and Lestrygonians, the two chapters in *Ulysses* in which the stream-of-consciousness technique is used most consistently and extensively. In addition to the traditional devices, however, the novelist now has available the stream-of-consciousness technique. The technique is thus not only a method of dramatizing the mind, to use Bowling's phrase; it is also a device which the novelist may use to aid him in one of his important problems, character projection and development.

13
The Sources of the Stream

Wassily Kandinsky has written:

> Inner necessity originates from three elements: (1) Every artist, as a creator, has something in him which demands expression (this is the element of personality). (2) Every artist, as a child of his time, is impelled to express the spirit of his age (this is the element of style)—dictated by the period and particular country to which the artist belongs (it is doubtful how long the latter distinction will continue). (3) Every artist, as a servant of art, has to help the cause of art (this is the quintessence of art, which is constant in all ages and among all nationalities).[1]

Let us first quickly acknowledge Joyce's contribution as both a servant and a help to art. By developing the stream-of-consciousness technique so completely and so imaginatively, he made available to the novelists who followed him a very sensitive and very useful method of delineating character and simulating consciousness.

Looking back at that development after the passing of half a century, however, one is tempted to ask questions arising from Kandinsky's first two points. Why Joyce? And why at that particular time? Since the second question is easier to deal with than the first, let us begin with that one.

Perhaps a good place to start would be with Arthur Symons's *The Symbolist Movement in Literature*, which appeared in 1899. According to Mary Colum, it was widely read among university students in Dublin. It is not clear when Joyce read the book. Richard Ellmann suggests 1900. Tindall says flatly 1902, when Yeats introduced Joyce to Symons. (We can be reasonably sure that Joyce did read the book because Mary Colum reports that "he had picked up some of his knowledge of the French symbolists, particularly Mallarmé" from Symons.)[2]

Whether he actually read the book, however, and, if so, when, is not important. I am not trying to prove Joyce derivative. Rather I am trying to show that an important part of his talent was the ability to translate some of the intellectual and aesthetic ideas of his day into imaginative fictional techniques. If he had not met the ideas in Symons's book, he would have heard them from his fellow students in Dublin; and if not in Dublin, then later in Paris. Symons shows us what some of those ideas were.

In his introductory chapter to *The Symbolist Movement*, Symons says, "In speaking to us so intimately, so solemnly, as only religion had hitherto spoken to us, [literature] becomes itself a kind of religion, with all the duties and responsibilities of the sacred ritual." He repeats the prayer of Gérard de Nerval "that I might have the power to create my own universe about me, to govern my dreams instead of enduring them." And he quotes Mallarmé's dictum that "the pure work implies the elocutionary disappearance of the poet."[3] (In the full French text Joyce might also have found "encore la faut-il, pour omettre l'auteur.")[4]

Those ideas, of course, were available elsewhere. In 1857, Gustave Flaubert had written, "An artist must be in his work like God in creation, invisible and all-powerful: he should be everywhere felt, but nowhere seen."[5] And in the preface to *The Picture of Dorian Gray*, published in 1891, Oscar Wilde had written, "The artist is the creator of beautiful things. To reveal art and conceal the artist is art's aim."[6]

It is not surprising, therefore, that in *A Portrait*, Joyce should have characterized the girl in the stream who inspired Stephen "To live, to err, to fall, to triumph, to recreate life out of life!" as a "wild angel . . . , the angel of mortal youth of beauty," or that the image he used to describe Stephen's entry into a new way of life should be throwing open "the gates." Thus Joyce is not propounding a new aesthetic principle when he has Stephen tell Lynch, "The artist, like the God of the creation, remains within or behind or beyond or above his handiwork, invisible, refined out of existence, indifferent, paring his fingernails," or when he has Stephen think of himself as "a priest of the eternal imagination, transmuting the daily bread of experience into the radiant body of everlasting life."[7]

What is unusual is the emotional energy with which Joyce

manages to infuse the individual images and the extended metaphor by reserving them for the climax of the novel, by clustering them in highly emotional passages, and finally by establishing the explicit parallelism of the two priesthoods. And for the purposes of this study what is even more important, what is also unusual, is the degree that he was able to implement his definition of the artist, the degree to which he was able to refine himself out of existence in the first half of *Ulysses*, to make himself as author invisible by the use of the stream-of-consciousness technique.

There also runs through Symons's *Symbolist Movement in Literature* the awareness that writers were striving for a greater subjectivity, a more explicit reflection of consciousness, that they were attempting to present to their readers their characters' very souls:

> Here, then, in this revolt against exteriority, against rhetoric, against a materialistic tradition; in this endeavour to disengage the ultimate essence, the soul, of whatever exists and can be realized by the consciousness; in this dutiful waiting upon every symbol by which the soul of things can be made visible; literature, bowed down by so many burdens, may at last attain liberty, and its authentic speech.

> "Sincerity and the impression of the moment followed to the letter": that is how [Verlaine] defined his theory of style, in an article written about himself.

> That the novel should be psychological was a discovery as early as Benjamin Constant, whose *Adolphe* anticipates *Le Rouge et le Noir*, that rare, revealing, yet somewhat arid masterpiece of Stendahl. But that psychology could be carried so far into the darkness of the soul, that the flaming walls of the world themselves faded to a glimmer, was a discovery which has been made by no novelist before Huysmans wrote *En Route*.

> Huysmans has found words for even the most subtle and illusive aspects of that inner life which he has come, at last, to apprehend.[8]

Again, it is only a short step to Joyce's attempt to record "what a man says, sees, thinks, and what such seeing, thinking, saying does, to what you Freudians call the subconscious," to Virginia Woolf's expression of interest in "the dark places of psychology," and to her charge to the novelist: "Let us record the atoms as they fall upon the mind in the order in which they fall, let us trace the pattern, however disconnected and incoherent in appearance, which each sight or incident scores upon the consciousness."[9] But again it is the degree to which Joyce was able to recognize the fruitfulness of the approach and to fulfill it that distinguishes him from other novelists.

Joyce may well have encountered the same interest in the impressions of the moment and their impact on consciousness among writers and painters when he was in Paris in 1902 and 1903. Herschel B. Chipp says:

> The artists participating in the subjectivist movement of about 1885-1900 may be grouped together only because they all rejected the realist conceptions or art that had prevailed for the preceding generation. . . . The movement was first heralded for the poets in the Symbolist Manifesto (1886) by Jean Moréas (1856-1910). . . . The Symbolist poets, grouped about Stéphane Mallarmé (1842-1898), developed theories of art which were to provide an ideological background for the thoughts of many of the artists. . . . Baudelaire's *Culte de moi* was revived; his concern with individuality of expression was transformed into an obsessive concern with the intimate, private world of the self that led to a rejection of the exterior world. . . .
> The Symbolist poet Gustave Kahn . . . wrote in *L'Evénement*, 1886, that "the essential aim of our art is to objectify the subjective (the externalization of the Idea) instead of subjectifying the objective (nature seen through the ideas of a temperament). Thus we carry the analysis of the Self to the extreme. . . ."
> The artists of this movement also wrote essays on their art, sometimes with great perception. . . . Most of them were prolific letter-writers, and they poured out their artistic struggles in the form of lengthy correspondence with their friends.[10]

Joyce should have encountered such discussions in Paris in the cafés, in at least one of which he "argued about literature in French, and when . . . knowledge of that language failed, in Latin," or in later years in Trieste, Paris again, and Zurich.[11] He probably also encountered them in the newspapers and magazines.

The impressionists were interested in sensations well before the symbolist manifesto. A critic wrote in 1875, "Manet paints as he sees, he reproduces the sensation his eye communicates to him."[12] As early as the 1880s, French artists were reading, debating, and trying to put into practice David Sutter's essays on phenomena of vision and the "scientific aesthetics" of Charles Henry, Ogdon N. Rood, and Michel E. Chevreul. The results were evident not only in their impressionistic paintings, but in what they wrote and said. Paul Gaugin, for example, wrote to a friend in 1885: "For a long time the philosophers have considered the phenomena which seem to us supernatural and yet of which we have the *sensation*. Everything is in that word. . . . All our five senses arrive *directly at the brain*, conditioned by an infinity of things which no education can destroy."[13] And Louis Le Bail learned from Pissarro: "Don't work bit by bit but paint everything at once by placing tones everywhere, with brushstrokes of the right color and value, while noticing what is alongside. Use small brushstrokes and try to put down your perceptions immediately. . . . Do not define too closely the outline of things: it is the brushstroke of the right value and color which should produce the drawing."[14] So much did the impressionists' paintings rely for their effect on the individual dab or dot of (often pure) color that they developed theories of retinal fusion and argued over the proper distance from which to view particular canvases.[15]

As late as 1912, Albert Gleizes and Jean Metzinger were writing, "To establish pictoral space, it is necessary to resort to tactile and motor sensations and to all our faculties" and "There is nothing real outside of us, there is nothing real but the coincidence of a sensation and an individual mental tendency. Far be it from us to throw doubt upon the existence of the objects which impinge upon our senses; but it is reasonable that we can only be certain of the image which they produce in our mind."[16]

The intimate world of the self; objectifying the subjective; visual, tactile, and motor sensations; the impact of minute impressions on the eye and mind; building a form from myriad brushstrokes instead of starting with the outline of things—all aspects of the stream-of-consciousness technique as Joyce developed it and as Virginia Woolf described it. Joseph Prescott reminds us that there are intimations of this interest even in *Stephen Hero*, where "we hear that 'Cranly grew used to having sensations and impressions recorded and analysed before him [by Stephen] at the very instant of their apparition.' The introspective habit, illustrated several times in the *Portrait*, is an appropriate base from which Joyce is later to find congenial

the internal monologue in Dujardin's *Les Lauriers sont coupés*
and the probings of modern psychologists."[17]

The artist himself, it was argued further, must be conscious
of sensations and impressions in order that his personality may
permeate the work of art. As we have seen, while Joyce was
writing *A Portrait*, Gleizes and Metzinger wrote: "To establish
pictoral space, it is necessary to restort to tactile and motor
sensations and to all our faculties." The rest of the paragraph
reads: "It is our entire personality which, contracting or
expanding, transforms the plane of the painting. As, reacting,
the plane reflects the painter's personality on the understanding
of the viewer, pictoral space defines itself: a sensitive pathway
between two subjective persons."[18] In *A Portrait* Joyce wrote:

> The simplest epical form is seen emerging out of lyrical literature
> when the artist prolongs and broods upon himself as the center
> of an epical event and this form progresses till the centre of
> emotional gravity is equidistant from the artist himself and from
> others. The narrative is no longer purely personal. The personality
> of the artist passes into the narration itself, flowing round and
> round the persons and the action like a vital sea.[19]

The cubist's personality "transforms" the painting, whereas the
personality of Joyce's artist "passes into the narration." Just as
the painter's personality and the viewer's understanding are
joined by "a sensitive pathway between two subjective persons,"
so, for Joyce's artist, "the centre of emotional gravity is
equidistant from . . . himself and from others."

Through those same years, writers and painters also sought
to develop new styles—styles appropriate to their subjects as
well as personal styles. They wrote and spoke about it
frequently. In 1852, Flaubert declared: "What seems beautiful
to me, what I should like to write, is a book about nothing,
a book dependent on nothing external, which would be held
together by the strength of its style, just as the earth, suspended
in the void, depends on nothing external for its support; a book
which would have almost no subject, or at least in which the
subject would be almost invisible, if such a thing is possible."[20]
In 1882, Gauguin wrote, "I have sacrificed everything this year,
execution, color, for the benefit of style, forcing upon myself
something different from what I know how to do. This is, I
believe, a transformation which hasn't yet borne its fruits, but

which will bear them."[21] In 1910, the futurists, in their technical manifesto, referred to "this truism, unimpeachable and absolute fifty years ago": "that the subject is nothing and that everything lies in the manner of treating it. That is agreed; we, too, admit that."[22] If one thinks of the artists and their paintings, one can trace in his mind's eye the individual struggles for style and how different were the individual styles that the painters developed—Manet, Monet, Renoir, Degas, Seurat, Van Gogh, Cézanne, Picasso. In Joyce one sees the same sort of struggle to develop a style as, under the early influence of Ibsen, he proceeds from the relative realism of *Dubliners* and *Stephen Hero* through the more subjective and impressionistic *A Portrait of the Artist as a Young Man* to the thoroughly subjective and impressionistic stream-of-consciousness technique in *Ulysses*. Indeed, Joyce told his brother, "Don't talk to me about politics. I am only interested in style."[23] In some ways Joyce's career is reminiscent of that of the French painter Manet a generation earlier, who began as a realist and developed into the father of impressionism.[24]

The symbolists and the impressionists maintained a balance, however, between subjectivism and realism. As we can see today, there is nothing "unreal" about the paintings of the impressionists. Symons quoted Huysmans to that effect, for Joyce to read:

> In *Là-Bas* [1891] . . . he had, indeed realized . . . that "it is essential to preserve the veracity of the document, the precision of detail, the fibrous nervous language of Realism, but it is equally essential to become the well-digger of the soul, and not to attempt to explain what is mysterious by mental maladies. . . . It is essential, in a word, to follow the great road so deeply dug out by Zola, but it is necessary also to trace a parallel pathway in the air, and to grapple with the within and the after, to create, in a word, a spiritual Naturalism."[25]

And as late as the 1920s Monet was saying: "I am simply expending my efforts upon a maximum of appearances in close relation with unknown realities. When one is on the plane of concordant appearances one can not be far from reality, or at least from what we know if it."[26]

Denis Rouart says of the *Water Lilies* that Monet was painting about the time Joyce was finishing *Ulysses*, "such is the distinctive feature of the last *Water Lilies,* which, while unquestionably representational paintings, yet attain a musicality of form and color sufficient to justify them independently of the subject. This fusion of realism and lyricism was the greatest achievement of Monet's old age, and the fulfillment of his Impressionism."[27] And Kenneth Clark says of the paintings: "This poem takes its point of departure from experience, but the stream of sensation becomes a stream of consciousness. And how does this consciousness become paint? That is the miracle. By a knowledge of each effect so complete that it becomes instinctive, and every moment of the brush is not only a record but also a self-revealing gesture."[28] Except for the references to old age and painting, these remarks would apply as well to Joyce's *Ulysses* as to Monet's *Water Lilies.*

This insistence on realism helps us to see that Joyce's concept of the epiphany was part of the same aesthetic that produced the stream-of-consciousness technique. In *Stephen Hero* Joyce wrote:

> Stephen as he passed on his quest heard the following fragment of colloquy out of which he received an impression keen enough to afflict his sensitiveness very severely.
> The Young Lady—(drawling discreetly). . . O, yes . . . I was . . . at the . . . cha . . . pel . . .
> The Young Gentlemen—(inaudibly) . . . I . . . (again inaudibly) . . . I . . .
> The Young Lady—(softly) . . . O . . . but you're . . . ve . . . ry . . . wick . . . ed . . .
> This triviality made him think of collecting many such moments together in a book of epiphanies. By an epiphany he meant a sudden spiritual manifestation, whether in the vulgarity of speech or of gesture or in a memorable phrase of the mind itself. He believed that it was for the man of letters to record these ephiphanies with extreme care, seeing that they themselves are the most delicate and evanescent of moments.[29]

Joyce himself wrote a series of such epiphanies.[30] A. Walton Litz says, "Many of the early *Epiphanies,*written in Paris during the winter and spring of 1902-03, eventually found their place in the texts of *Stephen Hero,* the *Portrait,* and *Ulysses,*" and he demonstrates the process.[31]

The impressionists also saw their work as recording "delicate and evanescent moments." Here are two descriptions by Monet

of his attempt to record a particular series of epiphanies, the
first statement from 1890 and the second from 1926:

> I am working terribly hard, struggling with a series of different
> effects (haystacks), but . . . the sun sets so fast that I cannot
> follow it. . . . I am beginning to work so slowly that I am
> desperate, but the more I continue, the more I see that a great
> deal of work is necessary in order to succeed in rendering that
> which I seek: "Instantaneity," especially the "enveloppe," the same
> light spreading everywhere, and more than ever I am dissatisfied
> with the easy things that come in one stroke.[32]

> At that time I was painting some haystacks forming a fine group
> not very far away. One day I noticed that my light had changed,
> so I said to my daughter-in-law, please go to the house and bring
> another canvas. She brought it, but in a few minutes it had
> changed again, than another, and another was begun! And I
> painted on each one only when the light was right. It's quite
> easy to understand.[33]

Guy de Maupassant also recorded the process:

> Last year . . . I often followed Claude Monet in his search of
> impressions. He was no longer a painter, in truth, but a hunter.
> He proceeded, followed by children who carried his canvases, five
> or six canvases representing the same subject at different times
> of day and with different effects.
> He took them up and put them aside in turn, following the
> changes in the sky. And the painter, before his subject, lay in
> wait for the sun and shadows, capturing in a few brushstrokes
> the ray that fell or the cloud that passed. . . .
> I have seen him thus seize a glittering shower of light on the
> white cliff and fix it in a flood of yellow tones that, strangely,
> rendered the surprising and fugitive effect of that unseizable and
> dazzling brilliance. On another occasion he took a downpour
> beating on the sea in his hands and dashed it on the canvas—and
> indeed it was the rain he had thus painted.[34]

Joyce and Monet each attempted to record "the most delicate
and evanescent of moments" as it flashes across the mind, to
capture the "unseizable" in a few impressionistic strokes. Once
again we are reminded of Virginia Woolf's statement: "Life is
not a series of gig lamps symmetrically arranged; but a luminous
halo, a semi-transparent envelope surrounding us from the
beginning of consciousness to the end. Is it not the task of the
novelist to convey this varying, this unknown and

uncircumscribed spirit, whatever aberration or complexity it may display, with as little mixture of the alien and external as possible?"[35] At least one writer, a member of the naturist movement, which opposed symbolist "decadence," had also enunciated the concept of the epiphany before Joyce did (although he did not use the term). At the Naturist Congress in Brussels (1896) a young disciple of Saint-Georges de Bouhélier declared: "A man appears on the scene—he is a mason, or a warrior, or a fisherman. The aim is to take him by surprise in a moment of eternity; the sublime instant when he leans forward to polish a cuirass or cast his net into the water. We know that his attitude at such a moment is in harmony with God."[36] Once again, however, who first enunciated the principle is less important than what Joyce did with it.

As Goldberg indicates, Joyce made the epiphany an important aspect of the stream-of-consciousness technique. After analyzing a passage of Bloom's stream of consciousness from Hades, Goldberg finds:

> Clearly this is far from the random, unorganized chaos it was once thought to be. It is certainly no mere record of a stream of passively registered "impressions" or "associations." . . . It is quite deliberately and artistically shaped and rendered. And the basis of organization is clearly the unit of the paragraph, and the paragraph in turn the expression of a separate mental act of apprehension. In short, the real artistic (and dramatic) unit of Joyce's "stream of consciousness" writing is the epiphany. What he renders dramatically are minds engaged in the apprehension of epiphanies—the elements of meaning in apprehended life.[37]

A glance at the passage Goldberg analyzes or at almost any paragraph in Proteus or Lestrygonians longer than three or four lines is enough to sustain this claim.

Monet's use of the word *instantaneity* also brings us to another problem faced by the stream-of-consciousness writer: that a moment of time is multidimensional, whereas language, in which the writer seeks to present that moment of time, is linear. It was not a new problem, of course. As Gleizes and Metzinger pointed out in 1913, Leonardo da Vinci alluded to "simultaneity" (as many of the painters referred to it) in the fifteenth century:

> We know well that the sight, by rapid observations, discovers in one point an infinity of forms: nevertheless it comprehends only

one thing at a time. Suppose, reader, that you were to see the whole of this written page at one glance, and were immediately to judge that it is full of different letters; you do not at the same moment know what letters they are, nor what they would say. You must go from one word to another and from line to line if you wish to attain a knowledge of these letters, as you must climb step by step to reach the top of a building, or you will never reach the top.[38]

Writers in the nineteenth century had begun experiments to overcome—or at least to alleviate—the linearity of language. In the famous episode at the fair in *Madame Bovary*, Flaubert alternated back and forth between the lovers and the ceremonies at the fair to approximate simultaneity. Dujardin's use of the internal monologue in *Les Lauriers sont coupés*, in its attempt to simulate what happened in a man's consciousness, could be considered another attempt to come to grips with the problem, as could some of Mallarmé's experiments with typography.[39]

There was also talk before World War I of cubist poetry, which attempted the simultaneity of cubist paintings. Thus Apollinaire's "Lundi Rue Christine," written in 1913, "is made up of simultaneous snatches of conversation, overheard, or invented, by the poet in the little Left Bank bar."[40] The ideograms of Apollinaire were also an attempt to adapt cubist techniques to poetry to achieve an effect of simultaneity. Here, for example, is his "Miroir":[41]

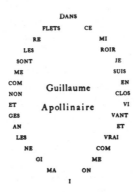

Ezra Pound's definition of an image in 1913, with its emphasis on instantaneity, also indicated a concern with the same phenomenon:

> An "Image" is that which presents an intellectual and emotional complex in an instant of time. I use the term "complex" rather in the technical sense employed by the newer psychologists, such as Hart, though we might not agree absolutely in our application.
> It is the presentation of such a "complex" instantaneously which gives that sense of sudden liberation; that sense of freedom from time limits and space limits; that sense of sudden growth, which we experience in the presence of the greatest works of art.[42]

Through most of the nineteenth century, painters, with their two-dimensional canvases and their ability to simulate a third dimension, did not think that their medium was faced with a problem of simultaneity. Indeed, in 1888 Paul Gauguin wrote of the obvious advantages of multidimensional painting over a linear medium like music:

> Painting is the most beautiful of all the arts. . . . Like music, it acts on the soul through the intermediary of the senses: harmonious colors correspond to the harmonies of sound. But in painting a unity is obtained which is not possible in music, where the accords follow one another, so that the judgment experiences a continuous fatigue if it wants to reunite the end with the beginning. The ear is actually a sense inferior to the eye. The hearing can only grasp a single sound at a time, whereas the sight takes in everything and simultaneously simplifies it at will.[43]

Seurat's satisfaction with the process of retinal fusion, in which the retina supposedly synthesized the individual dabs or dots of paint which artists applied to their canvases, was another example of how successfully painters felt simultaneity worked for them.

Joyce refers to the problem explicitly in *A Portrait:* "An aesthetic image is presented to us either in space or in time. What is audible is presented in time, what is visible is presented in space."[44] He considers it again at the beginning of Proteus:

> Stephen closed his eyes to hear his boots crush crackling wrack and shells. You are walking through it howsomever. I am, a stride at a time. A very short space of time through very short times of space. Five, six: the *nacheinander.* Exactly: and that is the ineluctable modality of the audible. Open your eyes. No. Jesus! If I fell over a cliff that beetles o'er his base, fell through the *nebeneinander* ineluctably. I am getting on nicely in the dark.

My ash sword hangs at my side. Tap with it: they do. My two
feet in his boots are at the end of his legs, *nebeneinander*.
(38:11/37:11)

Thus artists and other writers had worked with the problem
of simultaneity before Joyce faced it in attempting to present
"what a man says, sees, thinks, and what such seeing, thinking,
and saying does, to . . . the subconscious." Once again, however,
the measure of Joyce as an artist is not in the initial statement
of the problem, but in his responding to a challenge which his
predecessors had barely begun to meet, recognizing the promise
of what Dujardin and others had started, and developing
techniques to simulate multidimensional reality.

It is interesting to note how many of the ideas at the
beginning of Proteus which Stephen attributes to Aristotle
(*maestro di color che sanno*—38:8/37:8) and for which, indeed,
there are references in Aristotle were also matters of current
concern for the writers and artists at the end of the nineteenth
century and the beginning of the twentieth. Take just the
opening four lines of the chapter: "Ineluctable modality of the
visible: at least that if no more, thought through my eyes.
Signatures of all things I am here to read, seaspawn and
seawrack, the nearing tide, that rusty boot. Snotgreen,
bluesilver, rust: coloured signs." Now here are a series of
quotations from and about writers and painters of the period:

> That central secret of the mystics, from Pythagoras onwards, the
> secret which the Smaragdine Tablet of Hermes betrays in its "As
> things are below, so are they above"; which Boehme has classed
> in his teaching of "signatures." (Symons, 1899)[45]

> To discern a form implies, beside the visual function and the
> faculty of movement, a certain development of the imagination.
> (Gleizes and Metzinger, 1912)[46]

> Let the forms which [the artist] discerns and the symbols in
> which he incorporates their qualities be sufficiently remote from
> the imagination of the vulgar to prevent the truth which they
> convey from assuming a general character. (Gleizes and
> Metzinger, 1912)[47]

> The picture will exist ineluctably. [Le tableau existera
> inéluctablement.] (Apollinaire, 1913)[48]

[Braque] has taught the aesthetic use of forms so hidden that only certain poets had intimations of them. These luminous signs flare around us, but only a handful of painters have grasped their plastic significance. (Apollinaire, 1913)[49]

Red, the most powerful of all colors, is the symbol of height, force, and authority; lilac or violet of the solar spectrum, the symbol of coquetry, instability, and weakness. Orange is the image of pride and vanity; blue, that of modesty and candor, etc. (David Sutter, 1880)[50]

Since plastic form is the basis of all enduring art, and since the creation of intense form is impossible without color, I first determined, by years of color experimentation, the relative spatial relation of the entire color gamut. (Stanton MacDonald Wright, 1916)[51]

Forms and objects as signs and signatures, the ineluctability of visible forms, the signification of colors, the relation between color and form—it is all there. Joyce may have turned to Aristotle for solutions to aesthetic problems, but the problems themselves, and possible solutions to them, had been matters of intense interest to writers and painters for some years before he became a writer and continued to be while he was writing *Ulysses*. Stephen's experiment at the beginning of Proteus and Joyce's development of the stream-of-consciousness technique reflected clearly the aesthetic interests of the times.

Also relevant to this discussion is the interest among novelists of the second half of the nineteenth century in point of view. The obviously intrusive author who spoke directly to the reader was rejected, and many writers insisted on the importance of telling their story from the point of view of one of the characters involved, even to the point of having one of the characters tell the story. I need only mention here the novels of Joseph Conrad and Henry James as the most obvious examples. Percy Lubbock in *The Craft of Fiction*, Melvin J. Friedman in *Stream of Consciousness: A Study in Literary Method*, Leon Edel in *The Psychological Novel, 1900-1950*, and Wayne Booth in *The Rhetoric of Fiction* have all told this story and discussed its meaning too well for me to repeat it here.[52] The painters, of course, from the early impressionists to the late cubists (that is, from Joyce's birth to the completion of *Ulysses*) also wrote and talked about point of view and undertook endless experiments in point of view on their canvasses. Once again, Joyce's development of the stream-of-consciousness technique, a technique for viewing the world through the eyes and mind of a particular character, was a culminating and fulfilling step in a long trend.

We should also note movements parallel to those in aesthetics among the sciences, philosophy, psychology, music, and the popular arts. Indeed, many claim that new discoveries in science around the turn of the century gave new direction and new thrust to the aesthetics of the day. As a result of the discoveries of men like Thompson, Planck, and Rutherford,

> the generation that grew to manhood about 1900 realized that the ground which their forbears had confidently trod was now giving way beneath their own feet; reality was everywhere breaking up into elusive, impalpable fragments. Disbelief in the solidity of the world—formerly the subject of paradoxical discussions on the part of philosophers, or of wild conjectures by more or less unbalanced individuals—became an actual issue, an urgent, crucial, and compelling problem. The intellectual conceptions which for centuries had been man's stay and support in hours of doubt and trial, now suddenly collapsed, encumbering the path of progress with their débris.[53]

Wassily Kandinsky remembered that when Rutherford and Soddy reported the radioactive disintegration of the atom in 1903 there was a "terrific impact, comparable to the end of the world. . . . All things became flimsy, with no strength or certainty. I would hardly have been suprised if the stones had risen in the air and disappeared. To me, science had been destroyed. In its place—a mere delusion, guesswork."[54]

George Bernard Shaw has one of his characters in *Too True To Be Good* (1932) make much the same statement:

> Yes, sir: the universe of Isaac Newton, which has been an impregnable citadel of modern civilization for three hundred years, has crumbled like the walls of Jericho before the criticism of Einstein. Newton's universe was the stronghold of rational Determinism: the stars in their orbits obeyed immutably fixed laws; and when we turned from surveying their vastness to study the infinite littleness of the atoms, there too we found the electrons in their orbits obeying the same universal laws. Every moment of time dictated and determined the following moment, and was itself dictated and determined by the moment that came

before it. Everything was calculable: everything happened because
it must: the commandments were erased from the tables of the
law; and in their place came the cosmic algebra: the equations
of the mathematicians. Here was my faith: here I found my
dogma of infallibility: I, who scorned alike the Catholic with his
vain dream of responsible Free Will, and the Protestant with his
pretence of private judgment. And now—now—what is left of it?
The orbit of the electron obeys no law: it chooses one path and
rejects another: it is as capricious as the planet Mercury, who
wanders from his road to warm his hands at the sun. All is
caprice: the calculable world has become incalculable: Purpose and
Design, the pretexts for all the vilest superstitions, have risen
from the dead to cast down the mighty from their seats and put
paper crowns on presumptuous fools.[55]

Armand Siegel explains the impact this way:

The impact of the success of science, or what amounts to the
same thing for purposes of this discussion, its *intensity* as a
functioning social institution, may also help to resolve the
following paradox: That art seemed less alienated by the
mechanistic, literal theories of earlier eras of science than it is
by the seemingly more cautious operational theories of the current
era. Although a man was represented as a sort of elaborate
clockwork by the science of the nineteenth century, this was not
so disturbing, in view of the extent to which this earlier science
fell short of precisely implementing this picture, as the modern
description, which is in less literal terms but is far more advanced
in its empirical progress.[56]

At the very time, then, that aesthetics had become interested
in exploring below the surface of reality, in questioning
traditional materialism, science exploded that reality and that
materialism and to the short strokes, dabs, and dots of the
impressionists added invisible particles and waves. Once again
reality proved to be not palpable and solid in outline but hidden,
evanescent, mysterious—like the fleeting, darting, suggestive
sensations, images, and perceptions in the flow of consciousness.

There were similar tendencies in philosophy and psychology.
Bergson's ideas, as we know from Wyndham Lewis's *Time and
Western Man* and from Shiv K. Kumar's *Bergson and the
Stream of Consciousness Novel*, were important in developing
many of the concepts behind the stream-of-consciousness
technique.[57] The philosopher-psychologist William James devoted
an important section of his major work, *The Principles of*

Psychology (1890), to the stream of consciousness. An important tool for the German psychologists for the ten years before and ten years after the turn of the century was introspection. Before World War I, T. E. Hulme was telling artists to place themselves "inside the object instead of surveying it from outside."[58] Joyce may not have read about or discussed the works or specific ideas of any of these men, but they were very much part of the intellectual world in which he lived.

Joyce did know something, however, about C. G. Jung and Sigmund Freud, whose explorations into depth psychology made an important impact on the intellectual life of Europe after the turn of the century. Jung published a study on word association in 1913, and Freud's entire theory was based on free association. In 1920 Freud published (anonymously) "A Note on the Prehistory of the Technique of Analysis" in which he noted recommendations to writers on the use of free association by Schiller (1788), by J. J. Garth Wilkinson (1857), who was a physician, a poet, and a Swedenborgian mystic, and by Ludwig Börne, whom Freud had read as a boy.[59] "The Art of Becoming an Original Writer in Three Days," an essay written by Börne in 1823 and published in the first volume of the 1962 edition of his collected works, ends:

> And here follows the practical application that was promised. Take a few sheets of paper and for three days on end write down, without fabrication or hypocrisy, everything that comes into your head. Write down what you think of yourself, of your wife, of the Turkish war, of Goethe, of Fonk's trial, of the Last Judgment, of your superiors—and when three days have passed you will be quite out of your senses with astonishment at the new and unheard-of thoughts you have had. This is the art of becoming an original writer in three days.[60]

Again, whether or not Joyce read any of the documents of the psychoanalytic movement, with its interest in free association, dream symbols, and other processes of the mind, it was part of the world which made the stream-of-consciousness technique possible.

Music also contributed to the stream-of-consciousness technique, particularly the Wagnerian concept of the leitmotif: "In *Ulysses* . . . Joyce constructs, as Wagner had done in the *Ring*, a major, an all-inclusive work resting upon carefully placed leitmotifs as upon steel reinforcements. There are more than 150 motifs in the book, and of its 786 pages," says William Blisset, "I have found fewer than fifty without the sounding of at least one."[61] Blisset's analysis of the impact of Wagner on the symbolists and on Joyce's works is particularly thorough. Clive Bell, just before the publication of *Ulysses*, also saw the reflections of jazz in that novel:

> In literature Jazz manifests itself both formally and in content. Formally its distinctive characteristic is the familiar one—syncopation. It has given us a ragtime literature which flouts traditional rhythms and sequences and grammar and logic. . . . In prose I think Mr. Joyce will serve as a perhaps not very good example. . . . In his later publications Mr. Joyce does deliberately go to work to break up the traditional sentence, throwing overboard sequence, syntax, and, indeed most of those conventions which men habitually employ for the exchange of precise ideas. Effectually and with a will he rags the literary instrument.[62]

There were also reverberations between jazz and the films—and Sergei Eisenstein's discussion of the relationship between film and jazz techniques contains phrases and concepts we have encountered elsewhere: "repetition of identical elements . . . the intensity of contrast"; "several perspectives, simultaneously employed"; "A man enters his environment—the environment is seen through his eyes"; "intricate synthesis."[63] Joyce, of course, was interested in the film, at least commercially, and may have been influenced by techniques in the newly developing popular art.[64] Eisenstein made his first film in 1920, while Joyce was writing *Ulysses*.

The concept of montage as it developed in the films is reminiscent of both Joyce's use of the epiphany and Pound's definition of the image. In Eisenstein's *The Film Sense*, appear such statements as:

> two film pieces of any kind, placed together, inevitably combine into a new concept, a new quality, arising out of that juxtaposition.

> The juxtaposition of two separate shots by splicing them together resembles not so much a simple sum of one shot plus another shot—as it does a *creation*.

A work of art, understood dynamically, is just this process of arranging images in the feelings and mind of the spectator. It is this that constitutes the peculiarity of a truly vital work of art and distinguishes it from a lifeless one.

Before the inner vision, before the perception of the creator, hovers a given image, emotionally embodying his theme. The task that confronts him is to transform this image into a few basic *partial representations* which, in their combination and juxtaposition, shall evoke in the consciousness and feelings of the spectator, reader, or auditor, that same initial general image which originally hovered before the creative artist.[65]

The last statement sounds much like T. S. Eliot's concept of the objective correlative, enunciated in 1919: "The only way of expressing emotion in the form of art is by finding an 'objective correlative'; in other words, a set of objects, a situation, a chain of events which shall be the formula of that *particular* emotion; such that when the external facts, which must terminate in sensory experience, are given, the emotion is immediately evoked."[66] The similarity of Eisenstein's concept of the image and Eliot's concept of the objective correlative thus shows the latter also to be related to Joyce's concept of the epiphany.

Finally, we must come to the other question raised at the beginning of the chapter: why Joyce? One answer may be, as we shall see in the next chapter, that it was partly a matter of personality. A simpler answer is that at least two people very close to Joyce used the interior monologue, a special form of the stream-of-consciousness technique—one quite consciously as an experiment in writing, the other quite unconsciously, but regularly in her letters. In the diary of Joyce's younger brother, Stanislaus, which Joyce read regularly, is a long passage on the working of the mind, a passage too long to quote here except in part:

The mind "sees," that is is conscious of the image the eye reflects for it, and says continually within itself: "This is a road, the Malahide Rd. I know it well now that I see it. There are high broken hedges on both sides of it, and a few trees. Where the road branches an irregular dwelling-house with an orchard about it, sidles [?] to an arm and before pointing the bifurcation, is an old gate entrance. There is a young fellow on the opposite side going in the same direction as I am"; thinking not in sentences as in a book, but thought succeeding thought without

utterance like harmonies in music, while conveying a more
definite impression to the mind.[67]

Phillip Herring also says, "Those letters of Nora [Joyce's wife]
which survive are written in a style so strikingly similar to
Molly's interior monologue that she probably surpasses Edouard
Dujardin in importance as a stylistic influence on the 'Penelope'
episode." He then quotes part of a letter from Nora in support
of his contention: "My darling Jim since I left Trieste I am
continually thinking about you how are you getting on without
me or do you miss me at all. I am dreadfully lonely for you
I am quite tired of Ireland already well I arrived in Dublin
on Monday night your father charley Eva Florrie were at the
Station all looking very well we all went on to Finn's Hotel
I stayed two nights."[68]*

Why Joyce? And why at that particular time? He had
models—from members of his family and in literature already
written. And the times conspired to provide him with the
philosophy and psychology and aesthetics necessary to develop
the stream-of-consciousness technique. But other people had
those same models and lived in the same times; so ultimately,
as we shall see, the answer must be: because he was Joyce.

---

*Modern Fiction Studies, © 1969, by Purdue Research Foundation, Lafayette,
Indiana.

14
From Stream to Torrent

As one follows the story of the writing of *Ulysses* in Richard Ellmann's admirable biography *James Joyce*, it is interesting to note the responses of Ezra Pound and Harriet Weaver to the various chapters of *Ulysses* as they appeared.[1] Pound was clearly delighted with the early sections of the book when he received them late in 1917.[2] He wrote to Joyce:

> Pages 1-17, in duplicate rec'd. Since you will get yourself reviewed in modern Greek and thereby suggest new spelling of the name Daedalus. All I can say is Echt Dzoice, or Echt Joice, or however else you like it.

> Hope to forward a few base sheckles in a few days time. Wall Mr Joice, I recon you a damn fine writer, that's what I recon'. An' I recon' this here work o' yourn is some concarned litterchure. You can take it from me, an' I'm a jedge.[3]

In the spring of 1918, probably after he had read Calypso, Pound expressed concern that Joyce's explicitness about Bloom's bodily functions might cause trouble with the censor; but in November of that year, after having read not only Calypso but Lotus-eaters, Hades, Aeolus, Lestrygonians, and Scylla and Charybdis, he was enthusiastic about Bloom: "Bloom is a great man, and you have almightily answered the critics who asked me whether having made Stephen, more or less autobiography, you could ever go on and create a second character. . . . I looked back over Bouvard and Pecuchet last week. Bloom certainly does all Flaubert set out to do and does it on one tenth the space."[4]

With the appearance of the Sirens, however, Pound began to protest. Joyce wrote Budgen, "Pound writes disapprovingly of the *Sirens*, then modifying his disapproval and protesting against the close and against 'obsession' and wanting to know whether Bloom (prolonged cheers from all parts of the house) could not be relegated to the background and Stephen Telemachus brought forward."[5] What was bothering Pound is clear: he wrote, "A new style per chapter not required."[6] Harriet Weaver did not like the Sirens either, although she was gentler in her disapproval. She liked Nausicaa; but she registered some unhappiness (again gently) with Oxen of the Sun.[7]

The complexities of *Finnegans Wake* disturbed Pound even more. When Joyce sent him the Shawn book and asked him for his opinion, he replied: "I will have another go at it, but up to present I make nothing of it whatever. Nothing so far as I make out, nothing short of divine vision or a new cure for the clapp can possibly be worth all the circumambient peripherization."[8] Harriet Weaver's dismay with the opening passage of the book was equally clear. She wrote to Joyce: "But, dear sir, (I always seem to have a 'but') the worst of it is that without comprehensive key and glossary, such as you very kindly made out for me, the poor hapless reader loses a very great deal of your intention; flounders, helplessly, is in imminent danger, in fact, of being as totally lost to view as that illfated vegetation you mentioned."[9]

Looking back now at Joyce's writing, it is clear that Ezra Pound, Harriet Weaver, and others were reacting to a signal in the opening pages of The Sirens that Joyce was leaving the stream-of-consciousness technique behind and moving on to further experimentation, experimentation that was, perhaps, not predictable from Joyce's earlier statements on writing. As a young man in Paris, Joyce had written:

> There are three conditions of art: the lyrical, the epical and the dramatic. That art is lyrical whereby the artist sets forth the image in immediate relation to himself; that art is epical whereby the artist sets forth the image in mediate relation to himself and to others; that art is dramatic whereby the artist sets forth the image in immediate relation to others.[10]

And he repeated that statement in almost identical language in *A Portrait*.[11] In his play *Exiles* and in the first half of *Ulysses*, with the stream-of-consciousness technique, Joyce had moved to dramatic art: like God, he was invisible, had refined himself (the omniscient author) out of existence, had set forth his image (his work of art) in immediate relation to others. By

the middle of *Ulysses*, however, Joyce was ready to move on
to something new. The change had actually been signalled
before The Sirens—two chapters earlier, in fact.

When the reader turns to the ninth chapter, Scylla and
Charybdis, he has been carefully conditioned, for twice he has
experienced a movement from rather traditional fictional
presentations to an almost complete immersion in a stream of
consciousness. By the ninth chapter he should be prepared to
settle himself comfortably behind the eyes of any character and
experience the world as that character experiences it.

However, in Scylla and Charybdis there is a subtle shift in
technique.[12] Until now the omniscient author's sentences have
been unobtrusive because they have appeared in the innocuous
guise of stage directions or have been camouflaged by the idiom
and speech rhythms of the character whom they have located
or described. As the reader settles himself once more in
Stephen's mind at the beginning of Scylla and Charybdis,
however, he finds the omniscient author's sentences calling
attention to themselves in a way that they did not in Proteus:

> He came a step a sinkapace forward on neatsleather
>   creaking and a step backward a sinkapace on the solemn
>   floor. (182:6/184:6)
> Twicreakingly analysis he corantoed off. (182:14/184:14)

Stephen's idiom, we might say. Perhaps, but also a display of
virtuosity that reminds us that the author, who seemed to have
all but refined himself out of existence, is back there behind
his characters after all.

The stream of consciousness and dialogue quickly flow in,
however, and wash away the traces of the author; once again
the occasional omniscient author's sentence becomes a modest
stage direction:

> He laughed again at the now smiling bearded face.
>   (183:28/185:28)
> Mr Best came forward, amiable, towards his
>   colleague. (184:20/186:21)

A dozen pages later, however, the reader's eye encounters for
the first time a nonverbal image: a passage from a medieval
musical score (195:22/197:34). A little later Joyce suddenly
changes the layout on the page to a mock verse-play format

which forces the reader to puzzle out not only who is speaking but where the dialogue stops and the stream of consciousness begins, up to this point not a problem:

> To whom thus Eglinton:
>   You mean the will.
>   That has been explained, I believe, by jurists.
>   She was entitled to her widow's dower
>   At common law. His legal knowledge was great
>   Our judges tell us.
>   Him Satan fleers,
>   Mocker:
>   And therefore he left out her name
>   From the first draft but he did not leave out
>   The presents for his granddaughter, for his daughters,
>   For his sister, for his old cronies in Stratford
>   And in London. And therefore when he was urged,
>   As I believe, to name her
>   He left her his
>   Secondbest
>   Bed.
>   *Punkt*
>   Leftherhis
>   Secondbest
>   Bestabed
>   Secabest
>   Leftabed   (200:30/203:8)

Half a dozen pages later the dialogue suddenly shifts into the format of an opera libretto, complete with appropriate directions in Italian: *Piano, diminuendo. . . . A tempo. . . . Stringendo* (208/209).

In The Wandering Rocks and The Sirens (episodes ten and eleven), the narrative techniques become more and more complex. The former offers the reader fragments of Dublin life at midafternoon on 16 June 1904. Bloom appears in one vignette, Stephen in two. Otherwise the narrative for essentially the first time—and the only time until Penelope—moves beyond the consciousness of either Bloom or Stephen.[13] But Joyce does not here abandon the techniques of the first half of the book. Thirteen of the sections, most of which consist largely of conversations involving more than two people, are presented as they might have been by an omniscient author. But in six, each of which presents an individual observing the world around him, there are substantial passages of stream-of-consciousness writing.[14] The inclusion of these passages maintains continuity with the earlier sections without being obstrusive, and the stream of consciousness in each instance seems a natural product of the individual's situation at the moment.[15]

In this episode on the other hand, Joyce introduces one new technique which, like the headlines of Aeolus, is unnatural in the light of conventional narrative practice. As one reads along in one of the vignettes, he is surprised suddenly to be faced with an omniscient author's statement from another vignette which seems to have no relevance to the vignette being read. As we follow Stephen down Bedford Row in the city, for example, we are suddenly asked to leap two and a half miles to where "Father Conmee, having read his little hours, walked through the hamlet on Donnycarney, murmuring vespers" (239:11/242:33), after which without transition we return to Stephen's thoughts about the books on a cart and continue through the vignette with him. These suddenly inserted statements by the omniscient author, which are much like stage directions, are designed to let us know that certain events of the episode are occurring simultaneously. At the moment when Stephen bends over the book cart, Father Conmee is walking through Donnycarney. At the moment when Simon Dedalus puts coins in his pocket, the viceregal cavalcade passes out of Parkgate (234:29/239:4). As Boylan talks to the salesgirl in Thornton's, Bloom scans the books in a hawker's cart several blocks away (224:20/227:27). There are similar intrusive references also to concurrent activities of characters met in earlier episodes (the two midwives—238:24/242:7; the reverend Hugh C. Love—241:25/245:8; Councillor Nannetti—242:29/246:15; Denis Breen—237:31/240:40; 250:2/253:32) as well as to Miss Kennedy and Miss Douce (242:21/246:7; 249:4/252:30), whom the reader has not yet encountered but who will figure prominently in the next episode.

These brief stage directions—at least thirty of them, with twenty-three concentrated in nine of the central vignettes—are far more intrusive than the newspaper headlines of Aeolus. Joyce does attempt to ease the reader into this new technique by making the first insertion involving Professor Maginni so much like a description of something the strolling Father Conmee might see that the unwary reader may not realize that the professor is several blocks away (217:22/220:24). The second indication that two events are occurring simultaneously—this time separated in space by over a mile—is direct: "Corny Kelleher sped a silent stream of hayjuice arching from his mouth while a generous white arm from a window in Eccles street flung forth a coin" (222:3/225:9). Thereafter, however, Joyce omits the *while,* and the insertions are unprepared for.

By the time he reaches The Sirens, even the unwary reader must be aware of authorial intrusion. The chapter begins:

> Bronze by gold heard the hoofirons, steelyringing
>   Imperthnthn thnthnthn.
> Chips, picking chips off rocky thumbnail, chips.
> Horrid! And gold flushed more.
> A husky fifenote blew.
> Blew. Blue bloom is on the
> Gold pinnacled hair. (252:1/256:1)

And it continues on that way for a page and a half.

Cyclops begins like a monologue ("I was just passing the time of day with old Troy of the D. M. P."—287:1/292:1); but the reader is soon reminded of the author, for at the bottom of the first page he finds, "For nonperishable goods bought of Moses Herzog, of 13 Saint Kevin's parade, Wood quay ward, merchant, hereinafter called the vendor, and sold and delivered to Michael E. Geraghty, Esquire, of 29 Arbour Hill in the city of Dublin, Arran quay ward, gentleman, hereinafter called the purchaser" (287:35/292:38). At the bottom of the second page he finds a second intrusion: "In Inisfail the fair there lies a land, the land of holy Michan. There rises a watchtower beheld of men afar. There sleep the mighty dead as in life they slept, warriors and princes of high renown" (288:36/293:38). Later pages contain such interpolations as a séance with the ghost of Paddy Dignam, a report of a meeting on the revival of ancient Gallic sports, and a report of a wedding in which the participants bear the names of trees and flowers.

Nausicaa, the thirteenth chapter, suggests a return to the approach of the first half of *Ulysses.* Told by an omniscient author or narrator, the first half of the chapter is written "in a namby-pamby jammy marmalady drawersy (alto la!) style" appropriate to Gerty MacDowell, whose story it tells

(340-61/346-67).[16] The second half is written in the familiar
stream-of-consciousness style of Leopold Bloom (361-76/367-82).
Only the very last paragraph suggests an intrusive author
(376/382).

Since Circe, the fifteenth chapter, is presented as a drama,
one could argue that in that chapter, too, the author is invisible.
But in Oxen of the Sun, Eumaeus, and Ithaca, chapters
fourteen, sixteen, and seventeen, an intruding and manipulating
author is clearly present. His presence is evident in Penelope,
the last chapter, too, even though it is presented as Molly's
internal monologue, because Joyce wrote the chapter without
punctuation. Constantly feeling for the ends of sentences as he
progresses, the reader is continually aware of the difficulty of
the reading and conscious of the fact not only that he is reading
but that he is solving a puzzle. This awareness, of course, keeps
him aware of the author, who presented the difficulty.

There is another kind of change in *Ulysses* at about mid-novel
which roughly parallels the change from invisible to intrusive
author. In the early chapters, Joyce's experiments with words
and sound tend to be experiments in onomatopoeia. The
incoming sea makes "a fourworded wavespeech: seesoo, hrss,
rsseeiss ooos. . . . In cups of rocks it slops: flop, slop, slap:
bounded in barrels" (50:20/49:29). A cat cries, "Mkgnao! . . .
Mrkgnao! . . . Mrkrgnao!" (55/55). A machine goes, "Sllt"
(120:19/121:22). "Davy Byrne smiledyawnednodded all in
one:/—Iiiiiichaaaaaaach!" (175:16/177:38).

By The Sirens, however, Joyce is experimenting with more
complicated combinations: "Bald Pat who is bothered mitred the
napkins. Pat is a waiter hard of his hearing. Pat is a waiter
who waits while you wait. Hee hee hee hee" (276:17/280:36);
"he held a shield of hand beside his lips that cooed a moonlight
nightcall, clear from anear, a call from afar, replying"
(274:27/279:3); "Bronzedouce, communing with her rose that
sank and rose sought Blazes Boylan's flower and eyes"
(262:9/266:19); "Croak of vast manless moonless womoonless
marsh" (278:42/283:22). The author is clearly manipulating the
sentences; in keeping with the music in the chapter, the
language is obviously musical; and the pun appears as a poetic
device—not as a joke by one of the characters, as it functions
earlier ("*The Rose of Castille.* See the wheeze? Rows of cast

steel"—133:4/134:19), but as a device to add an additional level of meaning "in an instant of time."

Word echoes and puns appear even more frequently in later chapters. In Cyclops there is a parody of the Apostles' Creed which depends for its effectiveness largely on echoes of words and sound correspondences, a technique much like punning:

> They believe in rod, the scourger almighty
> *I believe in God, the Father Almighty,*
> creator of hell upon earth and in Jacky Tar,
> *Creator of heaven and earth and in Jesus Christ,*
> the son of a gun, who was conceived of
> *His only Son, our Lord: Who was conceived by*
> unholy boast
> *the Holy Ghost* (323:32/329:23)

And in that chapter and later ones there are puns: "Pan Poleaxe Paddyrisky" (302:17/307:30); "Tell her I was axing at her" (418:27/425:41); "See him today at a runefal [funeral]" (420:12/427:26); "Haltyaltyaltyall" (428:4/435:6); "With all my worldly goods I thee and thou [I thee endow]" (434:28/442:9); "We'll bury you in our shrubbery jakes . . . in the one cesspool. . . . We'll manure you, Mr Flower!" (531:21/544:3). From here to *Finnegans Wake*, where Joyce turns "the verbal unit into a polysemantic vehicle capable of producing polyphonic effects," may be a big step—but it is just a step.[17]

A. Walton Litz demonstrates another way in which Joyce can be seen moving toward the polysemantic/polyphonic effect in *Ulysses*:

> One of the last entries in the overture [to the Sirens] provides a neat example of Joyce's interweaving of motifs:
> Last rose Castille of summer left bloom I feel so sad alone. [253:15/257:15]
> This line is actually a compound of several motifs suggested earlier in the overture, and it anticipates important relationships in the narrative. A partial catalogue of its components would include: "rose of Castille," an allusion to Lenehan's riddle . . . ; Molly as a rose, a "Flower of the mountain" at Gibraltar [768:11/783:6]; and the "jumping rose" on Miss Douce's blouse [252:8/256:8, 256:31/260:32]. The extreme compression of this line, the "interweaving" of motifs, reflects Joyce's movement toward simultaneous presentation; but he retains the integrity of the individual word, although conventional syntax has been abandoned.[18]

Joyce even violates "the integrity of the word," however, in such constructions as Pokethankertscheff, Putrápesthi, Karamelopulos, and Paddyrisky (302/307).

Enough has been written about the polysemantic/polyphonic aspects of Joyce's prose in *Finnegans Wake* that there is no need for an extended analysis of its effects here. A single example will be enough to show not only what it is but also how Joyce increased the density of individual lines over the years as he worked on them:

1. Tell me, tell me, how could she cam through all her fellows, the daredevil? Linking one and knocking the next and polling in and potoring out and clyding by in the eastway. Who was the first that ever burst? Someone it was, whoever you are. Tinker, tailor, soldier, sailor, Paul Pry or polishman. That's the thing I always want to know. (*Navire D'Argent*, 1925)[19]

2. Tell me, tell me, how could she cam through all her fellows, the neckar she was, the diveline? Linking one and knocking the next, tapping a flank and tipping a jutty and palling in and petering out and clyding by on her eastway. Wai-whou was the first that ever burst? Someone he was, whoever they were, in a tactic attack or in single combat. Tinker, tailor, soldier, sailor, Paul Pry or polishman. That's the thing I always want to know. (*transition*, 1927)[20]

3. Tell me, tell me, how cam she camlin through all her fellows, the nektar she was the diveline? Linking one and knocking the next, tapting a flank and tipting a jutty and palling in and pietaring out and clyding by on her eastway. Whaiwhou was the first thurever burst? Someone he was, whuebra they were, in a tactic attack or in single combat. Tinker, tilar, souldrer, salor, Pieman Peace or Polistaman. That's the thing I always want to know. (*Anna Livia Plurabelle*, 1928)[21]

4. Tell me, tell me, how cam she camlin through all her fellows, the nektar she was, the diveline? Casting her perils before our swains from Fonte-in-Monte to Tidingtown and from Tidingtown tilhavet. Linking one and knocking the next, tapting a flank and tipting a jutty and palling in and pietaring out and clyding by on her eastway. Whaiwhou was the first thurever burst? Someone he was, whuebra they were, in a tactic attack or in single combat. Tinker, tiler, souldrer, salor, Pieman Peace or Polistaman. That's the thing I'm elwys on edge to esk. (*Finnegans Wake*, 1939)[22]

On the basis of the changes in this passage over fourteen years, one can notice several principles of the development of *Finnegans Wake*. In original conception, the passage was closer to monologue than to polysemantic/polyphonic prose. As in *Ulysses*, Joyce tended to add and complicate, not to prune. He added not only words, phrases and sentences, but also, by punning, gave additional meaning to words and phrases already in the text; and many of his additions were river names, for which he had a passion, particularly in this section, which is about the River Liffey.[23] Thus "polling in and petering out" becomes "palling in and petering out" in order to add *Paul* to *Peter*, and perhaps also to suggest *pall* and *appall*. The phrase then becomes "palling in and pietaring out" to suggest *pietà*, a representation of the Virgin Mary mourning over the dead Christ, and *piety*, two words quite appropriate to Peter and Paul. There may also be an echo of the Pie-ta Ho River in China. "Whoever" becomes "whuebra" to include the Huebra River in Spain and perhaps also to suggest *hubris*. "I always want to know" becomes "I'm elwys on edge to esk" to include the Ely River in Wales, the Elle River in France, and the Esk River in Scotland and to provide the repetition of the initial *e*.

Signals of the change which occurred in *Ulysses* can also be found in the manuscripts and in Joyce's letters. At the end of one draft of Scylla and Charybdis, Joyce wrote, "End of First Part of 'Ulysses,' James Joyce, Universitätstrasse, Zurich, New Year's Eve, 1918." Two years later in a letter to John Quinn in which he listed the eighteen chapters, he drew a line between Scylla and Charybdis and the chapter following, The Wandering Rocks, and commented, "The dotted line represents the first half, but not part or division—that is, 9 episodes of the 18."[24] His letters also became very explicit about the style of individual chapters. For example, he wrote about modelling Sirens on the *fuga per canonem*, about his tracing in Oxen of the Sun the history of the English language, about writing Ithaca "in the form of a mathematical catechism," and about Penelope's turning "like the huge earth ball slowly surely and evenly."[25] There are similarly explicit statements characterizing the style of the other chapters in the second half of *Ulysses*.

Style was becoming a major preoccupation with writers and painters alike.[26] At the same time, perhaps as part of the same trend, writers and painters began to look upon language as a medium to be manipulated physically, irrespective of its meaning. (Mallarmé's typographical experiments in *Un coup de dés* and Apollinaire's ideograms foretold the trend. They attempted, however, to make typography reflect or reinforce meaning.) Thus we find lettering in Braque's *Guitar Player,* painted about 1910;[27] and in 1912 Wassily Kandinsky wrote:

> If the reader looks at any letter of these lines naively, that is: as an object instead of as a familiar symbol of a part of a word; as something other than the practical-purposeful abstract form which man has created as a fixed symbol for a definite sound; then he will see in this letter a physical form which makes a definite external and internal impression. This impression is independent of the abstract form just mentioned. In this sense the letter consists of:
>
> 1. the main form (the whole appearance) which, quite roughly termed, appears "gay," "sad," "striving," "receding," "defiant," "ostentatious," and so forth;
>
> 2. and consists of individual lines curved this way or that, which always make a certain impression, that is, they are just as "gay," "sad," and so forth.
>
> When the reader has felt these two elements of the letter, there arises in him immediately the feeling which is caused by this letter as a being with an inner life.[28]

Therefore, the letter acts not only as a symbol, but also "as a form first and later as an inner resonance of this form, self-supporting and completely independent. . . . The *external effect can be a different one from the inner effect:* the inner effect is caused by the *inner resonance*; and this is *one of the most powerful* and deepest *means of expression* in every composition."[29]

The founders and followers of Dada, which was established at the Cabaret Voltaire in Zurich in the spring of 1916 also considered "language . . . no longer a means; it is an entity." Jean (Hans) Arp wrote: "From 1915 to 1920 I wrote my *Wolkenpumpe* (Cloud Pump) poems. In these poems I tore apart sentences, words, syllables. I tried to break down language into atoms, in order to approach the creative."[30] And Albert Gleizes wrote in 1920: "The Dadaists no longer organize ideas by arranging words according to an ordering syntax. They have not yet destroyed the word itself, but they will do so yet. I know of certain Dadaists in New York, bolder or more naive than the others, who have attained this summit."[31]

The "summit," however, had been attained earlier, even before Dada, by Hugo Ball, one of its founders:

> I invented a new species of verse: "Verse Without Words," or sound poems, in which the balancing of the vowels is gauged and distributed only to the value of the initial line. The first of these I recited tonight [1915] . . . . I recited the following:
>
> > gadji beri bimba
> > glandridi lauli lonni cadori
> > gadjama bim beri glassala
> > glandridi glassala tuffm i zimbrabim
> > blassa galassasa tuffm i zimbrabim
>
> The accents became heavier, the expression increased an intensification of the consonants. I soon noticed that my means of expression (if I wanted to remain serious, which I did at any cost), was not adequate to the pomp of my stage-setting. I feared failure and so concentrated intensely.[32]

Other theories of language and literature being propounded in Paris in the early years of the twentieth century contain many aspects of the system Joyce developed in *Finnegans Wake.* Marcel Duchamp, reminiscing about those days, told James Johnson Sweeney: "[Jean-Pierre] Brisset and [Raymond] Roussel were the two men in those years whom I most admired for their delerium of imagination. . . . Brisset's work was a philological analysis of language—an analysis worked out by means of an incredible network of puns. . . . Roussel thought he was a philologist, a philosopher, and a metaphysician. But he remains a great poet."[33] Here is a passage from Brisset's *La Science de Dieu*, published originally in 1890, and then republished in 1913 when it appeared under the title *Les Origines Humaines:*

> Voyons où ces ancêtres étaient *logés*: *l'eau j'ai* = j'ai l'eau ou je suis dans l'eau. *L'haut j'ai* = je suis haut, au-dessus l'eau, car les ancêtres construisirent les premières loges sur les eaux. *L'os j'ai* = j'ai l'os ou les os; on les mangeait où l'on était logé. L'ancêtre était carnivore. *Le au jet* = où je jette cet objet; où est le jet d'eau, *l'eau jet*, je suis *logé*. *Loge ai* = j'ai une loge. La première loge (*l'eau-jeu, l'eau je* = *l'eau à moi*) était un lieu arrangé dans l'eau. *Lot j'ai* = je tiens mon lot. Être *logé* est le lot naturel. Qui n'est pas logé a perdu son lot. *L'auge ai* = j'ai mon auge.[34]

The puns are clear even to one with a minimum of French. Raymond Roussel wrote poems containing pairs of lines like

> Avec un parti pris de rudesse ses gens
> *Ave* cote part type rit des rues d'essai suage. En
> (type des rues rit d'essai sauge)[35]

And his short story "Parmi les Noirs" began and ended:

> Les lettres du blanc sur les bandes du vieux billard formaient un incomprehensible assemblage.
>
> LES . . . LETTERS . . . DU . . . BLANC . . . SUR . . . LES . . . BANDES . . . DU . . . VIEUX . . . PILLARD.
> (The spots made by the white chalk on the borders of the old billiard formed an incomprehensible collection.)
> (THE . . . LETTERS . . . OF THE . . . WHITE MAN . . . ABOUT . . . THE . . . HORDES . . . OF THE . . . OLD . . . PLUNDERER)[36]

Roussel described his method at some length in *Comment j'ai écrit certains de mes livres.* He explained: "I chose two words almost alike (making one think of metagrams). For example, *billard,* and *pillard.* Then I added to each of them similar words but in two different senses, and I thus obtained almost identical phrases. . . . The two phrases found, [it] was than a question of writing a story which could begin with the first and end with the second."[37] "Parmi les Noirs" is one of many examples of such by Roussel. Another is "Chiquenaude," which begins, "Les vers de la doublure dans la pièce du *Forban talon rouge* avaient été composés par moi" and ends, " 'Les vers de la doublure dans la pièce du fort pantalon rouge!' "[38] "Creativity," Roussel felt, was "based on the coupling of two words taken in two different senses": "This process . . . is closely related to rhyme. In both cases there is an unexpected creation as a result of phonic ingenuity. It is essentially a poetic process."[39]

Still other writers were concerned with the problems of simultaneity. Richard Huelsenbeck, Marcel Janko, and Tristan Tzara performed and published (in 1916) "a simultaneous poem" which begins:

RH	Ahoi	ahoi	Des	Admirals	gwirktes	Beinkleid
MJ			Where the honey		suckle	wine twines
TT	Boum	boum boum	il	déshabilla	sa chair	quand les

RH	schnell	zerfällt				
MJ	itself	arround	the door	a		swetheart . . .
TT	grenouilles	humides	commancerent		à	bruler[40]

Janko sang his part, and Huelsenbeck and Tzara presumably spoke theirs.

In 1925, Jean-Richard Bloch published *La Nuit Kurde*, which contains a chapter in which he presents simultaneously the speech, thoughts, and dreams of two characters in conversation.[41] On the left-hand page appears:

> *Speech*:
> What do they say down below?
>
> *Thought*:
> He is here, a ravening beast, come to gorge himself with my unhappiness.
>
> *Dream*:
> Why are your eyes blue? They say that blue eyes in a woman are a sign of weakness. . . . You are not weak.

On the right-hand page opposite appears:

> *Speech*:
> Do not bother about it, they cannot understand.
>
> *Thought*:
> How thin he is! He does not eat enough. His eyes are quite hollow. By this life on the mountain. . .
>
> *Dream:*
> When shall we reach the top? This mountain is endless. It climbs up thus for the length of three men's lives.[42]

The chapter continues in this fashion for ten pages.

Thus there were two parallel trends: an interest in language as entity, as material to be used for shape and sound, but not for meaning; and an interest in overcoming or compensating for the linearity of language to provide multiple simultaneous meanings or understandings. The first movement peaked in 1926 with a manifesto of the Revolution of the Word, not published until 1929:

PROCLAMATION

Tired of the spectacle of short stories, novels, poems and plays still under the hegemony of the banal word, monotonous syntax, static psychology, descriptive naturalism, and desirous of crystallizing a viewpoint . . .

We hereby declare that:

1. THE REVOLUTION IN THE ENGLISH LANGUAGE IS AN ACCOMPLISHED FACT.

2. THE IMAGINATION IN SEARCH OF A FABULOUS WORLD IS AUTONOMOUS AND UNCONFINED.

> (*Prudence is a rich, ugly old maid courted by Incapacity*
> *. . .* Blake)

3. PURE POETRY IS A LYRICAL ABSOLUTE THAT SEEKS AN A PRIORI REALITY WITHIN OURSELVES ALONE.

> (*Bring out number, weight and measure in a year of dearth*
> *. . .* Blake)

4. NARRATIVE IS NOT MERE ANECDOTE, BUT THE PROJECTION OF A METAMORPHOSIS OF REALITY.

> (*Enough! Or Too Much!* . . . Blake)

5. THE EXPRESSION OF THESE CONCEPTS CAN BE ACHIEVED ONLY THROUGH THE RHYTHMIC "HALLUCINATION OF THE WORD".

> (Rimbaud)

6. THE LITERARY CREATOR HAS THE RIGHT TO DISINTEGRATE THE PRIMAL MATTER OF WORDS IMPOSED ON HIM BY TEXT-BOOKS AND DICTIONARIES.

> (*The road of excess leads to the palace of Wisdom* . . . Blake)

7. HE HAS THE RIGHT TO USE WORDS OF HIS OWN FASHIONING AND TO DISREGARD EXISTING GRAMMATICAL AND SYNTACTICAL LAWS.

> (*The tigers of wrath are wiser than the horses of instruction*
> \ . . . Blake)\

8. THE "LITANY OF WORDS" IS ADMITTED AS AN INDEPENDENT UNIT.

9. WE ARE NOT CONCERNED WITH THE PROPAGATION OF SOCIOLOGICAL IDEAS, EXCEPT TO EMANCIPATE THE CREATIVE ELEMENTS FROM THE PRESENT IDEOLOGY.

10. TIME IS A TYRANNY TO BE ABOLISHED.

11. THE WRITER EXPRESSES. HE DOES NOT COMMUNICATE.

12. THE PLAIN READER BE DAMNED.

> (*Damn braces! Bless relaxes!* . . . Blake)

Signed: Kay Boyle, Whit Burnett, Hart Crane, Caresse Crosby, Harry Crosby, Martha Foley, Stuart Gilbert, A. L. Gillespie, Leigh Hoffman, Eugene Jolas, Elliot Paul, Douglas Rigby, Theo Rutra, Robert Sage, Harold J. Salemson, Laurence Vail.[43]

The proclamation was written by Eugene Jolas. Ellmann says, "It was a time to be revolutionary, and Jolas centered his revolution in language."[44]

Joyce was thoroughly acquainted with both movements. For example, Louis Gillet reported:

> In the last few years he showed himself very much occupied with a certain Jesuit priest, whose name unfortunately escapes me. Joyce had heard him at the Salle de Geographie in a very curious lecture on comparative phonetics and linguistics, and

these new ideas expressed seemed to him most daring. According
to this clergyman, all languages constitute a system of the
Revelation, and their history in the world is the history of the
Logos, the history of the Holy Spirit. Perhaps this is somewhat
of a logomachy. I do not guarantee that the speaker really said
all that Joyce quoted of him. One feels, however, that such a
speech offered Joyce material for long reveries.[45]

The theories of Gillet's "Jesuit priest" are much like those of
Jean-Pierre Brisset. If Joyce did not hear Brisset, he seems
certainly to have heard one of his followers.

Joyce also knew Eugene Jolas quite well. In December 1926,
Joyce invited the Jolases and several others to hear him read
portions of what at that time was known as "Work in Progress,"
and, says Ellmann, "Jolas found in *Finnegans Wake* the
principal text for his revolution of the word."[46] As a result of
the meeting, the Jolases published "Opening pages of a Work
in Progress" in the first number of *transition* in April 1927 and
continued to publish sections of it through 1927, 1928, and 1929,
and again in 1933, 1935, 1937, and 1938.[47]

Painting was undergoing a parallel revolution during the same
years, a revolution of which Joyce must have heard at least
echoes. From 1909 until World War I, discussions of the works
and theories of the cubists and the futurists appeared regularly
in books, magazines and journals, and in the popular press on
the Continent in many languages. Both groups were much
concerned with simultaneity. The cubists went through an initial
period (1907-09) during which they studied and adapted
Cézanne's methods and theory. In their studies of the contrast
of surface and volume and in their concept of *passage*, the
presentation of several views of a single object on a flat canvas,
they sought both to capitalize on and to overcome the
restrictions of their two-dimensional medium, just as some of
the writers of the time were struggling to capitalize on and
to overcome the linearity of their medium. Their echoes of
shapes and outlines and playing with repetitions and near
repetitions of forms can be considered visual puns. By 1910 their
paintings had become objects in their own right, entities rather
than representations. Like the cubists, the futurists were also
concerned with simultaneity, but they rejected what they felt
to be the static aspects of cubism and emphasized dynamism,
motion, and energy. By 1913 in many of the major cities of

Europe there had been cubist and futurist exhibitions which were given coverage by the press.

Thus well before Joyce had Stephen do his experiment with the difference between *nacheinander* and *nebeneinander*, the difference between "one after the other" and "one beside the other" (38/37), painters had made the discovery that although simultaneity had some advantages, linearity had others. If writers had difficulty in presenting "an intellectual and emotional complex in an instant of time," painters had difficulty expressing duration in their medium. They began to experiment, for example, with presenting all sides of a guitar or mandolin simultaneously on a flat canvas, as Braque and Picasso did. Or they attempted to paint movement, as Marcel Duchamp did in his *Nude Descending the Staircase* (1913) or as Bala, the futurist, did in his *Dynamism of a Dog on a Leash* (1912). "My problem was kineticism—movement," Duchamp said. "My aim was a static representation of movement—a static composition of indications of various positions taken by a form in movement."[48]

It is interesting in this connection to look further at the career of Marcel Duchamp, many of the aspects of which paralleled aspects of Joyce's. For example, Duchamp gave considerable time and energy to puns and other plays on words. Beginning in the 1920s, he published puns under his own name and under the pseudonym Rrose Sélavy (*éros c'est la vie*): *Une nymphe amie d'enfance* (*une infamie d'enfance;* also echoes of *en famille); Nous nous cajolions* (*nounou; cage aux lions*); *Rrose Sélavy inscrira-t-elle longtemps au longtemps au cadran des astres le cadastre des ans?*[49] (The French refer to the spoonerism-like play on words in the last example as *contrepèterie.*)

Duchamp also produced ideograms. For example, he made a design of the letters MAGE completely encircled by the following string of letters and dashes: I-DOM-FRO-RA-PLU-HOM- (that is, *images, domages, fromages, ramages, plumages,* and *homages).* And he manufactured discs inscribed with plays on words: BAINS DE GROS THÉ POUR GRAINS DE BEAUTÉ SANS TROP DE BENGUÉ, and ON DEMANDE DES MOUSTIQUES DOMESTIQUES (DEMI-STOCK) POUR LA CURE D'AZOTE SUR LA COTE D'AZURE.[50]

Like some of Joyce's titles, *Chamber Music* and *Finnegans Wake,* the titles of some of Duchamp's paintings were puns. Schwarz says, "The 1919 bearded and moustached *Mona Lisa,*

L. H. O. O. Q. . . . when read in French . . . becomes 'she
has a hot bottom.' " And the *même* in *La Mariée mise à nu
par ses célibataires, même* can be read *m'aime,* so that "the bride
stripped bare by her bachelors, even" becomes "the bride
stripped bare by her bachelors is in love with me." Like Joyce,
Duchamp felt that titles were very important: "There is a
tension set up between my titles and the pictures," Duchamp
wrote. "The titles are not the pictures nor vice versa, but they
work on each other. The titles . . . may be compared to varnish
through which the picture may be seen and amplified."[51]

Duchamp was also quite serious about his word games; and
his admirers also took them seriously. For example, in December
1922 André Breton published an article in *Littérature* on
Duchamp's *jeu de mots,* in which he praised their "mathematical
rigor" and seriousness (*l'absence de l'élément comique*). He said
further:

> Some [people] thought that by dint of use [words] had been very
> much refined; others that their essence could legitimately allow
> them to aspire to a different position; briefly, the problem was
> to set them free. The "alchemy of the word" was followed by
> a veritable "chemistry" that first of all went about the task of
> discovering the properties of the word—only one of which,
> "meaning," is specified in the dictionary. The need was, first, to
> consider the word in itself, and second, to study the reactions
> of words one upon another as exhaustively as possible. Only at
> this price was it possible to hope to reinvest language with its
> fully destiny, which, for some—and I was among them—was a
> matter not only of making consciousness take a great leap
> forward, but also of exalting life itself.[52]

(I should stop to point out here that Joyce was living in Paris
at the time, regathering his energies after the publication of
Ulysses and preparing to start his "Work in Progress" and could
easily have read or heard about the article. Whether he did
or not, however, is irrelevant. The most important point is that
in *Finnegans Wake,* Joyce put into practice many of the ideas
and principles that were exciting artists and other writers of
the same period, particularly those in Paris.)

Duchamp also called his readymades "three dimensional puns."
According to André Breton, readymades were "manufactured
objects promoted to the dignity of objects of art through the
choice of the artist."[53] George Heard Hamilton says of them:

Probably the most "difficult" of Duchamp's concepts and creations
are the "readymades." They are outrageous yet logical
demonstrations of his suspension of the laws of artistic causality,
for he has substituted for the traditional "handmade" work of
art such ordinary, mass-produced, machine-made articles as a
snow shovel, a comb, a bottle rack, or a bicycle wheel (set upside
down on a kitchen stool). And the more commonplace they are
the better since they make no appeal to the aesthetic of "good
design" or "machine art," principles which were only defined long
after he had made his decisions. The substitution of an
anonymous article of everyday use for the conventional painting
or sculpture can be understood only as an intellectual or
philosophical decision.[54]

The Breton and Hamilton definitions remind one of Joyce's
definition of an epiphany, "a trivial incident" which is "a sudden
spiritual manifestation, whether in the vulgarity of speech or
gesture or in a memorable phase of the mind itself"; particularly
when one remembers that Stephen tells Cranly that "the clock
of the Ballast Office was capable of an epiphany": "Yes, said
Stephen. I will pass it time after time, allude to it, refer to
it, catch a glimpse of it. It is only an item in the catalogue
in Dublin's street furniture. Then all at once I see it and I
know at once what it is: epiphany."[55]

When critics objected to Duchamp's *Fountain* at the Society
of Independent Artists in New York in 1917, he wrote: "Whether
Mr. Mutt [Duchamp's pseudonym in this instance] with his own
hands made the fountain or not has no importance. He CHOSE
it. He took an ordinary article of life, placed it so that its useful
significance disappeared under the new title and point of
view—created a new thought for that object."[56] The artist's
recognition and presentation of the artifact made it a work of
art, not his creation of it, just as recognition and recording of
an epiphany by the man of letters made it a work of art "worthy
of being sent to all the great libraries of the world including
Alexandria" (41:34/40:35).

There are some differences in the two concepts, to be sure.
The first is, of course, that the media concerned are
different—literature and three-dimensional artifacts. The other
is that whereas Joyce thought of epiphanies as moments upon
which writers stumble, Duchamp thought of readymades as
things to be planned for in "a moment to come (on such a day,
such a date, such a minute). . . . The readymade can later be

looked for."[57] But even in this disagreement there is agreement on the importance of "the moment," "the instant of time," and perhaps even on the epiphany and the readymade being "out there" waiting to be found. Stephen speaks of epiphanies as "the most delicate and evanescent of moments" and says of the epiphany of the Ballast Office clock, "Then all at once I see it and I know at once what it is."[58] Duchamp wrote: "The important thing . . . is just this matter of timing, this snapshot effect, like a speech delivered on no matter what occasion *at such and such an hour. It is a kind of rendezvous.*"[59]

Duchamp's last and most controversial work, *La Mariée mise à nu par ses célibataires, même,* known as the "Large Glass," was, like both *Ulysses* and *Finnegans Wake,* a project of many years. Duchamp began thinking about it in 1912 and worked on it from 1915 through 1923. Duchamp's abandoning the work in 1923 still unfinished, but showing it in 1926, again in 1943-44, and finally allowing it to be placed in the Arensberg Collection of Duchamp's works in the Philadelphia Museum of Art in 1953 is also reminiscent of Joyce, who seemingly never thought that either *Ulysses* or *Finnegans Wake* was finished, even though he arranged for both to be published, and kept making additions on the proofs of both quite literally until the very last minute. Also like both *Ulysses* and *Finnegans Wake,* various parts of the "Large Glass" appeared separately in several versions over the years, and again like both novels, there was a "long reluctance [by the public] to consider it anything more than a joke, largely incomprehensible and not very funny at that."[60]

Just as Joyce gave his friends information about his books, charts explaining *Ulysses,* and keys to passages of *Finnegans Wake* and sold copies of his manuscripts of various stages of his work, Duchamp kept and finally published in 1934 his notes and sketches for the "Large Glass" in three hundred numbered copies of the *Green Box,* "a flat case containing ninety-four loose items," including reproductions of earlier works, sketches, plan and elevation drawings, and handwritten notes "reproduced in exact facsimile including torn edges, blots, erasures and occasional illegibility."[61]

It is a long way from *Stephen Hero,* which Ellmann characterizes as "to a large extent a Victorian novel, with an interest in incident for its own sake," to *Finnegans Wake,* in which Litz says, "Narrative structure has disappeared, and with it the elements of suspense and action." As Litz points out, "We have seen that one may view Joyce's artistic development as an all-consuming movement toward simultaneity of effects."[62] But the cost was great, perhaps too great. The simultaneity is not immediately achieved in Pound's "instant of time." Each "intellectual and emotional complex" is so dense that one must labor over it. Often the best way to untangle a passage is to return for clues to an earlier version which more closely resembled monologue than "a polysemantic vehicle capable of producing polyphonic effects."[63] One could argue, as some critics do, that the simultaneity is achieved after the untangling, but since that can be said about any work of art, even one in which the author did not attempt to achieve simultaneity, the statement becomes so broad as to be virtually meaningless.

Traditionally, at least, novels have served as windows which allow the reader to see into the world of man—sometimes into private places, sometimes into public. The language and the structure of the novel, like the glass and the frame of the window, focus the reader's attention and facilitate his view. When a writer uses language that directs attention to itself, however, that becomes opaque or convoluted or poetic, he festoons the glass. The window thus becomes something to look at rather than to look through, an artifact rather than an opening upon the world. Joyce began by attempting to make the glass invisible so that through it the reader could see without distortion or intervening glare "the most delicate and evanescent of moments," which he believed it was the duty of the writer to catch and record. About halfway through *Ulysses*, however, he slipped beyond the aesthetic principles he had set down in his notebooks in 1903-04 and had reaffirmed—or at least repeated—in *Stephen Hero* and *A Portrait* and ended, in *Finnegans Wake*, by making the glass itself a work of art.

At the end of the last chapter I concluded that although the stream-of-consciousness technique reflected the aesthetics of Joyce's day, one must conclude ultimately that he developed the technique as fully as he did and in the way that he did because he was Joyce. When we seek to understand why he moved beyond the stream-of-consciousness technique to the densities of polysemantic/polyphonic prose, we can again point to the aesthetics of Joyce's day; but, again, we must also conclude,

"Because he was Joyce." Many critics have commented on the obsessive nature of Joyce's method of composition. Ellmann says that writing *A Portrait* gave Joyce "an opportunity to be passionately meticulous." Litz speaks of Joyce's "desperate and untidy passion for order of any kind." Pound's early protest against Joyce's "obsession" is repeated more than forty years later in Goldberg's statement that "the busy ant-like industry with which he piles in detail, his inability always to select the necessary from the available, the itch to get *everything* in, produces some maddening exhibitions of misdirected elaboration. He seems to worry his material almost obsessively at times." Speaking of Cyclops, Oxen of the Sun, Eumaeus, and Ithaca, Goldberg refers to Joyce's "evident love of pattern for its own sake, and in particular his tendency to rely on purely verbal arrangements of his material." Jacques Mercanton describes Joyce and Stuart Gilbert elaborating a passage of *Finnegans Wake* because, as Joyce said, it was "still not obscure enough."[64] And one remembers the signs of endless elaboration and embroidery as they appear in the manuscripts and proofs of *Ulysses* and *Finnegans Wake* and the way Joyce kept adding material in the proofs until the very last moment.[65]

Ultimately, therefore, the literary scholar and critic can only describe Joyce's aesthetic odyssey; he cannot explain it. Explanations must come from scholars in other disciplines.[66]

Appendix
Notes
Index

Appendix

The analyses in Part Two are based largely on three chapters of *Ulysses*—Proteus (Stephen), Lestrygonians (Bloom), and Penelope (Molly)—because these chapters contain long and uninterrupted passages of the streams of consciousness of the three characters under investigation. (See chapter 5.)

The three were designated as stream-of-consciousness chapters early in the history of Joyce criticism, and critics have continued to accept that designation. For example, one of the early writers on Joyce, Frank Budgen, finds "nothing from beginning to end of *Proteus* that is not thought or sensation. Other characters who come into the picture do so only as part of the content of Stephen's mind." And he continues: "The greater part of *Lestrygonians* is Bloom's unspoken thoughts on his way to lunch. It differs from the other interior monologue in substance and rhythm." Of Penelope, he says, "Marion's monologue snakes its way through the last forty pages of *Ulysses* like a river winding through a plain." For Budgen, "interior monologue," the translation of the French *monologue intérieur,* is equivalent to "stream of consciousness."[1]

Gilbert, another early writer on Joyce, characterizes the chapters similarly. His chart of *Ulysses,* given to him by Joyce, lists the "Technic" of Proteus as "Monologue (male)" and that of Penelope as "Monologue (female)." And although he says that the "Technic" of Lestrygonians is "Peristaltic," his discussion of that chapter is a discussion of Bloom's thoughts.[2] Later critics have similarly accepted these chapters as the ones containing stream-of-consciousness technique. Proteus, Lestrygonians, and Penelope, therefore, contain the streams of consciousness of the three main characters: the contents of their minds, and their thoughts and monologues. The three chapters thus serve quite adequately for the analysis of the three streams of consciousness.

In Proteus (chapter 3, pp. 38-51/37-51), Stephen walks along Sandymount strand, looking about him and thinking. In Lestrygonians (chapter 8, pp. 149-81/151-83), Bloom wanders through the streets of Dublin searching for a restaurant in which to eat and thinking of his problems. In Penelope (chapter 18, pp. 723-68/738-83), Molly lies in bed thinking over the occurrences of the day and of her lifetime. All three chapters provide examples that are typical of the unfettered flow of the consciousness. Each chapter is long enough to give a good picture of the character concerned, and the ideas which reoccur in each character's simulated stream of consciousness throughout the day appear and reappear in these passages just as they do elsewhere in the novel.

For the analysis of sentence lengths in chapter six of this study and for most of the analyses in chapters eight and nine, I used a sampling technique rather than the full chapters. Where the text indicates that I have used samples, I used three full pages from each of the three chapters of *Ulysses* (Proteus, Lestrygonians, and Penelope): six half pages distributed at equal periods through the chapter. Analyzing six half pages rather than three complete pages provides a better sampling through each chapter; using six disconnected samples rather than three satisfies better the statistical need for independent passages; and choosing the samples at even intervals through each chapter assures that the passages will be chosen objectively and not because they support a particular thesis. The analyses were originally undertaken in the 1950s, before the appearance of the revised Random House edition of *Ulysses*, which appeared in 1961. They were made, therefore, on the 1934 Random House edition. In that edition, the passages analyzed were:

Proteus: pages 38 (top half), 40 (bottom half), 43 (top half), 45 (bottom half), 48 (top half), and 50 (bottom half)

Lestrygonians: the top half of pages 149, 155, 161, 167, 173, and 179

Penelope: the top half of pages 723, 732, 741, 750, 759, and 768

A half page of the earlier Random House edition of *Ulysses*

generally consists of twenty-one lines of text. In most cases,
however, each sample passage consists of slightly more than
twenty-one lines, since I felt it better, for purposes of
interpreting meaning, not to begin or end sample passages in
the middle of sentences.

The actual sample passages, therefore, begin and end as
follows:

Sample Number	Begin	End
	Proteus	
1	Ineluctable modality (38:1/37:1)	Sandymount strand? (38:22/37:22)
2	He has nowhere to put it (40:22/39:22)	Paff! (40:42/40:1)
3	Shoot him (42:42/42:2)	mammoth skulls. (43:22/42:24)
4	A shut door (45:20/44:23)	of sand. (46:1/45:4)
5	Smiled: Creamfruit (47:42/47:7)	*dainty is.* (48:22/47:29)
6	Vehement breath (50:21/49:30)	Easy now. (50:42/50:10)
	Lestrygonians	
1	Pineapple rock (149:1/151:1)	the luminous crucifix? (149:22/151:22)
2	He died (154:42/157:7)	or pain is it? (155:22/157:29)
3	Vinegar (160:42/163:13)	Tobacco shopgirls. (161:21/163:35)
4	A man spitting (166:42/169:18)	wings of his nose. (167:22/169:40)
5	High (172:41/175:19)	remembered. (173:22/176:1)
6	See things (178:42/181:26)	in his mind's eye. (179:22/182:6)
	Penelope	
1	Yes (723:1/738:1)	everything is clean (723:22/738:23)

2	how could he (731:42/747:1)	boiling old stew (732:21/747:23)
3	then a girl Hester (740:42/756:3)	yards of it (741:23/756:27)
4	then it came on (749:40/764:39)	with the earrings (750:21/765:20)
5	well theyre (758:41/773:39)	voice (759:22/774:19)
6	and the big wheels (767:40/782:36)	yes I will Yes. (768:18/783:14)

Differences in sample size were dealt with by doing analyses in percentages. Because one of the analyses, the type-token ratio, required consistency in sample size, for that analysis I used the first 175 words of each sample; and in the two samples which did not have 175 words I added the consecutive words necessary from the text to bring the sample to 175. Statistical methodology is indicated in the appropriate footnotes.

Notes

Chapter 1: Introduction

1. Djuna Barnes, "James Joyce," *Vanity Fair* 18, no. 2 (April 1922): 65 and 104.

2. Frank Budgen, *James Joyce and the Making of "Ulysses"* (New York: Harrison Smith and Robert Haas, 1934), p. 94.

3. Mary Colum, *Life and the Dream* (Garden City, N.Y.: Doubleday, 1947), p. 305. Edmund Wilson, review of *Ulysses*, *New Republic* 31 (5 July 1922): 164.

4. Valery Larbaud, "James Joyce," *Nouvelle Revue Francaise* 18 (April 1922), in Robert H. Deming, ed., *James Joyce, The Critical Heritage*, 2 vols. (New York: Barnes & Noble, 1970), 1: 258-59.

5. Stuart Gilbert, "Ulysse," *Nouvelle Revue Francaise* 32 (April 1929): 571.

6. Frank Budgen, *Making of "Ulysses,"* p. 49.

7. Arnold Bennett, "James Joyce's *Ulysses*," *Outlook* (London) (29 April 1922), p. 337, in Deming, *Critical Heritage* 1: 220.

8. Louis Gillet, "Joyce's Way" (originally published 1 August 1925), in *Claybook for James Joyce* (New York: Abelard-Schuman, 1958), p. 40. See also a later statement in "The Extraordinary Adventures of James Joyce" (originally published 15 December 1940), in ibid.: "[The stream-of-consciousness technique] represented thought grasped in its nascent, elementary state and close to pure sensation, before it was clarified and solidified by the thinking mind" (p. 65).

9. Gillet, "The Extraordinary Adventures of James Joyce," in *Claybook*, p. 65.

10. Richard Ellmann, *James Joyce* (New York: Oxford University Press, 1959), p. 456.

11. Virginia Woolf, "Modern Fiction," *The Common Reader* (1925; reprint ed., New York: Harcourt, Brace, 1953), p. 154. A footnote (p. 155) says that it was "written April 1919." Deming says the article appeared originally as "Modern Novels," *Times Literary Supplement,* no. 899 (10 April 1919), pp. 189-90; in Deming, *Critical Heritage* 1: 125.

12. Woolf, ibid., pp. 154-57.

13. Wyndham Lewis, *The Art of Being Ruled* (New York: Harper, 1926), pp. 413-14; repeated in Lewis, *Time and Western Man* (New York: Harcourt, 1928), pp. 104-05.

14. Stuart Gilbert, *James Joyce's "Ulysses,"* rev. (New York: Alfred A. Knopf, 1952), p. 26.

15. Gilbert, ibid., p. 28.

16. William York Tindall, *James Joyce* (New York: Charles Scribner's Sons, 1950), p. 41.

17. René Wellek and Austin Warren, *Theory of Literature* (New York: Harcourt, Brace, 1949), pp. 87-88.

18. C. S. Lewis, *A Preface to "Paradise Lost"* (London: Oxford University Press, 1942), p. 2.

19. Gilbert, *James Joyce's "Ulysses,"* p. 26.

20. Mary Colum, "The Confessions of James Joyce," *Freeman* 5 (19 July 1922): 450-52, in Deming, *Critical Heritage* 1: 233.

21. Gilbert Seldes, review of *Ulysses, Nation* 115 (30 August 1922): 211-12, in Deming, *Critical Heritage* 1: 236.

22. (Berkeley: University of California Press, 1954).

23. (New Haven: Yale University Press, 1955).

24. (London: Blackie, 1962).

25. Thomas Merton, "News of the Joyce Industry," *Sewanee Review* 77 (1969): 546, 554.

Chapter 2: The Psychological Stream of Consciousness

1. W. Edgar Vinacke, *The Psychology of Thinking* (New York: McGraw-Hill, 1952), p. 44.

2. Benjamin Jowett, trans., *The Dialogues of Plato,* 2 vols. (New York: Random House, 1947), 1: 460.

3. Aristotle, "On Memory and Reminiscence," trans. J. I. Beaver, 451^b [10], *Great Books of the Western World,* 54 vols. (Chicago: Encyclopaedia Britannica, 1952), 8: 693.

4. Vinacke, *Psychology of Thinking,* p. 14.

5. William James, *The Principles of Psychology* (1890; reprint ed., New York: Dover Publications, 1950), pp. 224-90, James's italics. Although James is generally given credit for the introduction of this term, the metaphor is not new. For example, Samuel Taylor Coleridge wrote of "the streamy nature of association, which thinking curbs and rudders," of "streamy associations," and of the "streamy nature of the associative faculty" (*Animae Poetae* [London: Heinemann, 1895], pp. 55, 56, 65-66). He suspected that it was the source of "moral evil" and that "they labour under this defect [the streamy nature of the associative faculty] who are most reverie-ish and streamy—Hartley, for instance, and myself. This seems to me no common corroboration of my former thought or [on, of?] the origin of moral evil in general."

6. Howard C. Warren, *Dictionary of Psychology* (Boston: Houghton Mifflin, 1934), p. 263.

7. William James, *Talks to Teachers on Psychology; and to Students on Some of Life's Ideals* (New York: Henry Holt, 1921), p. 17.

8. James, *Principles,* p. 225.

9. Ibid., p. 237.

10. Ibid., p. 238.

11. Ibid., p. 224.

12. Harry Stack Sullivan, *Conceptions of Modern Psychiatry* (New York: W. W. Norton, 1953), pp. 105-07.

13. The reader will begin to notice here a difficulty in expressing many of the psychological concepts, and perhaps even some contradictions. For example, the items mentioned above are not really discrete items but more exactly overlapping and interrelated events and elements in a highly complex space-time continuum. The problem here is really twofold. In the first place, this sort of itemizing would seem to be necessary in order to introduce some of the basic concepts in relatively simple form so that ultimately more involved concepts may be discussed. However, whatever distortion inheres in this early presentation because of the necessity of breaking into the pattern somewhere

in order to describe it will be corrected by the end of the chapter. A second difficulty is more fundamental and more serious. The physicists have much the same problem:

> The fundamental difficulty of determining the place of an electron moving at a certain velocity is expressed in a general manner by the uncertainty relation originally formulated by Werner Heisenberg. This relation is characteristic of quantum physics and states among other things that the measurement of an electron's velocity is inaccurate in proportion as the measurement of its position in space is accurate, and vice versa. It is not hard to discover the reason. We can determine the position of a moving electron only if we can see it and in order to see it we must illuminate it, i.e., we must allow light to fall on it. The rays falling on it impinge upon the electron and thus alter its velocity in a way which it is impossible to calculate. The more accurately we desire to determine the position of the electron, the shorter must be the light waves employed to illuminate it, the stronger will be the impact, and the greater the inaccuracy with which the velocity is determined. (Max Planck, *The Philosophy of Physics* [New York: W. W. Norton, 1936], p. 58)

So too, throwing light on the psychological stream of consciousness creates inaccuracies: to discuss a moment of consciousness as Sullivan does is to halt the flow and thus give an erroneous picture; to analyze the moment of consciousness forces itemizing, which fails to show the complex interrelationships of the components of consciousness; but to describe merely the flow on the grounds that to halt it distorts the picture is equally bad because it results in only a partial picture.

C. S. Lewis, in his diatribe against stream-of-consciousness writers, raises precisely this problem. First he inveighs against introspection:

> The disorganized consciousness which it regards as specially real is in fact highly artificial. It is discovered by introspection—that is, by artificially suspending all the normal and outgoing activities of the mind and then attending to what is left. In that residuum it discovers no concentrated will, no logical thought, no morals, no stable sentiments, and (in a word) no mental hierarchy. Of course not; for we have deliberately stopped all these things in order to introspect.

And then he denies the possibility of putting it into words:

> For the very nature of such unfocused consciousness is that it is not attended to. Inattention makes it what it is. The moment you put it into words you falsify it. It is like trying to see what a thing looks like when you are not looking at it. (C. S. Lewis, *A Preface to "Paradise Lost"* [London: Oxford University Press, 1942], pp. 131-32)

Although Lewis may not have intended it so, this argument is also directed against any attempt to discuss the psychological stream of consciousness. For the psychologist too depends heavily upon introspection for his knowledge of the stream of consciousness andd must use language to describe his findings. And, indeed, many psychologists, impressed by the difficulties involved and fearful of possible resultant inaccuracies, avoid concepts like "consciousness" and "mind"; they prefer instead to adopt a behavioristic approach, discussing what they can see and measure. Many psychologists are not so behaviorist, however, and do deal directly with the stream of consciousness. We shall therefore examine what these psychologists have to say about both the components and the flow of the stream of consciousness fully conscious of the possible distortion involved.

The problem of the distortion resulting from putting the stream of consciousness into words will be discussed later at some length, since it is an important difficulty in the simulation of the psychological stream of consciousness.

14. Vinacke, *Psychology of Thinking*, p. 47.

15. Warren, *Dictionary of Psychology*, pp. 245, 196, 131. For a fuller definition of *image*, see Alan Richardson, *Mental Imagery* (New York: Springer Publishing Co., 1969), pp. 1-12. Richardson's concise definition is: "Mental imagery refers to (1) all those quasi-sensory or quasi-perceptual experiences of which (2) we are self-consciously aware, and which (3) exist for us in the absence of those stimulus conditions that are known to produce their genuine sensory or perceptual counterparts, and which (4) may be expected to have different consequences from their sensory or perceptual counterparts" (pp. 2-3).

16. George A. Miller, *Language and Communication* (New York: McGraw-Hill, 1951), p. 225.

17. Edward G. Boring, *A History of Experimental Psychology* (New York: Appleton-Century-Crofts, 1957), pp. 642-43.

18. J. B. Watson, *Psychology from the Standpoint of a Behaviorist* (Philadelphia: J. B. Lippincott, 1924), p. 104.

19. David Katz, *Gestalt Psychology* (New York: Ronald Press, 1950), p. 55.

20. Ibid., p. 55.

21. Robert R. Holt, "Imagery: the Return of the Ostracized," *American Psychologist* 19 (1964): 257. There was, of course, some disagreement. Vinacke wrote, for example: "We may certainly accept the reality of images and at the same time accept the facts uncovered by the exponents of imageless thought. Both are necessary for an understanding of thought (*Psychology of Thinking*, p. 52). But many psychologists explained perception, thinking, and imagination largely without images. For example, a code theory was presented (R. W. Perry, "Neurology and the Mind-Brain Problem," *American Scientist* 40 [April 1952]: 295) and a theory that "the entire output of our thinking machine consists of nothing but patterns of motor coordination" (pp. 297-98). Other psychologists argued that we think directly and not in terms of anything:

> We perceive objects directly, not through the intermediary of "presentations," "ideas," or "sensations." Similarly, we imagine objects directly, not through the intermediary of images, though images are present as an important part of the whole activity. In each of these two cases, we may assign an important part, though not all, of the activity to one or other of the sensory modalities. We may, however, think a proposition, or (draw) an inference . . . in such a way that the activity in question falls within none of the sensory modalities; though in general such activity is accompanied by either perception or imagination. This would be a fair conclusion, stated in more modern terms, from the experiments of which those of the Würzburg school are typical. (George Humphrey, *Thinking* [New York: John Wiley & Sons, 1951], p. 129)

Those psychologists who did not cast images "into outer darkness" tended not to find it profitable to do research on them or to include them in their systems or models.

22. Holt, "Imagery," pp. 254-64. Holt discusses the history of the banishment

and factors in the reemergence of imagery as well as important studies of imagery and their implications for further research.

23. Jerome L. Singer, *Daydreaming* (New York: Random House, 1966) pp. 44, 57. Singer summarizes his own studies and studies of others and concludes with a full and useful bibliography.

24. Richardson, *Mental Imagery*, p. ix, also includes a full and useful bibliography.

25. Ibid., pp. 70, 80.

26. Peter McKellar, *Imagination and Thinking* (New York: Basic Books, 1957), p. 34; Lois J. Michael, "A Factor Analysis of Mental Imagery," *Dissertation Abstracts* 27 (1967), 3761A (Auburn University).

27. Richardson, *Mental Imagery*, p. 70.

28. Alfred Korzybski, *Science and Sanity*, 3d ed. (Lakeville, Conn.: International Non-Aristotelian Library, 1948), p. 59.

29. Gotthold Ephraim Lessing, *Laokoon* (London: Bell, 1914), p. 101.

30. Benjamin Lee Whorf, "Language and Logic" (reprinted from *Technology Review* 43 (1941): 250), in *Language, Thought, and Reality*, ed. John B. Carroll (New York: Technology Press of M.I.T., 1956), pp. 240, 241, 242. One further quotation from Whorf containing examples may help the reader to understand specifically what he means:

> In Nootka, a language of Vancouver Island, all words seem to us to be verbs . . . ; we have, as it were, a monistic view of nature that gives us only one class of word for all kinds of events. "A house occurs" or "it houses" is the way of saying "house," exactly like "a flame occurs" or "it burns." These terms seem to us like verbs because they are inflected for durational and temporal nuances, so that the suffixes of the word for house event make it mean long-lasting house, temporary house, future house, house that used to be, what started out to be a house, and so on. ("Science and Linguistics," reprinted from *Technology Review* 42 [1940], pp. 229, in *Language, Thought, and Reality*, pp. 215-16)

31. Lessing, *Laokoon*, p. 91.

32. Virginia Woolf, "Modern Fiction," *The Common Reader* (1925; reprint ed., New York: Harcourt, Brace, 1953), p. 155.

33. A. A. Mendilow, *Time and the Novel* (London: Peter Nevill, 1952), p. 80.

34. Aldous Huxley, *Brave New World* (1932; reprint ed., New York: Harper, 1950), pp. 200-01.

35. Herbert J. Muller, *Science and Criticism* (New Haven: Yale University Press, 1950), p. 97.

36. James, *Principles*, pp. 224-25.

37. James Livingston Lowes, *The Road to Xanadu* (Boston: Houghton Mifflin, 1927), pp. 55-56, 405, 429-30. Lowes attributes this difficulty to "the limitations of our finite minds."

38. Korzybski, *Science and Sanity*, p. 179.

39. Mendilow, *Time and the Novel*, p. 81.

40. Gardner Murphy, *Personality* (New York: Harper, 1947), p. 353. Murphy says that "the thinker and the imaginer . . . can be understood in the same terms" (p. 391).

41. Vinacke, *Psychology of Thinking*, p. 160.

42. Ibid., pp. 218, 220, 233.

43. Singer, *Daydreaming*, pp. 77-78.

44. Murphy, *Personality*, pp. 998, 989, 991, 983, 996, 988.

45. Vinacke, *Psychology of Thinking*, pp. 19-20.

46. C. G. Jung, *Studies in Word-Association* (London: Heinemann, 1918), p. 167.

47. Fred Schwartz and Richard O. Rouse, "The Activation and Recovery of Associations," *Psychological Issues* 3, no. 1 (1961): 1-2.

48. H. A. Witkin et al., *Personality Through Perception* (New York: Harper, 1954), p. 479.

Chapter 3: Introducing the Stream-of-Consciousness Technique in *Ulysses*

1. (5:1-17/3:1-7) indicates p. 5, lines 1-17, of the 1934 Random House edition of *Ulysses* and p. 3, lines 1-17, of the 1961 Random House edition. This method of locating passages in *Ulysses* will be followed throughout.

2. My italics.

3. Even after one has read the book, the line is difficult to understand. It might simply mean that Mulligan is holding Stephen's arm (8:36/7:1) the way Cranly used to hold it. There are suggestions, however, that the line has another meaning. For example, in the Rosenbach manuscript, the line appears, turned around ("His arm: Cranly's arm"), on page 50/49, between "Wilde's love that dare not speak its name" and "He now will leave me" (50:14/49:23). It disappeared from there before the first galley. (For a description of the Rosenbach and other manuscript versions of *Ulysses*, see John J. Slocum and Herbert Cahoon, *A Bibliography of James Joyce,* 1882-1941 [New Haven: Yale University Press, 1953], pp. 138-43.) The reader of Joyce's earlier works knows that in the *Portrait,* Stephen, walking with Cranly, thinks: "His face was handsome: and his body was strong and hard. He had spoken of a mother's love. He felt then the sufferings of women, the weaknesses of their bodies and souls: and would shield them with a strong and resolute arm and bow his mind to them" (James Joyce, *A Portrait of the Artist as a Young Man* [New York: Viking Press, 1968], p. 245). In the same book, there are two earlier mentions of Cranly's hands (pp. 227-28) and one of Cranly's taking Stephen's arm "in a strong grip" (p. 238), both in connection with thoughts of women. One possible explanation, then, might be that Cranly's arm is a symbol for Stephen of aid to the weak in general, and to women in particular.

On this point, William M. Schutte has written to me: "There is probably also an implied comparison between the Cranly-Mulligan 'manliness' and attractiveness to women and Stephen's lack of both. There are certainly homosexual implications in the placing of the phrases in the Rosenbach manuscript. Joyce may have moved them to avoid (or greatly reduce) these implications." See "Cranly seized his arm. . . . Stephen . . . thrilled by his touch" (*A Portrait,* p. 247).

Joseph Prescott has shown how Joyce's constant revision of manuscript and proof sometimes obscured meaning. See his "Stylistic Realism in Joyce's *Ulysses,*" in *A James Joyce Miscellany,* ed. Marvin Magalaner, 2d series (Carbondale: Southern Illinois University Press, 1959), pp. 15-66, and his *Exploring James Joyce* (Carbondale: Southern Illinois University Press, 1964).

See also Robert M. Adams, *Surface and Symbol: The Consistency of James Joyce's "Ulysses"* (1962; reprint ed., New York: Galaxy-Oxford, 1967), pp. 166-67, and passim. And see the discussion of characteristic sentence patterns in Proteus and Lestrygonians in ch. 6.

4. This discussion is not meant to suggest that the reader is always completely prepared by Joyce for all stream-of-consciousness passages. Indeed, some of the

earlier discussion in this chapter shows that sometimes Joyce decidedly does not prepare his reader. (See, for example, the discussion of "Cranly's arm. His arm" in n. 3.) I simply want to show how Joyce generally prepares the reader for the stream-of-consciousness technique and how the reader gathers information as he goes along that enables him to understand later stream-of-consciousness passages.

5. James Joyce, *A Portrait*, p. 215.

6. Bloom enters on page 55. Lestrygonians, the first stream-of-consciousness chapter for Bloom, begins on page 149/151.

7. . A. Richards, "The Analysis of a Poem," *Principles of Literary Criticism* (New York: Harcourt, Brace, 1923), pp. 114-33, is helpful in understanding this process.

Chapter 4: Simulating the Psychological Stream of Consciousness

1. In "all flesh," Stephen may be referring to "*quidditas,* the *whatness* of a thing" (*A Portrait of the Artist as a Young Man* [New York: Viking Press, 1968], p. 213). See also "Unsheathe your dagger definitions. Horseness is the whatness of allhorse" (184:13/186:13).

2. *Iliad*, 40. 34. Traherne from "Third Century," *Centuries of Meditations,* quoted by Stuart Gilbert, *James Joyce's "Ulysses"* (New York: Alfred A. Knopf, 1952), p. 61.

3. Horatio: "It is a nipping and an eager air" (*Hamlet*, Act 1, sc. 4, line 2). Weldon Thornton, *Allusions in "Ulysses"* (Chapel Hill: University of North Carolina Press, 1968) provides many more allusions for this section. The ones given above suggest some of the breadth of allusion in Stephen's thoughts.

4. Robert Humphrey, in *Stream of Consciousness in the Modern Novel* (Berkeley: University of California Press, 1954), pp. 44-47, gives a detailed analysis of the associations in a passage of Molly's soliloquy. He finds that, as in the passage from Proteus analyzed above, a perception (the sound of a clock or the sight of the wallpaper) generally starts a particular train of thought, which continues on by association until another perception interrupts it to redirect the flow or to start another chain.

5. *Omnis caro ad te veniet* is recited in the Introit of the Requiem Mass.

O thou that hearest prayer, unto thee all flesh shall come. (Ps. 65:2, King James Version)

In the Catholic version the passage is placed and reads differently:

Exaudi, oreatinem meam; ad te omnis caro veniet. (Ps. 64:3, Vulgate)
O hear my prayer: all flesh shall come to thee. (Ps. 64:3, Douay Version)

6. William M. Schutte, *Joyce and Shakespeare: A Study in the Meaning of Ulysses* (New Haven: Yale University Press, 1957), pp. 104-05.

7. Ibid., pp. 105-06. For a full discussion of the vampire god, see Schutte's chapter 7, "The Artist's Role: The *Dio Boia.*" References to *Ulysses* are to the 1934 Random House edition; to *A Portrait,* the Modern Library edition.

8. Humphrey, *Stream of Consciousness,* pp. 66-70.

9. This is Epicurus' phrase by way of Poincaré. See John Livingston Lowes, *The Road to Xanadu* (Boston: Houghton Mifflin, 1927), p. 62.

10. Gardner Murphy, *Personality* (New York: Harper, 1947), p. 357.

11. Richard Ellmann, "The Background of *Ulysses,*" *Kenyon Review* 16 (1954): 361. Robert M. Adams, *Surface and Symbol: The Consistency of James Joyce's "Ulysses,"* (1962; reprint ed., New York: Galaxy-Oxford, 1967), provides many other examples.

12. "Mental processes in which the free activities of imagination are evoked primarily by external stimuli" (W. Edgar Vinacke, *The Psychology of Thinking* [New York: McGraw-Hill, 1952], p. 218).

13. "Mental processes in which the free activities of imagination are evoked or influenced primarily by internal stimuli" (ibid., p. 218).

14. "Past experience . . . revived or relived with a more or less definite realization that the present experience is a revival" (Murphy, *Personality*, p. 991). In the first memory passage quoted, Bloom is remembering an episode from the days when he was courting Molly. In the second, he is remembering a flirtation between Molly and her current lover, Blazes Boylan.

15. "The result of dwelling upon a train of images without much attempt to control their direction" (ibid., p. 996).

16. Carney Landis and William A. Hunt, *The Startle Pattern* (New York: Farrar and Rinehart, 1938), pp. 31, 21, 25.

17. Donald B. Lindsley, "Emotion," *Handbook of Experimental Psychology,* ed. S. S. Stevens (New York: John Wiley & Sons, 1951), pp. 507-08.

18. James Joyce, *Stephen Hero* (Norfolk, Conn.: New Directions, 1955), p. 211.

19. "May the lily-bearing host of glowing confessors surround you; may the chorus of exulting virgins welcome you" (taken from the ritual of annointing which is part of the sacrament of extreme unction of the Roman Catholic church).

20. Joyce first locates Bloom with an omniscient author's sentence before he attempts to simulate his stream of consciousness.

21. The reader discovers later (179:6/181:32) that the name is Penrose.

22. William James, *The Principles of Psychology* (1890; reprint ed., New York: Dover Publications, 1950), p. 251.

23. Stuart Gilbert, *James Joyce's "Ulysses,"* 2d ed., rev. (New York: Alfred A. Knopf, 1952), p. 187.

24. Humphrey, *Stream of Consciousness,* pp. 74-76.

25. Bloom's memory of the "schoolpoems" that he learned generally works to the disadvantage of the poem, as we shall see later in a discussion about Cormac McArt that he thinks he remembers (167:5/169:23).

26. Imaginative thinking in the sense of Vinacke: a mental process "in which the free activities of the imagination are evoked primarily by external stimuli" (*Psychology of Thinking*, p. 218).

27. Humphrey, *Stream of Consciousness,* pp. 80-81.

28. Ibid., p. 77.

Chapter 5: The Intellectual Content of Proteus, Lestrygonians, and Penelope

1. Stuart Gilbert, *James Joyce's "Ulysses"* (New York: Alfred A. Knopf, 1952), p. 121. For other comments on references to Berkeley in Proteus, see William T. Noon, *Joyce and Aquinas* (New Haven: Yale University Press, 1957), p. 113.

2. Aristotle, *De Anima*, bk. 2, ch. 7, 418a29, in Richard McKeon, ed., *Introduction to Artistotle* (New York: Modern Library, 1947), p. 188. S. L. Goldberg also sees echoes of 431b-432a; see his *The Classical Temper: A Study*

of James Joyce's "Ulysses" (New York: Barnes & Noble, 1961), p. 73. Arnold Goldman sees echoes of Aristotle's *Physics*, bk. 3, chs. 1-2, 201a10-202a and his *Metaphysics*, 1065b15-1066a5; see his *The Joyce Paradox* (Evanston: Northwestern University Press, 1966), pp. 141-44. And Joseph E. Duncan sees echoes of *Physics*, bk. 4, ch. 11; see his "Modality of the Audible in *Ulysses*," *PMLA* 72 (March 1957): 286-95.

3. Kenelm Foster and Sylvester Humphries, trans., *Aristotle's "De Anima" in the Version of William of Moerbeke and the "Commentary" of St. Thomas Aquinas* (New Haven: Yale University Press, 1951), p. 256. See also Noon, *Joyce and Aquinas*, pp. 22-24. Both Aristotle and Aquinas also discuss "the transparent" (or the diaphanum as Aquinas calls it), Aristotle in bk. 2 of *De Anima*, ch. 7, 418b4-12 (McKeon, *Introduction*, p. 189) and Saint Thomas in his *Commentary*, lectio 15, par. 428, on bk. II (Foster and Humphries, *"De Anima" and "Commentary,"* p. 273). Robert M. Adams notes about the opening passage of Proteus, however, that "Joyce . . . has Aristotle repeat, with his head, *Dr. Johnson's* famous experiment with his foot, to prove the solidarity of the external world" (italics added); see *Surface and Symbol: The Consistency of James Joyce's "Ulysses"* (New York: Oxford University Press, 1962), p. 134.

4. Aristotle, *De Anima*, bk. 3, ch. 8, 432a1-5, in McKeon, ed., *Introduction*, p. 225.

5. Ernst Cassirer, *Essay on Man* (New Haven: Yale University Press, 1945), pp. 2-3.

6. William York Tindall, *James Joyce* (New York: Charles Scribner's Sons, 1950), p. 111.

7. "Il [Boehme] appartenait à la classe des sages sortis du peuple. Il ne connaissait pas plus Aristote que le Pseudo-Denys l'Aréopagite, la scholastique et la mystique médiévales. On ne peut trouver en lui, comme chez la plupart des mystiques chretiens, des influences directes de néoplatonisme. La Bible etait sa principale nourriture spirituelle" (Etudes sur Jacob Boehme, A. "L' 'Ungrund et la Liberté,'" par Nicholas Berdiaeff, in Jacob Boehme, *Mysterium Magnum*, *Tome 1* [Paris: Aubier, 1945], p. 6).

8. Jacob Boehme, *The Signature of All Things* (New York: E. P. Dutton, 1926), p. 91.

9. Tindall, *James Joyce*, pp. 111-12.

10. Boehme, *Signature*, p. 12.

11. Neither "Los" nor "Demiurgos," however, is underlined. For a description of the manuscript, see John Slocum and Herbert Cahoon, *A Bibliography of James Joyce* (New Haven: Yale University Press, 1953), p. 140. In his lecture in Trieste on Blake, Joyce referred to "the hammer of Los" (James Joyce, *The Critical Writings of James Joyce*, ed. Ellsworth Mason and Richard Ellmann [New York: Viking Press, 1964], p. 222).

12. "The Book of Los," ch. 4, 2. 11-14, in Max Plowman, ed., *The Poems and Prophecies of William Blake* (New York: E. P. Dutton, 1927), p. 107.

13. "The Book of Urizen," ch. 4, 2. 1-2, ibid., p. 85.

14. "The Book of Los," ch. 4, 2. 25 and 29, ibid., p. 108.

15. Ernest Bernbaum, *A Guide to the Romantic Movement* (New York: Ronald Press, 1949), p. 46.

16. "The Book of Los," ch. 4, 2. 41-48, in Plowman, *William Blake*, p. 108.

17. I.e., the manuscript in the possession of the Philip and A. S. W. Rosenbach Foundation of Philadelphia (described by Slocum and Cahoon, *Bibliography*, pp. 138-40).

18. Plowman, *William Blake*, p. xii.

19. Ibid., p. 53.

20. Gilbert, *James Joyce's "Ulysses,"* p. 119.

21. Frank Budgen, *James Joyce and the Making of "Ulysses"* (New York: Harrison Smith and Robert Haas, 1934), p. 49.

22. Joyce told Budgen, "I like that crescendo of verbs. The irresistible tug of the tides" (ibid., p. 55). Joseph Prescott comments on another aspect of the change in this sentence: "The vowels of the verbs constitute a document in labor, growing steadily in shrillness from the groaning gutteral to an almost hysterical acuteness of effort"; see his *Exploring James Joyce* (Carbondale: Southern Illinois University Press, 1964), p. 11. Joyce remarked on another language oddity in Proteus, "almosting" (47:6): "Parts of speech change, too. Adverb becomes verb" (Budgen, *Making of "Ulysses,"* p. 54). Prescott calls "almosting" an "Elizabethanism" (p. 10).

23. Greek: *"Euge! Euge!"* (43:7/42:11); *"oinopa ponton"* (48:31/47:39).

Latin: *"lex eterna"* (39:14/38:14); *"Duces Tecum"* (40:8/39:8); *"Requiescat"* (40:9/48:9); *"Descende, calve, ut ne nimium decalveris"* (41:1/40:1); *"descende"* (41:3/40:3); *"Terribilia meditans"* (46:19/45:22); *"frate porcospino"* (48:20/47:28); *"Omnis caro ad te veniet"* (48:34/48:1); *"Et vidit Deus. Et erant valde bona"* (50:1/49:10); *"diebus ac noctibus inurias patiens ingemiscit"* (50:31/49:41).

French:*"—Qui vous a mis dans cette fichue position?/—C'est le pigeon, Joseph."* (42:12/41:14); *"lait chaud"* (42:16/41:18); *"lapin"* (42:17/41:19); *"Gros lots"* (42:18/41:20); *"La Vie de Jesus"* (42:19/41:21); *"—C'est tordant, vous savez. Mois je suis socialiste. Je ne crois pas en l'existence de Dieu. Faut pas le dire à mon père./—Il croit?/—Mon père, oui"* (42:21-24/41:23-26); *"physiques, chimiques et naturelles"* (42:29/41:31); *"mou en civet"* (42:30/41:32); *"boul' Mich'"*(42:32/41:34); *"Lui, c'est moi"* (42:36/41:38); *"Encore deux minutes"* (42:41/42:1); *"Fermé"* (42:42/42:2); *"Comment?"* (43:10/43:12); *"Le Tutu"* (43:10/43:13); *"Pantalon Blanc et Culotte Rouge"* (43:31/42:13); *"chaussons"* (43:31/42:34); *"'pus"* (43:31/42:34); *"flan breton"* (43:32/42:34); *"Un demi setier!"* (43:37/42:40); *"Il est irlandais. Hollandais? Non fromage. Deux irlandais, nous, Irlande, vous savez? Ah, oui! . . . hollandais"* (43:38-40/42:37-40); *"slainte!"* (44:2/43:4); *"Vielle ogresse"* (44:11/43:13); *"dents jaunes"* (44:2/43:14); *"La Patrie"* (44:12/43:14); *"bonne à tout faire"* (44:16/43:18); *"mon fils"* (44:41/44:1); *"Un coche ensablé"* (45:32/44:35); *"Bonjour"* (50:2/49:11); *"Tiens, quel petit pied!"* (50:13/49:22).

German: *"nacheinander"* (38:14/37:14); *"nebeneinander"* (38:17, 20/37:17, 26; 50:9); *"Schluss"* (42:25/41:27); *"Naturlich"* (46:31/45:34).

Italian: *"maestro di color che sanno"* (38:8/37:8); *"Basta!"* (38:29/37:30); *"O si, certo!"* (41:22/40:23); *"piuttosto"* (49:36/49:3).

And Spanish: *"Los Demiurgos"* (38:20/37:20).

24. Aristotle: see above.

Arnold: (50:25-35/49:35-50:3)—Critics see here echoes of "Dover Beach."

Blake: see above; in addition, as Gilbert, *James Joyce's "Ulysses,"* p. 133, notes, the passage "mouth to her womb. Ooomb, allwombing tomb" (48:40/48:8) carries echoes of Blake's "The Gates of Paradise":

> The Door of Death I open found
> And the Worm Weaving in the Ground:
> Thou'rt my Mother from the Womb,
> Wife, Sister, Daughter to the Tomb,
> Weaving to Dreams the sexual strife
> And weeping over the Web of Life.   (Plowman, *William Blake*, p. 310)

Dryden: "Cousin Stephen, you will never be a saint" (41:18/40:19)—Dryden is supposed to have said to Swift, "Cousin Swift. you will never be a poet."

Gray: "The simple pleasures of the poor" (47:33/46:39)—Gray's "Elegy," 1.

32: "The short and simple annals of the poor."

Milton: "Sunk though he be beneath the watery floor" (50:41/50:9)—exact quotation from "Lycidas," l. 167.

Shakespeare: It would be wasteful here to quote all the echoes from Shakespeare in Proteus. The list is long, and it is readily available in William M. Schutte, *Joyce and Shakespeare: A Study of the Meaning of "Ulysses"* (New Haven: Yale University Press, 1957), pp. 178-86. The reader should note that Schutte's references are to the 1934 Random House edition of *Ulysses*.

Swift: "Houyhnhnm" (40:40/39:40)—horses in the fourth book of *Gulliver's Travels*; see also Dryden, above.

Swinburne: "Like me, like Algy, coming down to our mighty mother" (38:36/37:36).

Tennyson: "Of all the glad new year, mother, the rum tum tiddledy tum. Lawn Tennyson, gentleman poet" (51:20/50:31)—the quotation is from Tennyson's "The May Queen," ll. 1-4 of which follow:

> You must wake and call me early, call me early, mother dear;
> Tomorrow 'ill be the happiest time of all the glad New-Year,
> Of all the glad New-Year, mother, the maddest merriest day,
> For I'm to be Queen of the May, mother, I'm to be Queen of the May.

Traherne: "whiteheaped corn, orient and immortal, standing from everlasting to everlasting" (39:8/38:8)—"The corn was orient and immortal wheat, which never should be reaped, nor was ever sown. I thought it had stood from everlasting to everlasting" (from "Third Century," *Centuries of Meditations*, quoted by Gilbert, *James Joyce's "Ulysses,"* p. 61).

Wilde: "Wilde's Requiescat" (40:9/39:9).

Yeats: "*And no more turn aside and brood*" (50:7/49:16)—line from a poem by Yeats, "Who Goes With Fergus?":

> Who will go drive with Fergus now,
> And pierce the deep wood's woven shade,
> And dance upon the level shore?
> Young man, lift up your russet brow,
> And lift your tender eyelids, maid,
> And brood on hopes and fears no more.
>
> And no more turn aside and brood
> Upon love's bitter mystery;
> For Fergus rules the brazen cars,
> And rules the shadows of the wood,
> And the white beasts of the dim sea
> And all dishevelled wandering stars.

(W. B. Yeats, *The Collected Poems* [New York: Macmillan Co., 1933], p. 49. Buck sings a part of this song earlier [11:12/9:22])

Head: "*White thy fambles*" (48:16/47:23)—appears in Richard Head's *The Canting Academy*, published in London in 1673.

25. The italics are Joyce's.

26. "Let the birds fly, and like the famous ape, / To try conclusions, in the basket creep, / And break your own neck down" (*Hamlet*, act 3, sc. 4, line 195).

27. For other recent analyses of Proteus, see Goldberg, *Classical Temper*, pp.

158-63, and Stanley Sultan, *The Argument of "Ulysses"* (Columbus: Ohio State University Press, 1964), pp. 51-62. Joseph Prescott discusses the changes (mostly additions) that Joyce made in Stephen through the various stages of *Ulysses* in manuscript and proof in "The Characterization of Stephen Dedalus in *Ulysses*," *Exploring*, pp. 59-76.

28. *De Anima*, bk. 2, ch. 6, 418a10-13, in McKeon, ed., *Introduction*, p. 201.

29. *De Anima*, bk. 2, ch. 7, 419a3-7, in ibid.

30. The phrase "whether on the scaffold high" is from "God Save Ireland," by T. D. Sullivan: "Whether on the scaffold high / Or on the battlefield we die, / Oh what matter, when for Erin dear we fall."

31. The phrase "foundation of a building" may be a reference to the building of the Israelites into the walls of houses by the Egyptians. Leonard Albert says this is an allusion to Masonic lore: "Ulysses, Cannibals, and Freemasons," *A.D.* 2 (1951): 265-83. The "kidney burntoffering" is a reference to Bloom's own cooking of that morning (66/65).

32. M. G. Edgar and E. Chilman, *A Treasury of Verse for School and Home* (New York: Thomas Y. Crowell, 1926), p. 373.

33. William Rose Benet, ed., *The Reader's Encyclopedia*, 4 vols. (New York: Thomas Y. Crowell, 1948), 4: 975-76.

34. Stephen later corrects this "anachronism" (650:36/666:37). Weldon Thornton says that "Cormac is often described as the last pagan king of Ireland," so Bloom was not the only one to make this mistake (*Allusions in "Ulysses"* [Chapel Hill: University of North Carolina Press, 1968], p. 461). The editors of an anthology which includes the poem say that "there is a Christian legend which tells that Cormac McArt, who ruled Ireland in the third century, had an early intuition of the true faith and turned away from paganism" (Edgar and Chilman, *Treasury of Verse*, p. 372).

35. Charles Welsh, *The Golden Treasury of Irish Songs and Lyrics*, 2 vols. (New York: Dodge, 1907), 1:177.

36. Bloom's memories of happier days with Molly serve a dual—and paradoxical—function. For Bloom, focusing on them rather than on Molly's current faithlessness, they provide a warm glow and seem to make the present bearable. In contrast, for the reader they point up the poignance of Bloom's situation.

37. Helen D. Sargent and Ernest A. Hirsch, "Projective Methods," *An Introduction to Clinical Psychology*, ed. L. A. Pennington and Irwin A. Berg (New York: Ronald Press, 1954), pp. 188-89. The italics are in the original.

38. Not all the evidence of parallels here comes from Proteus.

39. The sentence quoted and the one preceding, which introduces Stephen's "ash sword," are not in the original autograph manuscript at the State University of New York at Buffalo. They do appear, however, in the Rosenbach manuscript. Evidently Joyce added them after his first draft of Proteus, perhaps after he wrote the stripling episode.

40. In the parentheses, *S* will indicate Stephen's thoughts and actions, *B*, Bloom's.

41. R. P. Blackmur, "The Jew in Search of a Son," *Virginia Quarterly Review* 24 (1948): 110. Although the references in this quotation go beyond Proteus and Lestrygonians, the statement is certainly applicable here.

42. The word *meshuggah* means "crazy." Bloom's equivalent of "off his chump" (157:27/159:38) is local slang.

43. For a disussion of Bloom's "inescapable Jewishness" see Marvin Magalaner, "The Anti-Semitic Limerick Incidents and Joyce's 'Bloomsday,'" *PMLA* 18 (1953): 1219. Magalaner writes that Bloom is "first and foremost . . . a Jewish-born man." However, the evidence that he offers to support this statement is all

from situations in which this position is forced on Bloom by other people. None of the episodes that Magalaner mentions shows any Jewish feelings on Bloom's part, or, indeed, any particularly Jewish understandings. See also Joseph Prescott, "Notes on Joyce's *Ulysses*," *Modern Language Quarterly* 8 (1952): 149-62. This matter is discussed in a later chapter.

44. Frank Budgen, *James Joyce and the Making of "Ulysses"* (New York: Harrison Smith and Robert Haas, 1934), p. 20.

45. Stuart Gilbert, *James Joyce's "Ulysses,"* rev. (New York: Alfred A. Knopf, 1952), p. 206.

46. Pp. 319-20. The later and fuller biography by Richard Ellmann, *James Joyce* (New York: Oxford University Press, 1959), confirms Budgen on these matters. I have used Budgen as a reference because his index makes them readily apparent in a way that Ellmann's does not.

47. Bloom does know Aristotle by name (232:4/235:19). Aristotle's *masterpiece* is probably an illustrated version of portions of *On the Generation of Animals*. Three passages offer short descriptions of the *Masterpiece*: "Plates: infants cuddled in a ball in bloodred wombs like livers of slaughtered cows" (232:5/232:20); "multi-geminal, twikindled and monstrous births conceived during the catamenic period or of consanguineous parents—in a word all the cases of human nativity which Aristotle has classified in his masterpiece with chromolithographic illustration" (404:8/411:3); "rotten pictures children with two heads and no legs" (757:42/772:40). Book 2 of *On the Generation of Animals* discusses the development and nourishment of the embryo; book 4 discusses malformations.

48. Joseph Prescott, "The Characterization of Molly Bloom," *Exploring*, pp. 90-93. Both Random House editions of *Ulysses* read: "not like me getting all at school" (751:15/766:14). Joyce later deleted the apostrophe in "Skerry's," but the compositor seems to have misunderstood his other instructions about "1's," which resulted in a corruption of the text (ibid., p. 156, n. 116).

49. Bloom may well have misquoted; but even then, anyone who had read any poetry would recognize the phrase. Her impatient "nonsensical book" is also a comment on her love of poetry.

50. "The young May moon shes beaming love" (725:11/740:12); "*Ave Maria*" (730:31/745:33); "there is a charming girl I love" (732:33/747:36); "*Stabat Mater*" (733:30/748:33); "Lead Kindly Light" (733:31/748:34); "lead Thou me on" (733:33/748:36); "Loves old sweet sonnnng" (739:36/754:40); "in Old Madrid" (743:30/758:32; 760:27, 31-34/775:24, 28-31; 768:2/782:40); "there is a flower that bloometh" (744:35/759:37); "My Lady's Bower" (748:11/763:10); "winds that blow from the South" (748:13/763:12); "O how the waters come down at Lahore" (755:15/770:12); "the Huguenots" (756:22/756:20; 757:15/772:13); "Bill Bailey won't you please come home" (759:8/774:5); "the old love is the new" (759:18/774:15); "so sweetly sang the maiden on the hawthorne bough" (759:19/774:16); "Maritana" (759:20, 22, 25/774:17, 19, 22); "winds that waft my sighs to the" (763:10/778:5).

51. Spanish: "*O Maria Santissima*" (731:27/746:29); "como esta usted muy bien gracias y usted" (764:22/779:17); "dos huevos estrellados senor" (764:40/779:35).

Italian: "mi fa pieta Masetto" (780:18/765:23); "presto non son piu forte" (765:24/780:19).

52. I have in the past been accused of being unfair to Molly and of misunderstanding her (see Adams, *Surface and Symbol*, p. 42; more about this matter later). In defense against a possible charge that I have slighted Molly by not saying as much about Penelope as I have about Proteus and Lestrygonians; therefore, I offer the following table:

	Proteus	*Lestrygonians*	*Penelope*
Number of pages in *Ulysses*	14	33	48
Number of pages in Tindall*	5	5	5
Number of pages in Blamires†	7	17	17
Number of pages in Thornton‡	17	21	16

*William York Tindall, *A Reader's Guide to James Joyce* (New York: Noonday, 1959). Tindall does not give 5 pages for every chapter. He gives 11 each to Ithaca and Circe, for example.
†Harry Blamires, *The Bloomsday Book* (London: Methuen & Co., 1966).
‡Weldon Thornton, *Allusions in "Ulysses"* (Chapel Hill: University of North Carolina Press, 1968).

There are many pages of speculation written about Molly, some of which we shall examine later; but summaries of the contents of Penelope usually are not longer than summaries of the contents of Proteus and of Lestrygonians, and sometimes they are shorter. That this is so despite the fact that Penelope is more than three times as long as Proteus and half again as long as Lestrygonians is clear testimony, it seems to me, of the relative emptiness of Molly's thoughts.

Chapter 6: Paragraph and Sentence Structure

1. For the purpose of this analysis and discussion, a sentence will be any group of words which begins with a capital letter, follows a piece of terminal punctuation, and is closed by a piece of terminal punctuation (period, exclamation point, question mark). Thus all of the following would be considered sentences:

> If he . . . (151:36/153:39)
> O! (151:37/153:40)
> Kinch here. (39:3/38:4)
> Elijah thirty-two feet per sec is com. (150:25/152:28)
> His pace slackened. (39:28/38:28)

2. For purposes of analysis, all such omniscient author's sentences, i.e., all those which immediately follow an omniscient author's sentence which begins a paragraph, will also be considered "introductory" (*a*) sentences rather than "buried" (*b*) sentences. For an example of a buried sentence, see 45:11/46:5, quoted above. The designations *s*, *a1*, *a2*, *a3*, *a4*, *a5*, and *b* will be used in this chapter as indicated above.

More formal descriptions of Joyce's sentence structure in *Ulysses* are being worked on than what I will present in this chapter. For example, Roger Di Pietro feels that "Joyce's style consists, in no small part, of possible but unusual applications of transformational rules." He has therefore undertaken with Suzanne Podvoll "a long range project to treat in detail the syntactic properties of all types of written sentences in a single work by Joyce [presumably *Ulysses*] and to formalize his so-called 'stream-of-consciousness' technique." See Roger Di Pietro, "A Tranformational Note on a Few Types of Joycean Sentences," *Style* 3 (1969): 156-67, for "six stylistic features [already uncovered] in the sub-structure of innovative sentences." (All quotations are from p. 157.)

3. Percentages are determined by $(po) \div (p - c)$. The difference is statistically significant at the .05 level. If conversational paragraphs are included, $(po) \div (p)$, the percentages do not differ much between the two chapters: Proteus, 25 percent; Lestrygonians, 28.3 percent.

4. Percentages are determined by $(a + s) \div (To)$. The difference is statistically significant at the .01 level.

5. A further support for this contention is that, whereas, if one excludes conversational paragraphs, only 30.9 percent of the paragraphs in Proteus begin with omniscient author's sentences, in Lestrygonians 45.4 percent (or half again as many) begin with omniscient author's sentences. (Including conversational paragraphs, the percentages do not differ very much between chapters: Proteus, 30.9 percent; Lestrygonians, 28.3 percent.) The figures for this computation are not presented in the table.

6. In Lestrygonians 15 percent of the paragraphs which could contain omniscient author's sentences (i.e., $p-c$) are composed *entirely* of omniscient author's sentences—9.4 percent of the total number of paragraphs, including conversational paragraphs (see table 1: s and $s+$). Percentages are determined by $(s$ and $s+) \div (p-c)$. In Proteus there are no paragraphs composed entirely of omniscient author's sentences.

7. This passage is not a single sentence, of course. It illustrates, however, the use of three parallel items in series characteristic of Stephen's stream of consciousness.

8. Joyce's revisions helped to increase this difference in the number of the uses of the colon between the two chapters. In the manuscript and galleys, Joyce changed two semicolons in Proteus to colons (50:13/49:22; 50:28/49:38), but did not strike out any colons or change them to any other type of punctuation. In Lestrygonians, however, Joyce changed one comma to a colon (164:24/166:41) and added a colon (165:12/167:28); but he also changed a colon to a semicolon (162:3/164:18), changed five colons to periods (150:5/152:6; 160:12/162:25; 163:16/165:30; 167:40/170:15; 170:33/173:10), and simply took out five other colons (162:4/164:18; 155:9/157:15; 168:9/170:27; 178:33/181:17; 179:22/182:6). His revisions, then, added two colons to the total in Proteus and subtracted ten from the total in Lestrygonians. (The page and line numbers given in this footnote indicate the beginning of the sentence in which the punctuation referred to occurs and not necessarily the line on which the punctuation itself appears.)

9. That the colon is not necessarily a concomitant of the stream-of-consciousness technique can be seen by comparing the figures for the use of the colon in Proteus and Lestrygonians with the number of uses of the colon in the first section (sixteen and a half pages) of Virginia Woolf's *Mrs. Dalloway* (only three). Inspection of the rest of *Ulysses* indicates that the proportion of colons per page was about the same throughout. Mrs. Woolf, however, used semicolons heavily in *Mrs. Dalloway*: 131 in the first sixteen and a half pages—almost 8 per page. By comparison, Joyce used only 4 semicolons in the fourteen pages of Proteus and only 4 in the thirty-two and a half pages of Lestrygonians. A comparison of the use of the stream-of-consciousness technique by the two authors, a study beyond the scope of this one, might find this difference in punctuation a meaningful clue to differences between the authors' styles or concept formations.

Joyce sometimes uses colons where others would use commas or semicolons. This statement applies to six of the fifty-eight colons in Proteus (41:30/40:31; 46:17/45:20; 48:22/47:30; 50:27/49:38; 50:28/49:39; 50:31/49:42) and to seven of the seventy-five colons in Lestrygonians (152:25/154:29; 155:28/157:37; 156:20/158:29; 162:12/164:26; 173:27/176:7; 178:23/181:7; 180:5/187:32). Joyce's use of the colon where conventional usage would call for a semicolon seems to indicate a fondness for the pause of anticipation. In only one instance in the two chapters does Joyce use a semicolon where he could have used a colon (43:10/42:12).

William M. Schutte suggests that in the use of the colon Joyce may have been reverting to sixteenth- and seventeenth-century usage.

10. These means were determined from six sample passages from each chapter. Analysis for critical ratio shows them to be significant on the .01 level. Analysis of variance, however, shows no significant difference. For the sampling technique employed, see the appendix.

11. 150:34/152:38; 151:10/153:12; 155:22/157:30; 158:24/160:36; 158:28/160:40; 158:32/161:2; 158:41/161:12; 159:17/161:29; 159:30/162:1; 160:5/162:18; 166:3/168:21; 168:39/171:16; 169:23/172:1; 173:25/176:5; 173:29/176:8; 179:1/181:27; 180:17/183:3.

12. 165:35/168:11; 169:21/174:41; 172:26/175:3; 173:4/175:24; 173:25/176:5; 180:13/182:41.

13. 39:10/38:10; 39:18/38:18; 39:19/38:19; 39:23/38:23; 44:12/43:14; 46:22/45:25; 48:5/47:12; 50:30/50:1.

14. See references to Prescott and to Adams in ch. 3, n. 3.

15. The short line of dialogue (two sentences) between paragraphs two and three in this passage is not considered in these computations. The second figure is an approximation for the chapter based on the percentage of omniscient author's sentences in six sample passages. For the sampling technique employed, see the appendix.

16. I am indebted to William M. Schutte, who made this point while reading a draft of this chapter.

17. Joyce to Budgen, 12 August 1921, *The Letters of James Joyce*, vol. 1, ed. Stuart Gilbert (New York: Viking Press, 1957), p. 170.

18. Frank Budgen, *James Joyce and the Making of "Ulysses"* (New York: Harrison Smith and Robert Haas, 1934), p. 91.

19. William York Tindall, *James Joyce* (New York: Charles Scribner's Sons, 1950), p. 42.

20. Edmund Wilson, *Axel's Castel* (1931; reprint ed., New York: Charles Scribner's Sons, 1948), pp. 224, 204.

21. Rebecca West, *The Strange Necessity* (London: Jonathan Cape, 1931), p. 48.

22. From *Le Morte Darthur* (Malory), bk. 21, ch. 5.

23. A glance at the opening of Penelope in its various manuscript forms shows the amount of revising that Joyce did on the later chapters of *Ulysses*. In that connection, the following few figures complement the discussion of the various revisions of the first sentence of Penelope and in general support the discussion above.

Page 738 of the 1934 Random House edition of *Ulysses*, the opening page of Penelope, has 535 words. As this same passage appeared initially in the Rosenbach manuscript (i.e., without the additions made in that manuscript), it was only 200 words long, or 37.3 percent of the final version. Another 119 words, an additional 22.2 percent, were added in revision of the manuscript. The other 217 words, 40.5 percent of the passage as it was finally published, were added in the typescript and galleys.

In the manuscript, Joyce used apostrophes to indicate contractions. They were deleted before the first galley.

24. Better examples of the transitional *then* can be found later in the chapter: "we were like cousins what age was I then the night of the storm I slept in her bed she had her arms around me then we were fighting in the morning with the pillow" (741:3/756:6).

25. The difference between sentence length in Penelope and Proteus is significant at the .05 level, between Penelope and Lestrygonians at the .01 level.

The standard error is 1.63401. Because of the extremely long sentences in samples one and six of Penelope, the analysis was done by ranking.

26. David Hayman, "*Ulysses,*" *The Mechanics of Meaning* (Englewood Cliffs, N.J.: Prentice-Hall, 1970), p. 75. The italics here and in the next two paragraphs are mine.

27. James Joyce, *A Portrait of the Artist as a Young Man* (New York: Viking Press, 1968), p. 215.

28. Joyce did not intend that they be the same, for what that is worth. In a letter to Harriet Weaver on 24 June 1921, he wrote: "The task I set myself technically in writing a book from eighteen different points of view and in as many different styles . . . , that and the nature of the legend chosen would be enough to upset anyone's mental balance" (*Letters,* 1: 167).

Chapter 7: Patterns of Association

1. Fred Schwartz and Richard O. Rouse, "The Activation and Recovery of Associations," *Psychological Issues* 3, no. 1 (1961), monograph 9, pp. 108-09.

2. Phebe Cramer, *Word Association* (New York: Academic Press, 1968), p. 188.

3. James Deese, *The Structure of Associations in Language and Thought* (Baltimore: Johns Hopkins Press, 1965), p. 152: "The noun-noun relation in association is a very convenient and efficient way of dealing with the problem of multi-dimensional similarity in thought processes." For interword associative matrices, see, for example, p. 56 (insect names) and p. 149 (animal names).

4. James Joyce, *Exiles,* ed. Padraic Colum (New York: Viking Press, 1951), pp. 117, 119, 121.

5. Ibid., p. 121.

6. A. Walton Litz, *The Art of James Joyce* (New York: Oxford University Press, 1964), p. 18.

7. Joyce, *Exiles,* p. 122.

8. Litz, *The Art of James Joyce,* p. 134. Litz associates this cluster with an undated epiphany-like sketch of a kitchen by Joyce which contains many of the same phrases. It is not clear whether the sketch or the note came first. It is possible that Joyce first wrote the sketch and then reduced it to an associative cluster as a convenient set of notes.

9. Robert M. Adams, *Surface and Symbol: The Consistency of James Joyce's "Ulysses"* (1952; reprint ed., New York: Galaxy-Oxford, 1967), p. 146.

10. I.e., words in nominal position, *not* including nouns functioning as adjectives.

11. Litz, *The Art of James Joyce,* pp. 63-64.

12. James Prescott, "James Joyce: A Study in Words," *Exploring James Joyce* (Carbondale: Southern Illinois University Press, 1964), pp. 10-13.

13. Ibid., p. 10.

14. Litz, *The Art of James Joyce,* p. 18.

15. Joyce, *Exiles,* p. 122.

16. Aristotle, *Parva Naturalia,* "De Sensu et Sensibili," 437a1-10; *Metaphysics,* 980a25.

17. Thomas Aquinas, *Commentary on the Metaphysics of Aristotle,* trans. John P. Rowan (Chicago: Henry Regnery, 1961), I. L. 1C 6-7, p. 8.

18. Aristotle, *Parva Naturalia,* 437a10-12; Aquinas, *Commentary,* I. L. 1C 8, pp. 8-9.

Chapter 8: Words

1. Fillmore H. Sanford, "Speech and Personality," *Psychological Bulletin* 39 (1942): 840.
2. Ibid., p. 816.
3. Charles E. Osgood, "Some Effects of Motivation on Style of Encoding," *Style in Language,* ed. Thomas A. Sebook (Cambridge, Mass.: Technology Press of M.I.T., 1960), p. 293. Italics in original.
4. Ibid., p. 293.
5. For careful and at times devastating documentation of that charge, see Robert F. Lane, *The Liberties of Wit* (New Haven: Yale University Press, 1961). For example:

> So . . . we come to the verification of empirical generalizations in literary criticism. At the very beginning the difference between discovering these generalizations, uncovering the regularities that may reside in the poetic process, bringing probable causes for various effects to the light of day, are all very different from their testing and verification. It is confusion on this point that often sends the imaginative innovator into a state of shock about the usual verification procedures. Discovery and insight may come from a wholly subjective reference; testing and verification rarely if ever can be achieved in this way. (p. 61)

Lane says that as a result of lack of verification (as well as poorly thought through theories of criticism and loose use of language), literary criticism too frequently displays "a tendency to plain obscurantism," is full of "conflicting opinion," offers "apparent license, or at least lack of effective restraint, [to] eccentric and 'wild' judgments," and is subject to a "prevalence of fads and literary movements with some exaggerated proportions" (pp. 81-83).

For a recent critical view of Joyce scholarship, see Thomas Merton, "News of the Joyce Industry," *Sewanee Review* 77 (1969): 543-54.

6. The observed difference in one-syllable words between Penelope and Proteus is significant at the .05 level; between Penelope and Lestrygonians at the .10 level (standard error 2.9833). The differences in the other columns are not statistically significant.

7. The observed difference in the percentage of words derived from Greek, Latin, and the Romance languages between Penelope and Proteus is significant at the .02 level; between Penelope and Lestrygonians at the .01 level (standard error 2.4437).

8. The concept of levels of abstraction applied here to the vocabularies of Stephen, Bloom, and Molly is the one made familiar by the semanticists. See Alfred Korzybski, "On the Structural Differential," *Science and Sanity,* 3d ed. (Lakeville, Conn.: International Non-Aristotelian Library, 1948), pp. 386-411. Analysis of this sort cannot be as precise as the analysis of word length or of word derivation. In comparing the streams of consciousness for abstract words, I went through the three sets of six sample passages noting all of what I felt to be highly abstract words and phrases. These are all listed at this point in the chapter. I determined what was abstract on the basis of my understanding of Korzybski's structural differential. Others doing this same analysis might choose more, fewer, or different words or phrases. But from the listings above, the reader will see that unless I have seriously misunderstood Korzybski there are important differences among the three streams of consciousness in the abstractions they contain.

9. I noted in the three sets of sample passages all instances of what I felt

were slang, dialectal words, and trite expressions. They are listed in the text above, the appropriate list with the discussion of the character from whose stream of consciousness it comes. As with the listings of abstract words and phrases, another person might have chosen more, fewer, or different words and phrases. But from the listings in the text above, the reader will see that, unless I have seriously misunderstood the concept of levels of usage, there are important differences among the three streams of consciousness in their use of the vulgate.

10. Richard Head, *The Canting Academy* (London, 1673), p. 1.

11. Ibid., pp. 19-21.

12. Eric Partridge, *A Dictionary of Slang and Unconventional English* (London: Routledge and Kegan Paul, 1949).

13. Partridge's entry reads "bing a-vest."

14. Joyce strengthened this aspect of Molly's monologue by additions to the galleys. See Joseph Prescott, "The Characterization of Molly Bloom," *Exploring James Joyce* (Carbondale: Southern Illinois University Press, 1964), p. 92-93.

15. John B. Carroll, *Language and Thought* (Englewood Cliffs, N.J.: Prentice-Hall, 1964), p. 54. See also Wendell Johnson, "Studies in Language Behavior," *Psychological Monographs* 56, no. 2 (1944): 1-3.

16. Frederick Mosteller and David L. Wallace, *Inference and Disputed Authorship: The Federalist* (Reading, Mass.: Addison-Wesley, 1964), p. 16.

17. Miles Hanley, *Word Index to James Joyce's "Ulysses"* (1937; reprint ed., Madison: University of Wisconsin Press, 1951).

18. Johnson, "Studies in Language Behavior," p. 3.

19. Gustav Herdan, *The Advanced Theory of Language as Choice and Chance* (New York: Springer-Verlag, 1966), pp. 49-50. Herdan, however, prefers a more sophisticated analysis; see p. 50.

20. See, for example, Charles F. Hockett, *A Course in Modern Linguistics* (New York: Macmillan Co., 1958), p. 264. Hockett prefers "contentive" and "functor" to "content word" and "function word" (pp. 261-67).

21. The observed difference between Penelope and Telemachus is significant at the .02 level (standard error 8.843); between Penelope and Proteus and between Penelope and Lestrygonians at the .01 level (standard error 7.2179).

22. William A. Evans, "Wordagglutinations in James Joyce's *Ulysses*," *Studies in the Literary Imagination* 3, no. 2 (1970): 28.

23. Ibid., p. 29.

Chapter 9: Expressive Behavior

1. Maria Lorenz, "Expressive Behavior and Language Patterns," *Psychiatry* 18 (1955): 353-54. Also relevant here is:

> The teatimestained terminal (say not the tag, mummer, or our show's a failure!) is a cosy little brown study all to oneself and, whether it be thumbprint, mademark or just a poor trait of the artless, its importance in establishing the identities in the writer complexus (for if the hand was one, the minds of active and agitated were more than so) will be best appreciated by never forgetting that both before and after the battle of the Boyne it was a habit not to sign letters always. Tip. . . . So why, pray, sign anything as long as every word, letter, penstroke, paperspace is a perfect signature of its own? A true friend is known much more easily, and better into the bargain, by his personal touch, habits

of full or undress, movements, response to appeals for charity than by his footwear, say. (James Joyce, *Finnegans Wake* [New York: Viking Press, 1947], pp. 114-15)

2. Louis A. Gottschalk, Goldine C. Gleser, and Gove Hambidge, Jr., "Verbal Behavior Analysis," *A.M.A. Archives of Neurology and Psychiatry* 77, no. 1 (1957): 300.

3. Joyce to Budgen, 16 August 1921, *The Letters of James Joyce,* vol. 1, ed. Stuart Gilbert (New York: Viking Press, 1957), p. 170.

4. William York Tindall, *A Reader's Guide to James Joyce* (New York: Noonday, 1959), p. 232.

5. Gottschalk et al., "Verbal Behavior Analysis," pp. 300, 309-10. For the first two categories, P<.01-P<.05. For the third, the level of significance was .06.

6. Albert Gilman and Roger Brown, "Personality and Style in Concord," *Transcendentalism and Its Legacy,* ed. Myron Simon and Thornton H. Parsons (Ann Arbor: University of Michigan Press, 1966), pp. 107-08. Passages were paired according to subject. Gilman and Brown reported sentences in which pronouns and negatives occurred rather than occurrences of words. They report that "for the pronoun analysis," p=.007; for the analysis of "negative forms," p=.001. In the final case, p=.002.

7. H. Aronson and Walter Weintraub, "Sex Differences in Verbal Behavior Related to Adjustive Mechanisms," *Psychological Reports* 21 (1967): 968.

8. See n. 9 below.

9. Aronson and Weintraub, "Sex Differences in Verbal Behavior," p. 968. All of these categories were found to discriminate in at least one of the Aronson and Weintraub studies:

Walter Weintraub and H. Aronson, "The Application of Verbal Behavior Analysis to the Study of Psychological Defense Mechanisms, II: Speech Patterns Associated with Impulsive Behavior," *Journal of Nervous and Mental Disease* 139 (1964): 75-82. Negation, retraction, feelings, and evaluation discriminated between "impulsive" patients and "normal" controls at the .01 level (p. 79).

Walter Weintraub and H. Aronson, "The Application of Verbal Behavior Analysis to the Study of Psychological Defense Mechanisms, III: Speech Patterns Associated with Delusional Behavior," ibid., 141 (1961): 172-79. The following categories discriminated between "delusional" patients and "normal" controls at the levels of significance indicated: negation (.05), qualification (.10), retraction (.05), explaining (.001), and evaluation (.01).

In their unpublished scoring manual, Aronson and Weintraub indicate that they count as "explaining" not only an explanation by the speaker about his own actions, but also about someone else's: His purpose is to. . . .

See also H. Aronson and Walter Weintraub, "Personal Adaptation as Reflected in Verbal Behavior," *Studies in Dyadic Communication,* ed. Aron Siegman and Benjamin Pope (New York: Pergamon Press, in press).

10. Aronson and Weintraub, "Sex Differences in Verbal Behavior," p. 969.

11. Ibid.

12. H. Aronson and Walter Weintraub, "A Scoring Manual for Verbal Behavior Analysis," mimeographed (1961), unpaged, item 11.

13. Aronson and Weintraub, "Sex Differences in Verbal Behavior," p. 969. Of Aronson and Weintraub's twelve categories, I found six useful: negation, qualification, retraction, explaining, feelings, and evaluation. Five others were not applicable: number of words, long pauses and silence, rate of speech, and direct reference to the experimenter. A twelfth category, personal reference, taps many of the same characteristics as do the analyses of references to self and

to self and others.

14. Aronson and Weintraub, "A Scoring Manual," item 12.

15. The Aronson-Weintraub manual calls for scoring "exclamatory phrases of value" on the pleasant-unpleasant continuum (item 12).

Chapter 10: Poetic Devices

1. The poem itself appears on page 131/132.

2. Harry Levin, *James Joyce* (Norfolk, Conn.: New Directions, 1941), p. 85.

3. Richard M. Kain, *Fabulous Voyager: James Joyce's "Ulysses"* (Chicago: University of Chicago Press, 1947), p. 88.

4. William York Tindall, *James Joyce* (New York: Charles Scribner's Sons, 1950), p. 42.

5. S. L. Goldberg, *The Classical Temper: A Study of James Joyce's "Ulysses"* (London: Chatto & Windus, 1961), p. 110; Robert M. Adams, *Surface and Symbol: The Consistency of James Joyce's "Ulysses"* (1962; reprint ed., New York: Galaxy-Oxford, 1967), p. 120.

6. Edith Rickert, *New Methods for the Study of Literature* (Chicago: University of Chicago Press, 1927), p. 192.

7. Ezra Pound, *Literary Essays of Ezra Pound*, ed. T. S. Eliot (Norfolk, Conn.: New Directions, 1954), p. 4.

8. This whole passage was quoted for two reasons: 1) the images are thoroughly interwoven, and separating would destroy them, and 2) if the images were listed separately most of the passage would be quoted anyway.

9. The one image of the eight which does not indicate change or the result of change directly is "entombing their blind bodies" (45:21/44:24). And even there, "entombing" suggests death and decay.

10. Kristian Smidt, *James Joyce and the Cultic Use of Fiction* (Oxford: Blackwell, 1955), p. 64.

11. The italics are mine.

12. Stuart Gilbert, *James Joyce's "Ulysses,"* 2d ed., rev. (New York: Alfred A. Knopf, 1952), p. 41.

13. Helen D. Sargent and Ernest A. Hirsch, "Projective Methods," *An Introduction to Clinical Psychology*, ed. L. A. Pennington and Irwin A. Berg (New York: Ronald Press, 1954), p. 189.

14. Caroline Spurgeon, "Leading Motives in the Imagery of Shakespeare's Tragedies," *Shakespeare Criticism, 1919-1935*, ed. A. Bradby (New York: Oxford University Press, 1949), pp. 18, 20.

15. Ibid., pp. 60-61.

16. Gordon W. Allport, *Personality* (New York: Henry Holt, 1937), pp. 172-73.

Chapter 11: Synthesis: Stephen, Bloom, and Molly

1. Frank Budgen, *James Joyce and the Making of "Ulysses"* (New York: Harrison Smith and Robert Haas, 1934), p. 50.

2. William York Tindall, *James Joyce* (New York: Charles Scribner's Sons, 1950), p. 42.

3. Stanley Sultan, *The Argument of "Ulysses"* (Columbus: Ohio State University Press, 1964), p. 52.

4. S. L. Goldberg, *The Classical Temper: A Study of James Joyce's "Ulysses"* (London: Chatto & Windus, 1961), p. 110; Robert M. Adams, *Surface and*

Symbol: The Consistency of James Joyce's "Ulysses" (1962; reprint ed., New York: Galaxy-Oxford, 1967), p. 120; Sultan, *The Argument of "Ulysses,"* p. 463.

5. Sultan, *The Argument of "Ulysses,"* pp. 463-64; Joseph Prescott, *Exploring James Joyce* (Carbondale: Southern Illinois University Press, 1964), pp. 73-74.

6. Thomas F. Staley, "Stephen Dedalus and the Temper of the Modern Hero," *Approaches to "Ulysses": Ten Essays,* ed. Thomas F. Staley and Bernard Benstock (Pittsburgh: University of Pittsburgh Press, 1970). pp. 6-8.

7. According to Richard Ellmann (*James Joyce* [New York: Oxford University Press, 1959], pp. 431-32), the first three chapters were written between mid-October and the end of December. As we shall see later, it took Joyce from February to the end of October to write Ithaca and Penelope, and he amplified them both greatly in proof.

8. C. P. Curran, *James Joyce Remembered* (New York: Oxford University Press, 1968), p. 32. William York Tindall, *Forces in Modern British Literature* (New York: Alfred A. Knopf, 1947), pp. 196-98, 204. See also *Ulysses,* 139:4-8/140:29-33.

9. Sheldon R. Brivic, "James Joyce: From Stephen to Bloom," in *Psychoanalysis and Literary Process,* ed. Frederick Crews (Cambridge, Mass.: Winthrop Publishers, 1970), p. 144-46. I have presented a very short—and probably inadequate—summary of a much longer and carefully drawn analysis by Brivic. For a discussion of Stephen's conception of God as *dio boia,* see William M. Schutte, *Joyce and Shakespeare: A Study of the Meaning of "Ulysses"* (New Haven: Yale University Press, 1957), ch. 7, pp. 95-120.

10. C. Day Lewis, *The Poetic Image* (London: Cape, 1947), p. 34.

11. Adams, *Surface and Symbol,* pp. 120-21.

12. Sultan, *The Argument of "Ulysses,"* p. 60.

13. Ibid., p. 61.

14. Goldberg, *The Classical Temper,* p. 163.

15. Ibid., p. 158.

16. Adams, *Surface and Symbol,* pp. 97-98.

17. Goldberg, *The Classical Temper,* p. 191.

18. Sultan, *The Argument of "Ulysses,"* pp. 452-53.

19. Goldberg, *The Classical Temper,* p. 179.

20. Sultan, *The Argument of "Ulysses,"* p. 453.

21. Goldberg, *The Classical Temper,* p. 179.

22. Brivic, "James Joyce," p. 162.

23. J. P. Guilford, "Three Faces of Intellect," *American Psychologist* 14 (1959): 474. Wouldn't Joyce have loved such a test! Note also the statement by Jacques Mercanton: "When I spoke of the artist's nature of the hero, Leopold Bloom, he lent an ear: 'you must have been one of the first to have noticed it. In general, readers have looked down on Bloom' " (Mercanton, "The Hours of James Joyce, Part I," *Kenyon Review* 24 [1962]: 702).

24. Once again, I am using here the Aronson-Weintraub categories and the results of the analyses made by means of the Aronson-Weintraub techniques.

25. For Joyce's remarks, see Ellmann, *James Joyce,* pp. 383-86, 407-08. Budgen, for example, has a great deal to say about Bloom's being Jewish. Unfortunately, however, Budgen's ideas about Jews give a peculiar distortion to the image of Bloom as it is refracted through the prism of *James Joyce and the Making of "Ulysses."* To Budgen, the "average" Jew is a good businessman—although, as he points out, Bloom is not (p. 277). He considers Jews oriental and thus "fatalistic in outlook," masochistic, and pessimistic (pp. 145-46). Finally, there is a "physical chemical repulsion" felt by the male Gentile for the male Jew, although it is not felt by the male Jew for the male Gentile or for either kind of men for women of either kind or at all

by female Gentiles or by Jewesses (p. 255). One wonders how much of this came from Joyce. See, for example, the passage in *Ulysses* which gave rise to this analysis by Budgen:

> Accordingly [Bloom] passed his left arm in Stephen's right and led him on accordingly.
> —Yes, Stephen said uncertainly, because he thought he felt a strange kind of flesh of a different man approach him, sinewless and wobbly and all that. (664:37/660:31)

A recent article is Robert Tracy, "Leopold Bloom Fourfold: A Hungarian-Hebraic-Hellenic-Hibernian Hero," *Massachusetts Review* 6 (1965): 523-38.

26. Joseph Prescott, "Notes on Joyce's *Ulysses*," *Modern Language Quarterly* 13 (1952): 151. See also other references on that same page and on pp. 150, 152, 156, 160; and Sultan, *The Argument of "Ulysses,"* pp. 99-106.

27. Prescott, "Notes on Joyce's *Ulysses*," p. 52.

28. Prescott points out that in the second line of Ha-Tikvah, the song on p. 673/689, the punctuation violates the meaning.

29. But Molly may have been: "I suppose on account of my being jewess looking after my mother" (756:16/771:14). If Molly's mother was Jewish, then by Jewish law she was born Jewish and Bloom was not.

30. Ellmann, *James Joyce*, p. 417; Tracy, "Leopold Bloom Fourfold," pp. 523-38. See *Ulysses*, pp. 672-73/688:89.

31. Sultan, *The Argument of "Ulysses,"* p. 106.

32. Sultan reports that Ellmann told him that Dodd (in real life) was probably not a Jew (p. 105 n. 6).

33. Joseph Prescott, "The Characterization of Leopold Bloom," *Literature and Psychology* 9, no. 1 (1959): 3-4.

34. Sigmund Freud, *A General Introduction to Psychoanalysis* (New York: Permabooks, 1953), pp. 314-15.

35. It might be argued here that until Rudy's death and the consequent cessation of marital relations between Molly and Bloom, Bloom was not so eccentric. But although marriage may have aggravated Bloom's sexual eccentricities, it did not cause them, as her memories of their courtship show.

36. Sigmund Freud, "The Economic Problem in Masochism," *Collected Papers*, 5 vols. (London: Hogarth, 1948), 2: 257-58.

37. This episode is a reflection of a thought that Bloom entertained earlier in the day (363:32/370:7).

38. For example, he points out to Henry Menton his crushed hat (114/115) and chases after Myles Crawford as the group from the newspaper office leaves for a drink (144-45/146-47). Again, he says to the Citizen "and the Saviour was a jew and his father was a jew" (336:18/342:25), a remark that anyone who had lived any time at all in Catholic Dublin would know better than to make to almost any Irishman, let alone to one who had been spending the afternoon drinking and getting himself excited in a political discussion.

39. Freud, "The Economic Problem in Masochism," p. 265.

40. Ibid., p. 258.

41. Freud, "The Sexual Aberrations," *The Basic Writings of Sigmund Freud*, trans. A. A. Brill (New York: Modern Library, 1938), p. 569.

42. Brivic, "James Joyce," p. 161.

43. Ibid., pp. 48, 127, 130, 133, 137, 148-52, 161.

44. Goldberg, *The Classical Temper*, p. 136.

45. Sultan, *The Argument of "Ulysses,"* pp. 106-07.

46. Leslie Fiedler, "Bloom on Joyce; Or, Jokey for Jacob," *Journal of Modern Literature* 1 (1970): 24.

47. Budgen, *Making of "Ulysses,"* p. 17.

48. Ibid., p. 16.

49. Phillip F. Herring, "The Bedsteadfastness of Molly Bloom," *Modern Fiction Studies* 15 (1969): 57.

50. Ibid., p. 58.

51. Adams, *Surface and Symbol*, p. 42.

52. Herring, "Molly Bloom," p. 53.

53. David Hayman, "The Empirical Molly," in *Approaches to "Ulysses": Ten Essays*, ed. Thomas F. Staley and Bernard Benstock (Pittsburgh: University of Pittsburgh Press, 1970), pp. 105, 133.

54. Darcy O'Brien, "Some Determinants of Molly Bloom," in *Approaches to "Ulysses,"* p. 143.

55. Herring, "Molly Bloom," pp. 58-60. I shall not argue the charge, but shall let the reader decide on the basis of what follows to what extent what Morse and I said "constitutes a rejection of Molly *on the basis of personal taste* and . . . seems to imply a *moral* judgment."

56. Goldberg, *The Classical Temper*, p. 296.

57. Adams, *Surface and Symbol*, p. 42.

58. Ellmann points out that the original binding of *Ulysses* "in the Greek colors—white letters on a blue field . . . suggested the myth of Greece and of Homer, the white island rising from the sea" (*James Joyce*, p. 539).

59. For a good recent discussion of the intentional fallacy, see Rosemarie Maier, " 'The Intentional Fallacy' and the Logic of Literary Criticism," *College English* 32 (1970): 135-45.

60. See also evidence from Ithaca, which suggests "deficient mental development" (670:22/686:15): inability to read, write, and compute adequately (670:24-38/686:17-30) and inability to learn (671:14/687:10).

61. The punctuation and capitalization are mine.

62. Goldberg, *The Classical Temper*, p. 296.

63. Phillip Toynbee, "A Study of James Joyce's Ulysses," *James Joyce: Two Decades*, ed. Sean Givens (New York: Vanguard Press, 1948), pp. 282-84; quoted by Goldberg, ibid., p. 296.

64. Hayman, "The Empirical Molly," p. 125.

65. Sultan, *The Argument of "Ulysses,"* p. 42. R. P. Blackmur, "The Jew in Search of a Son," *Virginia Quarterly Review* 24 (1948): 114-15; quoted by Goldberg, *The Classical Temper*, p. 292, who considers the Blackmur statement "sensitive," "sensible," and "persuasive."

66. Joyce to Claude W. Sykes, n.d. (early 1921), and Joyce to Budgen, February 1921, *The Letters of James Joyce*, vol. 1, ed. Stuart Gilbert (New York: Viking Press, 1957), pp. 157-59; Joyce to Carl Linati, 18 February 1921, ibid., vol. 3, ed. Richard Ellmann (New York: Viking Press, 1966), pp. 38-39.

67. Ellmann, *James Joyce*, p. 531.

68. *Letters* 1: 170; *The New Cassell's German Dictionary* (New York: Funk & Wagnalls Co., 1958).

69. Peter Spielberg, ed., *James Joyce's Manuscripts and Letters at the University of Buffalo: A Catalogue* (Buffalo: University of Buffalo, 1962), p. 50.

70. Ellmann, *James Joyce*, p. 536.

71. Two of the last twenty instances of negatives were added at this stage.

72. Joyce to Robert McAlmon, *Letters* 1: 157; Joyce to McAlmon, ibid., 3: 57; Ellmann, *James Joyce*, pp. 538-39.

73. Louis Gillet, *Claybook for James Joyce* (New York: Abelard-Schuman,

1958), p. 111.

74. Hugh Kenner, *Dublin's Joyce* (1956; reprint ed., Boston: Beacon Press, 1962), p. 262. Sultan, *The Argument of "Ulysses,"* p. 448. Goldberg, *The Classical Temper*, p. 297. O'Brien, "Some Determinants of Molly Bloom," p. 151. *James Joyce, "Ulysses"; Soliloquies of Molly and Leopold Bloom*, recorded by Siobhan McKenna, Caedmon TC-1063.

75. H. Aronson and Walter Weintraub, "Sex Differences in Verbal Behavior Related to Adjustive Mechanisms," *Psychological Reports* 21 (1967): 969.

76. William Smith, *A Classical Dictionary*, rev. by G. E. Marindin (London: John Murray, 1909), p. 350.

77. Harry Thurston Peck, ed., *Harper's Dictionary of Classical Literature and Antiquities* (New York: American Book Co., 1896), p. 702.

78. "Unam eandemque terram habere geminam vim, et masculinam, quod semina producat, et feminam, quod recipiat atque enutriat. Inde a vi feminina dictam esse Tellurem, a masculina Tellumonem" (from Varro, quoted by Augustine [*De Civitate Dei*, 7.23], from Andrew's Freund, *Harper's Latin Dictionary*, rev. by C. T. Lewis and C. Short [New York: American Book Co., 1907], p. 1847).

79. Bronislaw Malinowski, *Sex and Repression in Savage Society* (London: Routledge and Kegan Paul, 1949), pp. 19-20. I am using Malinowski here in response to the mythological archetype suggested by Joyce, not in any attempt to portray what woman's role should or should not be.

80. Ibid., p. 22.

81. Helen Deutsch, *Psychology of Women*, 2 vols. (London: Research Books, 1947), 2: 21, 41, 38.

82. Richard M. Kain, *Fabulous Voyager: James Joyce's "Ulysses"* (Chicago: University of Chicago Press, 1947), p. 100; Harry Levin, *James Joyce* (Norfolk, Conn.: New Directions, 1941), p. 126; Tindall, *James Joyce*, p. 38.

83. She seems to reserve humiliating Bloom, however, as her personal prerogative. When there is a possibility that others will make a fool of him, thus possibly reflecting on her, she bridles: "theyre not going to get my husband again into their clutches if I can help it making fun of him then behind his back I know well when he goes on with his idiotics" (758:41/ 773:39).

84. Geoffrey Chaucer, "The Wife of Bath's Prologue," 11. 113-14.

85. Ibid., ll. 481-88.

86. Ibid., l. 194.

87. Hayman, "The Empirical Molly," p. 117.

88. Ibid., pp. 125-26.

89. Hugh Kenner, "Joyce's *Ulysses:* Homer and Hamlet," *Essays in Criticism* 2 (1952): 94. The italics are Kenner's.

90. Stuart Gilbert, *James Joyce's "Ulysses"* (New York: Alfred A. Knopf, 1931), p. 68.

91. Unfortunately the critics did not follow closely the rest of what Gilbert says. Having pointed out that Stephen has earlier denied his own ("consubstantial") father, he goes on to explain that "after all, he is equally (indeed, more) aloof from, and ironic towards, his 'spiritual father' [i.e., Bloom]" (p. 70) and says that "even the meeting with Bloom is, for him, no release from his hopeless quest, no remedy for his future isolation. Stephen's attitude is really one of despair; he has not lost a father, like Telemachus, but he can never find one" (p. 71). Although calling Bloom Stephen's "spiritual father" is of a piece with saying that Stephen is "striving to be atoned with the father," the remarks about Stephen's lack of rapport with Bloom are well taken. Most of the critics, however, seem to have chosen to ignore them.

92. Levin, *James Joyce*, pp. 62, 83, 118.

93. Tindall, *James Joyce*, pp. 26-27, 29.

94. Staley, "Stephen Dedalus," p. 25.

95. Sultan, *The Argument of "Ulysses*," pp. 461-62.

96. Goldberg, *The Classical Temper*, pp. 168-69, 174, 178, 185, 190-93. Italics mine.

97. As will be seen from the discussion of the library scene below, attempts to equate Hamlet with Stephen, which might make this passage applicable to Stephen, rest on very shaky ground.

98. Description of lapwing from Levin, *James Joyce*, p. 80.

99. After all, Bloom persuades Stephen to go along with him while Stephen is still groggy (597:4/613:4). And Stephen's actions all through Eumaeus and Ithaca indicate his boredom and even lack of consideration: he wears a morose expression (605:16/621:14); he has "to make a superhuman effort of memory to try and concentrate and remember" to answer a question from Bloom (617:42/633:32); he refuses the well-meant, if unappetizing, food and drink offered him by Bloom in the cabman's shelter (618:40/634:35); he lets Bloom's conversation slide over the top of his head without paying much attention (628:34/644:26); he becomes "crosstempered" at a discussion of Ireland and suggests abruptly that they change the subject (629:23/645:15); he stifles a yawn (632:12/648:5); although Bloom disagrees with Stephen "tacitly," Stephen disagrees with him "openly" (650:32-34/666:33-35); and in general he acts in such a way as to make Bloom think that he is "standoffish" (641:40/658:34). Stephen goes home with Bloom not because he wants to or because he likes Bloom but because "Brazen Head or him or anywhere else was all more or less . . ." (642:40/658:35). Surely the only words that could be substituted for the three dots are "the same." Joyce is indicating here that Stephen would go anywhere with anyone and is not particularly interested in Bloom. Finally, Stephen leaves Bloom, declining his invitation to stay the night, without a word of explanation (680:13/695:35), although he knows that Bloom is aware that he has no place to spend the night.

100. The best discussion of this scene, the Scylla and Charybdis chapter, can be found in William M. Schutte, *Joyce and Shakespeare: A Study in the Meaning of "Ulysses"* (New Haven: Yale University Press, 1952); see especially chapters 4 and 5, pp. 52-80.

101. Speaking of Shakespeare, Stephen asks, "What softens the heart of a man, shipwrecked in storms dire, tried, like another Ulysses, Pericles, prince of Tyre?" (192:41/195:13). And again speaking of Shakespeare he says, "The tusk of the boar has wounded him there where love lies ableeding" (194:16/196:30); Eurycleia recognizes Odysseus by the scar of a wound made by the tusk of a wild boar.

Stephen argues that Shakespeare is "a ghost by absence" (i.e., from his home in Stratford) (186:38/189:1) and "a ghost by death" (playing the part of the ghost in *Hamlet*) (186:37/189:1). Eglinton: "He [Shakespeare] is the ghost and the prince." "He is, Stephen said" (210:1-3/212:28-30).

102. References to Hamlet in this chapter can generally be applied equally well to Stephen. See particularly p. 185/188 of *Ulysses*.

Shakespeare, playing the ghost, is "made up in the castoff mail of a court buck" (186:24/188:29). Stephen is wearing the castoff shoes of Buck Mulligan: "His gaze brooded on this broadtoed boots, a buck's castoffs" (50:8/49:17). See the second set of equations in the text.

103. This statement is true only if the argument of this paragraph, summarized in the last sentence, is accepted.

104. As he expounds his theory to the assemblage, he thinks to himself, "They list. And in the porches of their ears I pour" (194:23/196:38). The reference,

of course, is to the murder of Hamlet's father by having poison poured in his ear.

The whole discussion of the mocker (196/198) is double-edged, particularly since Stephen is referred to as "Mocker" later (200:39/203:16).

In another aside to himself, Stephen comments, "I think you're getting on very nicely. Just mix up a mixture of theolologicophilolological" (202:36/205:12). Later he says to himself, "What the hell are you driving at? I know. Shut up. Blast you! I have reasons" (205:9/207:31). At 207:30/210:11 he consciously withholds a piece of information that might damage his argument. Later he comments on the falseness of his voice (and by implication, what he is saying): "I am tired of my voice, the voice of Esau" (209:1/211:25). When asked by Eglinton whether he believes his own theory, he promptly says no (211:15/214:1). And immediately below, he says to himself, "I believe, O Lord, help my unbelief. That is, help me to believe or help me to unbelieve?" (211:29/214:15).

105. In "New Views on the Psychology and Psychopathology of Wit and the Comic," *Psychiatry* 13 (1950), Silvano Arieti points out that much wit is similar to the thinking of the schizophrenics in that it depends upon the confusion of "identity with similarity" (p. 62). This type of thinking Arieti calls *paleologic*. Thus, a 'schizophrenic was noticed to have the habit of wetting her body with oil. Asked why she would do so she replied, "The human body is a machine and has to be lubricated" (from Silvano Arieti, "Special Logic of Schizophrenic and Other Types of Autistic Thought," *Psychiatry* 11 [1948]: 325-38). Such a story could readily be told as a joke. Arieti also points out in his article on wit and the comic that puns belong to the paleologic type of thinking (p. 54). Joyce's puns in this section, his equating of everyone with everyone else (see p. 235, above), his weaving together of actually dissimilar items (see n. 102), his ribald play and cast of characters (214:5/216:37), all follow this paleologic pattern.

106. Bloom considers various courses of action, but not too seriously: "Assassination, never, as two wrongs did not make one right. Duel by combat, no. Divorce, not now" (718:24/733:35).

107. Jerome L. Singer, *Daydreaming* (New York: Random House, 1966), pp. 74, 77.

108. Ibid., pp. 56, 58.

109., Alan Richardson, *Mental Imagery* (New York: Springer Publishing Co., 1969), p. 70.

110. Hayman's quotation reads "Assuring," probably a typographical error. Both Random House editions read "Assuming" (716:17/731:25).

111. Hayman, "The Empirical Molly," pp. 105, 113-14.

112. The quotation from *Ulysses* is 727:9/742:10. O'Brien, "Some Determinants of Molly Bloom," pp. 143-44.

113. Joyce to Budgen, 28? February 1921, *Letters* 1: 159-60.

114. O'Brien, "Some Determinants of Molly Bloom."

Chapter 12: The Stream-of-Consciousness Technique Defined

1. Jacques Souvage, "The 'Dramatized' Novel," *An Introduction to the Study of the Novel* (Ghent: E. Story-Scientia P.V.B.A., 1965), p. 46. For this discussion, Souvage's sections " 'Telling' versus 'Showing' in the Novel," "Point of View," and "Point of View and Other Types of Narration" are helpful (pp. 48-62). Souvage's quotation from Leon Edel comes from *The Psychological Novel, 1900-1950* (New York and Philadelphia: J. B. Lippincott, 1955), p. 83. As the

spelling shows, Souvage used the British edition.

2. Edouard Dujardin, *Le Monologue intérieur* (Paris: Albert Messein, 1931), p. 59.

3. Ibid., p. 41.

4. Frank Budgen, *James Joyce and the Making of "Ulysses"* (New York: Harrison Smith and Robert Haas, 1934), p. 92; Djuna Barnes, "James Joyce," *Vanity Fair* 18, no. 2 (April 1922): 65, 104.

5. Virginia Woolf, "Modern Fiction," *The Common Reader* (1925; reprint ed., New York: Harcourt, Brace, 1953), pp. 154-55.

6. Lawrence E. Bowling, "What Is the Stream of Consciousness Technique?", *PMLA* 65 (1950): 345.

7. Robert Humphrey, *Stream of Consciousness in the Modern Novel* (Berkeley: University of California Press, 1954), p. 4.

8. Dujardin, *Le Monologue intérieur*, p. 58.

9. James Joyce, *A Portrait of the Artist as a Young Man* (New York: Viking Press, 1968), p. 215.

10. Alfred Korzybski, *Science and Sanity* (Lakeville, Conn.: International Non-Aristotelian Library, 1948), p. 179.

11. Phyllis Bentley, *Some Observations on the Art of Narrative* (New York: Macmillan Co., 1947), p. 9.

12. Edel, *The Psychological Novel*, p. 83. Edel does not use the concept of level of abstraction, but at the bottom of p. 84 he makes much the same point in other language.

13. Humphrey, *Stream of Consciousness*, pp. 36, 26.

14. Edel, *The Psychological Novel*, pp. 83, 23.

15. Stuart Gilbert, *James Joyce's "Ulysses"* (New York: Alfred A. Knopf, 1952), p. 255.

16. Dorrit Cohn, "Narrated Monologue: Definition of a Fictional Style," *Comparative Literature* 18 (1966): 97-98. Mrs. Cohn hesitates between "narrated consciousness" and "narrated monologue" as a translation for *erlebte Rede* and settles "tentatively" for "narrated monologue" (p. 104).

17. Joyce, *A Portrait*; Cohn, "Narrated Monologue," p. 98. Mrs. Cohn added the italics to indicate *erlebte Rede*.

18. Cohn, "Narrated Monologue," p. 98. "The deviation from past to conditional and pluperfect is explained in n. 23 [pp. 104-05 in Cohn]."

19. Edel, *The Psychological Novel*, p. 47.

20. Anthony Trollope, *Barchester Towers*, chapter 15; quoted by A. A. Mendilow in *Time and the Novel* (London: Peter Nevill, 1952), p. 101. For other discussions of the "intrusive author," see Mendilow's chapter by that title and Humphrey, *Stream of Consciousness*.

21. The italics are added.

22. Bentley, *Some Observations*, "Use of Summary."

23. From Stuart Gilbert's translation, entitled *We'll to the Woods No More* (Norfolk, Conn.: New Directions, 1938), p. 6.

24. For other attempts to sort out the various techniques generally lumped together by critics under the term "stream-of-consciousness technique," see Derek Bickerton, "Modes of Interior Monologue: A Formal Definition," *Modern Language Quarterly* 28 (1967): 229-39; Bickerton, "James Joyce and the Development of Interior Monologue," *Essays in Criticism* 18 (1968): 32-37; Bowling, "What Is the Stream of Consciousness Technique?" pp. 333-45; Liisa Dahl, *Linguistic Features of the Stream-of-Consciousness Technique in James Joyce, Virginia Woolf and Eugene O'Neill* (Turku, Finland: University of Turku, 1970); Melvin J. Friedman, *Stream of Consciousness: A Study in Literary Method* (New Haven: Yale University Press, 1955); Norman Friedman, "Point of View

in Fiction: The Development of the Critical Concept," *PMLA* 70 (1955): 1160-84; Humphrey, *Stream of Consciousness;* H. A. Kelly, "Consciousness in the Monologues of *Ulysses,*" *Modern Language Quarterly* 24 (1963): 3-12; Keith Leopold, "Some Problems of Terminology in the Analysis of the Stream of Consciousness Novel," *AUMLA,* no. 13 (May 1960), pp. 23-32; W. J. Lillyman, "The Interior Monologue in James Joyce and Otto Ludwig," *Comparative Literature* 23 (1971): 45-54; Robie Macauley and George Lanning, *Technique in Fiction* (New York: Harper & Row, 1964), pp. 88-94; John Spencer, "A Note on the 'Steady Monologuy of the Interiors,'" *Review of English Literature* 6 (1965): 32-41; William Flint Thrall and Addison Hibbard, *A Handbook to Literature,* rev. and enl. by C. Hugh Holman (New York: Odyssey Press, 1960), see "Interior Monologue" (p. 243) and "Stream-of-Consciousness Novel" (pp. 471-72).

The continuum above maintains a perfect correlation between the level of abstraction and the intrusiveness of the author: the lower the level of abstraction, the less intrusive the author; the higher the level, the more obvious the manipulations and judgments of the author become.

Chapter 13: The Sources of the Stream

1. Wassily Kandinsky, *Concerning the Spiritual in Art,* trans. Hilla Rebay (New York: George Wittenborn, 1947), p. 52; published originally in German in 1912.

2. Mary Colum, *Life and Dream* (London: Macmillan & Co., 1947), pp. 121, 129; Richard Ellmann, *James Joyce* (New York: Oxford University Press, 1959), p. 79; William York Tindall, *Forces in Modern British Literature* (New York: Alfred A. Knopf, 1947), p. 277. See also C. P. Curran, *James Joyce Remembered* (New York: Oxford University Press, 1968): Symons's book "introduced most of us to the movement abroad. It was ardently read. . . . Whether thanks to Symons or not, Joyce had acquaintance with Baudelaire, Verlaine, and the Symbolists in his earliest college years" (p. 31). Curran was a schoolfellow of Joyce.

3. Arthur Symons, *The Symbolist Movement in Literature,* 2d ed. rev. (New York: E. P. Dutton, 1908), pp. 9, 10, 131.

4. Stéphane Mallarmé, *Oeuvres complètes,* 2 vols. (Paris: Gallimard, 1945), p. 366; quoted by David Hayman, *Joyce et Mallarmé* (Paris: Lettres Modernes, 1965), p. 61.

5. Flaubert to Louise Colet, 8 March 1857, *The Selected Letters of Gustave Flaubert,* trans. and ed. Francis Steegmuller (London: Hamish Hamilton, 1954), p. 186.

6. Oscar Wilde, *The Picture of Dorian Gray* (New York: Modern Library, 1926), p. vii. Painters were saying the same sorts of things. In 1913, Guillaume Apollinaire wrote in *The Cubist Painters* (New York: Wittenborn, Schultz, 1949), "Each god creates in his own image, and so do painters. Only photographers manufacture duplicates of nature" (p. 11).

7. James Joyce, *A Portrait of the Artist as a Young Man* (New York: Viking Press, 1968), pp. 171, 172, 215, 221.

8. Symons, *The Symbolist Movement,* pp. 8-9, 85, 141, 143.

9. Djuna Barnes, "James Joyce," *Vanity Fair* 18, no. 2 (April 1922): 65 and 104; Virginia Woolf, "Modern Fiction," *The Common Reader* (1925; reprint ed., New York: Harvest-Harcourt, Brace, 1953), p. 155.

10. Herschel B. Chipp, *Theories of Modern Art* (Berkeley: University of California Press, 1968), pp. 48-51.

11. The quotation is from Ellmann, *James Joyce*, p. 128.

12. George Heard Hamilton, *Manet and His Critics* (New Haven: Yale University Press, 1954), p. 193.

13. Chipp, *Theories of Modern Art*, p. 58 n. and pp. 58-59 (italics in the original). See also William Innes Homer, *Seurat and the Science of Painting* (Cambridge, Mass.: M.I.T. Press, 1964), p. 44.

14. Homer, *Seurat*, p. 280.

15. Ibid., pp. 139ff., p. 172; Hamilton, *Manet*, p. 170. See also Seurat's letter to Maurice Beaubourgh, 28 August 1890, quoted in John Rewald, *Georges Seurat*, 2d rev. ed. (New York: George Wittenborn, 1946), p. 62.

16. Albert Gleizes and Jean Metzinger, *Du "Cubisme"* (Paris: Eugène Figuère, 1912), pp. 18, 30.

17. Joseph Prescott, *Exploring James Joyce* (Carbondale: Southern Illinois University Press, 1964), pp. 26-27.

18. Gleizes and Metzinger, *Du "Cubisme,"* p. 30.

19. Joyce, *A Portrait*, pp. 214-15.

20. Flaubert, to Louise Colet, 16 January 1852, in Steegmuller, *Selected Letters*, p. 131.

21. Gauguin to Emile Schuffenecker, 8 October 1888, in John Rewald, *Post Impressionism—from van Gogh to Gauguin*, 2d ed. (New York: Museum of Modern Art, 1962), p. 196.

22. "Futurist Painting: Technical Manifesto," 11 April 1910, in Joshua C. Taylor, *Futurism* (New York: Museum of Modern Art, 1961), p. 127. The futurists made one exception: "But this truism, unimpeachable and absolute fifty years ago, is no longer so today with regard to the nude, since artists obsessed with the desire to expose the bodies of their mistresses have transformed the Salons into arrays of unwholesome flesh!" (p. 127; the exclamation point is in the original).

23. Richard Ellmann in his introduction to Stanislaus Joyce's *My Brother's Keeper* (New York: Viking Press, 1958), p. 23.

24. Hamilton, *Manet*, traces this development. See especially p. 26, which records a critical opinion of an early (1861) painting: "But what a scourge to society is a realist painter! To him nothing is sacred! Manet tramples under foot even the most sacred ties." Grant Richards's printer evidently felt the same way about *Dubliners*; see Ellmann, *James Joyce*, pp. 227-31.

25. Symons, *The Symbolist Movement*, p. 137.

26. William Seitz, *Claude Monet* (New York: Harry N. Abrams, 1960), p. 44.

27. Denis Rouart, *Claude Monet* (New York: Skira Art Books, 1958), pp. 107-08.

28. Kenneth Clark, *Civilisation* (New York: Harper & Row, 1969), p. 290.

29. James Joyce, *Stephen Hero*, (New York: New Directions, 1944), p. 211.

30. Ellmann, *James Joyce*, pp. 87-89. See also James Joyce, *Epiphanies*, ed. O. A. Silverman (Buffalo: Lockwood Memorial Library of the State University of New York at Buffalo, 1956).

31. A. Walton Litz, *The Art of James Joyce* (New York: Galaxy-Oxford, 1964), pp. 132-39.

32. William C. Seitz, *Claude Monet—Seasons and Moments* (New York: Museum of Modern Art, 1960), p. 25. Many of the impressionists and the people who wrote about them made such statements. For example, Gustave Goetschy wrote in *La Vie moderne* for 17 April 1880: Manet "is concerned above all else with rendering in the most exact and direct way the object just as it was at the moment when he set himself to reproduce it. He tries to preserve faithfully and vividly the impression which he has felt and he believes he has done enough when he sincerely expressed it" (Hamilton, *Manet*, p. 228).

33. Daniel Wildenstein, *Monet: Impressions* (New York: French & European Publications, 1967), pp. 56-57.

34. Quoted in Seitz, *Claude Monet—Seasons and Moments*, p. 20.

35. Virginia Woolf, "Modern Fiction," p. 154. Note also Oscar Wilde's statement in "The Decay of Living" (1889): "Where, if not from the Impressionists, do we get those wonderful brown fogs that come creeping down our streets, blurring the gas-lamps and changing the houses into monstrous shadows? To whom, if not to them and their master, do we owe the lovely silver mists that brood over our river, and turn to faint forms of fading grace curved bridge and swaying barge?" (*The First Collected Edition of the Works of Oscar Wilde*, ed. Robert Ross, 15 vols. [London: Dawsons, 1969], 8:41).
Virginia Woolf not only repeats Monet's use of *envelope*, but her word *luminous* was also a favorite word of the painters. For example, Fénéon wrote about neoimpressionist paintings in 1887, "Take a few steps back and all the multicolored specks melt into undulant, luminous masses" (Homer, *Seurat*, p. 159); and the neoimpressionists developed a concept of chromoluminarism (ibid., p. 160). In 1910, the futurists declared: "Your eyes, accustomed to semi-darkness, will soon open to more radiant visions of light. The shadows which we shall paint shall be more luminous than the highlights of our predecessors, and our pictures, next to those of the museums, will shine like blinding daylight compared with deepest night" (Taylor, *Futurism*, p. 126). And in 1913, Guillaume Apollinaire wrote, "These luminous signs fare around us, but only a handful of painters have grasped their plastic significance" (*The Cubist Painters*, p. 25). ("Ces signes lumineux brillent autour de nous . . . ," Guillaume Apollinaire, *Les Peintres cubistes* [1913; reprint ed., Paris: Hermann, 1965], p. 69.) It also echoes, of course, the idea behind de Maupassant's phrases "a glittering shower of light" and "a flood of yellow tones." See also "the esthetic image is first luminously apprehended as selfbound and selfcontained upon the immeasurable background of space of time which is not it" (Joyce, *A Portrait*, p. 212).

36. Cecily Mackworth, *Guillaume Apollinaire and the Cubist Life* (New York: Horizon Press, 1963), p. 17.

37. S. L. Goldberg, *The Classical Temper* (London: Chatto & Windus, 1961), pp. 252-53.

38. The English translation is from Chipp, *Theories of Modern Art*, p. 215; for the French, see Gleizes and Metzinger, *Du "Cubisme,"* p. 34. For an early discussion of this matter, see Joseph Frank, "Spatial Form in Modern Literature," *Sewanee Review* 53 (1945): pp. 221-40, 443-56, 643-53; reprinted in *Critiques and Essays in Criticism*, ed. R. W. Stallman (New York: Ronald Press, 1949).

39. For the story of Joyce's debt to Dujardin, see Ellmann, *James Joyce*, pp. 534-35. See also Edouard Dujardin, *Le Monologue intérieur* (Paris: Albert Messein, 1931). David Hayman has written two volumes on Joyce's debt to Mallarmé: *Joyce et Mallarmé*.

40. Francis Steegmuller, *Apollinaire: Poet Among Painters* (New York: Farrar, Straus, 1963), p. 151.

41. First published in Guillaume Apollinaire, *Caligrammes* (Paris: Gallimard, 1918); reprinted in *The Cubist Painters*, p. 6.

42. First published in *Poetry* 1 (1913). Republished in Ezra Pound, *Pavannes and Divisions* (New York: Alfred A. Knopf, 1918), p. 96. See "The 'Image'" in Litz, *The Art of James Joyce*, pp. 53-61.

43. Chipp, *Theories of Modern Art*, p. 61.

44. Joyce, *A Portrait*, p. 212.

45. Symons, *The Symbolist Movement*, p. 30.

46. Quoted in Chipp, *Theories of Modern Art*, p. 210.

47. Quoted in ibid., p. 211.
48. Apollinaire, *The Cubist Painters*, p. 11; *Les Peintres cubistes*, p. 48.
49. Apollinaire, *The Cubist Painters*, p. 25; *Les Peintres cubistes*, p. 69.
50. David Sutter, "Les Phénomènes de la vision," *L'Art* 20 (1880): 216; quoted by Homer, *Seurat*, p. 44. Seurat and the neoimpressionists made much of Sutter's theories and tried to put them into practice. Joyce assigned colors to eight of the chapters in *Ulysses*: Telemachus, white and gold; Nestor, brown; Proteus, green; Calypso, orange; Hades, white and black; Aeolus, red; Nausicaa, grey and blue; Oxen of the Sun, white (Stuart Gilbert, *James Joyce's "Ulysses"* [New York: Alfred A. Knopf, 1952], p. 41). In *Ulysses*, Stephen thinks of words in a poem: "He saw them three by three, approaching girls, in green, in rose, in russet, entwining, *per l'aer perso* in mauve, in purple, *quella pacifica oriafiamma*, in gold or oriflamme, *di rimirar fe piu ardenti*" (137:4/138:26).
The artists (and Joyce) were continuing an idea set out by Baudelaire in "Correspondances" in 1857 and reinforced by Rimbaud in "Voyelles" in the early 1870s:

Correspondances
La Nature est un temple où de vivants piliers
Laissent parfois sortir de confuses paroles;
L'homme y passe à travers des forêts de symboles
Qui l'observent avec des regards familiers.
Comme de longs échoes qui de loin se confondent
Dans une ténébreuse et profonde unité,
Vaste comme la nuit et comme la clarté,
Les parfums, les couleurs et les sons se répondent.
Il est des parfums frais comme des chairs d'enfants,
Doux comme les hautbois, verts comme les praires,
—Et d'autres, corrompus, riches et triomphants,
Ayant l'expansion des choses infinies,
Comme l'ambre, le musc, le benjoin et l'encens,
Qui chantent les transports de l'esprit et des sens.

Voyelles
A noir, E blanc, I rouge, U vert, O bleu, voyelles,
Je dirai quelque jour vos naissances latentes.
A, noir corset velu des mouches éclatantes
Qui bombillent autour des puanteurs cruelles,

I have given just the first stanza of "Voyelles." Joyce could have read all four stanzas of the poem in Symons, however, and a discussion of it (*The Symbolist Movement*, pp. 68-69).
51. Quoted in Chipp, *Theories of Modern Art*, p. 320. I have chosen quotations from the beginning and end of a period of almost forty years, a period starting at about Joyce's birth and running to the time of the writing of *Ulysses*. Similar quotations are available—in abundance—from other writers, artists, and critics throughout those years.
52. Percy Lubbock, *The Craft of Fiction* (New York: Charles Scribner's Sons, 1921); Melvin J. Friedman, *Stream of Consciousness: A Study in Literary Method* (New Haven: Yale University Press, 1955); Leon Edel, *The Psychological Novel, 1900-1950* (Philadelphia: J. B. Lippincott, 1955); Wayne Booth, *The Rhetoric of Fiction* (Chicago: University of Chicago Press, 1961). See also Jacques Souvage, *An Introduction to the Study of the Novel* (Ghent, Belgium: Story, 1965).

53. Georges Lemaitre, *From Cubism to Surrealism* (Cambridge: Harvard University Press, 1947), p. 55.

54. Hilla Rebay, *In Memory of Wassily Kandinsky* (New York: Solomon R. Guggenheim Foundation, 1945), p. 49.

55. George Bernard Shaw, *Too True To Be Good, Village Wooing, and On the Rocks: Three Plays* (New York: Dodd, Mead, 1934), p. 105.

56. Armand Siegel, "Operational Aspects of Hidden-Variable Quantum Theories with a Postscript on the Impact of Recent Scientific Trends on Art," *Boston Studies in Philosophy of Science*, ed. Marx W. Wartofsky (Dordrecht, Holland: D. Reidel, 1963), p. 171.

57. Wyndham Lewis, *Time and Western Man* (New York: Harcourt, Brace, 1928); Shiv K. Kumar, *Bergson and the Stream of Consciousness Novel* (London: Blackie, 1962).

58. Quoted by Richard Ellmann in "Two Faces of Edward," *Edwardians and Late Victorians*, ed. Richard Ellmann (New York: Columbia University Press, 1960), pp. 205-06.

59. Sigmund Freud, *Collected Papers*, 5 vols. (London: Hogarth, 1953), 5: 101-04.

60. Quoted in ibid., p. 103.

61. William Blisset, "James Joyce in the Smithy of his Soul," *James Joyce Today*, ed. Thomas F. Staley (Bloomington: Indiana University Press, 1966), p. 115. See also "The Condition of Music" in Litz, *The Art of James Joyce*, pp. 62-74.

62. Clive Bell, "Plus de Jazz," *New Republic* 28 (21 September 1921): 94-95.

63. Sergei M. Eisenstein, *The Film Sense* (New York: Harcourt, Brace, 1942), pp. 95-97.

64. See Ellmann, *James Joyce*, pp. 310-13.

65. Eisenstein, *The Film Sense*, pp. 4, 7, 17, 30-31. Italics in the original.

66. T. S. Eliot, "Hamlet and His Problems," *Selected Essays* (New York: Harcourt, Brace, 1950), pp. 124-25.

67. Robert Scholes and Richard M. Kain, *The Workshop of Daedalus: James Joyce and the Raw Materials for "A Portrait of the Artist as a Young Man"* (Evanston: Northwestern University Press, 1965), pp. 78-79. See also two passages in Stanislaus Joyce, *The Dublin Diary of Stainislaus Joyce*, ed. George Harris Healey (Ithaca, N.Y.: Cornell University Press, 1962): (1) "The emotions Henry James chooses to deal with are slight, but in them his psychology is extraordinarily acute and full. He does not put you into the mind of his characters; you always feel you are reading about them, nor does he ever abandon his character of artist to disert upon what he has said—that habit of Meredith's which suggests the psychological essayist (Meredith's psychology always carries its own explanation with it)—but remains patiently impersonal. The Lord be thenkit!" (pp. 86-87). (2) Another passage of interior monologue at the top of p. 110.

68. Phillip F. Herring, "The Bedsteadfastness of Molly Bloom," *Modern Fiction Studies* 15 (1969): 51 n. The letter is dated 11 July 1912 and can be found in *The Letters of James Joyce*, vol. 2, ed. Richard Ellmann (New York: Viking Press, 1966), p. 296.

Chapter 14: From Stream to Torrent

1. Richard Ellmann, *James Joyce* (New York: Oxford University Press, 1959). The story is easier to follow here than in the three volumes of letters.

2. Ibid., p. 433.

3. Pound to Joyce, 19 December 1917, *The Letters of James Joyce*, vol. 2, ed. Richard Ellmann (New York: Viking Press, 1966), pp. 413-14.

4. Ellmann, *James Joyce*, pp. 456-57; Pound to Joyce, 22 November 1918, in *Letters*, 2: 423.

5. Joyce to Budgen, 19 June 1919. *The Letters of James Joyce*, vol. 1, ed. Stuart Gilbert (New York: Viking Press, 1957), p. 126; Ellmann, *James Joyce*, p. 473.

6. Ellmann, *James Joyce*, p. 473. By the time *Ulysses* appeared in book form, Pound seems to have recanted some—or was at least reluctant to be negative about the book in public. In an article in the *Mercure de France* on 1 June 1922, he wrote:

> [Joyce] expresses himself directly in different parts of his book (as even Aristotle permits), but this does not mean, as the distinguished Larbaud contends, that he abandons unity of style. Each character not only speaks in his own manner, but thinks in his own manner, and that is no more abandoning unity of style than when the characters of a novel in the so-called unified style speak in various ways: the quotation marks are left out, that's all. (Ezra Pound, "James Joyce and Pecuchet," trans. Fred Bornhauser, *Shenandoah* 3, no. 3 [1952]: 15)

7. Ellmann, *James Joyce*, pp. 474, 489, 490-91. Ellmann says, "Among Joyce's friends only Budgen responded to the *Sirens* with the admiration he expected and hoped for" (p. 474).

8. 15 November 1926; ibid., p. 597. A year later, Pound wrote to Joyce, "Nothing would be worth plowing through like this, except the Divine Vision—and I gather it's not that sort of thing" (ibid.).

9. 20 November 1926; ibid., p. 596. On 4 February 1927, Miss Weaver wrote, "Some of your work [in progress] I like enormously . . . but I am made in such a way that I do not care for the output from your wholesale pun factory nor for the darknesses and unintelligibilities of your deliberately-entangled language system" (ibid., pp. 602-03).

10. James Joyce, *The Critical Writings of James Joyce*, ed. Ellsworth Mason and Richard Ellmann (New York: Viking Press, 1964), p. 145.

11. James Joyce, *A Portrait of the Artist as a Young Man* (New York: Viking Press, 1968), p. 214.

12. A glance at Aeolus, an earlier chapter, suggests a major technical innovation—the newspaper headlines. They were a late addition, however. See Joyce to Harriet Weaver, 7 October 1921, *Letters* 1:172: "Eolus is recast." See also A. Walton Litz, *The Art of James Joyce* (New York: Galaxy-Oxford, 1964), p. 49.

13. In Lestrygonians the narrative leaves Bloom's consciousness for two and a half pages (174-76/177-79).

14. These vignettes are (1) Father Conmee; (7) Miss Dunne; (10) Bloom; (12) Kernan; (13) Stephen; (18) Master Dignam.

15. I have taken this paragraph and the two paragraphs following from William M. Schutte. See William M. Schutte and Erwin R. Steinberg, "The Fictional Technique of *Ulysses*," *Approaches to "Ulysses" : Ten Essays*, ed. Thomas F. Staley and Bernard Benstock (Pittsburgh: University of Pittsburgh Press, 1970), pp. 168-72.

16. Joyce to Budgen, 3 January 1920, *Letters* 1:135.

17. Litz, *The Art of James Joyce*, p. 71.

18. Ibid., pp. 69-70. Litz's whole second chapter, "New Bearings," pp. 44-75, is appropriate here.

19. Edmund Wilson, *Axel's Castle* (1931; reprint ed., New York: Charles Scribner's Sons, 1948), p. 301.

20. Ibid., pp. 301-02.

21. Ibid., p. 302. A version of *Anna Livia Plurabelle* was published earlier in the *Navire d'Argent*, 1 October 1925; but this version appeared separately as a small book in 1928.

22. James Joyce, *Finnegans Wake* (New York: Viking Press, 1939), p. 202.

23. For statements about rivers, see, for example, Jacques Mercanton, "The Hours of James Joyce, Part I," *Kenyon Review* 24 (1962): 714. See also Ellmann, *James Joyce*, p. 584.

24. 3 September 1920, *Letters* 1:145. See also his letter to Frank Budgen of 24 October 1940, ibid., p. 149: "Last night I thought of an *Entr'acte* for *Ulysses* in the middle of book after 9th episode *Scylla & Charybdis*. Short with absolutely no relation to what precedes or follows like a pause in the action of the play."

25. Joyce to Harriet Weaver, 6 August 1919, ibid., p. 129. Joyce to Budgen, 20 March 1920, ibid., pp. 139-40; February 1921, ibid., p. 159; 16 August 1921, ibid., p. 170.

26. I discussed the importance of style in the last chapter. For an excellent discussion of the awareness of style and changes in style among British writers from 1900 to 1910, see Richard Ellmann, "Two Faces of Edward," *Edwardians and Late Victorians*, ed. Richard Ellmann (New York: Columbia University Press, 1960), esp. p. 191.

27. Herschel B. Chipp, *Theories of Modern Art* (Berkeley: University of California Press, 1968), p. 254.

28. "On the Problem of Form," in ibid., p. 163.

29. Ibid. Italics in the original.

30. Jean (Hans) Arp, "Dada Was Not a Farce," *The Dada Painters and Poets: An Anthology*, ed. Robert Motherwell (New York: Wittenborn, Schultz, 1951), p. 294.

31. Albert Gleizes, "The Dada Case," *Action* (Paris), no. 3 (April 1920); Motherwell, *Painters and Poets*, p. 303.

32. Hugo Ball, "Sound Poems (Zurich, 1915)," trans. from *Flucht aus der Zeit* (Munich: Duncker and Humbolt, n.d.), *transition*, no. 25 (Fall 1936), p. 159; also in Motherwell, *Painters and Poets*, p. xix.

33. James Johnson Sweeney, "Eleven Europeans in America," *Bulletin of the Museum of Modern Art* 13 (1946), nos. 4-5, pp. 19-21; reprinted in Chipp, *Theories of Modern Art*, pp. 394-95.

34. Jean-Pierre Brisset, *La Science de Dieu* (1890; reprint ed., Paris: Chamuel, 1900), p. 10.

35. Raymond Roussel, *Comment j'ai écrit certain des mes livres* (Paris: Pauvert, 1963), p. 24. Georges Condominas kindly helped me with my translations from Roussel.

36. Ibid., pp. 11-12, 163, 170.

37. Ibid., pp. 11-12: "Je choisissais deux mots presque semblables (faisant penser aux métagrammes). Par example *billard* et *pillard*. Puis j'y ajoutais des mots pareils mais pris dans sens différents, et j'obtenais ainsi deux phrases presque identiques. . . . Les deux phrases trouvées, il s'agissait d'écrire un conte pouvant commencer par la première et finir par la seconde." I can find no satisfactory translation for "métagrammes," which is evidently a neologism.

38. Ibid., pp. 39, 48.

39. Ibid., p. 20: "Je m'en tiendrai donc là en ce qui concerne la création basée sur l'accouplement de deux mots pris dans deux sens différents." Ibid., p. 23: "Ce procédé . . . est parent de la rime. Dans les deux cas il y a création

imprévue due à des combinaisons phoniques. C'est essentiellement un procédé poétique." Note in *Ulysses*: "POST NO BILLS. POST NO PILLS" (151:34, 1934 edition) and "POST NO BILLS. POST 110 PILLS" (153:37, 1961 edition).

40. Richard Huelsenbeck, Marcel Janko, and Tristan Tzara, "L'Amiral cherche une maison à louer," *Cabaret Voltaire*, June 1916; Motherwell, *Painters and Poets*, pp. 106, 241; "vine," "around," and "sweetheart" are misspelled as indicated. In a footnote to the poem, Tzara relates it to the principles of simultaneity propounded in essays published on 1907 about the cubists Picasso, Braque, Picabia, Duchamp-Villon (the brother of Marcel Duchamp), and Delaunay; the tendency in the work of Villiers de l'Isle Adam in the theater toward a schematic simultaneity; Mallarmé's typographical experiments in "Un coup de dés"; and the work of Blaise Cendrars, Jules Romains, and Apollinaire, particularly the latter's ideograms. He puts his heaviest emphasis, however, on "un livre théoretique, 'Voix, Rythmes et chants Simultanés' [par Mr H. Barzun] où il cherchait une rélation plus étroite entre la symphonie polirythmique et le poéme." For a simultaneous poem by a Barzun (probably H. Barzun, but I am not sure), see "Fragment de l'universal poeme," *transition*, no. 27 (April-May 1938). It is printed on a foldout of several pages and looks as if it has been sprayed on the page. (I say this not with any deprecation, but merely to give a sense of the typography.)

41. Jean-Richard Bloch, *La Nuit Kurde* (Paris: Gallimard, 1925; reprint ed., Paris: Bibliothèque Francaise, 1933). I shall refer to the 1933 edition, pp. 192-93.

42. Jean-Richard Bloch, *A Night in Kurdestan*, trans. Stephen Haden-Guest (New York: Simon & Schuster, 1931), pp. 188-89.

43. "Revolution of the Word," *transition*, nos. 16-17 (June 1929), p. 13; also reprinted in Ellmann, *James Joyce*, pp. 600-01.

44. Ellmann, *James Joyce*, p. 600.

45. Louis Gillet, "The Living Joyce" (7 June 1941), *Claybook for James Joyce* (New York: Abelard-Schuman, 1958), p. 113. Brisset was born about 1850 and seems to have dropped out of sight in 1913, after the publication of his *Origines Humaines*; see Jean Schuster, "Parcours de Jean-Pierre Brisset," *La Quinzaine littéraire* (1-15 February 1971), pp. 10-11. See also in Gillet, "Desperate Words Call for Desperate Little Remedies," by André Gide (published originally in *Le Figaro*, 30/31 May 1942), which discusses the long tradition of puns among the French and in French literature, with particular reference to Rabelais and Victor Hugo (pp. 123-27).

46. Ellmann, *James Joyce*, p. 601.

47. Litz, *The Art of James Joyce*, pp. 146-148; part of Litz's chart is reprinted in Ellmann, *James Joyce*, pp. 802-03.

48. For a discussion by Duchamp of the *Nude* and its possible relation to futurism (none, he said), see Chipp, *Theories of Modern Art*, pp. 393-94; for other comments by Duchamp on the *Nude*, see also Arturo Schwarz, *The Complete Works of Marcel Duchamp* (New York: Harry N. Abrams, 1969), pp. 16-17, from which Duchamp's statement comes.

The Bala painting is reproduced in Joshua C. Taylor, *Futurism* (New York: Museum of Modern Art, 1958), p. 58. The futurist "Technical Manifesto" of 11 April 1910 proclaimed: "A profile is never motionless before our eyes, but it constantly appears and disappears. On account of the persistency of an image upon the retina, moving objects constantly multiply themselves, their form changes like rapid vibrations, in their mad career. Thus a running horse has not four legs, but twenty, and their movements are triangular" (ibid., p. 125). They painted accordingly.

49. Schwarz, *Marcel Duchamp*, pp. 80-81; Rrose Sélavy, *Littérature*, no. 7 (1 December 1922), p. 14.

50. Schwarz, *Marcel Duchamp*, pp. 534, 490.

51. Ibid., pp. 32, 79.

52. André Breton, "Les Mots sans rides," *Littérature*, no. 7 (1 December 1922), pp. 12-14. English from Schwarz, *Marcel Duchamp*, pp. 508-09.

53. Schwarz, *Marcel Duchamp*, pp. 37 n. 17, 43; see also p. 32.

54. George Heard Hamilton, third page of "Inside *The Green Box*," in Marcel Duchamp, *The Bride Stripped Bare by Her Bachelors Even*, a typographic version by Richard Hamilton of Marcel Duchamp's *Green Box*, trans. by George Heard Hamilton (London: Percy Lund, Humphries, n.d.), unpaged.

55. James Joyce, *Stephen Hero* (New York: New Directions, 1944), p. 211.

56. Schwarz, *Marcel Duchamp*, p. 43. Mr. Mutt suggests Mr. Jeff—another version of Shem and Shaun.

57. Marcel Duchamp, "Specifications for 'Readymades,'" in *The Bride*, unpaged.

58. Joyce, *Stephen Hero*, p. 211.

59. Duchamp, "Specifications for 'Readymades,'" in *The Bride*.

60. George Heard Hamilton, p. 1 of "Inside *The Green Box*," in ibid.

61. Richard Hamilton, p. 1 of "The Green Book," in Marcel Duchamp, *The Bride*.

62. Ellmann, "Two Faces of Edward," p. 201; Litz, *The Art of James Joyce*, pp. 73, 124.

63. Litz, *The Art of James Joyce*, p. 71.

64. Ellmann, "Two Faces of Edward," p. 202; Litz, *The Art of James Joyce*, p. 39; Joyce to Budgen, 19 June 1919, *Letters* 1:126; S. L. Goldberg, *The Classical Temper: A Study of James Joyce's "Ulysses"* (London: Chatto & Windus, 1961), p. 300 (italics in original); Jacques Mercanton, "The Hours of James Joyce, Part I," *Kenyon Review* 24 (1962): 710.

65. In *Ulysses*, almost to the very day of publication; see Ellmann, *James Joyce*, pp. 538, 727-28.

66. The literary scholar and critic may feel more free in a footnote than he would in the text, however, to suggest directions to scholars in other disciplines attempting such explanations. In quoting the following passage, I should stress first that, although it describes the language of a psychotic, I am *not* suggesting that Joyce was psychotic. I am suggesting that his personality seemed to tend in the direction of the pattern described. In "Expressive Behavior and Language Patterns," *Psychiatry* 18 (1955): 361, Maria Lorenz says:

> The recorded speech of the manic patient often shows a strong sense of movement and rhythm. The style may be deliberate and oratorical, or rapid, peremptory, and staccato. This seems to be brought about by the balancing of phrases in sentences, the repetition of words, alliteration, and plays on the sound of words. Even in his spoken language, the manic patient is more concerned with the external and perceptual facets of words and sentences than with the meaning conveyed. In language, as in dress, a liking for the decorative or bedecked is often obvious. Stylistic devices frequently employed are repetition, listing, enumerating, itemizing, and the use of rhetorical questions and direct quotations.
>
> To oversimplify, the figure that emerges in the language patterns of the manic is that of the realist, concerned with his status and role in life—the man of opinion and prejudice. This is brought about by the object-oriented quality of his speech, which produces rather than interprets objective reality. Common characteristics are the response to a stimulus

in terms of associations that are retrospectively directed, and the tendency to serial expansion of a topic or theme in terms of qualities contained within the topic or theme. There is a prevalence of opinions and pronouncements, with considerable use of words of denial, exaggeration, and emphasis. The language shows a rhythmic pattern, and stylistic devices include rhetorical questions, direct quotations, naming, listing and itemizing.

There is abundant evidence of Joyce's obssession with language, language rhythms, language patterns, and the sounds of words and as we have seen, through the years, Joyce became more and more concerned with those matters, frequently at the expense of meaning. There is also evidence that in dress Joyce liked the decorative. Ellmann quotes a passage from a letter by Thomas Wolfe that indicates that even when Joyce was a little shabby, he could be dramatic with his clothing: "Joyce got a bit stagey on the way home, draping his overcoat poetically around his shoulders" (*James Joyce*, p. 593 n.). In another place reporting on information he obtained in an interview with Samuel Beckett, Ellmann says, "Joyce formed a large collection of ties in Paris, and came to pay almost dandiacal attention to his clothes" (p. 546 n.). Joyce was certainly strenuously concerned with "his status and role in life," and he was a man of strong opinions and prejudices. Indeed, contradiction would rouse him to anger or set him to brooding—or both.

I have suggested a noticeable change in Joyce's writing around 1920. Litz, *The Art of James Joyce*, p. 87, suggests another in 1926-27. The Maria Lorenz passage, the two suggested turning points, the change in Joyce's style in a period of about seven years from the simplicity of dramatic presentation to the density of polysemantic/polyphonic prose—these offer the outlines of a hypothesis that someone trained in personality theory or depth pyschology might profitably pursue.

Appendix

1. Frank Budgen, *James Joyce and the Making of "Ulysses"* (New York: Harrison Smith and Robert Haas, 1934), pp. 48-49, 98, 262. See Budgen's discussion of the interior monologue, p. 91.

2. Stuart Gilbert, *James Joyce's "Ulysses"* (New York: Alfred A. Knopf, 1931), pp. 41, 199-207.

Index